Teacher Wraparound Edition

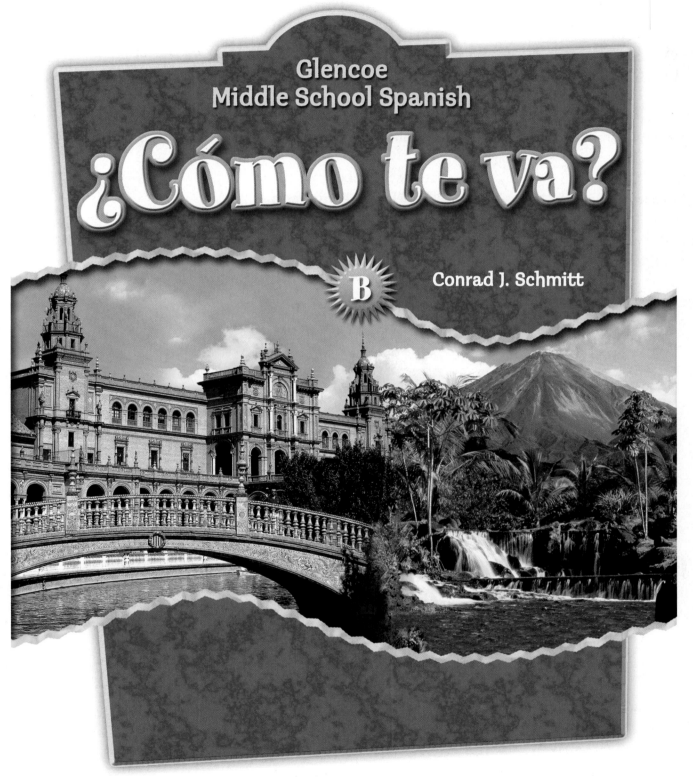

Glencoe
Middle School Spanish

¿Cómo te va?

B

Conrad J. Schmitt

McGraw Hill **Glencoe**

New York, New York   Columbus, Ohio   Chicago, Illinois   Peoria, Illinois   Woodland Hills, California

Teacher Reviewers

Jerry Block
Newbury Park, California

Gregg R. Juárez
Rockport, Texas

Ana Blount
Woodland Hills, California

Sandra Padró
Vineland, New Jersey

Ellen Cohen
Metairie, Louisiana

Susan Stranix
Philadelphia, Pennsylvania

Isabel Hines
Escondido, California

Dawn Uceda
Friendswood, Texas

The McGraw-Hill Companies

Send all inquiries to:
Glencoe/McGraw-Hill
8787 Orion Place
Columbus, OH 43240-4027

ISBN 0-07-860541-5 (Teacher Wraparound Edition)
ISBN 0-07-860351-X (Student Edition)

Printed in the United States of America

1 2 3 4 5 6 7   027   08 07 06 05 04 03

From the Author

Dear Spanish Teacher,

Welcome to Glencoe's **¿Cómo te va?** Middle School Spanish program. We hope that the way we have organized the presentation of the Spanish language and of Hispanic cultures will help you make this fascinating and important subject accessible and interesting to Middle School students and open up a whole new world of possibilities to students.

Upon completion of each unit of **¿Cómo te va?**, students will be able to communicate in Spanish in a real-life situation. **Paso 1** and **Paso 2** each begin with a presentation of new, high-frequency, productive vocabulary on a specific communicative topic. The vocabulary presentations focus on key situations where students would have to use Spanish to survive, and thus students become able to communicate in Spanish. Each vocabulary presentation is followed by structure points which enable students to expand from the situation presented, to learn to use their new words, and to communicate coherently.

In **Paso 1** and **Paso 2,** students acquire the essential vocabulary and structure needed to communicate in the given situations. We understand that giving students the opportunity to practice, a factor so often overlooked in many textbooks today, is crucial, so throughout **¿Cómo te va?** we provide students with many opportunities to use their Spanish in many kinds of activities especially tailored to their age group. The activities within each unit progress from simple, guided practice to more open-ended activities. Finally, especially in **Paso 3** and **Paso 4,** activities that encourage completely free communication enable students to recall and reincorporate all the Spanish they have learned up to that point.

In **Paso 3,** we present a realistic conversation that uses natural, colloquial Spanish and, most importantly, Spanish that students can readily understand. To introduce students to the culture of the Hispanic world, the unit topic is subsequently presented in a cultural milieu in narrative form. The **Cultura y lectura** reading recombines known language and enables students to read and learn—in Spanish—about the fascinating cultures of the people who speak Spanish. The topics presented in both the **Conversación** and the **Cultura y lectura** often involve the lifestyles and interactions of Middle School students in the Spanish-speaking world. In **Paso 3** students also have the opportunity to do review activities of a variety of scopes, from focused to broad.

In **Paso 4,** students review and strengthen the Spanish they have learned through many different types of fun activities such as music, theater, games, interviews, research, cultural readings, discussions, and **Plegables™** Study Organizers. Besides the additional opportunities this provides for reinforcement and review, we hope these activities will encourage students to have fun with the language and to connect it to the context of the world outside the classroom.

We are aware that Middle School students have varied learning styles and abilities. For this reason we have provided a great deal of optional material in **¿Cómo te va?** to permit you to pick and choose what is appropriate for the needs of different sets of learners. In this Teacher Wraparound Edition we have clearly outlined the material that is required, recommended, or optional in each unit, and we have also included Universal Access notes throughout the book to help you use specific types of activities to accommodate different learning styles.

Many resources accompany **¿Cómo te va?** to help you vary and enliven instruction. We hope these materials function as not only a useful but an integral part of the program. However, we trust many of you will agree that the Student Textbook is the lifeline of any program; the supporting materials can be used to reinforce and expand upon the themes of the main text.

We hope that **¿Cómo te va?** will be an exciting new avenue to both teaching and learning Spanish at the Middle School level.

Atentamente,

Conrad J. Schmitt

From Dinah Zike

Plegables are interactive graphic organizers that students can make themselves. They are a wonderful resource to help all types of learners, especially visual and kinesthetic learners, organize and retain information. **Plegables** have many purposes. Students can use them to remember vocabulary words or to organize more in-depth information on any given topic such as keeping track of what they know about a particular country. **Paso 4** of each unit of **¿Cómo te va?** contains instructions for making a **Plegable** which is specifically tailored to the information and skills learned in that unit.

You may have come across the **Plegables** used in this book before, in a supplemental program or staff-development workshop. My **Foldables** are used internationally. I present workshops and keynotes to over fifty thousand teachers and parents a year, sharing the **Foldables** that I began inventing, designing, and adapting over thirty years ago. Around the world, students of all ages are using them for daily work, note-taking activities, student-directed projects, forms of alternative assessment, journals, graphs, tables, and more.

Have fun using **Plegables** to help your students learn Spanish!

www.dinah.com

From Justo Lamas

I feel very blessed to be able to share these songs with you. I recorded them especially for young people who are learning Spanish, using the **¿Cómo te va?** program. Music can be a bridge between cultures, and I hope that my music helps young people to feel a sincere love for all peoples, regardless of cultural, racial, religious, and social differences. I hope to convey a sense of our rich Hispanic culture, but I am also sharing my feelings with you through my music. As a young person, I used music to gain self-esteem, and I hope that my songs will inspire young people today and help them find positive ways to feel good about themselves. These songs are also for Spanish teachers, who make important contributions to their students' lives every day, and I hope that they enjoy sharing these songs with their students.

justo-lamas.net

Table of Contents

Glencoe Spanish Program Articulation

We know that as a Middle School Spanish teacher you face unique challenges. For this reason Glencoe has developed a three-level Middle School Spanish program with a flexible format to meet your school's program configuration while providing your students with the content they need in a way that is manageable and fun. The flexibility built into this program is evident in the articulation from level to level as well as in the inclusion of required, recommended, and optional materials in the Student Editions.

You may begin the program with **¿Cómo te va? Intro, Nivel rojo** to introduce your students to Spanish. The content included in this level will be reintroduced and expanded upon in the next level. You may also choose to use **¿Cómo te va? Intro, Nivel rojo** if you teach an Exploratory Spanish course.

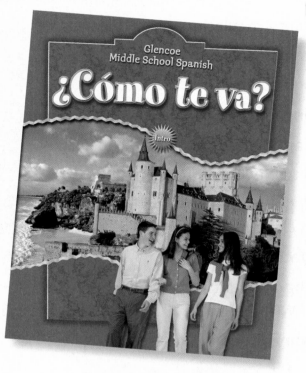

If your Middle School program is a two-year program you may begin with **¿Cómo te va? A, Nivel verde.** If you began your program with **¿Cómo te va? Intro, Nivel rojo,** the preliminary lessons will review and reinforce what you taught last year.

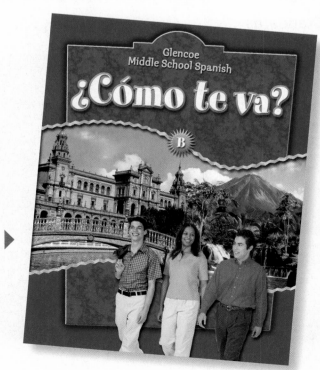

Your students will move seamlessly from **¿Cómo te va? A, Nivel verde** to **¿Cómo te va? B, Nivel azul.** Unit 6 of **Nivel verde** is repeated as Unit 1 of **Nivel azul.** In addition, **Repasos A, B, C** in **¿Cómo te va? B, Nivel azul** provide a review of what was taught in **Nivel verde.**

Your students are now prepared to begin Glencoe's **¡Buen viaje! Level 2.**

Scope and Sequence

Lesson 1
- Greeting people
- Greeting practices in the Spanish-speaking world
- Spain

Lesson 2
- Saying good-bye
- Names in Spanish
- Mexico

Lesson 3
- Counting from 1 to 30
- Finding out the price
- The numbers 1 and 7
- El Salvador

Lesson 4
- Speaking politely when ordering food
- Monetary systems
- Guatemala

Lesson 5
- Telling the days of the week
- Days of the week in the Spanish-speaking world
- Honduras

Lesson 6
- Months and seasons
- Finding out and giving the date
- Holidays in the Spanish-speaking world
- Nicaragua

Lesson 7
- Describing the weather
- Seasons in the Spanish-speaking world
- Costa Rica

Lesson 8
- Telling the time
- Counting from 31 to 60
- Telling what time something takes place
- The twenty-four-hour clock
- Panama

Lesson 9
- Telling what you speak
- Languages
- Cuba

Lesson 10
- Identifying classroom objects
- Identifying school supplies
- Telling what you need
- Asking what others need
- Dominican Republic

Lesson 11
- Identifying clothing
- Buying clothing
- Telling what clothing you are looking for
- Telling clothing sizes
- Puerto Rico

Lesson 12
- Reading in Spanish
- In a clothing store
- Talking about what others do
- Venezuela

Lesson 13
- Identifying colors
- Pablo Picasso
- Colombia

Lesson 14
- Telling who you are
- Finding out who someone is
- Names in Spanish
- Ecuador

Lesson 15
- Telling where you are from
- Finding out where someone is from
- Nationalities
- Peru

Lesson 16
- Telling what you study
- Asking what someone else studies
- Education in Spain and Latin America
- Bolivia

Lesson 17
- Reading some more in Spanish
- Students in the United States and in Mexico
- Chile

Lesson 18
- Identifying family members
- Finding out about someone's family
- Telling what you and others have
- Telling and finding out age
- The family in Hispanic culture
- Argentina

Lesson 19
- Describing your house
- Identifying rooms of a house or apartment
- Homes in the Spanish-speaking world
- Paraguay

Lesson 20
- Reading about a student in Puerto Rico
- Reading about biology
- Uruguay

Scope and Sequence

Nivel verde

Preliminary Lessons

Greeting people

Saying good-bye to people

Finding out and telling the days of the week

Finding out and telling the months of the year

Finding out and telling the date

Counting from 1 to 60

Telling time

Expressing simple courtesies

Telling about the seasons and weather

Unit 1

Topics
- Describing people and places
- Nationalities
- Numbers: 1–30
- School subjects and courses

Culture
- Carlos Irizarry, a student from San Juan, Puerto Rico
- Mara Crespo, a student from Santiago, Chile
- Schools in Spanish-speaking countries
- Enrique Iglesias, a famous Spanish singer
- Gloria Estefan, a famous Cuban American singer

Functions
- How to ask who someone is
- How to ask or tell what something is
- How to ask or tell where someone is from
- How to describe people or things
- How to identify people or things
- How to count from 1 to 30
- How to discuss classes in school
- How to express opinions about classes

Structure
- Singular and plural forms of definite and indefinite articles—**el, la, un, una**
- Singular and plural forms of adjectives
- Singular and plural forms of nouns
- Singular and plural forms of **ser**

Unit 2

Topics
- Family relationships
- Telling your age
- Numbers: 31–100
- Rooms in a house or an apartment

Culture
- The Garza family, from Miraflores, Lima, Peru
- **La quinceañera**
- Different types of houses in Peru
- *Las Meninas* by Diego Velázquez

Functions
- How to talk about your family
- How to count from 31 to 100
- How to describe your home
- How to tell and find out ages
- How to talk informally and formally
- How to talk about birthdays
- How to talk about what belongs to you and others
- How to talk about families in Spanish-speaking countries

Structure
- Singular and plural forms of the verb **tener**
- **Tú** versus **usted**
- Possessive adjectives

Unit 3

Topics
- Activities at home
- Going to school
- Activities at school
- Numbers: 100–1000
- Places you go

Culture
- Daily activities in the Spanish-speaking world compared to in the United States
- Schools in Spain and in Latin America
- The liberator Simón Bolívar
- A famous leader of Puerto Rico, Luis Muñoz Marín
- A famous Chilean poet, Gabriela Mistral
- Computer terms in Spanish

Functions
- How to talk about afterschool activities
- How to talk about what you and others do at home
- How to talk about going to school
- How to talk about school activities
- How to count from 100 to 1000
- How to say where you and others go
- How to say where you and others are

Structure
- Singular and plural forms of **-ar** verbs
- Singular and plural forms of **ir, dar,** and **estar**
- The contraction **al**

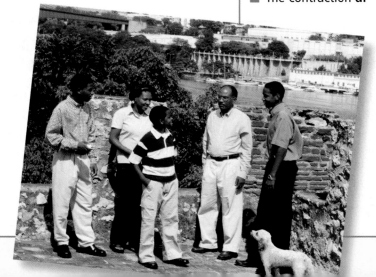

Nivel verde

Unit 4

Topics
- School supplies
- Shopping
- Numbers: 1,000 to 2,000,000
- Clothing
- Colors, sizes

Culture
- Similarities between the clothes young people wear in the United States and in Spanish-speaking countries
- Discussing school uniforms
- A famous clothing designer: Oscar de la Renta
- Indigenous clothing in Central and South America

Functions
- How to identify and describe school supplies
- How to count from 1,000 to 2,000,000
- How to describe articles of clothing
- How to state colors and sizes
- How to discuss what you are going to do
- How to tell what you have to do

Structure
- **Ir a; Tener que**
- Adjective agreement of colors
- Expressing amazement using **¡Qué... más... !**
- The contraction **del**

Unit 5

Topics
- Foods and beverages
- Eating at a café
- Shopping for food

Culture
- The importance of cafés
- Different types of popular Mexican and Spanish foods
- Open-air markets, indigenous markets, and supermarkets in Spain and in Latin America
- Eating habits in Spanish-speaking countries
- The metric system

Functions
- How to find a table at a café
- How to order in a café
- How to identify some foods
- How to shop for food
- How to talk about what you and others do

Structure
- Singular and plural forms of **-er** and **-ir** verbs

Unit 6

Topics
- Team sports
- Physical activities

Culture
- The importance of sports in the Spanish-speaking world
- The World Cup of soccer
- A famous baseball player from the Dominican Republic: Sammy Sosa
- A famous Spanish golfer: Sergio García
- Other famous sports stars from Spain and Latin America

Functions
- How to talk about sports
- How to talk about people's physical activities
- How to tell what you begin to, want to, and prefer to do
- How to express what interests, bores, or pleases you

Structure
- Stem-changing verbs **e → ie**
- Stem-changing verbs **o → ue**
- **Interesar, aburrir,** and **gustar**

Scope and Sequence

Nivel azul

Unit 1

Topics
- Team sports
- Physical activities

Culture
- The importance of sports in the Spanish-speaking world
- The World Cup of soccer
- A famous baseball player from the Dominican Republic: Sammy Sosa
- A famous Spanish golfer: Sergio García
- Other famous sports stars from Spain and Latin America

Functions
- How to talk about team sports
- How to talk about people's physical activities
- How to tell what you begin to, want to, and prefer to do
- How to express what interests, bores, or pleases you

Structure
- Stem-changing verbs **e → ie**
- Stem-changing verbs **o → ue**
- **Interesar, aburrir,** and **gustar**

Unit 2

Topics
- Minor illnesses
- Symptoms of a cold, flu, or fever
- Emotions
- Medical exams
- Parts of the body
- Prescriptions

Culture
- Adela goes to the doctor with a minor illness
- Comparisons between different types of **clínicas** in the Spanish-speaking world and in the United States
- Information about nutrition in Spanish

Functions
- How to explain a minor illness to a doctor
- How to describe some feelings
- How to have a prescription filled at a pharmacy
- How to describe characteristics or conditions
- How to tell where things are and where they're from
- How to tell where someone or something is now
- How to discuss what happens to you or to someone else

Structure
- **Ser** and **estar**
- **Me, te, nos**
- **Le** and **les**

Unit 3

Topics
- Air travel
- Travel-related activities

Culture
- The importance of air travel in South America
- The Andes Mountains
- The Amazon River
- The Nazca lines of Peru
- A Latin American astronaut: Elena Ochoa
- Differences between the twenty-four-hour clock and the system used in the United States

Functions
- How to check in for a flight
- How to tell what you and others are currently doing
- How to get through the airport after checking in for a flight
- How to tell what and whom you know

Structure
- **Hacer, poner, traer,** and **salir** in the present
- The present progressive
- **Saber** and **conocer** in the present

Unit 4

Topics
- Summer and winter weather
- Summer and winter sports and leisure activities

Culture
- Some typical Saturday activities for Iván, a Puerto Rican boy, and his friends
- Weather in Puerto Rico
- Stands that sell fresh snacks on the beach
- Resorts in the Spanish-speaking world
- Opposite seasons in the Northern and Southern Hemispheres
- A Cuban American speedskater: Jennifer Rodriguez

Functions
- How to describe summer and winter weather
- How to discuss past actions and events
- How to talk about summer sports and summer activities
- How to talk about winter sports
- How to refer to persons and things already mentioned

Structure
- Preterite of **-ar** verbs
- Direct object pronouns—**lo, la, los, las**
- **Ir** and **ser** in the preterite

Unit 5

Topics
- Going to a movie
- Renting a video
- Attending a concert
- Visiting a museum

Culture
- Antonio has some friends over for pizza
- The famous Spanish novel *Lazarillo de Tormes*
- A Spanish painter: Francisco de Goya
- A modern Spanish artist: Joan Miró
- A Mexican muralist: José Clemente Orozco
- A Mexican surrealist: Frida Kahlo
- A Puerto Rican singer: Ricky Martin
- A Spanish singer: Plácido Domingo
- Different types of Latin music

Functions
- How to discuss movies, museums, and concerts
- How to relate more past actions or events
- How to talk about what does not happen

Structure
- Preterite of **-er** and **-ir** verbs
- Negative words
- Preterite of **leer** and **oír**

Unit 6

Topics
- Daily routines
- Grooming habits
- Camping

Culture
- Camping in the Spanish-speaking world
- Comparisons between breakfast foods in the United States, Spain, and Latin America
- Ecology in the Spanish-speaking world

Functions
- How to describe your personal grooming habits
- How to talk about your daily routine
- How to tell some things you do for yourself
- How to talk about a camping trip

Structure
- Reflexive verbs
- Stem-changing reflexive verbs

Pacing and Priorities

Each unit of **¿Cómo te va?** contains required, recommended, and optional material. **Palabras, Formas, and Conversación** sections are always required. The recommended sections include the **Pronunciación, Cultura y lectura, Repaso, ¡Te toca a ti!, Assessment,** and **¡Hablo como un pro!** Optional material can be found in **Diversiones, Más cultura y lectura,** and **Conexiones.** The following chart provides you with a guide to the number of required, recommended, and optional pages in each of the six units.

Unit Planning in the Student Edition

Unit	required number of pages	recommended number of pages	optional number of pages
1	19	10	6
2	19	10	6
3	19	10	8
4	19	10	8
5	17	10	10
6	17	10	8
Total:	**110 required**	**60 recommended**	**46 optional**

Note: Unit 6 of **¿Cómo te va? A, Nivel verde** is repeated as Unit 1 of **¿Cómo te va? B, Nivel azul** for additional flexibility.

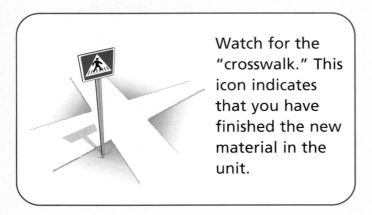

Watch for the "crosswalk." This icon indicates that you have finished the new material in the unit.

Helping Middle School Students Succeed

The organization of the text is the key to helping students succeed. The pages of **¿Cómo te va?** are colorful and inviting but never cluttered. Visuals are carefully placed to aid comprehension and to present the target culture. The topics presented in the text provide students with language they need to communicate in real-life situations.

Each **Unidad** is organized to lead students step-by-step to proficiency. At the beginning of each **Unidad** students see clearly stated objectives. The material in **¿Cómo te va?** is presented in chunks that will not overwhelm the Middle School student.

There are four **Pasos** in each **Unidad. Paso 1** and **Paso 2** contain the words and structures necessary to talk about the theme of the **Unidad.** Students learn to construct language by moving from words to phrases to paragraphs. This process gives students a real understanding of Spanish and an ability to create meaning.

The "crosswalk" is your signal that the new materials in the **Unidad** have been presented and that your students are moving ahead to polish their skills and to have fun with their newly learned language.

In **Paso 3** students fine-tune their spoken language skills in **Conversación** and in **Pronunciación.** They improve their reading skills while learning about culture. **Repaso, ¡Te toca a ti!,** and **Assessment** give students a chance to review, apply, and evaluate.

Paso 4 includes **Rompecabezas, Canciones, Teatro,** and **Plegables™** to meet the needs of the energetic Middle School student. Students will have so much fun with these activities that they will forget they are practicing their new skills.

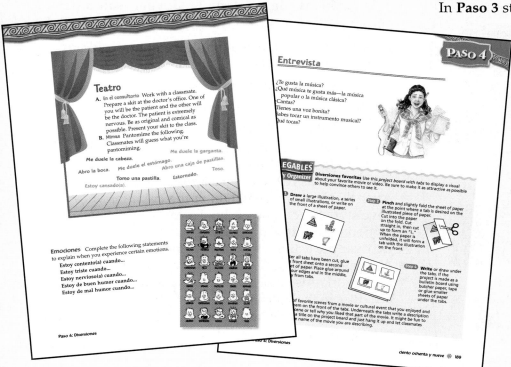

Helping Students Acquire Vocabulary

The students are introduced to new vocabulary in the **Palabras** section in **Paso 1** and in **Paso 2** of each unit. These sections contain a manageable number of new words that are all needed to communicate about a specific topic. The **Palabras** section always contains single words accompanied by an illustration that helps the student understand the meaning of the word without relying on translation. In addition, new words are contextualized in sentences. The structure that will be presented in the unit is presented lexically with the vocabulary.

Techniques for Presenting and Practicing Vocabulary

Glencoe provides several tools for presenting and practicing vocabulary. The Vocabulary Transparencies contain the illustrations from the vocabulary presentation in your text. You may wish to use these to present the new vocabulary. There are text overlays as well to offer you additional options. The vocabulary is also recorded on the Audio Program to help you vary presentation and practice. Additional practice for each **Palabras** section is included in the Workbook.

You may vary your presentation of **Palabras** to accommodate the learning styles of your students and to emphasize different skills by following the suggested techniques.

To emphasize oral and aural skills

Option 1 This option for the presentation of vocabulary best meets the needs of those teachers who consider the development of oral skills a prime objective.

- While students have their books closed, project the Vocabulary Transparencies. Point to the item being taught and have students repeat the word after you or the compact disc several times. After you have presented several words in this manner, project the transparencies again and ask questions such as:

  ¿Es un pasaporte?

  ¿Quién revisa el pasaporte?

  ¿Quién hace un viaje?

- To teach the contextualized segments on the **Palabras** pages, project the Vocabulary Transparency in the same way. Point to the part of the illustration that depicts the meaning of any new word in a sentence, be it an isolated sentence or a sentence from a conversation or narrative. Immediately ask questions about the sentence. For example, the following sentences appear in Unit 3:

  Los pasajeros están esperando en la puerta de salida. El avión sale de la puerta 14. El vuelo sale a tiempo.

  Questions to ask are:

  ¿Los pasajeros están esperando en el mostrador o en la puerta de salida?

  ¿Quiénes están esperando?

  ¿De qué puerta sale el avión?

  ¿Sale a tiempo el vuelo?

- Dramatizations by the teacher, in addition to the illustrations, can also help convey the meaning of many words such as **revisar el pasaporte, abordar,** etc.
- After this basic presentation of the **Palabras** vocabulary, have students open their books and read the **Palabras** section for additional reinforcement.
- Go over the activities in the **Palabras** section orally.
- Assign the activities in the **Palabras** section for homework. Also assign the corresponding vocabulary activities in the Workbook. If the **Palabras** section should take more than one day, assign only those activities that correspond to the material you have presented.

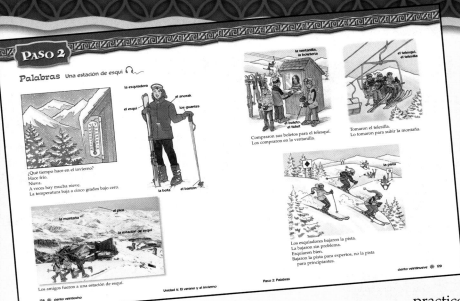

- The following day, go over the activities that were assigned for homework.

To balance oral, reading, and writing skills

Option 2 This option will meet the needs of those teachers who wish to teach the oral skills but consider reading and writing equally important.

- Project the Vocabulary Transparencies and have students repeat each word once or twice after you or the compact disc.
- Have students repeat the contextualized sentences after you or the compact disc as they look at the illustration.
- Ask students to open their books. Have them read the **Palabras** section. Correct pronunciation errors as they are made.
- Go over the activities in each **Palabras** section.
- Assign the activities in the **Palabras** section for homework. Also assign the vocabulary activities in the Workbook.
- The following day, go over the activities that were assigned for homework.

To emphasize reading and writing skills

Option 3 This option will meet the needs of those teachers who consider the reading and writing skills of utmost importance.

- Have students open their books and read the **Palabras** items as they look at the illustrations.
- Give students several minutes to look at the **Palabras** words and vocabulary activities. Then go over the activities.
- Go over the activities the following day.

    With all options you may wish to project the vocabulary overlays and point to words as students repeat them.

Practice Activities

The practice activities that follow each **Palabras** presentation give you the flexibility to customize to meet diverse student needs. The activities progress in difficulty. An easy activity may only require the student to produce a *yes* or *no* answer. As the activities progress in difficulty the student will be asked to produce single-word answers to phrases to sentences using a variety of forms. In the activities marked **Historieta**, each item is linked to create a story. If these activities are done orally in class, students must listen to their peers to correctly continue the story. Students who need extra practice can retell the story using the book as a guide. **Advanced learners** may retell the story without looking at the text. Once the story has been retold you may wish to extend the activity by having the students ask one another questions, give an oral synopsis of the story, or write a short paragraph about the story.

Additional Activities

You may use any of the following activities occasionally. These can be done in conjunction with the options previously outlined.

- After the vocabulary has been presented, project the Vocabulary Transparencies or have students open their books and make up as many original sentences as they can, using the new words. This can be done orally or in writing.
- Have students work in pairs or small groups. As they look at the illustrations in the textbook, have them make up as many questions as they can. They can direct their questions to their peers. It is often fun to make this a competitive activity. Individuals or teams can compete to make up the most questions in three minutes. This activity provides the students with an excellent opportunity to use interrogative words.
- Call on one student to read to the class one of the vocabulary activities that tells a story. Then call on an **advanced learner** to retell the story in his or her own words.
- With **students with learning difficulties** have one student go to the front of the room. Have him or her think of one of the new words. Let classmates give the student the new words from the **Palabras** until they guess the word the student in the front of the room has in mind. This is a very easy way to have the students recall the words they have just learned.

Helping Students Put Language Together

The **Formas** section of each **Paso** gives the students the tools they need to express their ideas coherently. Models in the **Formas** section are always presented using known vocabulary. Only those **Formas** needed to communicate about the topic are presented. Students will always see a purpose for the grammar they are learning. Grammar explanations are given in clear and simple English. Each explanation is accompanied by examples. Frequently, illustrations and graphic organizers are also used to support the explanations. **English language learners** and **students with learning difficulties** will find the **Formas** explanations accessible.

Certain structure points are taught more effectively in their entirety and others are more easily acquired if they are taught in segments. For example, the pronouns **me, te,** and **nos** are taught together, followed by the pronouns **le** and **les,** and later the pronouns **lo, la, los,** and **las** are taught. Irregular verb patterns are grouped together to make them appear more regular. For example, **hacer, poner, traer,** and **salir** are taught together in **Unidad 3.**

Whenever the contrast between English and Spanish poses problems for students in the learning process, a contrasting analysis between the two languages is made. An example of this is the **gustar** construction in **Unidad 1.**

Techniques for Presenting Formas

Option 1 Some teachers prefer the deductive approach to the teaching of grammar. When this is the preferred method, you can begin the **Formas** section of the unit by presenting the grammatical rule to students or by having them read the rule in their textbooks. After students have gone over the rule, have them read the examples in their textbooks or write the examples on the chalkboard. Then proceed with the activities that follow the grammatical explanation.

Option 2 Other teachers prefer the inductive approach to the teaching of grammar. If this is the case, begin the **Formas** section by writing the examples that accompany the rule on the chalkboard or by having students read them in their textbooks.

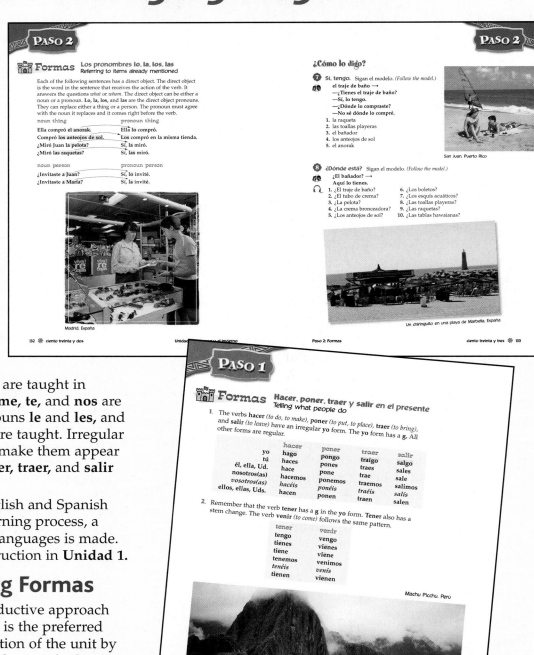

Specific Techniques for Practicing Formas

In the development of the Middle School series, we have purposely provided a wide variety of activities in the **Formas** section to meet the needs of all students and to keep them interested. The types of activities they will encounter are: reading and engaging in short conversations, answering questions, conducting or taking part in an interview, making up questions, describing an illustration, filling in the blanks, multiple choice, completing a narrative, etc. You may wish to choose to lead the activities or you may create a more student-centered activity by having the students work in pairs or small groups. The **Formas** activities can be done orally in class before they are assigned for homework or they may be assigned as written work before they are done orally. You may want to vary their approach to accommodate all learning styles.

All the **¿Cómo lo digo?** activities in the Student Edition can be done with books open. Many of the activities such as question-answer, interview, and transformation can also be done with books closed.

Practice Activities

As with the activities following **Palabras,** the **Formas** activities give you many options for targeting different levels of ability. The activities are presented from simple to more complex. In the case of verbs with an irregular form, for example, emphasis is placed on the irregular form, since it is the one students will most often confuse or forget. In all cases, students are given one or more activities that require them to use all forms at random. The first few activities that follow the **Formas** explanation assist the students in grasping and internalizing the new grammar concept. Subsequent activities require the students to recombine all aspects of the material they have learned. This format greatly assists teachers in meeting the needs of the various ability levels of students in their classes.

Certain activities from the Student Edition are recorded on the Audio Program. Whenever an activity is recorded, it is noted with an appropriate icon in the Teacher Edition.

The activities in the Workbook also parallel the order of presentation in the Student Edition. The Workbook is an essential tool for reinforcement of the material presented in the text.

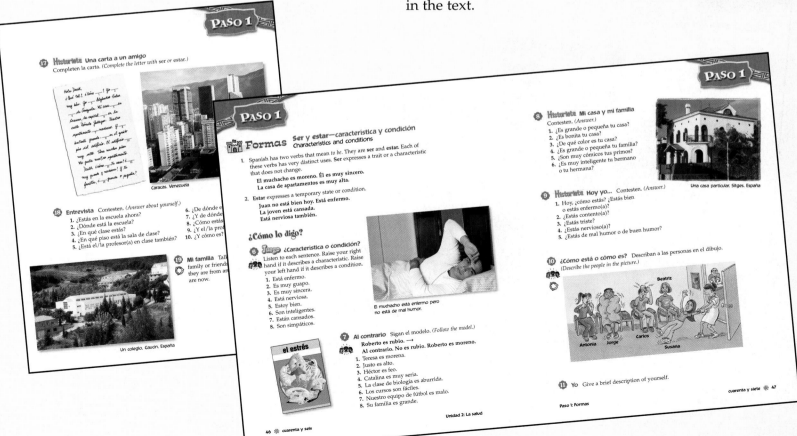

Helping Students Develop Speaking and Listening Skills

Students will begin to develop strong speaking skills from their first day with **¿Cómo te va?** The preliminary lessons launch the students into basic Spanish that will allow them to function in the classroom in Spanish. The program is designed so students will have minimal reliance on translation. Therefore, it is possible to conduct class almost exclusively in Spanish. To ensure that your students have exposure to other voices, it is suggested that you use the Audio Program to present vocabulary and to reinforce other skills. In addition, the varied accents on the Audio Program will acquaint students with accents from all parts of the Spanish-speaking world. All the practice activities in **¿Cómo te va?** can be done orally. You will optimize your students' speaking and listening skills if you practice orally with them in class. Activities that are practiced orally in class may also

be done as written assignments for reinforcement. **Un poco más** directs your students to *InfoGap* activities that allow them to practice speaking with a partner.

Palabras are often illustrated in conversation format. Your students are presented with a more extended conversation in the unit once they have learned the necessary words and forms. They will be able to comprehend this conversation easily and perform it or manipulate it to make it their own.

Pronunciation sections will help your students grasp the sound system and to produce more native Spanish.

The activities in **¿Cómo te va?** are intended to help Middle School students have fun and feel comfortable listening to and speaking Spanish. **Trabalenguas, Refranes,** and **Teatro** all give the students opportunities to practice and to perform. The songs on the **Canta con Justo CD** and the **¡En vivo! Justo Lamas music video** will help students sharpen their listening skills and develop fluidity in their spoken language.

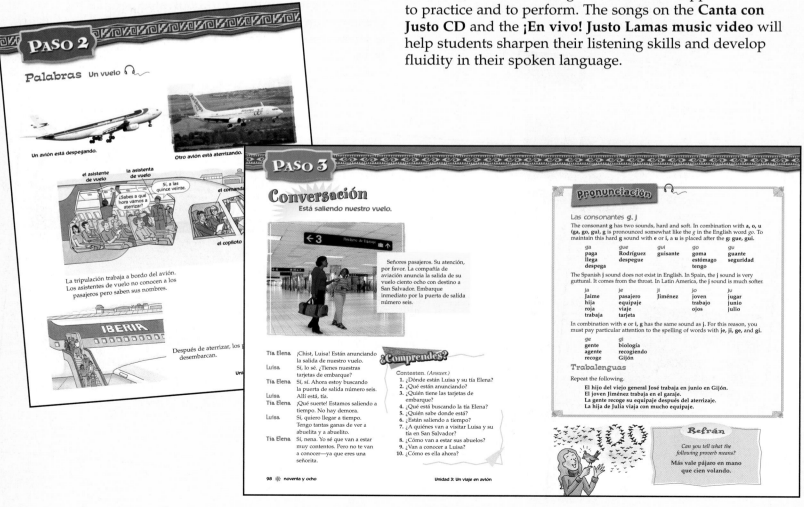

Integrating Culture

True competence in a foreign language cannot be attained without simultaneous development of an awareness of the culture in which the language is spoken. Culture is emphasized throughout ¿Cómo te va?

In **El mundo hispanohablante** the students are introduced to the vast Spanish-speaking world. This section of the text continues to serve as a reference as the students learn about the Spanish-speaking world in greater detail. The physical and linguistic diversity of the Spanish-speaking world is evident throughout **¿Cómo te va?**

In **¿Cómo te va?** language and culture are interwoven. Students learn language related to a particular topic and see how that topic is reflected in the Spanish-speaking world. In **Cultura y lectura** the students have the opportunity to expand their cultural knowledge while improving their reading skills.

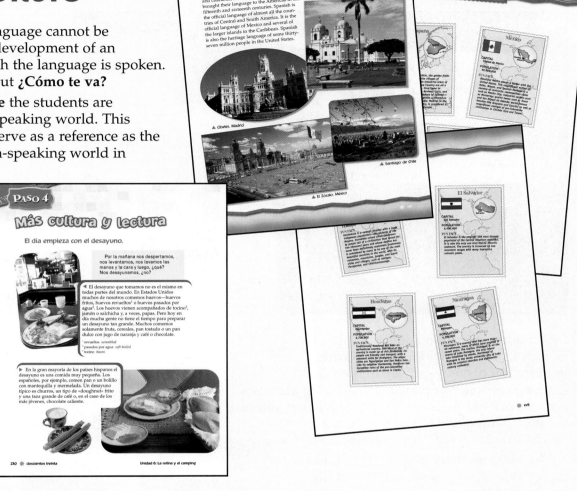

Helping Students Develop Reading and Writing Skills

¿Cómo te va? provides a strong foundation for students to develop reading skills in Spanish. From the very beginning students are led through the steps that help mold good reading skills. Careful attention was paid to developing considerate text. The visual context supports the meaning of the text. Readings include words and structures that were previously taught. The readings in the text are purposeful.

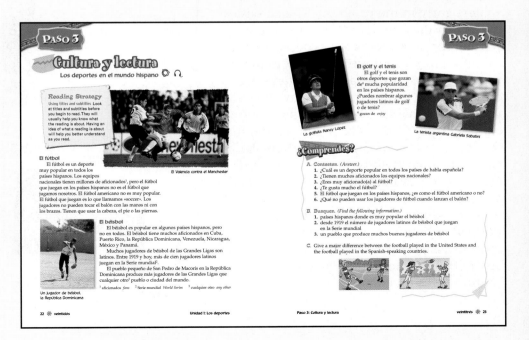

Helping Students Develop Reading and Writing Skills *(continued)*

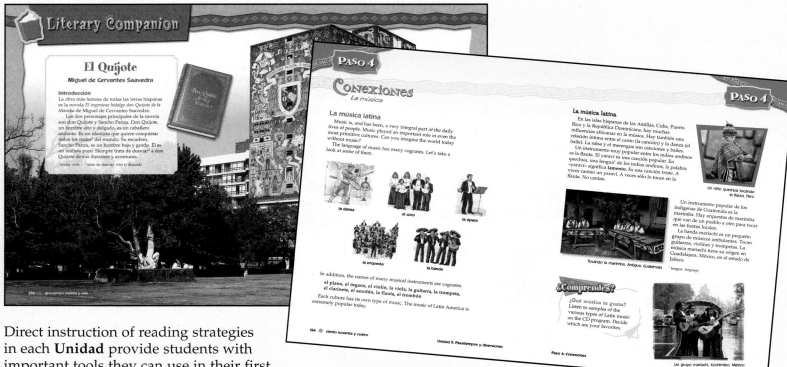

Direct instruction of reading strategies in each **Unidad** provide students with important tools they can use in their first language as well as Spanish. Pre-reading activities activate prior knowledge so the student can interact with the text. **¿Cómo te va?** students become successful readers of "real" literature.

The same methodology in **¿Cómo te va?** that enables students to understand the language system allows them to become writers early in the program. The activities in the text may be done either in oral or written form. Students are exposed to good, extended models of writing early in the program. Most importantly, students are only asked to produce written language when they have the tools to do so confidently. Activities help guide them from the smallest task of supplying letters to complete a word, to writing single-word answers, to writing lists, letters, paragraphs, and stories. Strategies for developing good writing skills are introduced in each unit. **Plegables**™ often help students organize their writing assignments. The Workbook provides an opportunity for students to practice their writing skills on a daily basis.

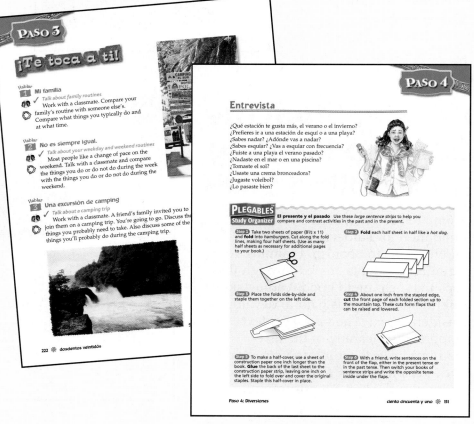

Assessing Students' Progress

Frequent and varied assessment will give you an accurate picture of student success and let you know when intervention is needed. The **¿Cómo te va?** program provides several tools for assessing students' progress in

all four skill areas. Checkups are presented throughout the Teacher Wraparound Edition.

The Assessment pages of **¿Cómo te va?** give students the opportunity to check their own mastery of the material. Assessment Answer worksheets and answers are provided in the Transparency Binder.

At the end of each **Unidad** there is an illustration that depicts the theme of the unit. This feature, **¡Hablo como un pro!,** provides an excellent opportunity for students to show their written or oral proficiency by telling as much as they can about the illustration. You may choose to use the rubrics on pages T22–T23 to assess their performance.

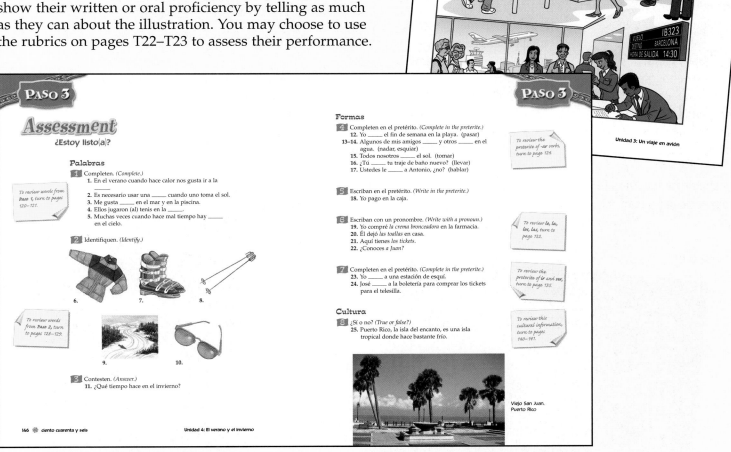

In addition to the many opportunities for assessment in the textbook, separate quizzes and reading, writing, listening, speaking, and proficiency tests are provided in the TeacherTools for each **Unidad.** You may create your own customized assessment tools using the ExamView Pro® Test Generator. Online quizzes are also available.

Rubric for Speaking

Analytic Scoring Guide for Rating Speaking Products

VOCABULARY

4 Vocabulary is generally accurate and appropriate to the task; minor errors, hesitations, and circumlocutions may occur.

3 Vocabulary is usually accurate; errors, hesitations, and circumlocutions may be frequent.

2 Vocabulary is not extensive enough for the task; inaccuracies or repetition may be frequent; may use English words.

1 Vocabulary inadequate for most basic aspects of the task.

0 No response.

GRAMMAR

4 Grammar may contain some inaccuracies, but these do not negatively affect comprehensibility.

3 Some grammatical inaccuracies may affect comprehensibility; some control of major patterns.

2 Many grammatical inaccuracies may affect comprehensibility; little control of major patterns.

1 Almost all grammatical patterns inaccurate, except for a few memorized patterns.

0 No response.

PRONUNCIATION

4 Completely or almost completely comprehensible; pronunciation errors, rhythm and/or intonation problems do not create misunderstandings.

3 Generally comprehensible, but pronunciation errors, rhythm and/or intonation problems may create misunderstandings.

2 Difficult to comprehend because of numerous pronunciation errors, rhythm, and intonation problems.

1 Practically incomprehensible.

0 No response.

MESSAGE CONTENT

4 Relevant, informative response to the task. Adequate level of detail and creativity.

3 Response to the task is generally informative; may lack some detail and/or creativity.

2 Response incomplete; lacks some important information.

1 Response not informative; provides little or no information.

0 No response.

Rubric for Writing

Analytic Scoring Guide for Rating Writing Products

VOCABULARY

4 Vocabulary is generally accurate and appropriate to the task; minor errors may occur.

3 Vocabulary is usually accurate; occasional inaccuracies may occur.

2 Vocabulary is not extensive enough for the task; inaccuracies may be frequent; may use English words.

1 Vocabulary inadequate for most basic aspects of the task.

0 No response.

GRAMMAR

4 Grammar may contain some inaccuracies, but these do not negatively affect comprehensibility.

3 Some grammatical inaccuracies may affect comprehensibility; some control of major patterns.

2 Many grammatical inaccuracies may affect comprehensibility; little control of major patterns.

1 Almost all grammatical patterns inaccurate, except for a few memorized patterns.

0 No response.

MECHANICS

4 Good control of the mechanics of Spanish; may contain occasional errors in spelling, diacritics, or punctuation, but these do not affect comprehensibility.

3 Some control of the mechanics of Spanish; contains errors in spelling, diacritics, or punctuation that sometimes affect comprehensibility.

2 Weak control of the mechanics of Spanish; contains numerous errors in spelling, diacritics, or punctuation that seriously affect comprehensibility.

1 Almost no control of the mechanics of Spanish.

0 No response.

MESSAGE CONTENT

4 Relevant, informative response to the task. Adequate level of detail and creativity.

3 Response to the task is generally informative; may lack some detail and/or creativity.

2 Response incomplete; lacks some important information.

1 Response not informative; provides little or no information.

0 No response.

Making Your Job Easier

Just as the **¿Cómo te va?** Student Edition is designed to make learning Spanish as easy as it can be for the student, the **¿Cómo te va? Teacher Wraparound Edition** is designed to help make teaching easier. We hope that we have been able to provide you with information, ideas, and organizational hints that will save you time and allow you to focus on your students.

The pages preceding each **Unidad** show you all the ancillary support for the **Unidad** and will help you plan effectively and easily. In these pages, we also show you the Correlations to the National Standards. The Pacing and Priorities Chart is here to remind you which pages in the text are required, recommended, or optional.

Preview The preview allows you to see at a glance what the students will learn in the unit.

Spotlight on Culture This feature gives you complete information about the photos and art used in the text pages. You may share this information with your students for enrichment without taking the time to do the research.

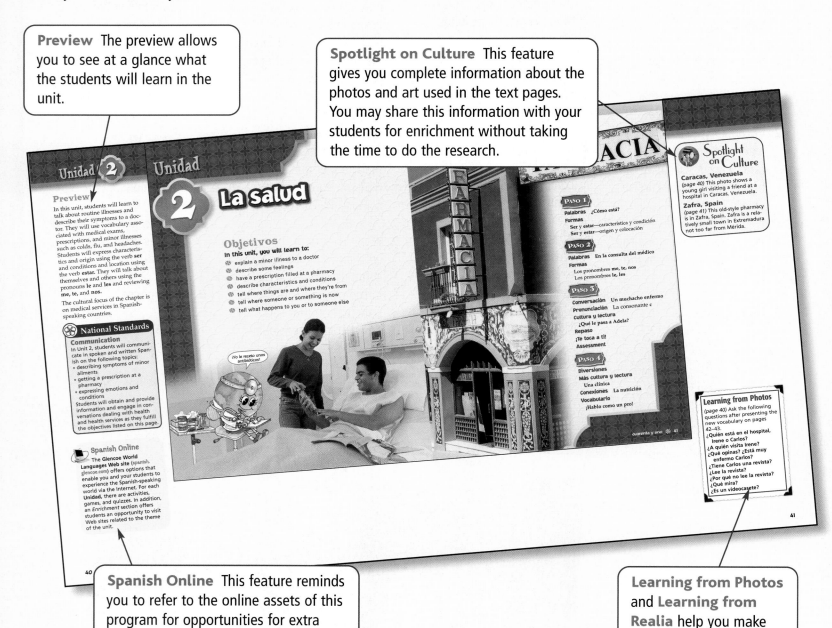

Spanish Online This feature reminds you to refer to the online assets of this program for opportunities for extra practice and for enrichment for **students with learning difficulties** as well as **advanced learners.**

Learning from Photos and **Learning from Realia** help you make the most of the visuals in the text.

Making Your Job Easier

Resource Manager lets you know which resources you will need for each **Paso**.

Bellringer Review (also available in the Transparency Binder) provides a quick review activity for the class.

About the Spanish Language points out interesting facts about language throughout the Spanish-speaking world.

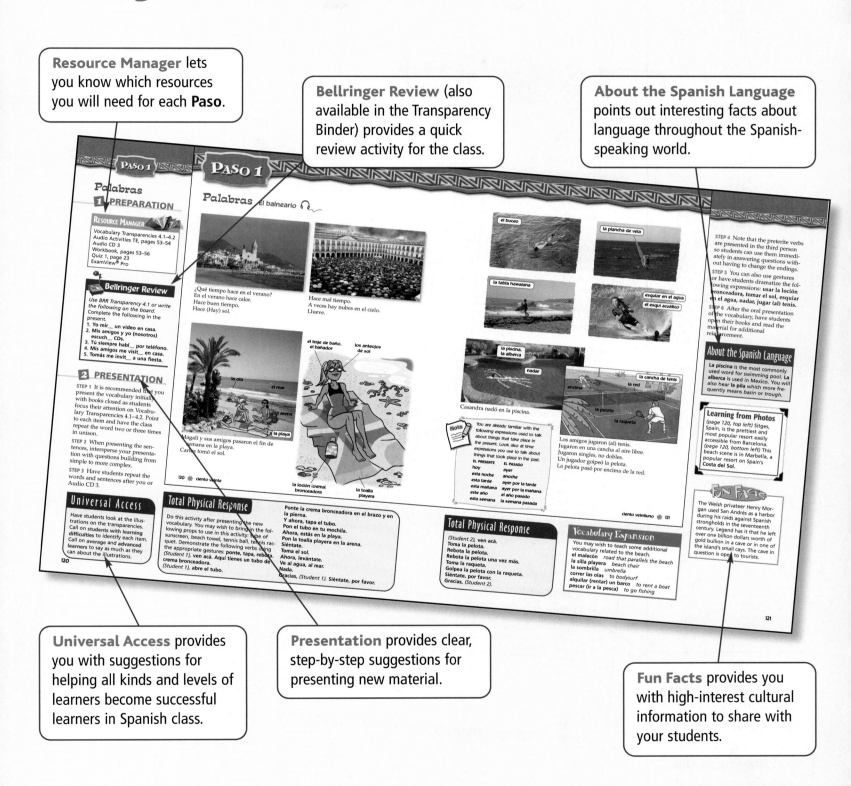

Universal Access provides you with suggestions for helping all kinds and levels of learners become successful learners in Spanish class.

Presentation provides clear, step-by-step suggestions for presenting new material.

Fun Facts provides you with high-interest cultural information to share with your students.

Making Your Job Easier

¡OJO! calls your attention to hints for avoiding potential pitfalls.

Writing Development gives you additional ideas for assigning and maintaining written work, particularly for portfolio assessment.

Answers are always provided at the bottom of the page for easy reference.

PASO 1

3 PRACTICE

¿Qué palabra necesito?

¡OJO! When students are doing the **¿Qué palabra necesito?** activities, accept any answer that makes sense. The purpose of these activities is to have students use the new vocabulary. They are not factual recall activities. Thus, it is not necessary for students to remember specific factual information from the vocabulary presentation when answering. If you wish, have students use the photos on this page as a stimulus, when possible.

Historieta Each time **Historieta** appears, it means that the answers to the activity form a short story. Encourage students to look at the title of the **Historieta,** since it can help them do the activity.

2 and **3** After going over Activities 2 and 3 on pages 4 and 5, call on one or more students to retell the stories in their own words.

Note: Activity 3 uses only the third person form of the stem-changing verbs so that the students can immediately answer questions and speak without having to change endings. Students will learn how to manipulate the stem-changing verbs in the **Formas** section of **Paso 1** of this unit.

Writing Development
Have students write the answers to Activity 2 in a paragraph to illustrate how the answers to all the items tell a story.

4

PASO 1

¿Qué palabra necesito?

1 Un partido de fútbol Completen según se indica.
(Answer as indicated.)

1. Diego lanza el balón con _____.

2. Él no lanza el balón con _____.

3. También lanza el balón con _____.

4. Pero no lanza el balón con _____.

5. Diego es un jugador muy bueno porque tiene _____ fuertes.

2 Historieta El fútbol Contesten según se indica.
(Answer as indicated.)

1. ¿Cuántos jugadores hay en el equipo de fútbol? (once)
2. ¿Cuántos tiempos hay en un partido de fútbol? (dos)
3. ¿Quién guarda la portería? (el portero)
4. ¿Cuándo mete un gol el jugador? (cuando el balón entra en la portería)
5. ¿Qué marca un jugador cuando el balón entra en la portería? (un tanto)
6. En el estadio, ¿qué indica el tablero? (el tanto)
7. ¿Cuándo queda empatado el tanto? (cuando los dos equipos tienen el mismo tanto)

Unidad 1: Los deportes

4 ❋ cuatro

ANSWERS TO ¿Qué palabra necesito?

1
1. el pie
2. la mano
3. la cabeza
4. el brazo
5. piernas

2
1. Hay once jugadores en el equipo de fútbol.
2. Hay dos tiempos en un partido de fútbol.
3. El portero guarda la portería.
4. El jugador mete un gol cuando el balón entra en la portería.
5. Un jugador marca un tanto cuando el balón entra en la portería.
6. El tablero indica el tanto.
7. El tanto queda empatado cuando los d...

Making Your Job Easier

Historieta gives you suggestions for using these special activities that enable students to tell a story as they practice.

PASO 2

¿Cómo lo digo?

8 **Historieta** **Juan lo leyó.**
Cambien **yo** a **Juan.** (*Change yo to Juan.*)

1. Yo leí el anuncio del concierto.
2. Yo lo leí en la revista *Tú.*
3. Yo oí el concierto.
4. Yo oí a Alejandro Sanz. Él cantó muy bien.

9 **¿Qué leíste?** Den el pretérito. (*Give the preterite.*)

1. Lo leo. No lo oigo.
2. Ella lo lee. No lo oye.
3. Lo leemos. No lo oímos.
4. ¿Lo lees? ¿No lo oyes?

10 **Ayer** Look at the following illustration. Tell a friend all that your sister and her friends did last weekend. Answer any questions your friend may have.

  For more practice using words and forms from **Paso 2,** do Activity 10 on page H11 at the end of this book.

Andas bien. ¡Adelante!

Paso 2: Formas

---

3 PRACTICE

¿Cómo lo digo?

8 and **9** These activities can be done with books open.

Universal Access

Have students bring in a book they read recently and a CD they like to listen to. Have them hold up the book or the CD and say they read or listened to it. Then have others in the class tell whether they have read the book or listened to the CD. This activity will be especially beneficial for kinesthetic learners.

✓ Assessment

You may wish to give the following dictations.

1. Lo leí.
2. Lo lee.

3. Lo leo.
4. Lo leyó.

or

1. Yo lo leí.
2. Ella lo lee.

3. Yo lo leo.
4. Él lo oyó.

Option 1 strictly tests sound/symbol. Option 2 with the subject pronouns gives grammatical assistance.

 This *InfoGap* activity will allow students to practice in pairs. The activity should be very manageable for them, since all vocabulary and structures are familiar to them.

¡Adelante! At this point, all new material has been presented. Students have learned all the vocabulary and structure necessary to complete the unit. The conversation, cultural readings, and activities in **Paso 3** and **Paso 4** recycle all the material learned up to this point.

Un poco más lets you know that there is an *InfoGap* activity that corresponds to the material the students are practicing. The *InfoGap* activities begin on page H2.

ANSWERS TO **¿Cómo lo digo?**

8
1. Juan leyó el anuncio del concierto.
2. Juan lo leyó en la revista *Tú.*
3. Juan oyó el concierto.
4. Juan oyó a Alejandro Sanz. Él cantó muy bien.

9
1. Lo leí. No lo oí.
2. Ella lo leyó. No lo oyó.
3. Lo leímos. No lo oímos.
4. ¿Lo leíste? ¿No lo oíste?

10 *Answers will vary. Students should use the preterite tense.*

Learning from Realia

(page 175, top left) Have students work in pairs. One student will pretend he or she attended this concert. The other will ask questions about the concert such as who, where, when, and whether he or she enjoyed it.

175

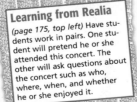

¡Adelante! signals you that you have presented all of the new material in the **Unidad.**

Program Resources

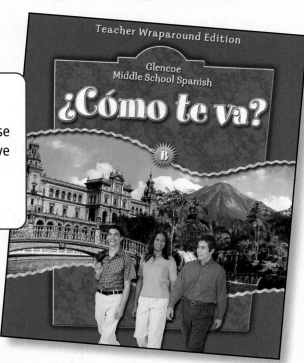

Teacher Wraparound Edition

Glencoe
Middle School Spanish

¿Cómo te va?

B

¿Cómo te va? Teacher Wraparound Edition

The **¿Cómo te va?** Teacher Wraparound Edition provides tips for presentation, pacing, and assessment to make it easy for you to use the text. Additional features in the Teacher Wraparound Edition give you cultural information about art and photos, facts about the Spanish language, ideas for Online activities and strategies for Universal Access to help you meet the needs of all learners.

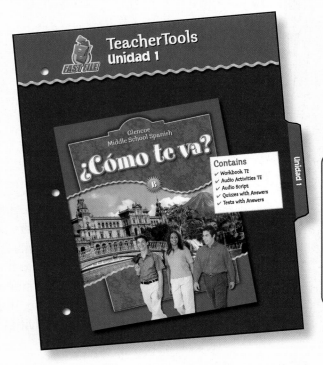

TeacherTools
Unidad 1

Glencoe
Middle School Spanish

¿Cómo te va?

B

Contains
- Workbook TE
- Audio Activities TE
- Audio Script
- Quizzes with Answers
- Tests with Answers

Unidad 1

TeacherTools

In **¿Cómo te va?** your teacher materials are organized by unit in FastFile booklets to make it easier for you to plan your classes and to maintain your materials. Each FastFile booklet contains Workbook TE, Audio Activities TE, Audio Script, Quizzes, and Tests.

Glencoe Exclusive!

TeacherWorks™

All-In-One Planner and Resource Center

Glencoe
Middle School Spanish

¿Cómo te va?

B

- Interactive Teacher Edition
- Interactive Lesson Planner with Calendar
- Point and Click Access to Teaching Resources
- Hotlinks to the Internet

P/N G00000.00

TeacherWorks™

All-In-One Planner and Resource Center

Windows/Macintosh
Version 1.0

0-07-860560-1
G05601.01
6/03

Mc Graw Hill Glencoe

Copyright © by The McGraw-Hill Companies Inc. All rights reserved

Glencoe Middle School Spanish

¿Cómo te va?

B

Software Support Hotline: 1-800-437-3715 or epgtech@mcgraw-hill.com

TeacherWorks™

The TeacherWorks™ All-In-One Planner and Resource Center will save you hours of planning time. This program will help you launch your program's software, view and add correlations, edit and modify teacher resources, create calendars, customize lesson planning, and organize your year.

Program Resources

Transparency Binder

The **¿Cómo te va?** Transparency Binder provides you with easy-to-use visual support for presentation, practice, and review. Transparencies include Maps, Songs, Alphabet, Bellringer Reviews, Vocabulary (art, photos, translated lists, and overlays with words), Pronunciation, and Assessment Answers.

Audio CD Program

The Audio CD Program includes additional activities to reinforce the material presented in **¿Cómo te va?** The Audio Program provides the opportunity for the students to hear a variety of voices and accents and to improve their listening and speaking skills.

Music

¿Cómo te va? is rich with musical resources that will help your students practice and remember their new language skills. **Canta con Justo** Music CD includes songs that were written or chosen to accompany each unit of **¿Cómo te va?** Your students can enjoy a live concert and interview without leaving the classroom with **Justo Lamas ¡En vivo!** Music video (available on VHS or DVD).

Program Resources

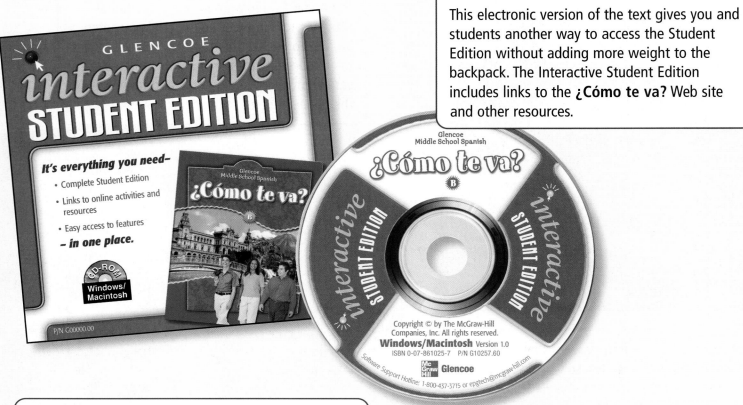

Interactive Student Edition

This electronic version of the text gives you and students another way to access the Student Edition without adding more weight to the backpack. The Interactive Student Edition includes links to the **¿Cómo te va?** Web site and other resources.

ExamView®Pro

ExamView®Pro allows you to create and customize quizzes, tests, and exams in a matter of minutes. Once you have created your assessment you can easily print several versions and answer keys. ExamView®Pro is an essential tool for easy customization of assessments for students with special learning needs.

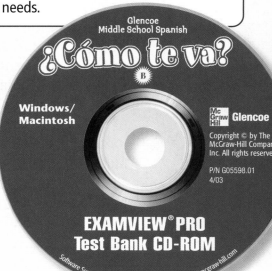

This test builder lets you...
- create tests easily and quickly
- customize tests using a full-feature editor
- select questions from existing test banks
- set up your own question test banks
- generate tests in Spanish

P/N G00000.00

Program Resources

Plegables™

¿Cómo te va? includes **Plegables™** Study Organizers. **Plegables™** are hands-on tools that will help students organize, study, and retain the Spanish they learn in each unit.

Manipulatives

Students learn by doing. The **¿Cómo te va?** manipulatives engage students in active learning and practice. Students will truly understand how language is built when they use the **¿Cómo te va?** manipulatives to construct their own words and sentences.

PLEGABLES™
Study Organizer

Para practicar más Use this *sentence strip* holder to practice your vocabulary, your verbs, or anything else you might feel you need extra help with.

Step 1 **Fold** a sheet of paper (8½" x 11") in half like a *hamburger*.

Step 2 **Open** the *hamburger* and fold the two outer edges toward the valley. This forms a shutter fold.

Step 3 **Fold** one of the inside edges of the shutter back to the outside fold. This fold forms a floppy L.

Step 4 **Glue** the floppy L tab down to the base so that it forms a strong straight L tab.

Step 5 **Glue** the other shutter side to the front of this L tab. This forms a tent that is the backboard for the flashcards or student work to be displayed.

Step 6 **Fold** the edge of the L up ¼" to ½" to form a lip that will keep the sentence strips from slipping off the holder.

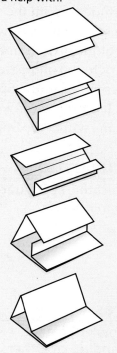

Vocabulary and spelling words can be stored inside the "tent" formed by this fold.

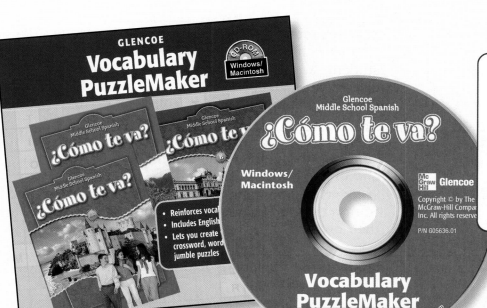

Vocabulary PuzzleMaker CD-ROM

This software allows you to quickly create and customize several kinds of puzzles. We have created vocabulary banks with the vocabulary from the entire **¿Cómo te va?** program to allow you the flexibility to create puzzles for students of all ability levels.

Standards

¿**Cómo te va?** has been written to help you meet the Standards for Foreign Language Learning as set forth by ACTFL. The focus of the program is to provide students with the skills they need to create language for communication. Culture is integrated throughout the text, from the basic introduction of vocabulary to the photographic contributions of images that represent the entire Spanish-speaking world. Special attention has been given to meeting the standard of Connections with a reading in Spanish in each unit about another discipline. Linguistic and cultural comparisons are made throughout the text. Suggestions are made for activities that encourage students to use their language skills in their immediate community and more distant ones. Students who complete the ¿**Cómo te va?** program are prepared to participate fully in life in the Spanish-speaking world.

Specific correlations to each unit are provided on the teacher pages preceding each unit.

Communication

Communicate in Languages Other than English	Standard 1.1	Students engage in conversations, provide and obtain information, express feelings and emotions, and exchange opinions.
	Standard 1.2	Students understand and interpret written and spoken language on a variety of topics.
	Standard 1.3	Students present information, concepts, and ideas to an audience of listeners or readers on a variety of topics.

Cultures

| Gain Knowledge and Understanding of Other Cultures | Standard 2.1 | Students demonstrate an understanding of the relationship between the practices and perspectives of the culture studied. |
| | Standard 2.2 | Students demonstrate an understanding of the relationship between the products and perspectives of the culture studied. |

Connections

| Connect with Other Disciplines and Acquire Information | Standard 3.1 | Students reinforce and further their knowledge of other disciplines through the foreign language. |
| | Standard 3.2 | Students acquire information and recognize the distinctive viewpoints that are only available through the foreign language and its cultures. |

Comparisons

| Develop Insight into the Nature of Language and Culture | Standard 4.1 | Students demonstrate understanding of the nature of language through comparisons of language studied and their own. |
| | Standard 4.2 | Students demonstrate understanding of the concept of culture through comparisons of the cultures studied and their own. |

Communities

| Participate in Multilingual Communities at Home and Around the World | Standard 5.1 | Students use the language both within and beyond the school setting. |
| | Standard 5.2 | Students show evidence of becoming life-long learners by using the language for personal enjoyment and enrichment. |

Glencoe
Middle School Spanish

¿Cómo te va?

B

Conrad J. Schmitt

McGraw Hill Glencoe

New York, New York   Columbus, Ohio   Chicago, Illinois   Peoria, Illinois   Woodland Hills, California

About the Front Cover

(left) **Plaza de España, Sevilla, España** The grandiose structure on the **Plaza de España** was Spain's pavilion at the 1928 Hispanic-American Exhibition. The brightly colored tile pictures in the arches represent what were the southern provinces of Spain. The four bridges over the lake represent the medieval kingdoms of the Iberian Peninsula.

(right) **Volcán Arenal, Costa Rica** This volcano is located in the southern part of the **Parque Nacional Rincón de la Vieja.** After a long dormant period, **el volcán Arenal** erupted in 1968 and has been quite active. Its cone has permanent flames and although there have been periods of inactivity, the volcano normally has eruptions every few hours spewing forth stone, ash, and gases. The volcano offers a particularly beautiful sight at nighttime. The **balneario de Tabacón** is famous for its hot springs. The water comes directly from the depths of the Arenal volcano.

Glencoe

The *McGraw-Hill* Companies

Printed in the United States of America.

Send all inquiries to:
Glencoe/McGraw-Hill
8787 Orion Place
Columbus, OH 43240-4027

ISBN: 0-07-860351-X (Student Edition)
ISBN: 0-07-860541-5 (Teacher Wraparound Edition)
1 2 3 4 5 6 7 8 9 10 027 10 09 08 07 06 05 04 03

ABOUT THE AUTHOR

Conrad J. Schmitt

Conrad J. Schmitt received his B.A. degree from Montclair State University in Montclair, New Jersey. He received his M.A. from Middlebury College, Middlebury, Vermont. He did additional graduate work at New York University.

Mr. Schmitt has taught Spanish and French at all levels from elementary school to university graduate courses. He taught at the Middle School in Hackensack, New Jersey, prior to becoming Coordinator of Foreign Languages for all the schools in the city. He also taught methodology at the Graduate School of Education, Rutgers University, New Brunswick, New Jersey.

Mr. Schmitt has authored or coauthored more than one hundred books, all published by the McGraw-Hill Companies. He has addressed teacher groups and given workshops throughout the United States. In addition, he has lectured and presented seminars in Japan, People's Republic of China, Taiwan, Philippines, Singapore, Thailand, Iran, Egypt, Spain, Portugal, Germany, Haiti, Jamaica, Mexico, Panama, Colombia, and Brazil.

Mr. Schmitt has traveled extensively throughout Spain and all of Latin America.

CONTENIDO

Repaso

Unidad ❶ Los deportes

Objetivos

In this unit, you will learn to:

- talk about sports
- talk about what you begin to, want to, and prefer to do
- talk about people's activities
- express what interests, bores, or pleases you
- discuss the role of sports in the Spanish-speaking world

Unidad 2 La salud

Objetivos

In this unit, you will learn to:

- explain a minor illness to a doctor
- describe some feelings
- have a prescription filled at a pharmacy
- describe characteristics and conditions
- tell where things are and where they're from
- tell where someone or something is now
- tell what happens to you or to someone else

Unidad 3 Un viaje en avión

Objetivos

In this unit, you will learn to:

- check in for a flight
- get through the airport after deplaning
- tell what you or others are currently doing
- tell what you know and whom you know
- discuss the importance of air travel in South America

CONTENIDO

Unidad 4 El verano y el invierno

Objetivos

In this unit, you will learn to:

- describe summer and winter weather
- talk about summer sports and summer activities
- talk about winter sports
- discuss past actions and events
- refer to people and things already mentioned
- talk about resorts in the Spanish-speaking world

GRANADA

SIERRA NEVADA

Unidad 5 Pasatiempos y diversiones

Objetivos

In this unit, you will learn to:

- discuss movies, museums, and concerts
- relate more past actions or events
- talk about what doesn't happen
- talk about cultural activities that are popular in the Spanish-speaking world
- discuss a famous Spanish novel

MUSEO DEL PRADO
CASON DEL BUEN RETIRO

CONTENIDO

Unidad 6 La rutina y el camping

Objetivos

In this unit, you will learn to:

- describe your personal grooming habits
- talk about your daily routine
- tell some things you do for yourself
- talk about a camping trip

Literary Companion

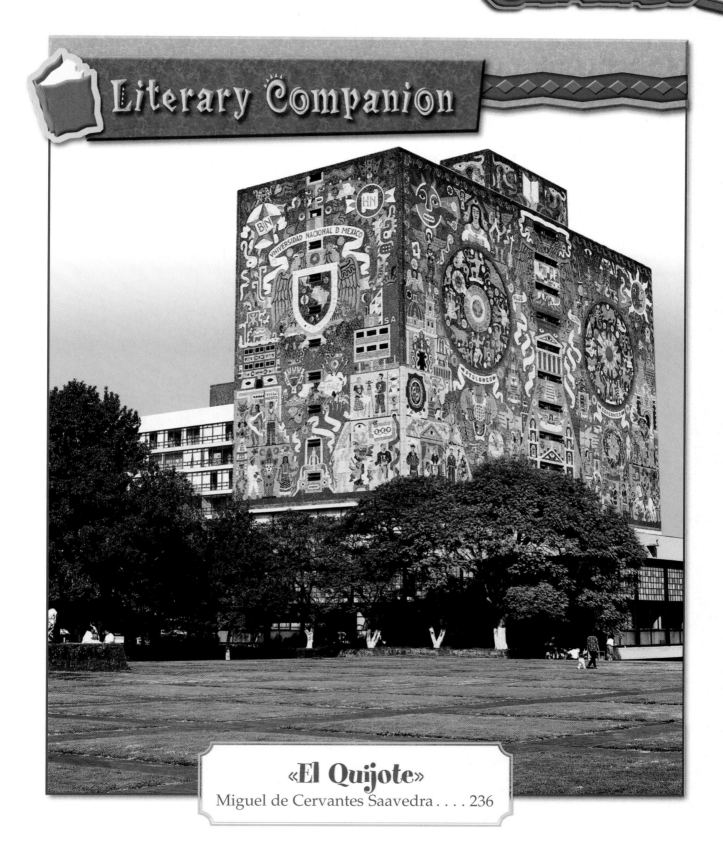

Handbook

Guide to Symbols

Throughout **¿Cómo te va?** you will see these symbols, or icons. They will tell you how to best use the particular part of the unit or activity they accompany. Following is a key to help you understand these symbols.

 Audio link This icon indicates material in the unit that is recorded on compact disc format.

 Recycling This icon indicates sections that review previously introduced material.

 Paired Activity This icon indicates sections that you can practice orally with a partner.

 Group Activity This icon indicates sections that you can practice together in groups.

 Un poco más This icon indicates additional practice activities that review knowledge from current units.

 ¡Adelante! This icon indicates the end of new material in each section and the beginning of the recombination section at the end of the unit.

El mundo hispanohablante

Spanish is the language of more than 350 million people around the world. Spanish had its origin in Spain. It is sometimes fondly called the "language of Cervantes," the author of the world's most famous novel and character, *Don Quijote*. The Spanish **conquistadores** and **exploradores** brought their language to the Americas in the fifteenth and sixteenth centuries. Spanish is the official language of almost all the countries of Central and South America. It is the official language of Mexico and several of the larger islands in the Caribbean. Spanish is also the heritage language of some thirty-seven million people in the United States.

▼ Trujillo, Perú

▲ Cibeles, Madrid

▲ El Zócalo, México

▲ Santiago de Chile

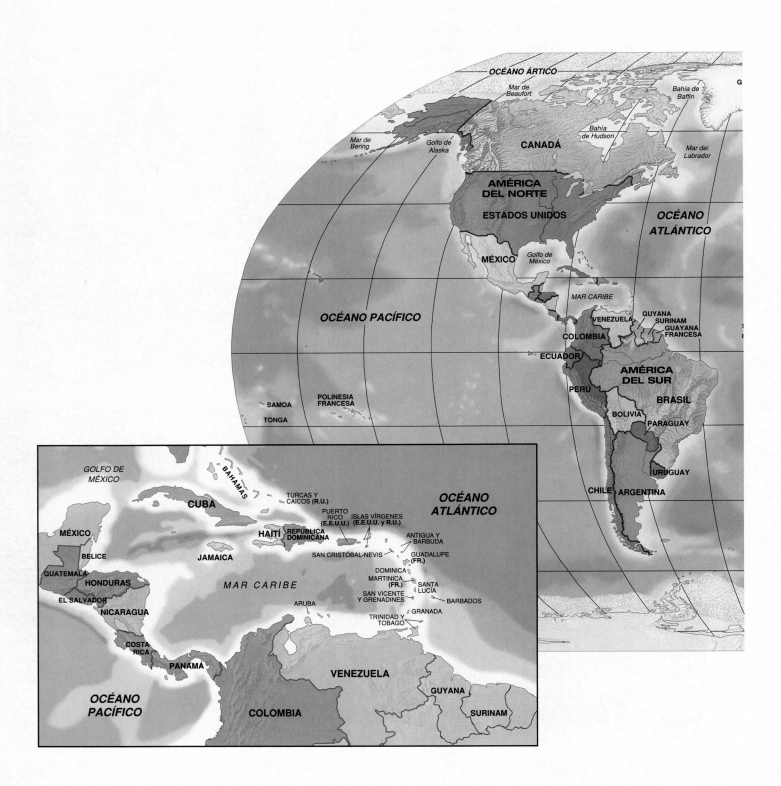

OCÉANO ÁRTICO

Mar de Beaufort

Bahía de Baffin

Mar de Bering

Golfo de Alaska

CANADÁ

Bahía de Hudson

Mar del Labrador

AMÉRICA DEL NORTE

ESTADOS UNIDOS

OCÉANO ATLÁNTICO

MÉXICO

Golfo de México

OCÉANO PACÍFICO

MAR CARIBE

VENEZUELA

GUYANA

SURINAM

GUAYANA FRANCESA

COLOMBIA

ECUADOR

PERÚ

AMÉRICA DEL SUR

BRASIL

BOLIVIA

PARAGUAY

SAMOA

POLINESIA FRANCESA

TONGA

URUGUAY

CHILE

ARGENTINA

GOLFO DE MÉXICO

BAHAMAS

TURCAS Y CAICOS (R.U.)

OCÉANO ATLÁNTICO

CUBA

PUERTO RICO (E.E.U.U.)

ISLAS VÍRGENES (E.E.U.U. y R.U.)

MÉXICO

HAITÍ

REPÚBLICA DOMINICANA

ANTIGUA Y BARBUDA

BELICE

JAMAICA

SAN CRISTÓBAL-NEVIS

GUADALUPE (FR.)

GUATEMALA

DOMINICA

HONDURAS

MARTINICA (FR.)

SANTA LUCÍA

EL SALVADOR

MAR CARIBE

SAN VICENTE Y GRENADINES

BARBADOS

NICARAGUA

ARUBA

GRANADA

TRINIDAD Y TOBAGO

COSTA RICA

PANAMÁ

OCÉANO PACÍFICO

VENEZUELA

GUYANA

COLOMBIA

SURINAM

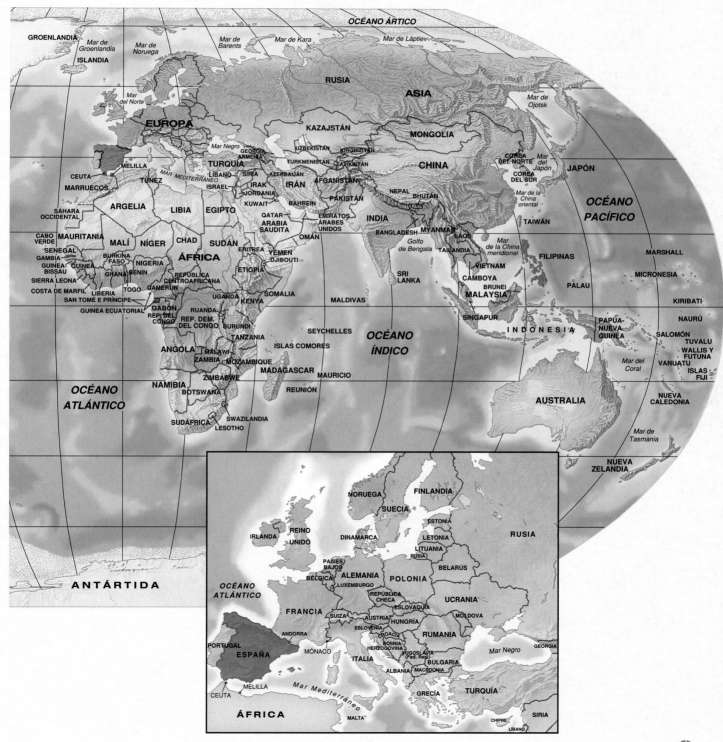

OCÉANO ÁRTICO

GROENLANDIA
Mar de Groenlandia
ISLANDIA
Mar de Noruega
Mar de Barents
Mar de Kara
Mar de Láptiev
Mar de Ojotsk

RUSIA

ASIA

Mar del Norte

EUROPA

Mar Negro
TURQUÍA
GEORGIA
ARMENIA
UZBEKISTÁN
KIRGUIZITÁN
TURKMENISTÁN
TAYIKISTÁN

KAZAJSTÁN

MONGOLIA

COREA DEL NORTE
Mar del Japón
JAPÓN
COREA DEL SUR

CEUTA
MELILLA
MARRUECOS
Mar MEDITERRÁNEO
LÍBANO
SIRIA
ISRAEL
IRAK
JORDANIA
AZERBAIJÁN
AFGANISTÁN
IRÁN

CHINA

OCÉANO PACÍFICO

TÚNEZ

KUWAIT
BAHREIN
PAKISTÁN
NEPAL
BHUTÁN
Mar de la China oriental

SÁHARA OCCIDENTAL
ARGELIA
LIBIA
EGIPTO
QATAR
ARABIA SAUDITA
EMIRATOS ÁRABES UNIDOS
OMÁN
INDIA
BANGLADESH
MYANMAR
TAIWÁN

CABO VERDE
MAURITANIA
MALÍ
NÍGER
CHAD
SUDÁN
ERITREA
YEMEN
DJIBOUTI

LAOS
Golfo de Bengala
TAILANDIA
Mar de la China meridional
FILIPINAS
MARSHALL

SENEGAL
GAMBIA
GUINEA-BISSAU
BURKINA FASO
NIGERIA
GUINEA
ÁFRICA
ETIOPÍA
VIETNAM
MICRONESIA

SIERRA LEONA
GHANA
BENIN
TOGO
REPÚBLICA CENTROAFRICANA
SRI LANKA
CAMBOYA
BRUNEI
PALAU

COSTA DE MARFIL
LIBERIA
CAMERÚN
MALDIVAS
MALAYSIA
KIRIBATI

SAN TOMÉ E PRÍNCIPE
GUINEA ECUATORIAL
GABÓN
REP. DEL CONGO
UGANDA
KENYA
SOMALIA
SINGAPUR
INDONESIA
PAPÚA-NUEVA GUINEA
NAURÚ

RUANDA
REP. DEM. DEL CONGO
BURUNDI
TANZANIA
SEYCHELLES
OCÉANO ÍNDICO
SALOMÓN
TUVALU

ANGOLA
MALAWI
ZAMBIA
MOZAMBIQUE
ISLAS COMORES
Mar del Coral
WALLIS Y FUTUNA
VANUATU

NAMIBIA
ZIMBABWE
MADAGASCAR
MAURICIO
ISLAS FIJI

OCÉANO ATLÁNTICO
BOTSWANA
REUNIÓN
AUSTRALIA
NUEVA CALEDONIA

SUDÁFRICA
SWAZILANDIA
LESOTHO

Mar de Tasmania

NUEVA ZELANDIA

ANTÁRTIDA

NORUEGA
FINLANDIA
SUECIA
ESTONIA
IRLANDA
REINO UNIDO
DINAMARCA
LETONIA
LITUANIA
RUSIA
RUSIA

PAÍSES BAJOS
BÉLGICA
ALEMANIA
POLONIA
BELARÚS

OCÉANO ATLÁNTICO
LUXEMBURGO
REPÚBLICA CHECA
UCRANIA

FRANCIA
SUIZA
ESLOVAQUIA
HUNGRÍA
MOLDOVA

ANDORRA
AUSTRIA
ESLOVENIA
CROACIA
RUMANIA

PORTUGAL
ESPAÑA
MÓNACO
BOSNIA-HERZOGOVINA
YUGOSLAVIA (Fed. Rep.)
BULGARIA
Mar Negro
GEORGIA

MELILLA
ITALIA
ALBANIA
MACEDONIA

CEUTA
Mar Mediterráneo
GRECIA
TURQUÍA

ÁFRICA
MALTA
CHIPRE
LÍBANO
SIRIA

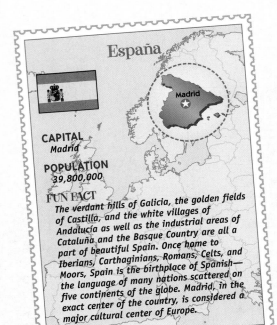

España

CAPITAL
Madrid

POPULATION
39,800,000

FUN FACT
The verdant hills of Galicia, the golden fields of Castilla, and the white villages of Andalucía as well as the industrial areas of Cataluña and the Basque Country are all a part of beautiful Spain. Once home to Iberians, Carthaginians, Romans, Celts, and Moors, Spain is the birthplace of Spanish— the language of many nations scattered on the five continents of the globe. Madrid, in the exact center of the country, is considered a major cultural center of Europe.

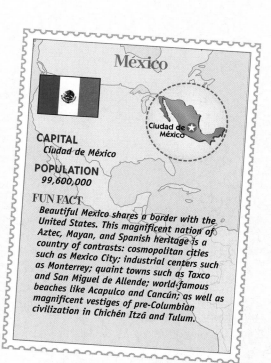

México

CAPITAL
Ciudad de México

POPULATION
99,600,000

FUN FACT
Beautiful Mexico shares a border with the United States. This magnificent nation of Aztec, Mayan, and Spanish heritage is a country of contrasts: cosmopolitan cities such as Mexico City; industrial centers such as Monterrey; quaint towns such as Taxco and San Miguel de Allende; world-famous beaches like Acapulco and Cancún; as well as magnificent vestiges of pre-Columbian civilization in Chichén Itzá and Tulum.

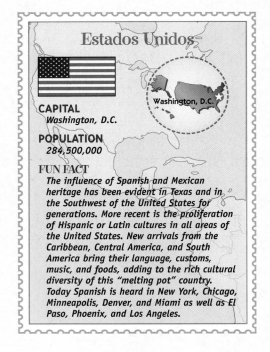

Estados Unidos

CAPITAL
Washington, D.C.

POPULATION
284,500,000

FUN FACT
The influence of Spanish and Mexican heritage has been evident in Texas and in the Southwest of the United States for generations. More recent is the proliferation of Hispanic or Latin cultures in all areas of the United States. New arrivals from the Caribbean, Central America, and South America bring their language, customs, music, and foods, adding to the rich cultural diversity of this "melting pot" country. Today Spanish is heard in New York, Chicago, Minneapolis, Denver, and Miami as well as El Paso, Phoenix, and Los Angeles.

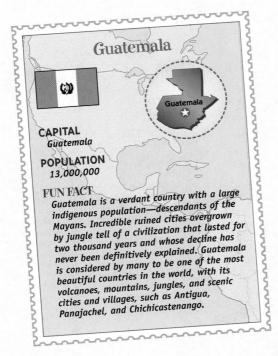

Guatemala

CAPITAL
Guatemala

POPULATION
13,000,000

FUN FACT
Guatemala is a verdant country with a large indigenous population—descendants of the Mayans. Incredible ruined cities overgrown by jungle tell of a civilization that lasted for two thousand years and whose decline has never been definitively explained. Guatemala is considered by many to be one of the most beautiful countries in the world, with its volcanoes, mountains, jungles, and scenic cities and villages, such as Antigua, Panajachel, and Chichicastenango.

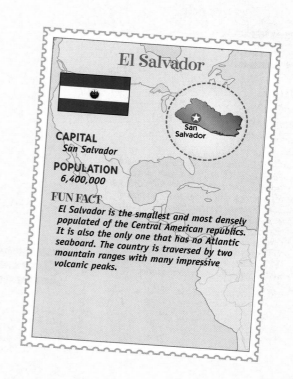

El Salvador

CAPITAL
San Salvador

POPULATION
6,400,000

FUN FACT
El Salvador is the smallest and most densely populated of the Central American republics. It is also the only one that has no Atlantic seaboard. The country is traversed by two mountain ranges with many impressive volcanic peaks.

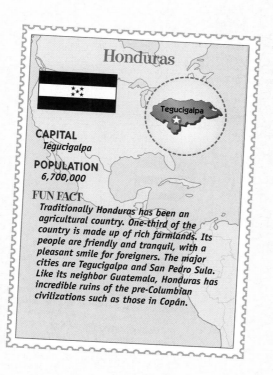

Honduras

CAPITAL
Tegucigalpa

POPULATION
6,700,000

FUN FACT
Traditionally Honduras has been an agricultural country. One-third of the country is made up of rich farmlands. Its people are friendly and tranquil, with a pleasant smile for foreigners. The major cities are Tegucigalpa and San Pedro Sula. Like its neighbor Guatemala, Honduras has incredible ruins of the pre-Columbian civilizations such as those in Copán.

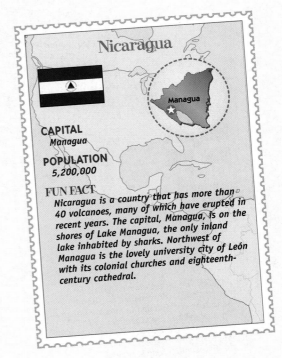

Nicaragua

CAPITAL
Managua

POPULATION
5,200,000

FUN FACT
Nicaragua is a country that has more than 40 volcanoes, many of which have erupted in recent years. The capital, Managua, is on the shores of Lake Managua, the only inland lake inhabited by sharks. Northwest of Managua is the lovely university city of León with its colonial churches and eighteenth-century cathedral.

El mundo hispanohablante

Costa Rica

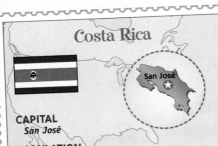

CAPITAL
San José

POPULATION
3,700,000

FUN FACT
Many consider Costa Rica a very special place. Its residents, Ticos, are polite, peaceful, and extremely friendly. Costa Rica has no army and prides itself on having more teachers than police officers. Costa Rica is a country of sun-drenched beaches on the Pacific, tropical jungles along the Caribbean coast, cosmopolitan cities such as San José, and high mountains in the central valley. Costa Rica is a tourist's paradise as well as home to many expatriates.

Panamá

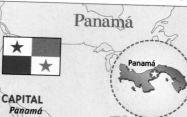

CAPITAL
Panamá

POPULATION
2,900,000

FUN FACT
Panama is a country of variety—a variety of races, customs, natural wonders, and attractions. It is a country of tropical forests, mountains, beautiful beaches, excellent fishing, picturesque lakes, rivers, two oceans, and—the most incredible engineering feat—the Panama Canal. Panama is also the largest financial center of Latin America. All this in a mere 77,432 square kilometers!

Cuba

CAPITAL
La Habana

POPULATION
11,300,000

FUN FACT
Havana, the capital of Cuba, is known for its gorgeous colonial architecture. This lush island, not far from Florida, is one of the world's greatest producers of sugar cane. Cuba has been ruled by Fidel Castro since 1959 when he overthrew the dictator Fulgencio Batista.

La República Dominicana

CAPITAL
Santo Domingo

POPULATION
8,600,000

FUN FACT
The Dominican Republic shares with Haiti the island of Hispaniola in the greater Antilles. The oldest university in our hemisphere, la Universidad de Santo Domingo, was founded in Santo Domingo. The Dominicans are ardent fans or aficionados of baseball, and this rather small island nation has produced some of the finest major league players.

Puerto Rico

CAPITAL
San Juan

POPULATION
3,900,000

FUN FACT
Puerto Ricans have an endearing term for their beloved island—la isla del encanto—island of enchantment. A commonwealth of the United States, Puerto Rico is a lush, tropical island with beaches along its Atlantic and Caribbean shores and gorgeous mountains with Alpine-like views in its interior. Puerto Rico is the home of the beloved coquí—a little frog that lives only in Puerto Rico and who lets no one see him.

Venezuela

CAPITAL
Caracas

POPULATION
24,600,000

FUN FACT
Venezuela was the name given to this country by Spanish explorers in 1499, when they came across indigenous villages where people lived on the water and where all commerce was conducted by dugout canoes. The waterways reminded them of Venice, Italy. Caracas is a teeming cosmopolitan city of high-rises surrounded by mountains and tucked in a narrow nine-mile valley. Angel Falls in southern Venezuela is the highest waterfall in the world, reaching a height of 3,212 feet with an unbroken fall of 2,648 feet.

Colombia

CAPITAL
Bogotá

POPULATION
43,100,000

FUN FACT
Colombia covers over 440,000 square miles of tropical and mountainous terrain. Bogotá is situated in the center of the country in an Andean valley 8,640 feet above sea level. The Caribbean coast in the North boasts many beautiful beaches; the South is covered by jungle, and the southern port of Leticia is on the Amazon River.

Ecuador

CAPITAL
Quito

POPULATION
12,900,000

FUN FACT
Ecuador takes its name from the equator, which cuts right across the country. Ecuador is the meeting place of the high Andean sierra in the center, the tropical coastal plain to the west, and the Amazon Basin jungle to the east. Snowcapped volcanoes stretch some 400 miles from north to south. The beautiful colonial section of the capital, Quito, is sometimes called "the Florence of the Americas."

Perú

CAPITAL
Lima

POPULATION
26,100,000

FUN FACT
Peru, like Ecuador, is divided into three geographical areas—a narrow coastal strip of desert along the Pacific, the Andean highlands where nearly half the population lives, and the Amazon jungle to the east. Lima is on the coast, and for almost nine months out of the year it is enshrouded in a fog called la garúa. Peru is famous for its Incan heritage. Nothing can prepare visitors for the awe-inspiring view of the Incan city of Machu Picchu, an imposing architectural complex high in the Andes.

Bolivia

CAPITAL
La Paz

POPULATION
8,500,000

FUN FACT
Bolivia is one of two landlocked countries in South America. Mountains dominate the Bolivian landscape. La Paz is the highest city in the world at an altitude of 12,500 feet. Bolivia also has the world's highest navigable lake, Lake Titicaca, which is surrounded by the picturesque villages of the Aymara Indians.

Chile

Santiago

CAPITAL
Santiago

POPULATION
15,400,000

FUN FACT
Chile, a "string bean" country never more than 111 miles wide, stretches 2,666 miles from north to south along the Pacific Coast. The imposing Andes isolate it from Bolivia and Argentina. The northern part of the country is characterized by the super-arid Atacama desert, the South by the spectacular wind-swept glaciers and fjords of Patagonia. Over one-third of the country's population lives in the Santiago area.

Argentina

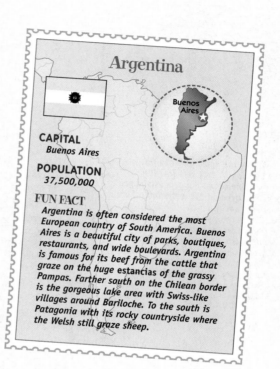

Buenos Aires

CAPITAL
Buenos Aires

POPULATION
37,500,000

FUN FACT
Argentina is often considered the most European country of South America. Buenos Aires is a beautiful city of parks, boutiques, restaurants, and wide boulevards. Argentina is famous for its beef from the cattle that graze on the huge estancias of the grassy Pampas. Farther south on the Chilean border is the gorgeous lake area with Swiss-like villages around Bariloche. To the south is Patagonia with its rocky countryside where the Welsh still graze sheep.

Paraguay

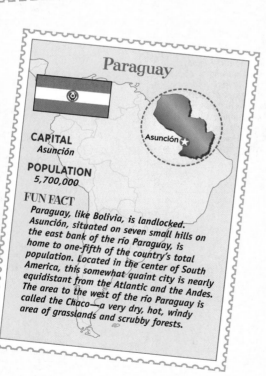

Asunción

CAPITAL
Asunción

POPULATION
5,700,000

FUN FACT
Paraguay, like Bolivia, is landlocked. Asunción, situated on seven small hills on the east bank of the río Paraguay, is home to one-fifth of the country's total population. Located in the center of South America, this somewhat quaint city is nearly equidistant from the Atlantic and the Andes. The area to the west of the río Paraguay is called the Chaco—a very dry, hot, windy area of grasslands and scrubby forests.

Uruguay

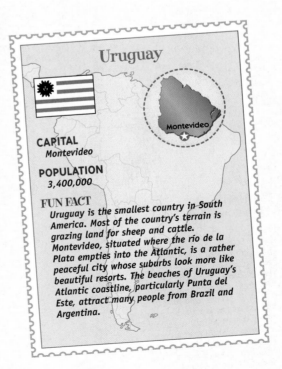

Montevideo

CAPITAL
Montevideo

POPULATION
3,400,000

FUN FACT
Uruguay is the smallest country in South America. Most of the country's terrain is grazing land for sheep and cattle. Montevideo, situated where the río de la Plata empties into the Atlantic, is a rather peaceful city whose suburbs look more like beautiful resorts. The beaches of Uruguay's Atlantic coastline, particularly Punta del Este, attract many people from Brazil and Argentina.

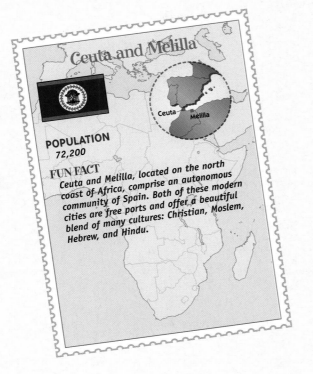

Ceuta and Melilla

POPULATION
72,200

FUN FACT
Ceuta and Melilla, located on the north coast of Africa, comprise an autonomous community of Spain. Both of these modern cities are free ports and offer a beautiful blend of many cultures: Christian, Moslem, Hebrew, and Hindu.

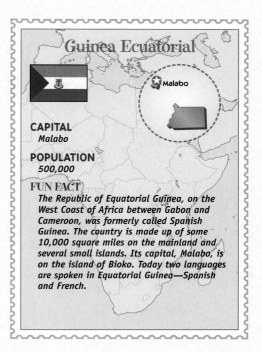

Guinea Ecuatorial

Malabo

CAPITAL
Malabo

POPULATION
500,000

FUN FACT
The Republic of Equatorial Guinea, on the West Coast of Africa between Gabon and Cameroon, was formerly called Spanish Guinea. The country is made up of some 10,000 square miles on the mainland and several small islands. Its capital, Malabo, is on the island of Bioko. Today two languages are spoken in Equatorial Guinea—Spanish and French.

Las Islas Filipinas

Manila

CAPITAL
Manila

POPULATION
77,200,000

FUN FACT
The Republic of the Philippines is an island nation in the South Pacific. The official language of the Philippines is Tagalog. Many people also speak Filipino—a language that has borrowed many words from Spanish. Spanish influence was extremely strong during the eighteenth and nineteenth centuries. Many Filipinos have Spanish names, and many can still speak Spanish.

España

OCÉANO ATLÁNTICO

FRANCIA

MAR CANTÁBRICO

Golfo de Vizcaya

La Coruña

Santiago de Compostela

Oviedo

Asturias

Santander

Cantabria

Bilbao

País Vasco

San Sebastián

Roncesvalles

ANDORRA

LOS PIRINEOS

Galicia

CORDILLERA CANTÁBRICA

León

Burgos

Pamplona

Navarra

Rioja

Cataluña

Castilla y León

Río Ebro

Zaragoza

Barcelona

Valladolid

Río Duero

Aragón

Salamanca

Segovia

SIERRA DE GUADARRAMA

Río Tajo

Ávila

Madrid

Madrid

PORTUGAL

E S P A Ñ A

Comunidad Valenciana

Islas baleares

Menorca

Palma

Mallorca

Castilla-la Mancha

Valencia

Ibiza

Río Guadiana

Formentera

Lisboa

Extremadura

MAR MEDITERRÁNEO

Río Guadalquivir

Alicante

Córdoba

Murcia

Murcia

Cartagena

Sevilla

Granada

Jerez de la Frontera

Andalucía

SIERRA NEVADA

Málaga

COSTA DEL SOL

Cádiz

Marbella

Estepona

Gibraltar (R.U.)

Estrecho de Gibraltar

Ceuta (Esp.)

Tánger

Melilla (Esp.)

OCÉANO ATLÁNTICO

ARGELIA

MARRUECOS

Islas Canarias

La Palma

Lanzarote

Santa Cruz de Tenerife

Fuerteventura

Gomera

Las Palmas

Tenerife

Hierro

Gran Canaria

MARRUECOS

ÁFRICA

OCÉANO ATLÁNTICO

SAHARA OCCIDENTAL

La América del Sur

MAR CARIBE

OCÉANO ATLÁNTICO

Barranquilla
Cartagena
Maracaibo
Caracas
Lago de Maracaibo
Río Orinoco

VENEZUELA

Medellín
Santafé de Bogotá
Río Magdalena
Cali

COLOMBIA

GUYANA
SURINAM
GUAYANA FRANCESA

Ecuador

Otavalo
Quito
ECUADOR
Guayaquil
Cuenca

Islas Galápagos (Ecuador)

Río Amazonas

PERÚ

El Callao
Lima
Cuzco
Lago Titicaca

CORDILLERA

BRASIL

BOLIVIA
La Paz
Cochabamba
Santa Cruz
Sucre

Brasília

Trópico de Capricornio

PARAGUAY
Asunción

CHILE

DE LOS ANDES

Río Paraná

Vicuña

Córdoba

OCÉANO PACÍFICO

Valparaíso
Santiago

Rosario
Buenos Aires
La Plata

URUGUAY
Montevideo
Río de la Plata

ARGENTINA

Mar del Plata

Puerto Montt

PATAGONIA

OCÉANO ATLÁNTICO

Estrecho de Magallanes
Islas Malvinas (R.U.)

Punta Arenas
Tierra del Fuego

Cabo de Hornos

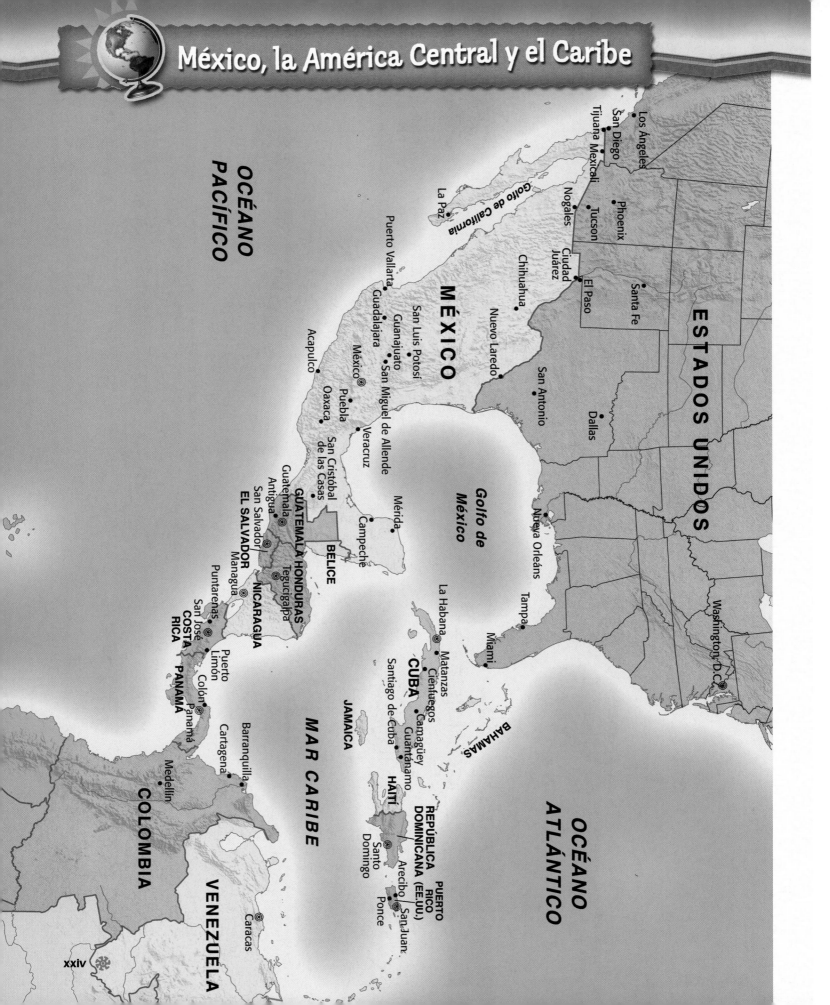

OCÉANO PACÍFICO

OCÉANO ATLÁNTICO

Golfo de California

Golfo de México

MAR CARIBE

MÉXICO

ESTADOS UNIDOS

Los Ángeles
San Diego
Tijuana
Mexicali
Nogales
Tucson
Phoenix
La Paz
Ciudad Juárez
El Paso
Chihuahua
Santa Fe
Nuevo Laredo
San Antonio
Dallas
Puerto Vallarta
Guadalajara
San Luis Potosí
Guanajuato
Acapulco
México
San Miguel de Allende
Oaxaca
Puebla
Veracruz
San Cristóbal de las Casas
Mérida
Campeche
Nueva Orleáns
Tampa
Miami
Washington, D.C.

BELICE

Guatemala
Antigua
GUATEMALA
San Salvador
EL SALVADOR
HONDURAS
Tegucigalpa
Managua
NICARAGUA
Puntarenas
San José
COSTA RICA
Puerto Limón
Colón
Panamá
PANAMÁ
Barranquilla
Cartagena
Medellín

COLOMBIA

VENEZUELA

Caracas

La Habana
Matanzas
Cienfuegos
CUBA
Camagüey
Santiago de Cuba
Guantánamo

BAHAMAS

JAMAICA

HAITÍ
REPÚBLICA DOMINICANA
Santo Domingo
PUERTO RICO (EE.UU.)
Arecibo
San Juan
Ponce

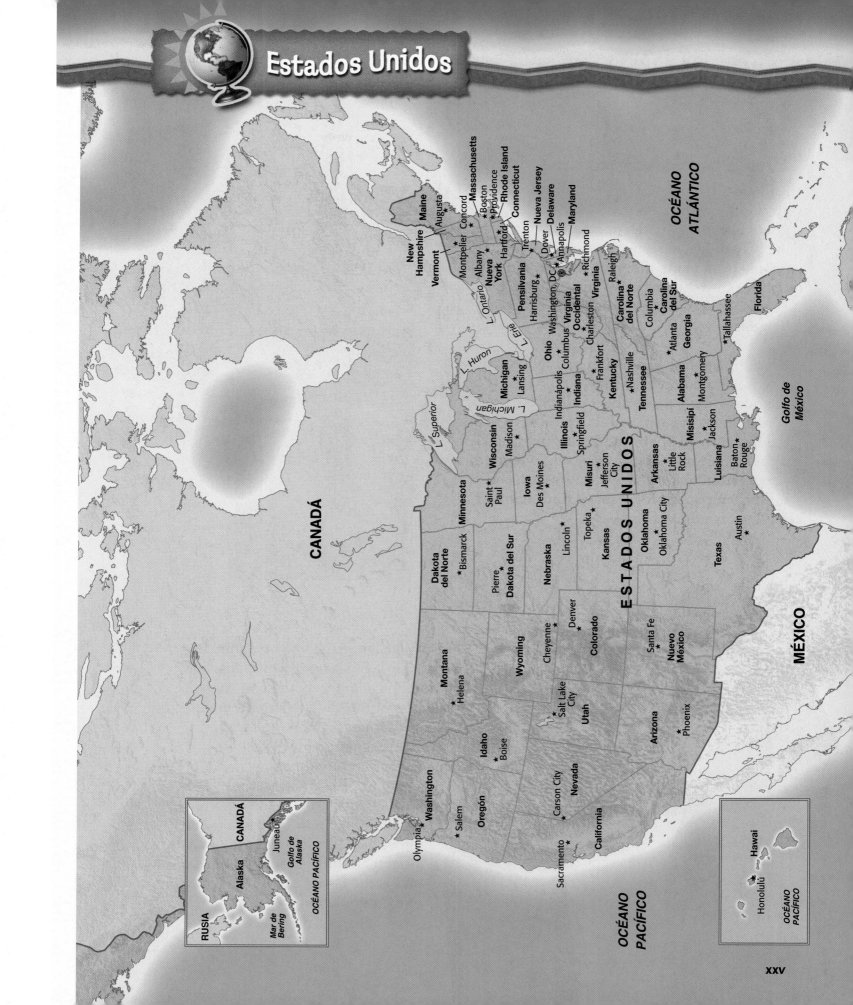

Estados Unidos

OCÉANO ATLÁNTICO

CANADÁ

Maine
Augusta ★
New Hampshire
Massachusetts
★ Boston
Concord
Providence
Rhode Island
Connecticut
Nueva Jersey
Delaware
Trenton ★
Dover ★
Maryland
★ Annapolis
Vermont
Montpelier ★
Albany ★
Nueva York
Hartford ★
Washington, DC ⊚
Richmond ★
Raleigh ★
L. Ontario
Pensilvania
Harrisburg ★
Virginia Occidental
Virginia
Carolina del Norte
L. Erie
Ohio
Columbus ★
Charleston ★
Columbia ★
Carolina del Sur
Huron
Columbus
Indianápolis ★
Frankfort ★
Nashville ★
Atlanta ★
Georgia
Florida
★ Tallahassee
Michigan
Lansing ★
Indiana
Kentucky
Tennessee
Alabama
Montgomery ★
L. Michigan
Illinois
Springfield ★
Misisipi
Jackson ★
Golfo de México
L. Superior
Wisconsin
Madison ★
Iowa
Des Moines ★
Misuri
Jefferson City ★
Arkansas
Little Rock ★
Luisiana
Baton Rouge ★
Minnesota
Saint Paul ★
Bismarck ★
Dakota del Norte
Pierre ★
Dakota del Sur
Nebraska
Lincoln ★
Topeka ★
Kansas
Oklahoma
Oklahoma City ★
Texas
Austin ★
ESTADOS UNIDOS
Cheyenne ★
Wyoming
Denver ★
Colorado
Santa Fe ★
Nuevo México
Montana
Helena ★
Salt Lake City ★
Utah
Arizona
Phoenix ★
MÉXICO
Idaho
Boise ★
Washington
Olympia ★
Salem ★
Oregón
Carson City ★
Nevada
California
Sacramento ★
CANADÁ

OCÉANO PACÍFICO

RUSIA
CANADÁ
Alaska
Juneau ★
Mar de Bering
Golfo de Alaska
OCÉANO PACÍFICO

Hawai
Honolulú ★
OCÉANO PACÍFICO

xxv

The Spanish-Speaking World

Knowing Spanish will open doors to you around the world. As you study the language, you will come to understand and appreciate the way of life, customs, values, and cultures of people from many different areas of the world. Look at the map on pages xiv–xv to see where Spanish is spoken, either as a first or second language.

Learning Spanish can be fun and will bring you a sense of accomplishment. You'll be really pleased when you are able to carry on a conversation in Spanish. You will be able to read the literature of Spain and Latin America, keep up with current events in magazines and newspapers from Spain and Latin America, and understand Spanish-language films without relying on subtitles.

The Spanish language will be a source of enrichment for the rest of your life—and you don't have to leave home to enjoy it. In all areas of the United States there are Hispanic radio and television stations, Latin musicians, Spanish-language magazines and newspapers, and a great diversity of restaurants serving foods from all areas of the Spanish-speaking world. The Latin or Hispanic population of the United States today totals more than thirty-five million people and is the fastest growing segment of the population.

Career Opportunities

Your knowledge of Spanish will also be an asset to you in a wide variety of careers. Many companies from Spain and Latin America are multinational and have branches around the world, including the United States. Many U.S. corporations have great exposure in the Spanish-speaking countries. With the growth of the Hispanic population in the United States, bilingualism is becoming an important asset in many fields including retail, fashion, cosmetics, pharmaceutical, agriculture, automotive, tourism, airlines, technology, finance, and accounting.

You can use your Spanish in all these fields, not only abroad but also in the United States. On the national scene there are innumerable possibilities in medical and hospital services, banking and finance, law, social work, and law enforcement. The opportunities are limitless.

Language Link

Another benefit to learning Spanish is that it will improve your English. Once you know another language, you can make comparisons between the two and gain a greater understanding of how languages function. You'll also come across a number of Spanish words that are used in English. Just a few examples are: **adobe, corral, meseta, rodeo, poncho, canyon, llama, alpaca**. Spanish will also be helpful if you decide to learn yet another language. Once you learn a second language, the learning process for acquiring other languages becomes much easier.

Spanish is a beautiful, rich language spoken on many continents. Whatever your motivation is for choosing to study it, Spanish will expand your horizons and increase your job opportunities. **¡Viva el español!**

El Alfabeto Español

a avión

b bebé

c cesta

d dedo

e elefante

f foto

g gemelos

h hamaca

i iglesia

j jabón

k kilo

l lago

m mono

n nariz

ñ
*ñ*ame

o
*o*so

p
*p*elo

q
*q*ueso

r
*r*ana

s
*s*ala

t
*t*é

u
*u*va

v
*v*aca

w
*W*ashington, D.C.

x
e*x*amen

y
*y*eso

z
*z*apato

ch
*ch*icle

ll
*ll*uvia

rr
guita*rr*a

Ch, ll, and *rr* are not letters of the Spanish alphabet. However, it is important for you to learn the sounds they represent.

Preview

There are three **Repasos (A–C)** at the beginning of **¿Cómo te va?, B Nivel azul.** In **Repaso A,** students review the vocabulary they need to describe people and things and to identify nationalities. In the **Formas** section, they review the verb **ser** and the agreement of nouns and adjectives. Students practice this vocabulary and these structures as they talk about their friends, classes, and teachers.

National Standards

Communication

In Review A, students will communicate in spoken and written Spanish on the following topics:
- Describing people
- Talking about their courses

Students will obtain and provide information and engage in conversations about friends, family, and school.

Repaso

A Amigos y alumnos

Utuado, Puerto Rico
(page R1) These boys are in Utuado, Puerto Rico. Utuado is a small town nestled in the lushly covered hills of the interior. Some of Puerto Rico's best musicians come from Utuado and their town is mentioned in many of their ballads.

The **colegio San Miguel** in Utuado is a private school. Note that many private schools in Puerto Rico use the terms **colegio** or **academia.** Public schools use the terms **escuela intermedia** and **escuela superior** or **secundaria.**

Spanish Online

The **Glencoe World Languages Web site** (spanish. glencoe.com) offers options that enable you and your students to experience the Spanish-speaking world via the Internet. For each **Unidad,** there are activities, games, and quizzes. In addition, an *Enrichment* section offers students an opportunity to visit Web sites related to the theme of the unit.

Palabras

1 PREPARATION

RESOURCE MANAGER

Workbook, pages R1–R4
Tests, pages R1–R2

Bellringer Review

Use BRR Transparency R.1 or write the following on the board. Write any words you can use to describe a person.

2 PRESENTATION

STEP 1 Students should be quite familiar with this vocabulary. It should be possible to review it very quickly.

STEP 2 Call on a student to read the sentences below or next to each photo.

STEP 3 Ask questions about the sentences. Then have students say anything they can about the photos.

Learning from Photos

(page R2, bottom) These students are from Hatillo, Puerto Rico.

The third largest underground river in the world, **el río Camuy** in Puerto Rico runs through a series of caves, canyons, and sinkholes. One of the sinkholes, called the Tres Pueblos Sinkhole, is 650 feet in diameter and 400 feet deep. Tres Pueblos lies on the boundaries of three municipalities: Hatillo, Camuy, and Lares.

R2

Palabras

Lupe Cárdenas es mexicana.
Es morena y bastante alta.
Lupe es de Guanajuato.
Ella es alumna en un colegio en Guanajuato.

José es dominicano.
Él es alumno en un colegio.
José es un alumno muy bueno.

Felipe y Maïte son amigos.
Son alumnos en la misma escuela.
Ellos son bastante cómicos.

Universal Access

The following are examples of categories of questions: (1) easy; (2) intermediate; (3) more difficult.

(1) **¿Es mexicana Lupe?**
¿Es morena ella?
(2) **¿Es mexicana o dominicana Lupe?**
¿Es rubia o morena ella?
(3) **¿De qué nacionalidad es Lupe?**
¿Cómo es ella?

As material is reviewed and reintroduced, **students with learning difficulties** can be called upon to answer the more challenging questions.

¿Qué palabra necesito?

1 Historieta Casandra Ramos

 Contesten. *(Answer.)*

1. Casandra Ramos es de Bogotá, Colombia. ¿De qué nacionalidad es ella?
2. No es rubia. ¿Cómo es ella?
3. No es muy baja. ¿Cómo es ella?
4. ¿De dónde es ella?
5. ¿Es Casandra alumna en un colegio de Bogotá?
6. Es ella una amiga sincera?

2 Historieta Fernando Arenal de San Juan

Contesten. *(Answer.)*

1. ¿De dónde es Fernando?
2. ¿Es él alumno en una escuela primaria o en un colegio?
3. Fernando no es un alumno malo. ¿Qué tipo de alumno es?
4. ¿Es él un amigo muy simpático?

3 Historieta Felipe y Maïte Completen. *(Complete.)*

1. Felipe y Maïte no son hermanos. Son _____.
2. Ellos no son alumnos en escuelas diferentes. Son alumnos en la _____ escuela.
3. Ellos no son alumnos malos. Son alumnos _____.
4. Ellos no son tímidos. Son _____.

✻ R3

ANSWERS TO ¿Qué palabra necesito?

1. Ella es colombiana.
2. Ella es morena.
3. Ella es alta.
4. Ella es de Bogotá, Colombia.
5. Sí, Casandra es alumna en un colegio de Bogotá.
6. Sí, ella es una amiga sincera.

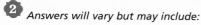 *Answers will vary but may include:*
1. Fernando es de San Juan.
2. Él es alumno en un colegio.
3. Es un alumno bueno.
4. Sí, (No, no) es un amigo muy simpático.

1. amigos
2. misma
3. buenos
4. cómicos (graciosos)

Conversación
PRESENTATION

STEP 1 Call on two students to come to the front of the class. Have them read the **Conversación** aloud using as much expression as possible.

STEP 2 Now quickly do the activity.

Universal Access

You may wish to allow **students with learning difficulties** and **average students** to read the conversation aloud with as much expression as possible. Then call on **advanced learners** to present the conversation without reading. They do not have to recite it from memory. Permit them to ad lib and say anything that makes sense.

Learning from Photos

(page R4) These young boys are in front of the **Parque de Bombas** in Ponce, Puerto Rico. Ponce, located on the southern Caribbean coast, is the second largest city of Puerto Rico. It was founded in 1692. It is a city of many plazas, parks, and public buildings.

The **Parque de Bombas** was constructed in 1882 for a twelve-day agricultural fair to promote the charms of Ponce. A year later it became the island's first permanent volunteer fire fighters' headquarters. It is known for its bright colors. Although there are still some fire engines in the building, the fire department has moved to modern quarters in another part of the city.

Conversación
¿De dónde son?

Lucas	¡Hola!
Mario	¡Hola! ¿Qué tal?
Lucas	Bien. ¿Y tú?
Mario	Bien. Oye, ¿eres un amigo de Cristina Irizarry, ¿no?
Lucas	Sí, soy un amigo de Cristina. Pero ella es mi prima también.
Mario	Ah, Cristina y tú son primos. Y tú, ¿eres de Ponce también?
Lucas	Sí, soy de Ponce.
Mario	Pues, todos (nosotros) somos ponceños.

¿Comprendes?

Contesten. *(Answer.)*

1. ¿Son puertorriqueños los dos muchachos?
2. ¿Es Lucas un amigo de Cristina Irizarry?
3. ¿Es también el primo de Cristina?
4. ¿Son primos Mario y Cristina?
5. ¿Es Mario de Ponce también?

R4

ANSWERS TO **¿Comprendes?**

1. Sí, los dos muchachos son puertorriqueños.
2. Sí, Lucas es un amigo de Cristina Irizarry.
3. Sí, es el primo de Cristina también.
4. No, Mario y Cristina no son primos.
5. Sí, Mario es de Ponce también.

Formas Presente del verbo **ser**

Review the forms of the irregular verb **ser**.

ser	
soy	somos
eres	*sois*
es	son

¿Cómo lo digo?

4 **Entrevista** Contesten. (*Answer about yourself.*)
1. ¿Quién eres?
2. ¿De qué nacionalidad eres?
3. ¿Dónde eres alumno o alumna?
4. ¿Cómo es tu escuela?

5 **Historieta** **El amigo de Andrés** Completen con **ser**. (*Complete with* ser.)

Yo __1__ un amigo de Andrés. Andrés __2__ muy simpático. Y él __3__ gracioso. Andrés y yo __4__ dominicanos. __5__ de la República Dominicana.

La capital de la República Dominicana __6__ Santo Domingo. Nosotros __7__ alumnos en un colegio en Santo Domingo. Nosotros __8__ alumnos de inglés. La profesora de inglés __9__ la señorita White. Ella __10__ americana.

Unos alumnos dominicanos.
Villa Fundación, la República Dominicana

✳ R5

Formas

1 PREPARATION

Bellringer Review

Use BRR Transparency R.2 or write the following on the board. Answer.
1. ¿Quién eres?
2. ¿De dónde eres?
3. ¿De qué nacionalidad eres?

2 PRESENTATION

Presente del verbo **ser**

STEP 1 Quickly go over the forms of **ser** and have students do the activities.

3 PRACTICE

¿Cómo lo digo?

4 Have students work in pairs and ask each other the questions in Activity 4.

Writing Development
After going over Activity 5 have students rewrite the story in their own words.

Universal Access

Give advanced learners the forms of **ser** and have them make up an original sentence with each one.

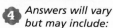 **ANSWERS TO** ¿Cómo lo digo?

4 Answers will vary but may include:
1. Soy ___.
2. Soy americano(a).
3. Soy alumno(a) en ___.
4. Mi escuela es grande (pequeña).

5
1. soy
2. es
3. es
4. somos
5. Somos
6. es
7. somos
8. somos
9. es
10. es

Formas

1 PREPARATION

Bellringer Review

Use BRR Transparency R.3 or write the following on the board.
Write the following in the plural.
1. **Él es americano.**
2. **La muchacha es bonita.**
3. **El colegio es moderno.**
4. **El curso es fácil.**

2 PRESENTATION

 Sustantivos, artículos y adjetivos

STEP 1 As you go over the explanation, have students repeat the words and phrases in Items 1–3 after you. Point to a specific person or object as you use the definite article.

Learning from Photos

(page R6) You may wish to ask the following questions about the girls in the **Parque Florida** in Buenos Aires.
¿Cuántas muchachas hay en la fotografía?
¿De dónde son ellas?
¿Están en el parque?
¿Tienen bicicletas?

Sustantivos, artículos y adjetivos

1. Spanish nouns are either masculine or feminine. Most nouns ending in **o** are masculine and most nouns ending in **a** are feminine. The definite articles **el** and **los** accompany masculine nouns; **la** and **las** accompany feminine nouns.

el alumno	**los alumnos**	**la amiga**	**las amigas**
el curso	**los cursos**	**la escuela**	**las escuelas**

2. An adjective must agree with the noun it describes or modifies. Adjectives that end in **o** have four forms.

el amigo sincero	**los amigos sinceros**
la amiga sincera	**las amigas sinceras**

3. Adjectives that end in **e** or in a consonant have only two forms.

el curso interesante	**los cursos interesantes**
la asignatura interesante	**las asignaturas interesantes**
el curso difícil	**los cursos difíciles**
la asignatura difícil	**las asignaturas difíciles**

Unas amigas argentinas, Buenos Aires

Learning from Photos

(page R7, bottom) American bush pilot Jimmy Angel was looking for a mountain of gold in an area some 160 miles south of Ciudad Guayana in Venezuela. As he attempted to land, his plane crashed. Some eleven days after the crash he and his small party, which included his wife, emerged from the forest not having discovered any gold but the highest waterfall in the world. Angel Falls are the highest in the world with an unbroken fall of 2,648 feet and a total height of 3,212 feet. The falls are 50 times higher than Niagara Falls.

¿Cómo lo digo?

6 Silvia Describan a la muchacha.
(Describe the girl.)

7 Los amigos
Describan a los amigos.
(Describe the friends.)

Hatillo. Puerto Rico

San Miguel de
Allende. México

8 Historieta Mis clases Contesten. *(Answer.)*

1. ¿Es grande o pequeña tu clase de español?
2. ¿De dónde es el/la profesor(a) de español?
3. ¿Es interesante la clase de español?
4. ¿Es difícil o fácil?
5. Las clases de ciencias y matemáticas, ¿son grandes o pequeñas?
6. Para ti, ¿los cursos de ciencias son fáciles o difíciles?
7. ¿Cuál es tu clase favorita?
8. ¿Quién es tu profesor(a) favorito(a)?

9 En Venezuela You are spending the summer with a family in Venezuela. Tell your Venezuelan "brother" or "sister" (your partner) all you can about your Spanish class and your Spanish teacher. Answer any questions he or she may have. Then reverse roles.

10 Cursos You are speaking with an exchange student from Peru (your partner). He or she wants to know about your school, your schedule, and your classes. Tell as much as you can about your school and then ask him or her about school life in Peru.

Amigos y alumnos

El Salto Ángel. Venezuela

Formas
3 PRACTICE

¿Cómo lo digo?

6 Have students say as much as they can about the girl.

Writing Development
After going over Activity 7 orally in class, have students write about what they see in the photo.

Universal Access

In Activities 6 and 7 you may wish to ask **students with learning difficulties** to give descriptions after hearing the descriptions given by **advanced learners and average students.**

9 and **10** These activities allow students to use the vocabulary and structures of the unit in open-ended, real-life situations. They also give students another opportunity to use words and structures learned in **¿Cómo te va? A, Nivel verde.** Have students work on as many activities as you wish. You may also allow them to select which activity they want to do. Different groups can work on each activity.

ANSWERS TO ¿Cómo lo digo?

6 Answers will vary, but students should correctly use singular forms of ser and descriptive adjectives with feminine singular endings.

7 Answers will vary, but students should correctly use plural forms of ser and descriptive adjectives with the masculine plural endings.

8 Answers will vary but may include:
1. Mi clase de español es grande (pequeña).
2. El/La profesor(a) de español es de ___.
3. Sí (No), la clase de español (no) es interesante.
4. Es fácil (difícil).
5. Las clases de ciencias y matemáticas son grandes (pequeñas).
6. Para mí, los cursos de ciencias son fáciles (difíciles).
7. Mi clase favorita es ___.
8. Mi profesor(a) favorito(a) es ___.

9 and **10** Answers will vary. Students will use vocabulary and structures previously learned in ¿Cómo te va? A, Nivel verde.

Preview

In **Repaso B**, students review vocabulary relating to school, getting to school, and buying school supplies and clothing. In the **Formas** section, students review the present tense of **-ar** verbs, the verbs **ir, dar,** and **estar,** and the contraction **al.**

Students practice this vocabulary and these structures as they talk about school, after-school activities, and shopping for clothes.

National Standards

Communication

In Review B, students will communicate in spoken and written Spanish on the following topics:
- School activities
- Buying clothing and supplies for school

Students will also narrate present events. They will obtain and provide information about school and shopping.

B De compras para la escuela

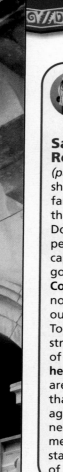

Spotlight on Culture

Santo Domingo, La República Dominicana
(pages R8–R9) These photos show **calle El Conde,** a very famous and traditional street that is mentioned in many Dominican songs. It is the sole pedestrian-only street in the capital, Santo Domingo. In days gone by no man would go to **El Conde** not wearing a jacket and no woman would appear without being beautifully attired. Today **El Conde** is a commercial street with many different types of shops, boutiques, cafés, and **heladerías.** Many of these shops are owned by Spanish families that arrived on the island years ago. In addition to these businesses there are many street merchants who set up their stands and sell an assortment of merchandise.

Spanish Online

The **Glencoe World Languages Web site** (spanish. glencoe.com) offers options that enable you and your students to experience the Spanish-speaking world via the Internet. For each **Unidad,** there are activities, games, and quizzes. In addition, an *Enrichment* section offers students an opportunity to visit Web sites related to the theme of the unit.

✽ R9

Palabras

RESOURCE MANAGER

Workbook, pages R5–R12
Tests, pages R3–R4

Bellringer Review

Use BRR Transparency R.4 or write the following on the board. Write as many words as you can think of associated with school.

2 PRESENTATION

 Before you begin your presentation, you may wish to ask students to say anything they can about the illustrations. If you find that they have a good command of the vocabulary, you can skip this review material and do the activities immediately.

STEP 1 Have students open their books. Point to individual items in the illustrations and have the class repeat **los alumnos, la escuela, el bus escolar,** for example. Then build to the complete sentences.

STEP 2 As you present the sentences, ask comprehension questions building from simple to more complex.

STEP 3 After reviewing the vocabulary orally, have students read the material for additional reinforcement.

Palabras

Los alumnos llegan a la escuela a las ocho menos cuarto.
Algunos toman el bus escolar.
Otros van a la escuela a pie.

Los alumnos estudian mucho.
Toman apuntes.
Escuchan a la profesora cuando habla.
La profesora enseña.

Teresa está en la papelería.
Necesita materiales escolares.
Compra un cuaderno, un lápiz y un bolígrafo (una pluma).
Paga en la caja.

José está en la tienda de ropa.
Compra unos pantalones para llevar a la escuela.
Mira los pantalones.

Universal Access

The following are examples of categories of questions.
(1) **¿Llegan los alumnos a la escuela?**
   ¿Llegan a las ocho menos cuarto?
(2) **¿Los alumnos llegan a la escuela o a la tienda de ropa?**
   ¿Llegan a las nueve menos cuarto o a las ocho menos cuarto?
(3) **¿Quiénes llegan?**
   ¿Adónde llegan?
   ¿A qué hora llegan?

¿Qué palabra necesito?

1 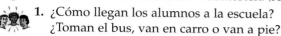 **En la escuela** Contesten. *(Answer.)*

1. ¿Cómo llegan los alumnos a la escuela? ¿Toman el bus, van en carro o van a pie?
2. ¿A qué hora llegan a la escuela?
3. ¿Con quién hablan los alumnos cuando entran en la sala de clase?
4. ¿Quiénes toman exámenes y quién da los exámenes?
5. ¿Sacan los alumnos notas altas?
6. ¿Prestan ellos atención cuando la profesora habla?

San Juan. Puerto Rico

2 **A la papelería** Escojan. *(Choose.)*

1. Alicia necesita materiales escolares. ¿Adónde va ella?
   a. a la cafetería   **b.** a la tienda de ropa   **c.** a la papelería
2. ¿Con quién hablan los alumnos cuando entran en la sala de clase?
   a. con el empleado   **b.** con el profesor   **c.** con el mesero
3. ¿Qué compra Alicia en la papelería?
   a. un refresco   **b.** un pantalón   **c.** un cuaderno
4. ¿Dónde paga Alicia?
   a. cien pesos   **b.** en la caja   **c.** en la cocina
5. ¿En qué lleva ella los materiales escolares?
   a. en una mochila   **b.** en un cuaderno   **c.** en un bolígrafo

Una tienda de departamentos.
Marbella. España

3 **Historieta** **En la tienda de ropa**
Contesten según se indica. *(Answer as indicated.)*

1. ¿Adónde va Roberto? (a la tienda de ropa)
2. ¿Qué necesita? (una camisa de mangas cortas)
3. ¿Busca una camisa verde? (no, roja y azul)
4. ¿Qué talla usa? (treinta y ocho)
5. ¿Compra Roberto una camisa? (sí)
6. ¿Cuánto cuesta? (veinticinco euros)
7. ¿Dónde paga Roberto? (en la caja)

De compras para la escuela

 R11

Conversación
PRESENTATION

STEP 1 Call on two students to read the **Conversación** aloud using as much expression as possible.

STEP 2 Have students make up their own conversations with similar information. Ask for volunteers to present their conversations to the class.

STEP 3 After the conversation has been read, go over the **¿Comprendes?** activity.

Universal Access

Allow shy students to read the conversation while in their seat. Have outgoing types perform it in front of the class.

Conversación
En la tienda de ropa

¿Comprendes?

Contesten. *(Answer.)*
1. ¿Dónde está Marcos?
2. ¿Qué desea?
3. ¿Qué talla usa él?
4. ¿Qué busca el dependiente?
5. ¿Compra Marcos el blue jean?
6. ¿Cuánto cuesta?
7. ¿Qué más necesita Marcos?
8. ¿Qué hay hoy en la tienda?
9. ¿Cómo son los precios?

ANSWERS TO ¿Comprendes?

1. Marcos está en la tienda de ropa.
2. Desea un blue jean.
3. Él usa talla treinta y dos.
4. El dependiente busca un treinta y dos.
5. Sí, Marcos compra el blue jean.
6. Cuesta mil quinientos pesos.
7. Marcos necesita una camisa (también).
8. Hoy hay una liquidación.
9. Los precios son muy bajos.

Formas Presente de los verbos en -ar

1. Review the forms of the present tense of regular **-ar** verbs.

mirar		tomar	
miro	miramos	tomo	tomamos
miras	*miráis*	tomas	*tomáis*
mira	miran	toma	toman

2. Remember that to make a sentence negative you put **no** before the verb.

No hablamos francés. Hablamos español.

3. Remember to use **tú** when talking to a friend, a family member, or a person your own age. Use **usted** when speaking to an adult, a person you do not know well, or someone to whom you wish to show respect.

¿Tú estudias español, Roberto?
¿Y usted, señora? ¿Usted también estudia español?

¿Cómo lo digo?

4 Entrevista Contesten. *(Answer about yourself.)*
1. ¿En qué escuela estudias?
2. ¿Cómo llegas a la escuela?
3. ¿Cuántos cursos tomas?
4. ¿En qué llevas los materiales escolares?
5. ¿Estudian mucho los alumnos de tu escuela?
6. ¿Sacan ustedes buenas notas?
7. ¿Toman ustedes muchos exámenes?
8. ¿Escuchan ustedes cuando la profesora habla?

Alumnos delante del colegio Francisco Febres Cordero La Salle, Quito, Ecuador

5 Historieta En la fiesta Completen. *(Complete.)*
1. Durante la fiesta todos nosotros _____. (bailar)
2. Felipe _____ el piano. (tocar)
3. Mientras él _____ el piano, Elena y Carlos _____. (tocar, cantar)
4. ¿_____ ustedes refrescos para la fiesta? (Preparar)
5. ¿_____ ustedes fotos durante la fiesta? (Tomar)
6. Sí, y todos nosotros _____ las fotografías. (mirar)

Nota You use **tocar** with a musical instrument.
Juan toca el piano.
Yo toco la guitarra.

De compras para la escuela   R13

REPASO B

Formas

1 PREPARATION

Bellringer Review

Use BRR Transparency R.5 or write the following on the board. Use the following expressions in a sentence.
estudiar mucho
tomar apuntes
prestar atención
sacar notas

2 PRESENTATION

Presente de los verbos en -ar

STEP 1 Have students read the forms of the **-ar** verbs aloud.

STEP 2 Write the two verbs on the board and underline the endings.

STEP 3 Read the information in Item 3 to the class. Review this point as quickly as possible.

3 PRACTICE

¿Cómo lo digo?

4 Activity 4 can be done as an interview. Have one student ask the questions and another respond.

5 Have students do Activity 5 with books open.

ANSWERS TO ¿Cómo lo digo?

4
1. Estudio en la escuela ___.
2. Llego a la escuela a pie (en carro, en el bus escolar).
3. Tomo ___ cursos.
4. Llevo los materiales escolares en una mochila.
5. Sí (No), los alumnos de mi escuela (no) estudian mucho.
6. Sí, (No, no) sacamos buenas notas.
7. Sí, (No, no) tomamos muchos exámenes.
8. Sí, (No, no) escuchamos cuando la profesora habla.

5
1. bailamos
2. toca
3. toca, cantan
4. Preparan
5. Toman
6. miramos

R13

REPASO B

Formas

PRESENTATION

 Los verbos **ir, dar, estar**

STEP 1 Have students look at the verbs on page R14. Point out to them that the endings are the same as regular **-ar** verbs except for the **yo** form.

STEP 2 Have students repeat **voy, doy, estoy.** Then have them repeat all the forms.

STEP 3 Read the explanation about **al** in Item 2 aloud.

Universal Access

Have students come up with as many place words as they can. Then call on students to make up sentences using **voy al** or **voy a la** and these place words. Allow **advanced learners** to add anything that makes sense at the end of the sentence. Have students also use plural forms.

Learning from Photos

(page R14) The **Retiro** is a large, popular park in the central part of Madrid. This lake or **estanque** is in the center of the park. It's fun to rent a boat here and row around the lake. The statue is of King Alphonso XII.

PRACTICE

¿Cómo lo digo?

6 Activity 6 can be done orally with books closed.

REPASO B

Los verbos **ir, dar, estar**

1. Note that the verbs **ir, dar,** and **estar** are the same as regular **-ar** verbs in all forms except **yo.**

ir	voy	vas	va	vamos	vais	van
dar	doy	das	da	damos	dais	dan
estar	estoy	estás	está	estamos	estáis	están

2. The preposition **a** often follows the verb **ir.** Remember that **a** contracts with **el** to form one word, **al.**

   Voy al parque.   *but*   **Voy a la tienda.**

El Parque del Retiro, Madrid, España

¿Cómo lo digo?

6 Historieta **Voy a la escuela.**

Contesten. *(Answer.)*
1. ¿Vas a la escuela?
2. ¿A qué hora vas a la escuela?
3. ¿Con quién vas a la escuela?
4. ¿Cómo van ustedes a la escuela?
5. ¿Están ustedes en la escuela ahora?
6. Después de las clases, ¿van ustedes al café?

ANSWERS TO ¿Cómo lo digo?

6
1. Sí, voy a la escuela.
2. Voy a la escuela a las ___.
3. Voy a la escuela con ___.
4. Vamos a la escuela a pie (en carro, en el bus escolar).
5. Sí, (No, no) estamos en la escuela ahora.
6. Sí, (No, no) vamos al café después de las clases.

REPASO B

7 Historieta En la papelería

Completen. *(Complete.)*

Yo __1__ (ir) a la papelería. Elisa __2__ (ir) también. Ella y yo __3__ (estar) en la tienda. Yo __4__ (necesitar) una calculadora para la clase de matemáticas. Yo __5__ (buscar) una calculadora. Elisa necesita solamente un cuaderno.

Yo __6__ (comprar) mi calculadora y Elisa __7__ (comprar) su cuaderno. Nosotros __8__ (pagar) en la caja. Nosotros __9__ (hablar) con la dependienta.

Una papelería. Santiago de Chile

8 Juego ¿Para qué clase? Name a school supply you need. Another classmate will try to guess which class you need it for.

Una librería en avenida Amazonas. Quito, Ecuador

9 Juego ¿Quién es? Work in small groups. One person tells what someone in the class is wearing. The others have to guess who it is. If several people are wearing the same thing, the person giving the clues will have to give more details.

De compras para la escuela

R15

Formas

7 Go over Activity 7 with books open.

Writing Development
Have students rewrite the information from Activity 7 in paragraph form.

Learning from Photos
(page R15, top) Have students look at the photo taken in Santiago, Chile, and say something about it in their own words. For example, they could say: **La muchacha busca materiales escolares. La muchacha habla con el dependiente. La muchacha mira un bolígrafo.**
(page R15, bottom) This **librería** is on **avenida Amazonas,** a main street with shops, restaurants, and cafés in Quito, Ecuador.

ANSWERS TO ¿Cómo lo digo?

7
1. voy
2. va
3. estamos
4. necesito
5. busco
6. compro
7. compra
8. pagamos
9. hablamos

8 *Answers will vary. Students will use vocabulary related to classes and school supplies.*

9 *Answers will vary. Students will use vocabulary related to clothing.*

Preview

In **Repaso C,** students review vocabulary relating to family and home; they also discuss some of their daily activities. In the **Formas** section, they review the present tense of **-er** and **-ir** verbs, the verb **tener,** and possessive adjectives.

Students practice this vocabulary and these structures as they talk about their families, homes, and neighbors.

National Standards

Communication

In Review C, students will communicate in spoken and written Spanish on the following topics:
- Describing their family
- Describing their home

Students will also learn to narrate present events. They will obtain and provide information and engage in conversations about home and family.

Repaso

C Mi familia y mi casa

Spotlight on Culture

Santa Domingo, La República Dominicana *(page R16)* This family is at the **Fortaleza de Santo Domingo,** a military fort built in 1502 to protect the city and guard entry to the Ozama River.

Cartagena, Colombia *(page R17)* These houses are in the walled city of Cartagena on the Caribbean coast of Colombia. Cartagena was an important port during the days of the Spanish conquest. The city was sacked by the privateer Sir Francis Drake in 1586, but fortunately he decided not to burn the city to the ground. The Spaniards then decided to build thick walls around the city.

Today Cartagena is a lovely city with wide avenues and elegant residential areas on the old walled citadel. Cartagena has been declared a World Cultural Heritage Site by UNESCO.

Spanish Online

The **Glencoe World Languages Web site** (spanish. glencoe.com) offers options that enable you and your students to experience the Spanish-speaking world via the Internet. For each **Unidad,** there are activities, games, and quizzes. In addition, an *Enrichment* section offers students an opportunity to visit Web sites related to the theme of the unit.

R17

Palabras

Bellringer Review

Use BRR Transparency R.6 or write the following on the board. Complete.

1. El hermano de mi padre es mi ___.
2. La hija de mis tíos es mi ___.
3. Yo soy ___ de los padres de mis padres.
4. Los padres de mis padres son mis ___.

2 PRESENTATION

STEP 1 Have students open their books to page R18. As you review the vocabulary, have students repeat the words and sentences after you.

STEP 2 You may wish to intersperse questions of varying difficulty levels in your vocabulary presentation.

Universal Access

Have **students with learning difficulties** give one sentence describing a house. Have **advanced learners** give a complete description of a house.

Palabras

Es la familia Suárez.
En la familia Suárez hay cinco personas.
Los señores Suárez tienen tres hijos.

Los Suárez tienen una casa en San Andrés.
Ellos viven en Colombia.

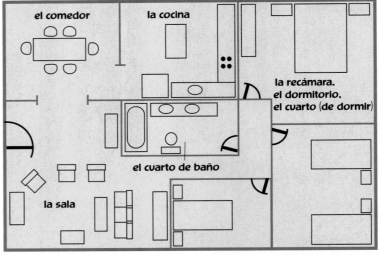

Su casa tiene siete cuartos.

Learning from Photos

(page R18) The house shown here is made of wood with a tin roof. It is characteristic of much of the housing on many Caribbean islands. The island of San Andrés belongs to Colombia.

Palabras

REPASO C

STEP 3 Once you have asked your questions about all the illustrations and photos, have students say everything they can about them.

La familia está en la sala.
La señora Suárez lee un libro.
Su esposo (marido) lee el periódico.
José ve la televisión.
Una hermana escribe una carta.
La otra habla por teléfono.

La familia va al mercado.
Compran comida.
En el mercado venden frutas y vegetales.
Venden carne también.
La señora compra un kilo de tomates.
Los tomates están a cincuenta pesos el kilo.

Mi familia y mi casa

Universal Access

Have **advanced learners** make up false statements about the illustrations. They can then call on classmates to correct the false statements.

Palabras

3 PRACTICE

¿Qué palabra necesito?

Historieta Each time **Historieta** appears, it means that the answers to the activity form a short story. Encourage students to look at the title of the **Historieta,** since it can help them do the activity.

¡OJO! Go over the activities as quickly as possible. If students appear to have a good command of the vocabulary, it is not necessary that they write the activities.

However, if you feel students need additional reinforcement of the vocabulary, have them write the activities after you go over them orally in class.

Learning from Photos

(page R20) This seafood restaurant is built over the water alongside a small fishing port of the Colombian island of San Andrés.

Universal Access

For each question in Activity 2, give **students with learning difficulties** a subject and have them give a complete sentence.

---

3 Juego You may wish to have students work in small groups to play this game. See which group can come up with the longest list for each category.

¿Qué palabra necesito?

1 **Historieta La familia López** Contesten según se indica. *(Answer as indicated.)*

1. ¿Cuántas personas hay en la familia López? (cinco personas)
2. ¿Tienen ellos una casa o un apartamento? (una casa)
3. ¿Dónde viven ellos? (San Andrés)
4. ¿Cuántos cuartos tiene su casa? (ocho)

Un restaurante de pescado.
San Andrés, Colombia

2 Expresiones Pareen. *(Match.)*

1. leer	a. mucho en la escuela
2. escribir	b. al quinto piso
3. vivir	c. una novela
4. aprender	d. un alumno bueno y serio
5. vender	e. una carta con bolígrafo (pluma)
6. comer	f. una limonada
7. ver	g. en una casa particular
8. ser	h. una emisión deportiva
9. subir	i. discos en una tienda
10. beber	j. carne, ensalada y papas

3 Juego ¿Cuáles son? Contesten. *(Answer.)*

1. ¿Cuáles son algunas cosas que comemos?
2. ¿Cuáles son algunas cosas que bebemos?
3. ¿Cuáles son algunas cosas que leemos?
4. ¿Cuáles son algunas cosas que escribimos?

ANSWERS TO ¿Qué palabra necesito?

1
1. Hay cinco personas en la familia López.
2. Ellos tienen una casa.
3. Ellos viven en San Andrés.
4. Su casa tiene ocho cuartos.

2 *(Please note that some numbers have more than one possible answer. However, for the activity to work as a whole, only one answer is possible for each item.)*

1. c	6. j
2. e	7. h
3. g	8. d
4. a	9. b
5. i	10. f

3 *Answers will vary. Students should recall vocabulary they have previously learned.*

Conversación

¿Vive en Caracas tu familia?

Conversación
PRESENTATION

STEP 1 Call on two students to read the **Conversación** aloud.

STEP 2 Then go over the **¿Comprendes?** activity.

Universal Access

Have two **advanced learners** prepare a similar conversation about their families and where they live. Have **average students** answer questions about it. Have **students with learning difficulties** give a summary.

Learning from Photos
(page R21, right) Caracas, the capital of Venezuela, is situated in the north of the country in a beautiful valley at the foot of Ávila Mountain.

Marisa Javier, ¿tienes una familia grande?

Javier Sí, bastante grande. Somos siete. Tengo cuatro hermanos.

Marisa ¿Viven ustedes aquí en la capital?

Javier Sí, vivimos en la capital. Tenemos un apartamento en el edificio Bolívar en la Castellana.

¿Comprendes?

Contesten. *(Answer.)*
1. ¿Tiene Javier una familia grande?
2. ¿Cuántos hermanos tiene Javier?
3. ¿Vive su familia en la capital?
4. ¿Dónde tienen un apartamento?
5. ¿En qué sección de la ciudad está el edificio Bolívar?

Mi familia y mi casa R21

ANSWERS TO ¿Comprendes?
1. Sí, Javier tiene una familia grande.
2. Javier tiene cuatro hermanos.
3. Sí, su familia vive en la capital.
4. Tienen un apartamento en el edificio Bolívar.
5. El edificio Bolívar está en la Castellana.

Formas

REPASO C

1 PREPARATION

Bellringer Review

Use BRR Transparency R.7 or write the following on the board. Do the following.
1. Write five things you can eat.
2. Write three things you can drink.
3. Write the names of the three meals.

2 PRESENTATION

 Presente de los verbos en -er e -ir

STEP 1 Have students repeat all the verb forms after you.

STEP 2 Write one **-er** and one **-ir** verb on the board and have students repeat all forms after you.

STEP 3 Read Item 2 aloud and underline the endings to emphasize that **-er** and **-ir** verbs have the same endings in all forms except **nosotros** (and **vosotros**).

3 PRACTICE

¿Cómo lo digo?

 Go over the activities orally in class. If you feel students need additional review, have them write the activities for homework.

Learning from Photos

(page R22) This outdoor café is in Ronda, Spain, an Andalusian town that clings to a clifftop with a very deep gorge. The history of Ronda, which today is a thriving town of some 35,000 inhabitants, dates back to the time of the ancient Iberians.

Formas Presente de los verbos en -er e -ir

1. Review the following forms of regular **-er** and **-ir** verbs.

comer		vivir	
como	comemos	vivo	vivimos
comes	*coméis*	vives	*vivís*
come	comen	vive	viven

2. Note that the **-er** and **-ir** verbs have the same endings in all forms except **nosotros** (and **vosotros**).

comemos	vivimos
coméis	*vivís*

Un café al aire libre. Ronda. España

¿Cómo lo digo?

4 **Tú y tus amigos** Contesten. *(Answer.)*
1. ¿Qué comes cuando vas a un café?
2. ¿Qué bebes cuando estás en un café?
3. ¿Qué aprenden tú y tus amigos en la escuela?
4. ¿Qué leen ustedes en la clase de inglés?
5. ¿Qué escriben ustedes?
6. ¿Comprenden los alumnos cuando la profesora de español habla?
7. ¿Reciben ustedes notas buenas en todos sus cursos?

5 **Historieta En un café** Completen. *(Complete.)*
En el café los clientes __1__ (ver) al mesero. Ellos __2__ (hablar) con el mesero. Los clientes __3__ (leer) el menú y __4__ (decidir) lo que van a tomar. Los meseros __5__ (tomar) la orden y __6__ (escribir) la orden en un cuaderno pequeño o en un bloc. Los meseros no __7__ (leer) el menú. Y los clientes no __8__ (escribir) la orden.

ANSWERS TO ¿Cómo lo digo?

4
1. Como ___ cuando voy a un café.
2. Bebo ___ cuando estoy en un café.
3. Mis amigos y yo aprendemos ___ en la escuela.
4. Nosotros leemos ___ en la clase de inglés.
5. Nosotros escribimos ___.
6. Sí (No), los alumnos (no) comprenden cuando la profesora de español habla.
7. Sí, (No, no) recibimos notas buenas en todos nuestros cursos.

5
1. ven
2. hablan
3. leen
4. deciden
5. toman
6. escriben
7. leen
8. escriben

El verbo tener

1. Review the forms of the irregular verb **tener.**

tener	
tengo	**tenemos**
tienes	***tenéis***
tiene	**tienen**

2. Note that the expression **tener que** followed by an infinitive means *to have to.*

Tenemos que estudiar y aprender mucho.

¿Cómo lo digo?

6 Historieta Mi familia Contesten. *(Answer.)*

1. ¿Tienes una familia grande o pequeña?
2. ¿Cuántos hermanos tienes?
3. ¿Cuántos años tienen ellos?
4. ¿Y cuántos años tienes tú?
5. ¿Tienen ustedes un perro o un gato?
6. ¿Tiene tu padre o tu madre un carro?
7. En la escuela, ¿tienes que estudiar mucho?
8. ¿Y tienen que trabajar mucho tus padres?

7 Historieta La familia Bravo

Completen con **tener.** *(Complete with* tener.*)*

La familia Bravo __1__ un piso o apartamento en Madrid. Su piso __2__ seis cuartos. Está en Salamanca, una zona muy bonita de la ciudad. Muchas calles en la zona Salamanca __3__ los nombres de artistas famosos—la calle Goya, la calle Velázquez.

Hay cuatro personas en la familia Bravo. Teresa __4__ diecisiete años y su hermano __5__ quince años. Ellos __6__ un perro adorable.

Una casa de apartamentos, barrio Salamanca, Madrid, España

ANSWERS TO ¿Cómo lo digo?

6

1. Tengo una familia grande (pequeña).
2. Tengo ___ hermano(s). (No tengo hermanos).
3. Ellos tienen ___ años.
4. Yo tengo ___ años.
5. Sí, nosotros tenemos un perro (un gato). (No, no tenemos un perro [un gato]).
6. Sí, mi padre (mi madre) tiene un carro.
7. Sí, (No, no) tengo que estudiar mucho en la escuela.
8. Sí (No), mis padres (no) tienen que trabajar mucho.

7

1. tiene
2. tiene
3. tienen
4. tiene
5. tiene
6. tienen

Formas

1 PREPARATION

Bellringer Review

Use BRR Transparency R.8 or write the following on the board. Write an original sentence using each of the following verbs.

1. **vivir**
2. **leer**
3. **escribir**
4. **aprender**

2 PRESENTATION

El verbo tener

STEP 1 Have students repeat the forms of the verb **tener.**

STEP 2 Read the information in Item 2 about **tener que** to the class.

STEP 3 Have students make up additional sentences using **tener que.**

3 PRACTICE

¿Cómo lo digo?

6 Activity 6 can be done in pairs as an interview.

Learning from Photos

(page R23) The architecture of this building is very typical of the apartment buildings of the Salamanca district of Madrid.

Formas

1 PREPARATION

Bellringer Review

Use BRR Transparency R.9 or write the following on the board. Answer.

1. **¿Dónde vives?**
2. **¿Tienes una familia grande o pequeña?**
3. **¿Cuántos años tienes?**
4. **Y tu hermano(a), ¿cuántos años tiene?**
5. **¿Tienen Uds. un perro o un gato?**

2 PRESENTATION

 Adjetivos posesivos

STEP 1 Have students open their books to page R24. Go over Items 1 and 2 with them. Have them read the model sentences aloud.

STEP 2 After you have gone over the explanation with them, ask students to make up some original sentences using the possessive adjectives.

STEP 3 Go over the activities orally in class. Assign them for written homework if you feel additional review and reinforcement are necessary.

3 PRACTICE

¿Cómo lo digo?

Writing Development
Have students use their answers to Activity 8 to create a paragraph about their home and family.

 **Adjetivos posesivos**

1. Review the forms of the possessive adjectives **mi, tu,** and **su.** These adjectives have only two forms.

> ¿Dan una fiesta **tu** hermana y **tus** primos?
> Sí, **mi** hermana y **mis** primos dan una fiesta.
> Todos **sus** amigos van a recibir una invitación a **su** fiesta.

2. The possessive adjective **nuestro** has four forms.

> **Nuestro** primo, **nuestra** tía, **nuestras** primas y **nuestros** abuelos viven todos en Madrid.

¿Cómo lo digo?

8 **Historieta Mi familia y mi casa** Contesten. *(Answer.)*

1. ¿Dónde está tu casa o tu apartamento?
2. ¿Cuántos cuartos tiene tu casa o tu apartamento?
3. ¿Cuántas personas hay en tu familia?
4. ¿Dónde viven tus abuelos?
5. Y tus primos, ¿dónde viven?

9 **Historieta Nuestra casa** Completen. *(Complete.)*

Nosotros vivimos en __1__ *(name of city or town).* __2__ casa está en la calle __3__ *(name of street).* __4__ padres tienen un carro. __5__ carro es bastante nuevo. Yo tengo una bicicleta. __6__ bicicleta está en el garaje con el carro de __7__ padres. Nosotros tenemos un perro. __8__ perro es adorable.

__9__ perro está en el jardín. Mi hermano y __10__ amigos siempre juegan en el jardín alrededor de __11__ casa.

ANSWERS TO ¿Cómo lo digo?

8
1. Mi casa (apartamento) está en ___.
2. Mi casa (apartamento) tiene ___ cuartos.
3. Hay ___ personas en mi familia.
4. Mis abuelos viven en ___.
5. Mis primos viven en ___.

9
1. *Answers will vary.*
2. Nuestra
3. *Answers will vary.*
4. Nuestros
5. Su
6. Mi
7. mis
8. Nuestro
9. Nuestro
10. sus
11. nuestra

Apartamentos With a classmate, look at this plan of the fourth floor of an apartment building. A different family lives in each of the two apartments. Give each family a name. Then say as much as you can about each family and their activities. Don't forget to describe their apartment. Be as original as possible.

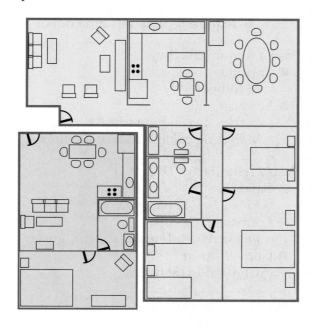

En el café Work in groups of three or four. You're all friends from Chile. After school you go to a café where you talk about lots of things—school, teachers, friends, home, family, etc. One of you will be the server. You have to interrupt the conversation once in a while to take the orders and serve. Take turns.

Un café al aire libre.
Valparaíso, Chile

Mi familia y mi casa

Formas

10 Encourage students to be as creative as possible when doing this activity. They can make up a lot of funny things.

11 Have students present their conversations to the class.

Universal Access

You may wish to ask **students with learning difficulties** questions about their descriptions in Activity 10 to help them add more details. Or, you may wish instead to have all students share their descriptions with partners or small groups who may then ask questions. Have students incorporate the answers to the questions into their descriptions.

Learning from Photos

(page R25) Valparaíso, Chile, is a port city that clings to hills that border the Pacific. Many of the streets are extremely steep. There are also several funiculars to help residents go from the lower to the upper town. With regard to its hills and steep streets, Valparaíso is often compared with San Francisco.

ANSWERS TO ¿Cómo lo digo?

9 *Answers will vary. Students will use vocabulary relating to houses and family.*

10 *Answers will vary. Students should use vocabulary they have previously learned.*

Planning for Unit 1

CORRELATIONS

National Standards

Communication Standard 1.1
pages 5, 7, 9, 10, 11, 14, 15, 17, 18, 19, 20, 26, 27, 32, 33

Communication Standard 1.2
pages 9, 11, 15, 20, 21, 23, 30, 34, 37

Communication Standard 1.3
pages 5, 7, 10, 15, 19, 26, 27, 32

Cultures Standard 2.1
pages 22–23, 27, 32, 34, 35

Cultures Standard 2.2
pages 22–23, 30, 32, 35

Connections Standard 3.1
pages 22–23, 27, 32, 34, 35, 36–37

Connections Standard 3.2
pages 27, 32, 34

Comparisons Standard 4.1
pages 16, 21, 37

Comparisons Standard 4.2
pages 22–23, 27, 32, 35

Communities Standard 5.1
pages 26, 27

PACING AND PRIORITIES

The unit content is color coded below to assist you in planning.

■ required   ■ recommended   ▨ optional

Paso 1 (required)   *Days 1–8*
■ Palabras
   El fútbol
■ Formas
   Verbos de cambio radical **e → ie**
   Verbos de cambio radical **o → ue**

Paso 2 (required)   *Days 9–16*
■ Palabras
   El béisbol, El básquetbol
■ Formas
   Los verbos **interesar, aburrir, gustar**
■ Conversación
   Un partido de fútbol

Paso 3 (recommended)   *Days 17–24*
■ Pronunciación
   Las consonantes **s, c, z**
■ Cultura y lectura
   Los deportes en el mundo hispano
■ Repaso
■ ¡Te toca a ti!
■ Assessment

Paso 4 (optional)
▨ Diversiones
▨ Más cultura y lectura
   La Copa mundial
   Personajes latinos famosos
▨ Conexiones
   La anatomía

SECTION		PAGES	SECTION RESOURCES
Paso 1			
Palabras	El fútbol	2–5	• Vocabulary Transparencies 1.1–1.2 • Audio CD 2 • Audio Activities TE, pages 1–3 • Workbook TE, pages 1–3 • Quiz 1, page 1 • ExamView® Pro
Formas	Verbos de cambio radical **e → ie** Verbos de cambio radical **o → ue**	6–7 8–11	• Audio CD 2 • Audio Activities TE, pages 3–6 • Workbook TE, pages 4–6 • Quizzes 2–3, pages 2–3 • ExamView® Pro
Paso 2			
Palabras	El béisbol El básquetbol, el baloncesto	12 13–15	• Vocabulary Transparencies 1.3–1.4 • Audio CD 2 • Audio Activities TE, pages 7–11 • Workbook TE, pages 7–9 • Quiz 4, page 4 • ExamView® Pro
Formas	Los verbos **interesar,** **aburrir, gustar**	16–19	• Audio CD 2 • Audio Activities TE, pages 12–13 • Workbook TE, pages 10–12 • Quiz 5, page 5 • ExamView® Pro
Paso 3			
Conversación	Un partido de fútbol	20	• Audio CD 2 • Audio Activities TE, pages 13–14 • Workbook TE, page 13
Pronunciación	Las consonantes **s, c, z**	21	• Pronunciation Transparency P 1 • Audio CD 2 • Audio Activities TE, page 15
Cultura y lectura	Los deportes en el mundo hispano	22–23	• Audio CD 2 • Audio Activities TE, page 16 • Workbook, page 14
Repaso		24–25	• Audio CD 2 • Audio Activities TE, pages 17–18 • Workbook TE, page 15 • Tests, pages 1–14
¡Te toca a ti!		26–27	• Audio CD 2 • Audio Activities TE, pages 19–20 • Workbook TE, pages 16–17
Assessment		28–29	• Vocabulary Transparency 1.5 • Tests, pages 1–14 • ExamView® Pro, Unit 1 • Performance Assessment, Tasks 1–2
Paso 4			
Diversiones		30–33	• Workbook, page 18
Más cultura y lectura	La Copa mundial Personajes latinos famosos	34 35	• Tests, page 6
Conexiones	La anatomía	36–37	• Tests, page 6

Using Your Resources for Unit 1

Transparencies

Bellringer 1.1–1.6

Vocabulary V 1.1–1.6

Assessment A 1

Songs S 1

Workbook

Paso 1 Vocabulary and Structure
pages 1–6

Paso 2 Vocabulary and Structure
pages 7–12

Conversation and Reading
pages 13–14

Repaso, ¡Te toca a ti!, Diversiones
pages 15–18

Audio Program and Audio Activities Booklet

Paso 1 Vocabulary and Structure
pages 1–6

Paso 2 Vocabulary and Structure
pages 7–13

Conversation, Pronunciation
pages 13–16

Repaso, ¡Te toca a ti!
pages 17–20

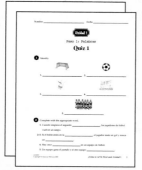
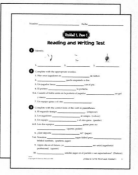
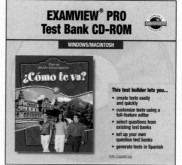

Vocabulary and Structure Quizzes, pages 1–8

Unit Tests, pages 1–14

ExamView® Pro, Unit 1

Timesaving Teacher Tools

TeacherWorks
All in One Teacher Planning

TeacherWorks™ is your all in one teacher resource center. Personalize lesson plans, access resources from the Teacher Wraparound Edition, connect to the Internet, or make a to-do list. These are only a few of the many features that can assist you in the planning and organizing of your lessons.

Includes:
- A calendar feature
- Access to all program blackline masters
- Standards correlations and more

Test Bank software for Macintosh and Windows makes creating, editing, customizing, and printing tests quick and easy.

FOLDABLES™
Study Organizer

Manipulatives The foldable activities give students of all learning styles the opportunity to excel in a nontraditional manner. Your students will love these hands-on activities!

Technology Resources

Spanish Online
In the Unit 1 online resources, you and your students will have a chance to learn more about sports in the Spanish-speaking world.

PuzzleMaker allows you to create crossword puzzles, jumble puzzles, and word searches in minutes or edit a database of key terms and puzzles to review unit vocabulary. You can choose English-Spanish puzzles or Spanish-English puzzles. The puzzles can be printed or played on the computer screen.

Canta con Justo This CD contains songs sung by a young Argentine singer, Justo Lamas, which are specifically geared to review and expand upon the vocabulary learned in each unit. Students will enjoy listening to these songs while they learn from them.

¡En vivo! This music video of Justo Lamas performing his songs live in concert gives your students a chance to experience the songs in a different way while reinforcing the language skills they are learning!

Unidad 1

Preview

In this unit, students will learn to discuss and describe team sports. To do this they will learn basic vocabulary related to soccer, basketball, and baseball. They will also learn some stem-changing verbs—**empezar, querer, preferir, perder, volver, poder,** and **jugar.** Students will be able to use these verbs when talking about team sports.

They will also learn verbs such as **interesar, aburrir,** and **gustar** so they can tell what sports interest them or bore them and which sports they like. Students will also learn about the popularity of sports in various areas of the Spanish-speaking world.

National Standards

Communication

In Unit 1 students will communicate in spoken and written Spanish on the following topics:
- describing team sports, namely soccer, basketball, and baseball
- expressing interests, likes, and dislikes

Students will obtain and provide information, express personal preferences and dislikes, and engage in conversations about sports events as they fulfill the objectives listed on this page.

Spanish Online

The **Glencoe World Languages Web site** (spanish. glencoe.com) offers options that enable you and your students to experience the Spanish-speaking world via the Internet. For each **Unidad,** there are activities, games, and quizzes. In addition, an *Enrichment* section offers students an opportunity to visit Web sites related to the theme of the unit.

Unidad 1 Los deportes

Objetivos

In this unit you will learn to:
- talk about sports
- talk about what you begin to, want to, and prefer to do
- talk about people's activities
- express what interests, bores, or pleases you
- discuss the role of sports in the Spanish-speaking world

¡Me gusta jugar al fútbol!

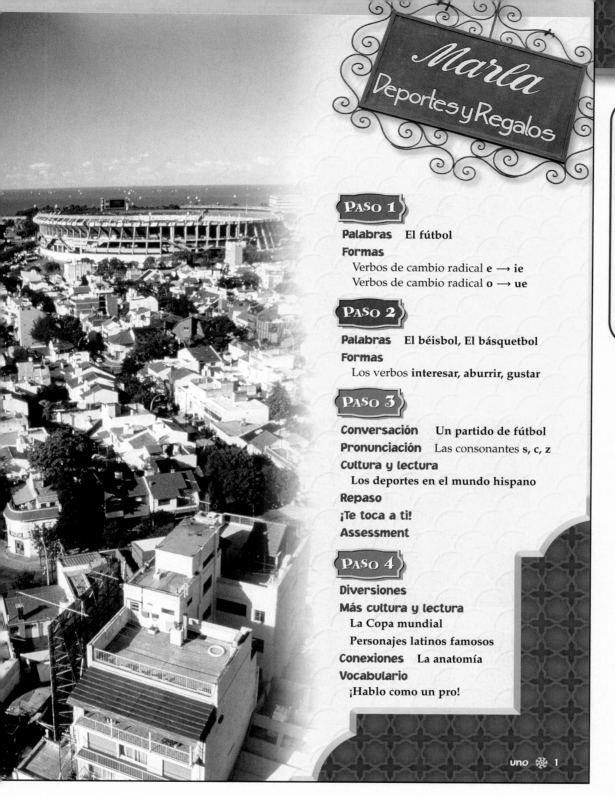

Marla

Deportes y Regalos

Spotlight on Culture

Santo Domingo, República Dominicana
(left) These students are members of the soccer team at **el Colegio Dominicano de la Salle** in Santo Domingo.

Buenos Aires, Argentina
(right) This stadium is in Buenos Aires, Argentina. In the background you can see the **río de la Plata.**

Palabras

Palabras El fútbol

- la cabeza
- el brazo
- la mano izquierda
- el equipo
- la mano derecha
- la rodilla
- la pierna
- el pie
- el jugador
- la jugadora

el estadio

- el tablero indicador
- 2do. TIEMPO
- el tanto
- el espectador, la espectadora
- la portería
- el portero

el campo de fútbol

1 PREPARATION

RESOURCE MANAGER

Vocabulary Transparencies 1.1–1.2
Audio Activities TE, pages 1–3
Audio CD 2
Workbook, pages 1–3
Quiz 1, page 1
ExamView® Pro

Bellringer Review

Use BRR Transparency 1.1 or write the following on the board.
Write three sentences about each of the following topics.
Mi casa
Mi familia

2 PRESENTATION

STEP 1 Use Vocabulary Transparencies 1.1–1.2 for the initial presentation of the new vocabulary.

STEP 2 After the oral presentation, as suggested in previous units, have students open their books and read the new vocabulary for additional reinforcement.

STEP 3 Project Vocabulary Transparency 1.1 again and let students ask one another questions about what they see. For example, they might ask: **¿Cuántas personas hay en el equipo? ¿Hay muchos espectadores en el estadio o pocos espectadores?**

Learning from Photos

(page 2) The game seen here between the teams Chivas and Atlas took place in Guadalajara, México, in front of a capacity crowd of 75,000 fans.

Total Physical Response

TPR 1 Teach **rebotar** *(bounce)*, **pelota** *(ball)*, **tirar** *(throw)*, and **atrapar** *(catch)* by using the appropriate gestures as you say each word.
(Student 1), **levántate. Ven acá.**
Cuenta: uno, dos, tres.
Ahora, toma la pelota.
Rebota la pelota cinco veces.
Ahora, tira la pelota. Tira la pelota a
(Student 2).

(Student 2), **atrapa la pelota.**
Y ahora, tira la pelota a *(Student 3)*. **Gracias.**

TPR 2 The following TPR activity can be done with the entire class participating.
Indíquenme la mano derecha.
Indíquenme la mano izquierda.
Indíquenme la rodilla.
Indíquenme la pierna.
Levanten la mano derecha.
Y ahora levanten el pie derecho.
Levanten el pie izquierdo. Gracias.

2

Hoy hay un partido.
El Real Madrid juega contra el Barcelona.

STEP 4 Model the sentences under each illustration on page 3. Have students repeat the sentences after you or Audio CD 2. As they do, intersperse your presentation with questions.

Universal Access

As you ask questions during the vocabulary presentation, you may wish to ask questions of varying difficulty levels to accommodate differences in students' abilities. The first time you present this vocabulary, ask **students with learning difficulties** only the easier questions. Ask them the more difficult questions after they have had more time to become familiar with the vocabulary and after they have had the opportunity to hear other students' responses.

Have students answer with the complete sentence or sometimes have them use just the specific word or expression that responds to the question word.

Los jugadores juegan al fútbol.
Un jugador lanza el balón.
Lanza el balón con el pie.
El portero guarda la portería.

El segundo tiempo empieza.
Los dos equipos vuelven al campo.
El tanto queda empatado a cero.

El portero no puede bloquear
    (parar) el balón.
El balón entra en la portería.
López mete un gol.
Él marca un tanto.

El Real Madrid gana el partido.
El Barcelona pierde.
Los espectadores no duermen
    durante el partido.

Paso 1: Palabras

tres 🌸 3

About the Spanish Language

- The verb **jugar** can be followed by **a,** or the **a** can be eliminated. It is probably safe to say that the **a** is more commonly used in Spain, but it is also heard in areas of Latin America.
- Another commonly used term for scoreboard is **el marcador.**
- **El partido** is used to refer to a sports match

or game. **La partida** is used for a card game, for example.
- Note the use of the article **el** with **el Real Madrid** and **el Barcelona.** The article **el** is used because **el equipo** is understood. However, when talking about the **Copa mundial** the article refers to the country instead of the team, for example **(la) Argentina ante (el) Perú.**

3

3 PRACTICE

¿Qué palabra necesito?

¡OJO! When students are doing the **¿Qué palabra necesito?** activities, accept any answer that makes sense. The purpose of these activities is to have students use the new vocabulary. They are not factual recall activities. Thus, it is not necessary for students to remember specific factual information from the vocabulary presentation when answering. If you wish, have students use the photos on this page as a stimulus, when possible.

Historieta Each time **Historieta** appears, it means that the answers to the activity form a short story. Encourage students to look at the title of the **Historieta,** since it can help them do the activity.

2 and 3 After going over Activities 2 and 3 on pages 4 and 5, call on one or more students to retell the stories in their own words.

Note: Activity 3 uses only the third person form of the stem-changing verbs so that the students can immediately answer questions and speak without having to change endings. Students will learn how to manipulate the stem-changing verbs in the **Formas** section of **Paso 1** of this unit.

¿Qué palabra necesito?

1 **Un partido de fútbol** Completen según se indica.
(Answer as indicated.)

1. Diego lanza el balón con _____.

2. Él no lanza el balón con _____.

3. También lanza el balón con _____.

4. Pero no lanza el balón con _____.

5. Diego es un jugador muy bueno porque tiene _____ fuertes.

2 **Historieta El fútbol** Contesten según se indica.
(Answer as indicated.)

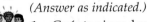

1. ¿Cuántos jugadores hay en el equipo de fútbol? (once)
2. ¿Cuántos tiempos hay en un partido de fútbol? (dos)
3. ¿Quién guarda la portería? (el portero)
4. ¿Cuándo mete un gol el jugador? (cuando el balón entra en la portería)
5. ¿Qué marca un jugador cuando el balón entra en la portería? (un tanto)
6. En el estadio, ¿qué indica el tablero? (el tanto)
7. ¿Cuándo queda empatado el tanto? (cuando los dos equipos tienen el mismo tanto)

Writing Development
Have students write the answers to Activity 2 in a paragraph to illustrate how the answers to all the items tell a story.

ANSWERS TO ¿Qué palabra necesito?

1
1. el pie
2. la mano
3. la cabeza
4. el brazo
5. piernas

2
1. Hay once jugadores en el equipo de fútbol.
2. Hay dos tiempos en un partido de fútbol.
3. El portero guarda la portería.
4. El jugador mete un gol cuando el balón entra en la portería.
5. Un jugador marca un tanto cuando el balón entra en la portería.
6. El tablero indica el tanto.
7. El tanto queda empatado cuando los dos equipos tienen el mismo tanto.

3 Historieta Un partido de fútbol

Contesten. (Answer.)

1. ¿Cuántos equipos de fútbol hay en el campo de fútbol?
2. ¿Cuántos jugadores hay en cada equipo?
3. ¿Qué tiempo empieza, el primero o el segundo?
4. ¿Vuelven los jugadores al campo cuando empieza el segundo tiempo?
5. ¿Tiene un jugador el balón?
6. ¿Lanza el balón con el pie o con la mano?
7. ¿Para el balón el portero o entra el balón en la portería?
8. ¿Mete el jugador un gol?
9. ¿Marca un tanto?
10. ¿Queda empatado el tanto?
11. ¿Quién gana, el Valencia o el Liverpool?
12. ¿Qué equipo pierde?
13. ¿Siempre pierde?

El estadio de Mestalla. Valencia. España

Learning from Photos
(page 5) This game is between Valencia and Liverpool, England in **el Estadio de Mestalla** in Valencia, Spain.

Universal Access

After going over Activity 3, call on **students with learning difficulties** to give some random sentences about a soccer game. Have **advanced learners** give a thorough description in their own words.

4 Un partido de fútbol
Work with a classmate. Take turns asking and answering each other's questions about the illustration below.

Paso 1: Palabras

cinco 5

ANSWERS TO ¿Qué palabra necesito?

3
1. Hay dos equipos de fútbol en el campo de fútbol.
2. Hay once jugadores en cada equipo.
3. El primer (segundo) tiempo empieza.
4. Sí, los jugadores vuelven al campo cuando empieza el segundo tiempo.
5. Sí, un jugador tiene el balón.
6. Lanza el balón con el pie.
7. El balón entra en la portería. (El portero para el balón.)

8. Sí (No), el jugador (no) mete un gol.
9. Sí, (No, no) marca un tanto.
10. Sí (No), el tanto (no) queda empatado.
11. El Valencia (El Liverpool) gana.
12. El Liverpool (El Valencia) pierde.
13. Sí, (No, no) pierde siempre.

4 Answers will vary, but students should use the vocabulary from Paso 1.

5

Formas

1 PREPARATION

RESOURCE MANAGER

Audio Activities TE, pages 3–6
Audio CD 2
Workbook, pages 4–6
Quizzes 2–3, pages 2–3
ExamView® Pro

Bellringer Review

Use BRR Transparency 1.2 or write the following on the board.
Write as many parts of the body in Spanish as you can.

2 PRESENTATION

 Verbos de cambio radical
e → ie

STEP 1 Write the verb forms on the board. Have students repeat them aloud.

STEP 2 You may wish to start with the **nosotros** form to show that it is different.

STEP 3 Use different colored chalk for **nosotros** (and **vosotros**) to emphasize the difference in sound and spelling in comparison to the other forms.

STEP 4 Read the information to the students about the use of **a** + *infinitive* from the **Nota** box on page 6.

 Formas — **Verbos de cambio radical e → ie**
Telling what you begin to, want to, or prefer to do

1. Some verbs in Spanish are called stem-changing verbs. The verbs **empezar, querer, perder,** and **preferir** are examples of stem-changing verbs. All forms, except the **nosotros** (and **vosotros**) forms, change the **e** of the infinitive to **ie**. The endings of these verbs are the same as those of a regular verb.

	empezar	querer	preferir
yo	empiezo	quiero	prefiero
tú	empiezas	quieres	prefieres
él, ella, Ud.	empieza	quiere	prefiere
nosotros(as)	empezamos	queremos	preferimos
vosotros(as)	*empezáis*	*queréis*	*preferís*
ellos, ellas, Uds.	empiezan	quieren	prefieren

2. The verbs **empezar, querer,** and **preferir** are often followed by an infinitive.

Prefieren ganar. No quieren perder.

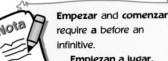

Nota

Empezar and **comenzar** require **a** before an infinitive.
Empiezan a jugar.
Comienzan a jugar.

Los muchachos juegan fútbol en
Tortuguero, Costa Rica

Universal Access

Kinesthetic learners may need to copy (write) the verb forms to help them retain them.

Learning from Photos

(page 6) This informal game is being played in Tortuguero, Costa Rica. The small town of Tortuguero is located north of Puerto Limón on the intricate Tortuguero canal system. The town has very few residents, most of whom are employed at the **Parque Nacional Tortuguero.**

¿Cómo lo digo?

5 **Historieta** **Queremos ganar.**

 Contesten. *(Answer.)*

1. ¿Empiezan ustedes a jugar?
2. ¿Empiezan ustedes a jugar a las tres?
3. ¿Quieren ustedes ganar el partido?
4. ¿Quieren ustedes marcar un tanto?
5. ¿Pierden ustedes a veces o ganan siempre?
6. ¿Prefieren ustedes jugar en el parque o en la calle?

Papá y su hijo juegan fútbol.
Plaza Catedral. Cádiz. España

6 **Historieta** **El partido continúa.**

Formen oraciones según el modelo.
(Form sentences according to the model.)

el segundo tiempo / empezar →
El segundo tiempo empieza.

1. los jugadores / empezar a jugar
2. los dos equipos / querer ganar
3. ellos / preferir marcar muchos tantos
4. Sánchez / querer meter un gol
5. el portero / querer parar el balón
6. el equipo de Sánchez / no perder

7 **Historieta** **¿Un(a) aficionado(a) a los deportes?**

Contesten. *(Answer about yourself.)*

1. ¿Prefieres jugar al béisbol o al fútbol?
2. ¿Prefieres jugar con un grupo de amigos o con un equipo formal?
3. ¿Prefieres jugar en el partido o prefieres mirar el partido?
4. ¿Prefieres ser jugador(a) o espectador(a)?
5. ¿Siempre quieres ganar?
6. ¿Pierdes a veces?

El *estadio* Atahualpa.
Quito. Ecuador

1 PREPARATION

Bellringer Review

Use BRR Transparency 1.3 or write the following on the board. Change the following to **nosotros.**
1. Yo empiezo a jugar.
2. Yo quiero ganar.
3. Yo no pierdo.

2 PRESENTATION

 Verbos de cambio radical
o → ue

STEP 1 Write the verb forms from page 8 on the board and have students repeat them after you.

STEP 2 To give visual assistance for the spelling, use different colored chalk when writing the **nosotros** and **vosotros** forms on the board.

STEP 3 Have students open their books to page 8 and lead them through Items 1 and 2.

Learning from Realia

(page 8) Ask students what they think this advertisement is for. *(an airline)* Then ask students the following questions: **¿Juega fútbol el muchacho? ¿Qué juega el muchacho? ¿Lanza el balón con el pie o con la cabeza?**

Verbos de cambio radical o → ue
Describing more activities

1. The verbs **volver** *(to return to a place)*, **devolver** *(to return a thing)*, **poder** *(to be able to)*, and **dormir** *(to sleep)* are also stem-changing verbs. The **o** of the stem changes to **ue** in all forms except **nosotros** (and **vosotros**). The endings are the same as those of the regular verbs. Study the following forms.

	volver	poder	dormir
yo	vuelvo	puedo	duermo
tú	vuelves	puedes	duermes
él, ella, Ud.	vuelve	puede	duerme
nosotros(as)	volvemos	podemos	dormimos
vosotros(as)	*volvéis*	*podéis*	*dormís*
ellos, ellas, Uds.	vuelven	pueden	duermen

2. The **u** in the verb **jugar** changes to **ue** in all forms except **nosotros** (and **vosotros**).

   jugar   **juego, juegas, juega, jugamos,** *jugáis,* **juegan**

Nota

Jugar is sometimes followed by **a** when a sport is mentioned. Both of the following are acceptable:

Juegan al fútbol.
Juegan fútbol.

ES INCREÍBLE LO QUE PUEDE HACER CON MÁS ESPACIO.

¿Cómo lo digo?

8 **¿Qué juegan?**   Practiquen la conversación.

(Practice the conversation.)

Ana y Paco, ¿juegan Uds. al fútbol?

Sí, jugamos mucho. ¿Y Uds.?

No, jugamos más al béisbol. Cuando Uds. juegan al fútbol, no pueden usar las manos, ¿no?

No. Tenemos que lanzar el balón con los pies o con la cabeza. ¿Quieren Uds. jugar con nosotros?

No. Preferimos ser espectadores y mirar el partido.

9 **Historieta** **¿Qué quieren jugar?**

Contesten. *(Answer based on the conversation.)*

1. ¿Quiénes juegan mucho al fútbol?
2. ¿A qué juegan Tomás y Elena?
3. ¿Pueden los jugadores usar las manos cuando juegan al fútbol?
4. ¿Con qué tienen que lanzar el balón?
5. ¿Quieren jugar Tomás y Elena?
6. ¿Prefieren jugar o mirar?

Paso 1: Formas

---

3 PRACTICE

¿Cómo lo digo?

8 First have students repeat after you. Then have pairs of students role-play the conversation.

9 This activity can be done orally with books closed as a follow-up to student presentations of the conversation.

Universal Access

You may wish to allow **students with learning difficulties** and **average students** to read the conversation aloud with as much expression as possible. Then call on **advanced learners** to present the conversation without reading. They do not have to recite it from memory. Permit them to say anything that makes sense.

ANSWERS TO **¿Cómo lo digo?**

9

1. Ana y Paco juegan mucho al fútbol.
2. Tomás y Elena juegan al béisbol.
3. No, los jugadores no pueden usar las manos cuando juegan al fútbol.
4. Tienen que lanzar el balón con los pies o con la cabeza.
5. No, Tomás y Elena no quieren jugar.
6. Prefieren mirar.

PASO 1

3 PRACTICE (continued)

 This activity can be done orally with books closed.

Writing Development
Have students write a paragraph about **un partido de fútbol** after going over Activity 10.

Learning from Photos
(page 10) These young boys are playing football in the yard in front of their home which leads directly to the beach in Casares, Spain.

 Historieta Un partido de fútbol   Contesten. *(Answer.)*

1. ¿Juegan ustedes (al) fútbol?
2. ¿Juegan con unos amigos o con el equipo de su escuela?
3. ¿Vuelven ustedes al campo cuando empieza el segundo tiempo?
4. ¿Pueden ustedes usar las manos cuando juegan (al) fútbol?
5. ¿Tienen ustedes que lanzar el balón con los pies o el brazo?
6. ¿Duermen ustedes bien después de jugar (al) fútbol?

Los niños juegan al fútbol. Casares. España

 Historieta En la clase de español
Contesten. *(Answer.)*

1. ¿Juegas al Bingo en la clase de español?
2. ¿Puedes hablar inglés en la clase de español?
3. ¿Qué lengua puedes o tienes que hablar en la clase de español?
4. ¿Duermes en la clase de español?
5. ¿Devuelve el/la profesor(a) los exámenes pronto?

ANSWERS TO ¿Cómo lo digo?

10
1. Sí, (No, no) jugamos al fútbol.
2. Jugamos con unos amigos (con el equipo de nuestra escuela).
3. Sí, volvemos al campo cuando empieza el segundo tiempo.
4. No, no podemos usar las manos cuando jugamos (al) fútbol.
5. Tenemos que lanzar el balón con los pies.
6. Sí, dormimos bien después de jugar (al) fútbol.

11
1. Sí, (No, no) juego al Bingo en la clase de español.
2. Sí, (No, no) puedo hablar inglés en la clase de español.
3. Puedo (Tengo que) hablar español en la clase de español.
4. No, no duermo en la clase de español. (Sí, duermo en la clase de español.)
5. Sí (No), el/la profesor(a) (no) devuelve los exámenes pronto.

12 **Historieta** **Sí, pero ahora no puede.**
Completen. *(Complete.)*

Yo __1__ (jugar) mucho al fútbol y Diana __2__ (jugar) mucho también, pero ahora ella no __3__ (poder).

—Diana, ¿por qué no __4__ (poder) jugar ahora?

—No __5__ (poder) porque __6__ (querer) ir a casa.

Sí, Diana __7__ (querer) ir a casa porque ella __8__ (tener) un amigo que __9__ (volver) hoy de Puerto Rico y ella __10__ (querer) estar en casa. Pero mañana todos nosotros __11__ (ir) a jugar. Y el amigo puertorriqueño de Diana __12__ (poder) jugar también. Su amigo __13__ (jugar) muy bien.

Un estadio de fútbol. San Juan, Puerto Rico

13 **Quiero pero no puedo.** A classmate will ask you if you want to do something or go somewhere. Tell him or her that you want to but you can't because you have to do something else. Tell what it is you have to do. Take turns asking and answering the questions.

14 **¿Es así o no?** Choose one of the illustrations below and make a statement about it. Your partner will look at the other illustration and agree with your statement or correct you if his or her picture is different.

For more practice using words and forms from **Paso 1,** do Activity 1 on page H2 at the end of this book.

Paso 1: Formas

once ✳ **11**

12 In this activity, students have to use all the different forms of the various stem-changing verbs.

13 Tell students to be as creative as possible. They can make up some outlandish reasons why they can't do something.

UN POCO MÁS This *InfoGap* activity will allow students to practice in pairs. The activity should be very manageable for them, since all vocabulary and structures are familiar to them.

 ANSWERS TO **¿Cómo lo digo?**

12
1. juego
2. juega
3. puede
4. puedes
5. puedo
6. quiero
7. quiere
8. tiene
9. vuelve
10. quiere
11. vamos
12. puede
13. juega

13 *Answers will vary. Students should begin their question with:* ¿Quieres + *infinitive...?* Their partner will answer with: Sí, quiero... pero no puedo porque...

14 *Answers will vary but may include:*
—El portero se llama Rodríguez.
—No, el portero se llama García.
—Los Toros ganan.
—No, los Águilas ganan.

Palabras

1 PREPARATION

RESOURCE MANAGER

Vocabulary Transparencies 1.3–1.4
Audio Activities TE, pages 7–11
Audio CD 2
Workbook, pages 7–9
Quiz 4, page 4
ExamView® Pro

Bellringer Review

Use BRR Transparency 1.4 or write the following on the board.
¿Sí o no?
1. El jugador de fútbol tiene que tirar el balón con las dos manos.
2. Hay ocho tiempos en un partido de fútbol.
3. Hay once jugadores en un equipo de fútbol.

2 PRESENTATION

STEP 1 Model the new words and phrases on pages 12 and 13 using Vocabulary Transparencies 1.3–1.4 and Audio CD 2.

STEP 2 Have students repeat each word or expression two or three times.

STEP 3 As you present the vocabulary with the overhead transparencies you may wish to ask the following questions:

¿Lleva un guante un jugador de béisbol?
¿Quién lanza la pelota, el pícher o el cátcher?
Si el bateador no batea la pelota, ¿quién devuelve la pelota?
¿De dónde batea el bateador?
Del platillo, ¿corre a la primera base o a la tercera base?
Cuando el bateador batea, ¿quién atrapa la pelota con frecuencia? ¿El receptor o el jardinero?

Palabras El béisbol

el campo de béisbol

la base

el bateador

el jugador de béisbol

el pícher, el lanzador

la pelota

El pícher lanza la pelota.

el cátcher, el receptor

El cátcher devuelve la pelota.

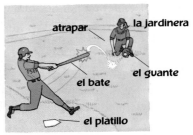

atrapar
la jardinera
el guante
el bate
el platillo

La jugadora atrapa la pelota.
Atrapa la pelota con el guante.

correr

El bateador batea.
Batea un jonrón.
El jugador corre de una base a otra.

En un juego de béisbol hay nueve entradas.
Si después de la novena entrada el tanto queda empatado, el partido continúa.

Total Physical Response

TPR1 You may wish to bring in some props (glove, bat, baseball, basketball, hoop) to use with these activities.
(Student 1), **ven acá. Tú vas a ser el pícher.**
Ponte el guante.
Toma la pelota.
(Student 2), **ven acá. Tú vas a ser el bateador.**
Toma el bate.
(Student 1), **tira la pelota a** *(Student 2).*
(Student 2), **batea la pelota.**
La pelota vuela. *(Student 2),* **corre.**
Corre a la primera base.
Gracias, *(Student 1)* **y** *(Student 2).* **Siéntense.**

El básquetbol, El baloncesto

pasar el balón

Son campeones.
Ganan un trofeo.

driblar con
el balón

la cancha de básquetbol

el balón

el cesto,
la canasta

meter el balón
en el cesto

encestar

tirar el balón

About the Spanish Language

- Most baseball vocabulary in Spanish is similar to the English because baseball is a sport that originated in the United States.
- **La pelota** refers to a small ball. **El balón** refers to a larger ball. A very small ball such as a golf ball is **la bola**.
- There is no definite rule as to when to use **el campo** vs. **la cancha**. In Spain, however, **el campo** is heard in many instances where **la cancha** would be preferred in Latin America.

FUN FACTS

El básquetbol After soccer, the sport that has reached the highest worldwide popularity is basketball. The professional basketball league in Spain is one of the best in Europe. Many American college players that are not able to play in the NBA (National Basketball Association) in the United States are able to obtain lucrative contracts in European leagues, especially in Italy and Spain. In South America and the Caribbean, the sport has reached its highest levels respectively in Brazil and in Puerto Rico.

Total Physical Response

TPR2 *(Student 1)* y *(Student 2)*, **vengan aquí. Vamos a jugar al básquetbol.**
(Student 1), **toma el balón. Dribla con el balón. Dribla cinco veces.**
Y ahora, pasa el balón a *(Student 2)*.

(Student 2), **dribla y corre con el balón.**
Tira el balón.
No, no encesta. Toma el balón de nuevo.
Dribla con el balón.
Tira el balón y encesta.
Gracias, *(Student 1)* y *(Student 2)*. **Siéntense.**

Universal Access

As you ask questions using the new vocabulary, direct your questions to the various ability levels in the class:
1) *easy*
   ¿Batea el bateador?
   ¿Batea un jonrón?
   ¿Corre?

2) *intermediate*
   ¿Quién batea?
   ¿Qué batea el bateador?
   ¿Corre de una base a otra?
3) *difficult*
   ¿Adónde corre el bateador?
   ¿Cuándo corre de una base a otra?

13

3 PRACTICE

¿Qué palabra necesito?

❶ Have students do Activity 1 with books open.

❷ and ❸ It is recommended that you go over the activities orally in class before assigning them for homework.

Writing Development

After going over Activity 3, have students write a short description of a basketball game.

Learning from Photos

(page 14) Here we see the ball court among the famous Mayan ruins in Copán, Honduras. Thousands of spectators attended the games, the object of which seems to have been to bounce the ball up the walls and hit one of the carved stone goals seen here. Players were not allowed to use hands, arms, or feet. The ball was very large and made of solid rubber.

The court seen here dates from 775 A.D.

¿Qué palabra necesito?

❶ **¿Qué deporte es?** Escojan. *(Choose.)*

1. El jugador lanza el balón con el pie.
2. Hay cinco jugadores en el equipo.
3. Hay nueve entradas en el partido.
4. El jugador corre de una base a otra.
5. El portero para o bloquea el balón.
6. El jugador tira el balón y encesta.

Una cancha de pelota. Copán. Honduras

❷ **Historieta El béisbol** Escojan. *(Choose.)*
1. Juegan (al) béisbol en _____ de béisbol.
   a. un campo   **b.** una pelota   **c.** una base
2. El pícher _____ la pelota.
   a. lanza   **b.** encesta   **c.** batea
3. El jardinero atrapa la pelota en _____.
   a. una portería   **b.** un cesto   **c.** un guante
4. El jugador _____ de una base a otra.
   a. tira   **b.** devuelve   **c.** corre
5. En un partido de béisbol hay _____ entradas.
   a. dos   **b.** nueve   **c.** once

❸ **Historieta El baloncesto** Contesten. *(Answer.)*

1. ¿Es el baloncesto un deporte de equipo o un deporte individual?
2. ¿Hay cinco o nueve jugadores en un equipo de baloncesto?
3. Durante un partido de baloncesto, ¿los jugadores driblan con el balón o lanzan el balón con el pie?
4. ¿El jugador tira el balón en el cesto o en la portería?
5. ¿El encestado (canasto) vale dos puntos o seis puntos?

ANSWERS TO ¿Qué palabra necesito?

❶
1. el fútbol
2. el básquetbol (el baloncesto)
3. el béisbol
4. el béisbol
5. el fútbol
6. el básquetbol (el baloncesto)

❷
1. a
2. a
3. c
4. c
5. b

❸
1. El baloncesto es un deporte de equipo.
2. Hay cinco jugadores en un equipo de baloncesto.
3. Durante un partido de baloncesto los jugadores driblan con el balón.
4. El jugador tira el balón en el cesto.
5. El encestado (canasto) vale dos puntos.

4 **Historieta** **Los campeones**

Contesten. *(Answer.)*

1. ¿Juegan muy bien los Leones?
2. ¿Tienen un equipo muy bueno?
3. ¿Ganan o pierden muchos partidos?

4. ¿Son campeones?
5. ¿Ganan un trofeo?
6. ¿Duermen los espectadores cuando miran un partido de los Leones?

Un partido entre Yugoslavia y España

5 **Juego** **¿Qué deporte es?** Work with a classmate. Give him or her some information about a sport. He or she has to guess what sport you're talking about. Take turns.

6 **Juego** **¡Adivina quién es!** Think of your favorite sports hero. Tell a classmate something about him or her. Your classmate will ask you three questions about your hero before guessing who it is. Then reverse roles and you guess who your classmate's hero is.

7 **Pobre Mario** Work with a partner. One of you can be Mario and the other, María. Mario is confused. He wants to do everything but he always makes mistakes. Mario will explain what he wants to do and María tells him why he cannot.

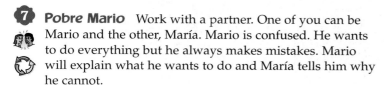

Quiero jugar baloncesto.

Quiero jugar béisbol.

Quiero jugar fútbol.

¡Ay, Mario!

Paso 2: Palabras

quince 15

4 After going over Activity 4, have one student retell the story in his or her own words.

5 **Juego** This is a good activity to use when students need a "break" during the class period, or as an opening or closing activity.

6 **EXPANSION** You may wish to have students bring in pictures of their favorite sports figures. Have other students say something about them. Ask the student who brought in the photo or picture why he or she is so fond of this player: **¿Por qué eres (es Ud.) muy aficionado(a) a ___?**

Class Motivator

¿Sí o no? Divide the class into two teams and play the following *true/false* game.

1. **Es necesario tener un cesto para jugar al voleibol.**
2. **Es necesario tener una red para jugar al voleibol.**
3. **El jugador de básquetbol puede correr con el balón en la mano.**
4. **El jugador de básquetbol tiene que driblar con el balón.**
5. **El balón de voleibol tiene que pasar por encima de la red.**
6. **El voleibol no puede tocar la red.**
7. **Los jugadores de básquetbol llevan guantes.**
8. **Los jugadores de béisbol corren de un canasto a otro.**

ANSWERS TO **¿Qué palabra necesito?**

4
1. Sí, los Leones juegan muy bien.
2. Sí, tienen un equipo muy bueno.
3. Ganan muchos partidos.
4. Sí, son campeones.
5. Sí, ganan un trofeo.
6. No, los espectadores no duermen cuando miran un partido de los Leones.

5 *Answers will vary, but students should use vocabulary presented in Paso 2.*

6 *Answers will vary, but students should use vocabulary presented in Paso 2.*

7 *Answers will vary but may include:*
—Quiero jugar (al) baloncesto.
—¡Ay, Mario! No puedes jugar (al) baloncesto con un balón de fútbol. Necesitas un balón de baloncesto y zapatos de tenis.

15

Formas

1 PREPARATION

RESOURCE MANAGER

Audio Activities TE, pages 12–13
Audio CD 2
Workbook, pages 10–13
Quiz 5, page 5
ExamView® Pro

Bellringer Review

Use BRR Transparency 1.5 or write the following on the board. Answer.

1. **¿Qué comes en el desayuno?**
2. **¿Qué comes en el almuerzo?**
3. **¿Qué comes cuando quieres tomar un refresco?**
4. **¿Qué comes cuando tienes mucha hambre?**

2 PRESENTATION

 Interesar, aburrir, gustar

¡OJO! English-speaking students often have a problem grasping the concept of **gustar.** Introducing **interesar** and **aburrir** in conjunction with **gustar** makes it much easier for students since we do have an exact parallel construction in English.

STEP 1 As you go over the explanation and **¿Cómo lo digo?** activities, have students point to themselves as they say **me** and have them look at a friend as they say **te.**

 **Formas**   **Los verbos interesar, aburrir, gustar**
Expressing what interests, bores, or pleases you

1. The verbs **interesar** and **aburrir** function the same in English and in Spanish. Study the following examples.

¿Te aburre el béisbol?	*Does baseball bore you?*
No, el béisbol me interesa.	*No, baseball interests me.*
¿Te aburren los deportes?	*Do sports bore you?*
No, los deportes me interesan.	*No, sports interest me.*

2. The verb **gustar** in Spanish works (functions) the same as **interesar** and **aburrir. Gustar** conveys the meaning *to like*, but its true meaning is *to please*. The Spanish way of saying *I like baseball* is *Baseball pleases me*.

   ¿Te aburre el béisbol? No, no. Me interesa.
   ¿Te gusta el béisbol? Sí, me gusta mucho el béisbol.
   ¿Te gustan los deportes en general? Sí, me gustan.

El *colegio San José, Estepona, España*

3. **Gustar** is often used with an infinitive to tell what you like to do.

   ¿Te gusta ganar? Sí. No me gusta perder.
   ¿Te gusta comer?

 **Nota**

Mí and ti are used after a preposition: **para mí** and **para ti.**
   A mí me gustan.
   ¿A ti también?
   A mí no me gustan.
   Ni a mí tampoco.

¿Cómo lo digo?

8 **¿Qué cursos te interesan y qué cursos te aburren?** Contesten. *(Answer.)*

1. ¿Te interesa la historia?
2. ¿Te interesa la geografía?
3. ¿Te interesa la biología?
4. ¿Te interesa la educación física?
5. ¿Te interesan las matemáticas?
6. ¿Te interesan las ciencias?

9 **¿Te interesan o te aburren?**
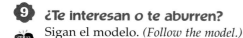
Sigan el modelo. *(Follow the model.)*

las ciencias →
Las ciencias me interesan. No me aburren.

1. las matemáticas
2. los estudios sociales
3. mis cursos
4. los deportes

10 **¿Te interesa o te aburre?**
Contesten. *(Answer.)*

1. ¿Te interesa o te aburre el béisbol?
2. ¿Te interesa o te aburre el arte?
3. ¿Te interesan o te aburren los partidos de fútbol?
4. ¿Te interesan o te aburren las emisiones deportivas?

11 **Los deportes** Contesten. *(Answer.)*

1. ¿Te gusta el fútbol?
2. ¿Te gusta el béisbol?
3. ¿Te gusta el voleibol?
4. ¿Te gusta más el béisbol o el fútbol?
5. ¿Te gusta más el voleibol o el básquetbol?
6. ¿Te gusta el golf?
7. ¿Te gusta el tenis?

¿Es una clase interesante?
Santiago de Chile

Paso 2: Formas

diecisiete ✦ 17

---

3 PRACTICE

¿Cómo lo digo?

8 Note that questions 1–4 have singular subjects and Items 5–6 have plural subjects. We have separated them to help students understand the concept.

9 Note that Activity 9 uses only plural subjects to reinforce this concept.

Learning from Photos

(page 17) These students are listening to a lecture on Chilean contemporary history in a class at a public high school in Santiago de Chile.

Universal Access

Give **students with learning difficulties** more practice contrasting singular and plural. You may ask questions such as:
   ¿Te gusta el deporte?
   ¿Te gustan los deportes?
   ¿Te gusta el curso?
   ¿Te gustan los cursos?
Or, just say **el curso** and students respond.
   ¿El curso? Sí, me gusta el curso.
Use the following.
   el curso/los cursos, el deporte/ los deportes, el cuadro/los cuadros, el bocadillo/los bocadillos, la fruta/las frutas

---

ANSWERS TO ¿Cómo lo digo?

8
1. Sí, (No, no) me interesa la historia.
2. Sí, (No, no) me interesa la geografía.
3. Sí, (No, no) me interesa la biología.
4. Sí, (No, no) me interesa la educación física.
5. Sí, (No, no) me interesan las matemáticas.
6. Sí, (No, no) me interesan las ciencias.

9
1. Las matemáticas me interesan. No me aburren.
2. Los estudios sociales me interesan. No me aburren.
3. Mis cursos me interesan. No me aburren.
4. Los deportes me interesan. No me aburren.

10
1. Me interesa (Me aburre) el béisbol.
2. Me interesa (Me aburre) el arte.
3. Me interesan (Me aburren) los partidos de fútbol.
4. Me interesan (Me aburren) las emisiones deportivas.

11
1. Sí, (No, no) me gusta el fútbol.
2. Sí, (No, no) me gusta el béisbol.
3. Sí, (No, no) me gusta el voleibol.
4. Me gusta más el béisbol (el fútbol).
5. Me gusta más el voleibol (el básquetbol).
6. Sí, (No, no) me gusta el golf.
7. Sí, (No, no) me gusta el tenis.

3 PRACTICE (continued)

13 After doing Activity 13, quickly review the colors students learned in Unit 4 of **¿Cómo te va? A, Nivel verde.**

¿Quieres un helado? Plasencia, España

12 **Los alimentos** Contesten. (Answer.)

1. ¿Te gusta la ensalada?
2. ¿Te gusta un sándwich de jamón y queso?
3. ¿Te gusta el pescado?
4. ¿Te gusta el helado?
5. ¿Te gusta la torta?
6. ¿Te gustan las frutas?
7. ¿Te gustan los tomates?
8. ¿Te gustan las hamburguesas?
9. ¿Te gustan los mariscos?

13 **¿Te gusta la ropa?**

 Sigan el modelo. (Follow the model.)

—¿Te gusta la gorra? →
—Sí, a mí me gusta.

1.

2.

3.

4.

5.

6.

18 ✵ dieciocho

Unidad 1: Los deportes

ANSWERS TO ¿Cómo lo digo?

12

1. Sí, (No, no) me gusta la ensalada.
2. Sí, (No, no) me gusta un sándwich de jamón y queso.
3. Sí, (No, no) me gusta el pescado.
4. Sí, (No, no) me gusta el helado.

5. Sí, (No, no) me gusta la torta.
6. Sí, (No, no) me gustan las frutas.
7. Sí, (No, no) me gustan los tomates.
8. Sí, (No, no) me gustan las hamburguesas.
9. Sí, (No, no) me gustan los mariscos.

13

1. ¿Te gusta la camisa?
   Sí, a mí me gusta.
2. ¿Te gusta la corbata?
   Sí, a mí me gusta.
3. ¿Te gusta el T-shirt (la camiseta)?
   Sí, a mí me gusta.

4. ¿Te gustan los calcetines?
   Sí, a mí me gustan.
5. ¿Te gusta el pantalón corto?
   Sí, a mí me gusta.
6. ¿Te gustan los zapatos?
   Sí, a mí me gustan.

¿Qué te gusta hacer?

 Contesten. *(Answer.)*

1. ¿Te gusta cantar?
2. ¿Te gusta bailar?
3. ¿Te gusta comer?
4. ¿Te gusta leer?
5. ¿Te gusta más hablar o escuchar?
6. ¿Te gusta más jugar o ser espectador(a)?

Gustos Work with a classmate. Tell one another some things you like and don't like. Let one another know when you agree. Following are some categories you may want to explore.

ropa   comida   deportes   cursos   actividades

Los niños juegan baloncesto. Quetzalan, México

 *For more practice using words and forms from **Paso 2,** do Activity 2 on page H3 at the end of this book.*

Paso 2: Formas

Andas bien. ¡Adelante!

---

14 Ask students to think of additional verbs of action they have learned. Write these on the board for all students to see.

15 After doing Activity 15, follow up by having each pair of students report to the class those things that interest them, those things that bore them, those things they like, and those they dislike.

UN POCO MÁS This *InfoGap* activity will allow students to practice in pairs. The activity should be very manageable for them, since all vocabulary and structures are familiar to them.

¡Adelante! At this point, students have learned all the vocabulary and structure necessary to complete the unit. The conversation, cultural readings, and activities in **Paso 3** and **Paso 4** recycle all the material learned up to this point.

ANSWERS TO **¿Cómo lo digo?**

14

1. Sí, (No, no) me gusta cantar.
2. Sí, (No, no) me gusta bailar.
3. Sí, (No, no) me gusta comer.
4. Sí, (No, no) me gusta leer.
5. Me gusta más hablar (escuchar).
6. Me gusta más jugar (ser espectador[a]).

15 *Answers will vary, but students should use* gustar, interesar, *and* aburrir *to describe clothing, food, sports, courses, and activities they like and don't like.*

Conversación

Conversación

1 PREPARATION

RESOURCE MANAGER

Audio Activities TE, pages 13–15
Audio CD 2
Workbook, page 13

Bellringer Review

Use BRR Transparency 1.6 or write the following on the board.
Write down two things that you like and two things that you don't like.

2 PRESENTATION

STEP 1 Have students open their books to page 20. Half the class will take the part of **Madela,** the other half will take the part of **Alicia.** Each half will read in unison.

STEP 2 Now call on one individual to be **Madela** and another to be **Alicia.** Have them read the conversation aloud.

STEP 3 You may wish to play Audio CD 2 for them.

STEP 4 Go over the **¿Comprendes?** activity.

STEP5 Call on students to present a similar conversation of their own.

Conversación
Un partido de fútbol

¿Comprendes?

Contesten *(Answer.)*

1. ¿Va a jugar fútbol Madela?
2. ¿Quiere jugar Alicia?
3. ¿Cuándo van a jugar?
4. ¿Puede jugar la amiga de Alicia?
5. Si juega Alicia, ¿cuántas jugadoras tienen?
6. ¿Cuándo puede jugar la amiga de Alicia?
7. Y, ¿quién juega hoy?

ANSWERS TO ¿Comprendes?

1. Sí, Madela va a jugar fútbol.
2. Sí, Alicia quiere jugar.
3. Van a jugar ahora.
4. No, la amiga de Alicia no puede jugar.
5. Si juega Alicia (ya) tienen once jugadoras.
6. La amiga de Alicia puede jugar mañana.
7. Madela y Alicia juegan hoy.

Universal Access

Have **advanced learners** retell the information in the conversation in narrative form in their own words. Call on **students with learning difficulties** to answer questions about the narrative.

Pronunciación

Las consonantes s, c, z

The consonant **s** is pronounced the same as the *s* in *sing*. Repeat the following.

sa	se	si	so	su
sala	base	sí	peso	su
pasa	serio	simpático	piso	Susana
saca	seis	siete	sopa	supermercado
mesa	mesero		sobrino	

The consonant **c** in combination with **e** or **i** (**ce, ci**) is pronounced the same as an *s* in all areas of Latin America. In many parts of Spain, **ce** and **ci** are pronounced like the *th* in English. Likewise, the pronunciation of **z** in combination with **a, o, u** (**za, zo, zu**) is the same as an *s* throughout Latin America and as a *th* in most areas of Spain. Repeat the following.

za	ce	ci	zo	zu
cabeza	cero	cinco	zona	zumo
empieza	encesta	ciudad	almuerzo	Zúñiga
lanza	cena		venezolano	Venezuela

Trabalenguas

Repeat the following.

González enseña en la sala de clase.
El sobrino de Susana es serio y sincero.
La ciudad de Zaragoza tiene cinco zonas.
Toma el almuerzo a las doce y diez en la cocina.

Refrán

Can you guess what the following proverb means?

Perro que ladra no muerde.

Pronunciación

STEP 1 Have students repeat the consonant sounds after you or the recording on Audio CD 2. Have them imitate very carefully.

STEP 2 Be sure students do not make an English *z* sound when pronouncing words with the letter **z**.

STEP 3 Have students open their books to page 21. Call on individuals to read the sentences.

STEP 4 The words and sentences presented here can also be used for dictation. It is important to bring these sounds and their spellings back frequently since they are very often misspelled.

Refrán

If students cannot guess what the proverb means, tell them, "His bark is worse than his bite."

Cultura y lectura

1 PREPARATION

RESOURCE MANAGER

Audio Activities TE, page 16
Audio CD 2
Workbook, page 14

National Standards

Cultures
In the reading on this page students learn about sports that are popular in the Spanish-speaking world. They will gain insight into the importance of these sports in Hispanic culture.

2 PRESENTATION

 If your students are not interested in sports, you can go over the **Lectura** quickly. If your class is rather sports-minded, you may wish to do the **Lectura** more thoroughly.

PRE-READING

Give students a brief oral synopsis of the reading in Spanish.

READING

STEP 1 Ask students to open their books to page 22. Call on individuals to read two or three sentences. After each student reads, ask the others follow-up questions. Continue in this manner through the entire reading.

STEP 2 Ask five or six questions that review the main points of the reading. The answers to these questions will give a coherent oral summary of the **Lectura.**

STEP 3 With advanced classes, have students write their own summary. This should take approximately seven minutes.

Cultura y lectura

Los deportes en el mundo hispano

Reading Strategy
Using titles and subtitles Look at titles and subtitles before you begin to read. They will usually help you know what the reading is about. Having an idea of what a reading is about will help you better understand as you read.

El Valencia contra el Manchester

El fútbol

El fútbol es un deporte muy popular en todos los países hispanos. Los equipos nacionales tienen millones de aficionados[1], pero el fútbol que juegan en los países hispanos no es el fútbol que jugamos nosotros. El fútbol americano no es muy popular. El fútbol que juegan es lo que llamamos «soccer». Los jugadores no pueden tocar el balón con las manos ni con los brazos. Tienen que usar la cabeza, el pie o las piernas.

Un jugador de béisbol, la República Dominicana

El béisbol

El béisbol es popular en algunos países hispanos, pero no en todos. El béisbol tiene muchos aficionados en Cuba, Puerto Rico, la República Dominicana, Venezuela, Nicaragua, México y Panamá.

Muchos jugadores de béisbol de las Grandes Ligas son latinos. Entre 1919 y hoy, más de cien jugadores latinos juegan en la Serie mundial[2].

El pueblo pequeño de San Pedro de Macorís en la República Dominicana produce más jugadores de las Grandes Ligas que cualquier otro[3] pueblo o ciudad del mundo.

[1] aficionados *fans*   [2] Serie mundial *World Series*   [3] cualquier otro *any other*

Learning from Photos

(page 23, left) Nancy López, the daughter of hardworking parents Domingo and Marina López, was born in Torrance, California. At age three she moved to Roswell, New Mexico. Nancy started to play golf when she was very young, and throughout her extraordinary career she became a true leader in advocating women's golf. López has devoted herself to many children's causes, especially to those dealing with children with special needs.

(page 23, right) Gabriela Sabatini was born on May 16, 1970 in Buenos Aires, Argentina. She became a professional tennis player at fourteen. During her career, she was ranked among the top ten female tennis players in the world until a few months before her retirement in 1996. She won three titles, including the U.S. Open in 1990.

El golf y el tenis

El golf y el tenis son otros deportes que gozan de[4] mucha popularidad en los países hispanos. ¿Puedes nombrar algunos jugadores latinos de golf o de tenis?

[4] gozan de *enjoy*

La golfista Nancy López

La tenista argentina Gabriela Sabatini

¿Comprendes?

A. Contesten. *(Answer.)*
1. ¿Cuál es un deporte popular en todos los países de habla española?
2. ¿Tienen muchos aficionados los equipos nacionales?
3. ¿Eres muy aficionado(a) al fútbol?
4. ¿Te gusta mucho el fútbol?
5. El fútbol que juegan en los países hispanos, ¿es como el fútbol americano o no?
6. ¿Qué no pueden usar los jugadores de fútbol cuando lanzan el balón?

B. Busquen. *(Find the following information.)*
1. países hispanos donde es muy popular el béisbol
2. desde 1919 el número de jugadores latinos de béisbol que juegan en la Serie mundial
3. un pueblo que produce muchos buenos jugadores de béisbol

C. Give a major difference between the football played in the United States and the football played in the Spanish-speaking countries.

POST-READING

STEP 1 Have students form three groups. Have each group write a brief news announcement for a different type of sporting event and present their announcement to the class.

STEP 2 Now have students do the **¿Comprendes?** activities on page 23.

¿Comprendes?

A. Activity A will help students prepare an oral or written summary of the **Lectura.**

C. Have students give the answer in Spanish.

Universal Access

Call on an **advanced learner** to give a summary of the **Lectura** in his or her own words. Call on **average students** or **students with learning difficulties** to answer questions about the oral summary just given. Then have a **student with learning difficulties** give an oral summary based on the summary of the **advanced learner.**

ANSWERS TO ¿Comprendes?

A.
1. El fútbol es un deporte popular en todos los países de habla española.
2. Sí, los equipos nacionales tienen millones de aficionados.
3. Sí, (No, no) soy muy aficionado(a) al fútbol.
4. Sí, (No, no) me gusta mucho el fútbol.
5. No, el fútbol que juegan en los países hispanos no es como el fútbol americano.
6. Los jugadores no pueden usar las manos ni los brazos cuando lanzan el balón.

B.
1. Cuba, Puerto Rico, la República Dominicana, Venezuela, Nicaragua, México y Panamá
2. San Pedro de Macorís
3. más de cien

C. *Answers will vary, but students should talk about differences such as using your hands for throwing and catching the ball in U.S. football compared to using your feet to pass the ball in fútbol (soccer).*

23

Repaso

Repaso

This section reviews the salient points from Unit 1. Students will review and practice stem-changing verbs and the verbs **interesar, aburrir,** and **gustar.**

1 PREPARATION

RESOURCE MANAGER

Audio Activities TE, pages 17–18
Audio CD 2
Workbook, page 15

2 PRESENTATION

STEP 1 Write the verbs in Item 1 on the board and have students read all forms aloud.

STEP 2 Have students give another **e → ie** stem-changing verb and another **o → ue** stem-changing verb and supply the endings.

STEP 3 Read Item 2 aloud with students.

STEP 4 Have students identify the subject of each sentence in Item 2. Point out to them that if the subject is plural, the verb is plural.

STEP 5 Have students do Activities 1 and 2 orally before assigning them for homework. Students may do Activity 2 in pairs.

Learning from Realia

(page 24) Ask students the following questions: **¿Cuándo juegan México y Honduras? ¿Dónde juegan México y Honduras? ¿Juegan al fútbol o al baloncesto? ¿Qué deporte juegan?**

---

1. In this unit, I learned stem-changing verbs **e ⟶ ie, o ⟶ ue.** Stem-changing verbs with **e** change to **ie** in all forms except **nosotros** (and **vosotros**); **o** changes to **ue.**

querer (e ⟶ ie)		poder (o ⟶ ue)	
quiero	queremos	puedo	podemos
quieres	*queréis*	puedes	*podéis*
quiere	quieren	puede	pueden

2. The verb **gustar** *(to like)* functions the same in Spanish as the verbs **interesar** and **aburrir.**

> Me interesan los deportes. ¿Te interesan a ti?
> No me aburren los deportes. ¿Te aburren a ti?
> Me gustan mucho los deportes. Y, ¿a ti te gustan?

Nota

Mi and **ti** are used following a preposition. **A mí me gustan los deportes. ¿Y a ti también?**

Un estadio de fútbol.
Barcelona, España

¡Pongo todo junto!

1 ¡A jugar! Completen. *(Complete.)*

1. Ellos _____ fútbol. (jugar)
2. Y nosotros _____ béisbol. (jugar)
3. ¿Qué _____ ustedes jugar? (preferir)
4. ¿Tú _____ jugar con nosotros? (poder)
5. Si yo _____, nuestro equipo gana. Nosotros no _____. (jugar, perder)
6. ¿A qué hora _____ el partido? (empezar)

2 Intereses y gustos
Sigan el modelo. *(Follow the model.)*

los deportes →

¿Te aburren los deportes?
Sí, me aburren.

¿Te interesan los deportes?
Sí, me interesan.

¿Te gustan mucho
los deportes? Sí, me
gustan mucho.

1. el béisbol y el básquetbol
2. el fútbol
3. la televisión
4. las emisiones deportivas
5. los cursos

FÁBRICA DE UNIFORMES DEPORTIVOS
La casa de las urgencias
27 años de experiencia nos respaldan
Pedidos al interior de la República
y en los Estados Unidos

Fabricante de balones de Futbol, Voli,
Basket, Pelotas de Beisball, Gorras,
Playeras y todo para el deporte.

UNIFORMES SUBLIMADOS DE EQUIPOS NACIONALES
Y EXTRANJEROS A PRECIOS MUY BAJOS. CONSÚLTANOS
SCHUMANN No. 165-2o PISO, COL, VALLEJO MÉXICO D.F. 07870
55-17-24-25 /57-59-21-71 / 55-17-53-29

3 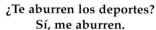 **yo practic o**

Work with a partner. Practice your
verbs using your manipulatives.

3 PRACTICE

¡Pongo todo junto!

2 After students have completed this activity in written form, have them review this activity with a classmate by asking each other the questions.

Learning from Realia
(page 25) Have students look at the ad and tell what this factory manufactures.

ANSWERS TO ¡Pongo todo junto!

1
1. juegan
2. jugamos
3. prefieren
4. puedes
5. juego, perdemos
6. empieza

2
1. ¿Te aburren el béisbol y el básquetbol? Sí, me aburren.
¿Te interesan el béisbol y el básquetbol? Sí, me interesan.
¿Te gustan mucho el béisbol y el básquetbol? Sí, me gustan mucho.
2. ¿Te aburre el fútbol? Sí, me aburre.
¿Te interesa el fútbol? Sí, me interesa.
¿Te gusta mucho el fútbol? Sí, me gusta mucho.

3. ¿Te aburre la televisión? Sí, me aburre.
¿Te interesa la televisión? Sí, me interesa.
¿Te gusta mucho la televisión? Sí, me gusta mucho.
4. ¿Te aburren las emisiones deportivas? Sí, me aburren.
¿Te interesan las emisiones deportivas? Sí, me interesan.
¿Te gustan mucho las emisiones deportivas? Sí, me gustan mucho.

5. ¿Te aburren los cursos? Sí, me aburren.
¿Te interesan los cursos? Sí, me interesan.
¿Te gustan mucho los cursos? Sí, me gustan mucho.

25

¡Te toca a ti!

Recycling

These activities allow students to use the vocabulary and structure from this unit in completely open-ended, real-life situations.

Encourage students to say as much as possible when they do these activities. Tell them not to be afraid to make mistakes, since the goal of the activities is real-life communication. If someone in the group makes an error, allow the others to politely correct him or her. Let students choose the activities they would like to do.

You may wish to divide students into pairs or groups. Encourage students to elaborate on the basic theme and to be creative. They may use props, pictures, or posters if they wish.

Learning from Photos

(page 26, top) This swimming pool is in the **Polideportivo,** a sports complex in the small town of Ojén, Spain. Even many small towns in Spain have a public swimming pool.

¡Te toca a ti!

Hablar

1 **Mi(s) deporte(s) favorito(s)**

✓ *Discuss a sport or sports you like*

Pick your favorite sport or sports. Get together with a classmate who likes the same sport or sports as you. Take turns describing the sport or sports you like best.

Hablar

2 **Intereses y gustos**

✓ *Discuss what does or does not interest you and what you like to do*

Work with a classmate. Share with one another things that interest you and that you like to do.

El polideportivo de Ojén, España

Hablar

3 **Un partido de fútbol**

✓ *Describe a soccer game*

You are at a soccer match with a friend (your classmate). He or she has never been to a soccer game before and doesn't understand the game. Your friend has a lot of questions. Answer the questions and explain the game. You may want to use some of the following words.

ganar   empezar   lanzar

marcar   jugar

meter   volver   perder

Mia Hamm, futbolista popular de Estados Unidos

ANSWERS TO ¡Te toca a ti!

1 *Answers will vary. Students should use* gustar, interesar, *and the sports-related vocabulary learned in this unit.*

2 *Answers will vary. Students should use* gustar *and* interesar *to talk about their interests.*

3 *Answers will vary. Students should use the words given and the soccer-related vocabulary learned in this unit.*

Una calle de Ceuta. África del Norte

4 El béisbol

 ✓ *Write about baseball*

You have a key pal from Ceuta in Africa. He or she e-mails you and tells you he or she doesn't know anything about baseball. E-mail him or her describing important things about a baseball game.

5 Un reportaje

✓ *Describe a sporting event*

You went to a sporting event at your school. Write an article about the event for the "Spanish Corner" in your school newspaper. You can write your report in the present tense.

Writing Strategy

Gathering information If your writing projects deal with a subject you are not familiar with, you may need to gather information before you begin to write. Some of your best sources are the library, the Internet, and people who know something about the topic. Even if you plan to interview people about the topic, it may be necessary to do some research in the library or on the Internet to acquire enough knowledge to prepare good interview questions.

6 La Copa mundial

Many of you already know that the World Cup is a soccer championship. Try to give a description of the World Cup as best you can in Spanish. If you are not familiar with it, you will need to do some research. It might be interesting to take what you know or find out about the World Cup and compare it to the World Series in baseball. Gather information about both these championships and write a report in Spanish.

Writing Development

Have students keep a notebook or portfolio containing their best written work from each unit. These selected writings can be based on assignments from the Student Textbook and the Writing Activities Workbook. The activities on page 27 are examples of writing assignments that may be included in each student's portfolio.

In the Workbook, students will develop an organized autobiography **(Mi autobiografía)**. These workbook pages may also become a part of their portfolio.

Learning from Photos

(page 27) This is a street scene in the **comunidad autónoma de Ceuta** in North Africa. Situated just across from Algeciras and **el peñón de Gibraltar,** Ceuta is an attractive city where many cultures, Christian, Islamic, and Jewish, converge.

Universal Access

Advanced learners can say quite a bit about each activity. **Students with learning difficulties** may give only two or three sentences, but both groups should feel good about their performance.

Paso 3: ¡Te toca a ti! veintisiete 27

ANSWERS TO ¡Te toca a ti!

4 *Answers will vary. Students should use the baseball-related vocabulary learned in this unit.*

5 *Answers will vary. Students should use the sports-related vocabulary learned in this unit. Encourage students to be as creative as possible.*

6 *Answers will vary but may include:*
The World Cup is a soccer tournament played every four years. After qualifying rounds are finished, thirty-two countries compete in this event to determine the world champion. It is a very popular tournament throughout the world. Baseball's World Series is the annual championship tournament of Major League Baseball. Despite the name, it is not a true world championship, since the league is comprised only of teams from the United States and Canada.

27

PASO 3

Assessment

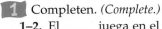

¿Estoy listo(a)?

RESOURCE MANAGER

Vocabulary Transparency 1.5
Tests, pages 1–14
ExamView® Pro, Unit 1
Performance Assessment,
   Tasks 1–2

 Assessment

This is a pretest for students to take before you administer the unit test. Note that each section is cross-referenced so students can easily find the material they have to review in case they made errors. You may use Assessment Answers Transparency A 1 to do the assessment in class, or you may assign this assessment for homework. You can correct the assessment yourself, or you may prefer to project the answers on the overhead in class.

Spanish Online

For additional practice, students may wish to do the online games and quizzes on the **Glencoe Spanish Web site** (spanish.glencoe.com). Quizzes are corrected instantly and results can be sent via e-mail to you.

Palabras

1 Completen. *(Complete.)*

To review words from **Paso 1,** *turn to pages 2–3.*

1–2. El _____ juega en el partido y el _____ mira el partido.

3–4. Dos partes del cuerpo humano son _____ y _____.

5. El portero _____ la portería.

6. Un equipo _____ y el otro pierde.

7–8. El jugador _____ un gol y marca un _____.

2 Identifiquen. *(Identify the player.)*

9.

To review words from **Paso 2,** *turn to pages 12–13.*

10–11.

3 Identifiquen. *(Identify the sport.)*

12. Corren de una base a otra.

13. Dribla con el balón.

14. Tira el balón y encesta.

15. Lanza el balón con el pie.

ANSWERS TO *Assessment*

1
1. jugador
2. espectador
3. *Answers will vary but may include:* la cabeza, la pierna, el brazo, la mano, la rodilla, el pie
4. *Answers will vary but may include:* la cabeza, la pierna, el brazo, la mano, la rodilla, el pie

5. guarda
6. gana
7. mete
8. tanto

2
9. el pícher
10. el bateador
11. la jardinera

3
12. el béisbol
13. el básquetbol (baloncesto)
14. el básquetbol (baloncesto)
15. el fútbol

28

Formas

4 Completen. *(Complete.)*
16. Los jugadores _____ al campo. (volver)
17. Nosotros _____ jugar. (querer)
18. Nuestro equipo no _____. (perder)
19. Tú _____ jugar si quieres. (poder)
20. Nosotros _____ bastante bien. (jugar)

To review stem-changing verbs, turn to pages 6 and 8.

5 Completen. *(Complete.)*
21. ¿Te gust__ los deportes? Sí, _____ gust__ mucho.
22. _____ gust__ el pescado pero a ti no _____ gust__.
23. El arte me interes__ pero los deportes me aburr__.

To review verbs like *interesar*, *aburrir*, and *gustar*, turn to page 16.

Cultura

6 Den la información. *(Give the following information.)*
24. el deporte número uno en los países hispanos
25. dos países donde hay muchos aficionados al béisbol

To review this cultural information, turn to pages 22–23.

El canal de Panamá

Learning from Photos

(page 29) Here we see a ship in the Gatún lock on the Panama Canal. The ships in the background are waiting to enter one phase of the lock to be lifted to the next level. The water seen in the foreground will flow out of the lock. The water will lower to the level of the ship. The ship will enter the lock aided by **mulas** (today *tractors*), the doors will close, and the lock will fill with water lifting the ship to the next level.

Paso 3: Assessment

ANSWERS TO *Assessment*

 4
16. vuelven
17. queremos
18. pierde
19. puedes
20. jugamos

 5
21. ¿Te gustan los deportes? Sí, me gustan mucho.
22. Me gusta el pescado pero a ti no te gusta.
23. El arte me interesa pero los deportes me aburren.

 6
24. el fútbol
25. *Answers should include any two of the following:* Cuba, Puerto Rico, la República Dominicana, Venezuela, Nicaragua, México, *and* Panamá.

Diversiones

Paso 4 of each **Unidad** includes a **Diversiones** section. As the title indicates, this section contains different types of activities that students in Middle School should enjoy. They also take into account the various learning modalities.

The many types of activities included are:

Canciones This section entitled **Canta con Justo** contains songs performed on the music CD by Justo Lamas, a young singer from Argentina who has written songs specifically for **¿Cómo te va?**

Teatro These activities provide students the opportunity to get up and perform. They give suggestions for short skits, pantomimes, and dramatizations. These activities are particularly helpful for **kinesthetic learners.**

Manos a la obra

These activities enable students to get involved and use their hands. Some examples are: drawing cards or pictures, preparing ads and brochures, and preparing schedules and announcements.

Rompecabezas
Some units contain riddles or puzzles that reinforce language in a fun way.

Diversiones

Canta con Justo
El gran campeón

Pa - ra triun - far hay que sa - ber. Pue - des ga - nar pue - des per - der. Si an - das

bien, o an - das, mal, muy bue - no es po - der lle - gar y con - ti - nuar ha - cia el fi - nal. La

vi - da es un par - ti - do, tú tie - nes que ga - nar. Si quie - res ser un gran cam - peón de - bes co -

rrer y no pa - rar. Tus ma - nos, pier - nas y tus pies, tie - nes que u - sar pa - ra ju -

gar. No es im - po - si - ble, fá - cil es Siem - pre ha - cia ade - lan - te por la Co - pa mun - dial.

Levanta un brazo y celebra el gol	Para triunfar, hay que saber	Levanta un brazo y celebra el gol
Canta muy fuerte con esta canción	Que puedes ganar, puedes perder	Canta muy fuerte con esta canción
Este trofeo es para el mejor	Si andas bien, o andas mal	Este trofeo es para el mejor
Y nuestro equipo es el gran campeón	Divino es poder llegar	Y nuestro equipo es el gran campeón
Sube tu brazo, luego bájalo	Y continuar hacia el final	Sube tu brazo, luego bájalo
Mueve tu cuerpo, vamos muévelo	La vida es un partido	Mueve tu cuerpo, vamos muévelo
Este trofeo es para el mejor	tú tienes que ganar	Este trofeo es para el mejor
Y nuestro equipo es el gran campeón		Y nuestro equipo es el gran campeón.

Investigaciones

This little research section allows those students who like to work on their own to get involved in some research projects that add another dimension to the cultural material of the unit.

Music Connection

Canta con Justo
The song **El gran campeón** will be easy for learners of all ability levels. It will help students practice the sports vocabulary introduced in **Unidad 1** of **¿Cómo te va? B, Nivel azul.** You can find this song on Track 1 of the music CD.

Teatro

Stand up and act out the following "plays."

lanzar el balón con el pie

bloquear el balón   lanzar el balón con la cabeza

correr   pasar el balón   batear

driblar con el balón

atrapar la pelota   tirar el balón

Teatro Encourage students to be as expressive as possible when performing these activities.

Juego

Play this version of **Simón dice.**

Levanta la mano.
Levanta la mano izquierda.
Levanta el brazo derecho.
Levanta la pierna derecha.
Levanta la rodilla izquierda.

Universal Access

You may wish to call on several **advanced learners** to take a turn as the leader in this game of **Simón dice.**

Manos a la obra

Encourage students to illustrate their posters and to make them visually appealing. You may wish to display them in the classroom or on a school bulletin board.

Investigaciones

You may wish to encourage students to research this topic via the Internet. This can be done at home or as an in-class activity if your school has a computer lab.

Spanish Online

Students will find links dealing with Hispanic athletes to help them with their research project should they choose to do one.

Learning from Photos

(page 32, top) Roberto Clemente is considered by some to be baseball's greatest right fielder ever. He was known for making spectacular catches and then throwing immediately to home plate to keep runners from scoring. He also won four batting titles and finished with 3,000 hits.

Clemente was born on August 18, 1934 in Carolina, Puerto Rico. He was a talented baseball player from an early age, and he played in the major leagues for the Pittsburgh Pirates. In 1966 he was the National League's Most Valuable Player. In 1960 and 1971, he helped lead his team to victory in the World Series, winning MVP honors in 1971.

Tragically, Clemente was killed in a plane crash while trying to deliver relief supplies to earthquake victims in Nicaragua. He was the first Latino to be inducted into baseball's Hall of Fame.

Manos a la obra

Carteles Make a poster indicating in Spanish all the sporting events that will take place in your school next month.

 Los deportes Work with a classmate. Take turns saying something about a sport. Your classmate will tell what sport you're talking about.

El beisbolista y héroe puertorriqueño Roberto Clemente

Investigaciones

Look up some information about any one of the following famous Hispanic athletes. You may choose from the list below or write about any others you know.

Béisbol
José Canseco
Bobby Bonilla
Fernando Valenzuela

Fútbol
Claudio Reyna
Carlos Llamosa
Jaime Moreno

Tenis
Mary Joe Fernández
Gigi Fernández
Gabriela Sabatini

Golf
"Chi Chi" Rodríguez
Nancy López
Lee Trevino

Spanish Online

For more information about sports in the Spanish-speaking world, go to the Glencoe Spanish Web site: spanish.glencoe.com.

La tenista Gigi Fernández

32 treinta y dos

Unidad 1: Los deportes

(page 32, bottom) Gigi Fernández was born in San Juan, Puerto Rico in 1964. Her father was a very prominent physician in San Juan. She was the first female professional athlete from Puerto Rico, and she became one of the greatest female tennis doubles players ever. Her career lasted from 1983 to 1997, and in that time she won twenty-one Grand Slam doubles titles, including six in a row, and two Olympic gold medals. She was often ranked first in the world.

After retiring, she took up golf and almost joined the LPGA tour before becoming a tennis coach. She began coaching the Puerto Rican National Team in 1999. Fernández enrolled at the University of South Florida for her bachelor's degree in 2001 and took a job coaching the school's tennis team in 2002.

32

Entrevista

¿Te gustan los deportes?
¿Cuál es tu deporte favorito?
¿Juegas con un equipo de tu escuela?
¿Con qué equipo juegas?
¿Prefieres jugar o ser espectador(a)?
¿Tiene tu escuela un equipo muy bueno?
¿En qué deporte?
¿Cuántos partidos gana el equipo?
Y, ¿cuántos pierde?

PLEGABLES™
Study Organizer

Mi autobiografía Use this *minibook* organizer to write and illustrate your autobiography. Before you begin to write, think about the many things concerning yourself that you have the ability to write about in Spanish. On the left pages, draw the events of your life in chronological order. On the right, write about your drawings.

Step 1 **Fold** a sheet of paper (8½" x 11") in half like a *hot dog*.

Step 2 **Fold** it in half again like a *hamburger*.

Step 3 Then **fold** in half again, forming eights.

Step 4 **Open** the fold and cut the eight sections apart.

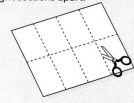

Step 5 **Place** all eight sections in a stack and fold in half like a hamburger.

Step 6 **Staple** along the center fold line. Glue the front and back sheets into a construction paper cover.

Entrevista

The **Entrevista** activity reinforces students' ability to interact with peers in Spanish in a real-life situation. This task recombines material the student has already learned. Students of all ability levels will be able to perform this task.

PLEGABLES™
Study Organizer

This foldable will help students organize, display, and arrange data as they learn about new topics in Spanish. You may wish to encourage them to add information from each unit as they continue to learn how to discuss many different aspects of their lives in Spanish.

Encourage students to keep this *minibook* foldable in a safe place so they can refer to it and add content as they acquire more knowledge.

Más cultura y lectura

¡OJO! The readings on pages 34–35 are optional. You may skip them completely, have the entire class read them, have only several students read them and report to the class, or assign them for extra credit.

PRESENTATION

STEP 1 Have students read the passage quickly as they look at the photos that accompany it. Have students discuss whatever information they find interesting.

STEP 2 Have students do the **¿Comprendes?** activities that follow the reading.

La Copa mundial The World Cup matches were played in the United States for the first time in 1994. The first World Cup matches were held in Uruguay in 1930. The Uruguayan national team won. Uruguay and Argentina have each won twice. Three-time winners are Italy and Germany. Brazil has won the cup four times. The World Cup competition takes place every four years.

La Copa mundial

Fernando Hierro y Roberto Carlos da Silva son dos jugadores de fútbol muy buenos. Los dos juegan con el mismo equipo profesional, el Real Madrid. Es un equipo español muy popular e Hierro y da Silva tienen muchos aficionados.

Los dos van a jugar en la Copa mundial[1]. Pero no van a jugar con el mismo equipo. Cada uno va a jugar con un equipo diferente. ¿Cómo es posible? Pues, da Silva juega con el equipo español, el Real Madrid. Pero él no es español. Es del Brasil y en la Copa mundial él tiene que jugar con el equipo de su país. Él va a jugar con el equipo brasileño. Hierro es español y él va a jugar con el equipo de España. Así, los dos compañeros tienen que jugar en equipos contrarios.

▲ El equipo nacional de España

Cada cuatro años las estrellas[2] de cada país forman parte de su equipo nacional. Hay treinta y dos equipos nacionales que juegan en la Copa mundial.

[1] Copa mundial *World Cup*
[2] estrellas *stars*

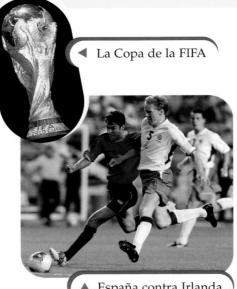

◀ La Copa de la FIFA

▲ España contra Irlanda

¿Comprendes?

Busquen *(Find the following information.)*
1. con qué equipo juegan Hierro y da Silva
2. la nacionalidad de da Silva
3. la nacionalidad de Hierro
4. con qué equipo tiene que jugar da Silva en la Copa mundial
5. con qué equipo juega Hierro en la Copa mundial
6. el número de equipos nacionales que participan en la Copa mundial

Unidad 1: Los deportes

Learning from Photos

(page 34) You may wish to have students say as much as they can about the photos on this page.

ANSWERS TO ¿Comprendes?

1. el Real Madrid
2. brasileño
3. español
4. el equipo de Brasil
5. el equipo de España
6. treinta y dos

Personajes latinos famosos

◄ Sammy Sosa es un jardinero derecho con los Chicago Cubs. En tres temporadas consecutivas Sosa golpea más de cincuenta jonrones.

¿De dónde es Sammy Sosa? Es de San Pedro de Macorís en la República Dominicana. Es el pueblo que produce más jugadores de las Grandes Ligas que cualquier otro pueblo o ciudad.

Sosa es un jugador popular y es también una persona muy buena. En 1998, él funda la Fundación Sammy Sosa para ayudar[1] a niños necesitados[2] en Chicago y en la República Dominicana. En 1999 la Fundación establece el Centro Médico Sammy Sosa para niños en su pueblo natal, San Pedro de Macorís.

[1] ayudar *to help* [2] necesitados *needy*

▶ El joven español Sergio García es un jugador de golf muy famoso. Es de Castellón en España. Tiene el apodo[3] «el Niño» porque empieza a jugar cuando es muy joven. Su objetivo es de «ser el mejor[4] del mundo». Como en el caso de Tiger Woods, el padre de Sergio es un entrenador[5].

[3] apodo *nickname*
[4] mejor *best*
[5] entrenador *trainer, coach*

¿Comprendes?

Tell all you knew about Sammy Sosa or Sergio García before you read about them. Then tell what you learned from the reading.

Paso 4: Más cultura y lectura

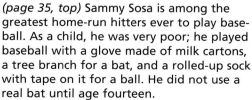

Personajes latinos famosos

❀ National Standards

Cultures
Students become familiar with the backgrounds of Sammy Sosa and Sergio García, two famous sports stars from Spanish-speaking countries.

PRESENTATION

STEP 1 Have students read the passage quickly as they look at the photos that accompany it. Have students discuss whatever information they find interesting.

Learning from Photos

(page 35, bottom) Sergio García was born in Castellón, Spain on January 9, 1980. Sergio began to play golf at age three, soon competing for a coke or some ice cream. By the time he was twelve, he was the champion of his club. In 1999 he turned professional and ended that year ranked twelfth in the world and third on the European Tour. He was the captain of Spain's Dunhill Cup team and led them to their first victory ever. In 2002, he finished first in the Mercedes Championship. He is known to be very energetic. As a young star, he has often been in the limelight for both success and failure. He plays on both the European and U.S. Tours, and says he loves Spanish food and the lifestyle in Spain as well as many parts of American pop culture.

(page 35, top) Sammy Sosa is among the greatest home-run hitters ever to play baseball. As a child, he was very poor; he played baseball with a glove made of milk cartons, a tree branch for a bat, and a rolled-up sock with tape on it for a ball. He did not use a real bat until age fourteen.

In 1993, his first full season with the Cubs, he became an All-Star. During the 1998 season, he and Mark McGuire both broke the record for home runs in a single season in an historic competition—McGuire finishing with 70 and Sosa with 66 home runs. That year, Sosa was the MVP in the National League. Sosa is also the only player ever to hit more than 60 home runs in multiple seasons. Sosa wears number 21 in honor of his hero, another great Latino baseball player, Roberto Clemente.

When a hurricane hit the Dominican Republic in 1998, Sosa donated food and raised over $700,000 for the victims.

Conexiones

PASO 4

Conexiones
Las ciencias

 ¡OJO! The readings in the **Conexiones** section are optional. They focus on some of the major disciplines taught in schools and universities. The vocabulary is useful for discussing such topics as history, literature, art, economics, business, science, etc. You may choose any of the following ways to do the readings in the **Conexiones** sections.

Independent reading Have students read the selections and do the post-reading activities as homework, which you collect. This option is least intrusive on class time and requires a minimum of teacher involvement.

Homework with in-class follow-up Assign the readings and post-reading activities as homework. Review and discuss the material in class the next day.

Intensive in-class activity This option includes a pre-reading vocabulary presentation, in-class reading and discussion, assignment of the activities for homework, and a discussion of the assignment in class the following day.

La anatomía

Staying in good physical shape is important for all athletes. To do so, they have to know how to care for their bodies. They also have to know something about their bones and muscles to avoid injuries. All athletes should have some basic knowledge of anatomy. Anatomy is the branch of science that studies the structure of humans and animals.

Before reading this selection on anatomy, study the diagrams of the human body.

El esqueleto

El esqueleto humano tiene doscientos seis huesos. Hay treinta y dos huesos en cada brazo y treinta y uno en cada pierna. El cuerpo cuenta con más de seiscientos músculos. Algunos músculos están conectados a un hueso. Pueden estar conectados directamente a un hueso o por medio de un tendón.

Además de[1] los músculos esqueléticos, hay muchos músculos internos. El corazón es un ejemplo.

[1] Además de *Besides*

un hueso

un músculo

un tendón

el pecho

el cuerpo humano

el esqueleto

Unidad 1: Los deportes

El corazón

El corazón es un órgano muscular. Es el órgano principal de la circulación de la sangre[2]. Está situado más o menos en el centro del pecho.

Los pulmones

Los dos pulmones están situados a cada lado[3] del corazón. El pulmón es el órgano principal del aparato respiratorio. El aire llega a cada pulmón por un bronquio. La sangre llega por la artería pulmonar. La sangre, cuando llega, está cargada de dióxido de carbono. Cuando sale[4] de las venas pulmonares la sangre está purificada.

No hay duda[5] que el cuerpo humano es una máquina[6] extraordinaria.

el corazón

los pulmones

[2] sangre *blood*
[3] a cada lado *on each side*
[4] sale *it leaves*
[5] duda *doubt*
[6] máquina *machine*

¿Comprendes?

A. Busquen. *(Find all the cognates in the reading.)*

B. Busquen. *(Find the following information.)*
1. el número de huesos en cada brazo
2. el número de huesos en cada pierna
3. lo que puede conectar un músculo a un hueso
4. un músculo interno, un órgano vital
5. el órgano principal del aparato respiratorio

NOTE: It is suggested that you have students who are interested in science, particularly biology, read this selection.

STEP 1 Have students read the introduction in English on page 36.

STEP 2 Have students look at the callout words in the illustrations to familiarize themselves with the new vocabulary they will encounter in the reading.

STEP 3 As students read about these parts of the body, have them study the illustrations on pages 36–37.

STEP 4 Have students read the selection quickly or have them skim it.

Universal Access

You may wish to have students draw and label an illustration of the body. This activity is particularly beneficial for **visual** and **kinesthetic learners**.

ANSWERS TO ¿Comprendes?

A. *Answers should include:* esqueleto, humano, músculos, conectados, directamente, tendón, esqueléticos, internos, ejemplo, órgano, muscular, principal, circulación, situado, centro, aparato, respiratorio, aire, bronquio, artería, pulmonar, dióxido de carbono, venas, purificada, extraordinaria

B.
1. treinta y dos
2. treinta y uno
3. un tendón
4. el corazón
5. el pulmón

¡Hablo como un pro!

This unique section gives students the opportunity to speak freely and say whatever they want on their own. The illustrations serve to remind students of precisely what they know how to say in Spanish. There are no depictions of activities that students do not have the ability to describe or talk about in Spanish. The art in this section recombines all that the students learned in the particular unit and in addition frequently recombines the topic or situation of the unit with that of another unit for additional reinforcement.

You can use this section in many ways. Some possibilities are:
1. Have students look at the illustrations and just identify items by giving the correct Spanish words.
2. Have students make up sentences about what they see in the illustrations.
3. Have students make up questions about the illustrations. They can call on another class member to respond if you do this as an entire class activity, or you may prefer to allow students to work in small groups. This activity is extremely beneficial because it enables students to actively use the interrogative words.
4. You may wish to ask questions and call on students to answer.
5. Have students look at the illustrations and give a complete oral review of what they see.
6. Have two students work together and make up a conversation based on the illustrations.
7. Have students look at the illustrations and write a paragraph (or paragraphs) about them in class.

You can also use this section as an assessment or testing tool, taking into account individual differences by having students go from simple to quite complicated tasks.

38

¡Hablo como un pro! Tell all you can about the following illustration.

38 ✹ treinta y ocho   Unidad 1: Los deportes

The assessment can be either oral or written. You may wish to use the rubrics provided on pages T22–T23 as you give students the following directions.
1. Identify the topic or situation of these illustrations.
2. Identify as many items as you can and give the Spanish words. Don't forget to include actions you see.
3. Give as many sentences as you can to describe the illustrations.
4. Go over your sentences and put them in the best sequence possible.
5. Polish your sentences and sequencing to give a coherent story based on the illustrations.

Universal Access

When talking about the illustration, **students with learning difficulties** may just give random sentences. **Advanced students** will give a coherent story. You may wish to have **advanced students** write a paragraph about the illustration.

Vocabulario

Identifying sports
el deporte   el fútbol   el béisbol   el básquetbol, el baloncesto

---

Describing a sporting event in general
el estadio	el equipo	jugar	lanzar
el/la espectador(a)	el tablero indicador	empezar	correr
el campo	el tanto	continuar	guardar
la cancha	empatado	indicar	perder
el partido	el/la campeón(ona)	entrar	ganar
el/la jugador(a)	un trofeo	tirar	contra

Describing a football (soccer) game
el fútbol	el/la portero(a)	parar	usar
el balón	la portería	tocar	marcar un tanto
el tiempo	bloquear	poder	meter un gol

Describing a baseball game
el béisbol	el/la cátcher,	la base	el bate
el/la bateador(a)	el/la receptor(a)	un jonrón	el guante
el/la pícher,	el/la jardinero(a)	la entrada	batear
el/la lanzador(a)	el platillo	la pelota	atrapar
			devolver

Describing a basketball game
el básquetbol,	driblar
el baloncesto	pasar
el cesto, la canasta	encestar
el balón	meter

Identifying some parts of the body
el pie	la mano
la pierna	el brazo
la rodilla	la cabeza

Expressing likes and dislikes
gustar
interesar
aburrir

Other useful expressions
derecho(a)	volver
izquierdo(a)	quedar
durante	dormir

Vocabulario

Vocabulary Review
The words and phrases in the **Vocabulario** have been taught for productive use in this unit. They are summarized here as a resource for both student and teacher. This list also serves as a convenient resource for the **¡Te toca a ti!** activities on pages 26–27. There are approximately twenty-two cognates in this vocabulary list. Have students find them.

¡OJO! You will notice that the vocabulary list here is not translated. This has been done intentionally, since we feel that by the time students have finished the material in the unit they should be familiar with the meanings of all the words. If there are several words they still do not know, we recommend that they refer to the **Paso 1 Palabras** and **Paso 2 Palabras** sections in the unit or go to the dictionaries at the end of this book to find the meanings. However, if you prefer that your students have the English translations, please refer to Vocabulary Transparency 1.6, where you will find all these words with their translations.

Los estadios de fútbol The largest sports stadiums in the world are soccer stadiums in Hispanic countries, with capacities in excess of 100,000 spectators. Among the largest stadiums are **el Estadio Azteca** in Mexico City (see page 24) and **el Estadio del Boca Juniors,** nicknamed **la Bombonera** *(The Candy Store),* in Buenos Aires.

Universal Access

Tarjetas de colección Many students collect baseball and football cards. You may have them bring some to class and talk about their favorite teams and players. This will be especially useful for **visual learners.**

Afiches Have groups of students make posters for a sports day at your school. They should include the date, event(s), team names, times, etc. **Kinesthetic learners** will benefit most from this activity.

Biografías Have **advanced learners** choose their favorite athlete. Have them prepare a short biography of him or her.

Planning for Unit 2

CORRELATIONS

National Standards

Communication Standard 1.1
pages 44, 45, 47, 49, 50, 51, 54, 55, 56, 57, 58, 59, 60, 66, 71, 73

Communication Standard 1.2
pages 45, 46, 48, 49, 55, 62–63, 66, 74, 75

Communication Standard 1.3
pages 44, 45, 47, 51, 55, 59, 66, 67, 71, 72, 73

Cultures Standard 2.1
pages 49, 62–63

Cultures Standard 2.2
pages 70, 74

Connections Standard 3.1
page 75

Connections Standard 3.2
page 74

Comparisons Standard 4.1
pages 46, 48, 53, 61

Comparisons Standard 4.2
page 74

Communities Standard 5.1
page 67

PACING AND PRIORITIES

The unit content is color coded below to assist you in planning.

■ required ■ recommended ▨ optional

Paso 1 (required) *Days 1–8*
- ■ Palabras
  - ¿Cómo está?
- ■ Formas
  - **Ser** y **estar**—característica y condición
  - **Ser** y **estar**—origen y colocación

Paso 2 (required) *Days 9–16*
- ■ Palabras
  - En la consulta del médico
- ■ Formas
  - Los pronombres **me, te, nos**
  - Los pronombres **le, les**
- ■ Conversación
  - Un muchacho enfermo

Paso 3 (recommended) *Days 17–24*
- ■ Pronunciación
  - La consonante **c**
- ■ Cultura y lectura
  - ¿Qué le pasa a Adela?
- ■ Repaso
- ■ ¡Te toca a ti!
- ■ Assessment

Paso 4 (optional)
- ▨ Diversiones
- ▨ Más cultura y lectura
  - Una clínica
- ▨ Conexiones
  - La nutrición

SECTION		PAGES	SECTION RESOURCES

PASO 1

Palabras	¿Cómo está?	42–45	📖 Vocabulary Transparencies 2.1–2.2 💿 Audio CD 2 🎧 Audio Activities TE, pages 21–23 📘 Workbook TE, pages 19–20 📘 Quiz 1, page 9 💿 ExamView® Pro
Formas	**Ser** y **estar**— característica y condición **Ser** y **estar**— origen y colocación	46–47 48–51	💿 Audio CD 2 🎧 Audio Activities TE, pages 24–27 📘 Workbook TE, pages 21–24 📘 Quizzes 2–3, pages 10–11 💿 ExamView® Pro

PASO 2

Palabras	En la consulta del médico	52–55	📖 Vocabulary Transparencies 2.3–2.4 💿 Audio CD 2 🎧 Audio Activities TE, pages 28–29 📘 Workbook TE, pages 25–27 📘 Quiz 4, page 12 💿 ExamView® Pro
Formas	Los pronombres **me, te, nos** Los pronombres **le, les**	56–57 58–59	💿 Audio CD 2 🎧 Audio Activities TE, pages 29–30 📘 Workbook TE, pages 27–28 📘 Quiz 5, page 13 💿 ExamView® Pro

PASO 3

Conversación	Un muchacho enfermo	60	💿 Audio CD 2 🎧 Audio Activities TE, pages 31–32 📘 Workbook TE, page 29
Pronunciación	La consonante **c**	61	📖 Pronunciation Transparency P 2 💿 Audio CD 2 🎧 Audio Activities TE, page 33
Cultura y lectura	¿Qué le pasa a Adela?	62–63	💿 Audio CD 2 🎧 Audio Activities TE, page 34 📘 Workbook TE, page 30
Repaso		64–65	💿 Audio CD 2 🎧 Audio Activities TE, page 35 📘 Workbook TE, page 31 📘 Tests, pages 15–28
¡Te toca a ti!		66–67	💿 Audio CD 2 🎧 Audio Activities TE, page 36 📘 Workbook TE, pages 32–33
Assessment		68–69	📖 Vocabulary Transparency 2.5 📘 Tests, pages 15–28 💿 ExamView® Pro, Unit 2 📘 Performance Assessment, Tasks 3–4

PASO 4

Diversiones		70–73	📘 Workbook TE, page 34
Más cultura y lectura	Una clínica	74	📘 Tests, page 21
Conexiones	La nutrición	75	📘 Tests, page 21

Using Your Resources for Unit 2

Transparencies

Bellringer 2.1–2.8

Vocabulary V 2.1–2.6

Assessment A 2

Songs S 2

Workbook

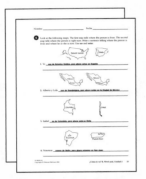

Paso 1 Vocabulary and Structure pages 19–24

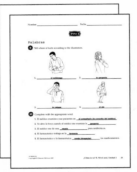

Paso 2 Vocabulary and Structure pages 25–28

Conversation and Reading pages 29–30

Repaso, ¡Te toca a ti!, Diversiones pages 31–34

Audio Program and Audio Activities Booklet

Paso 1 Vocabulary and Structure pages 21–27

Paso 2 Vocabulary and Structure pages 28–30

Conversation, Pronunciation pages 31–34

Repaso, ¡Te toca a ti! pages 35–36

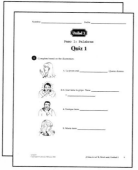

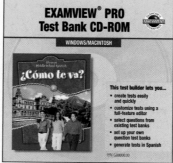

Vocabulary and Structure Quizzes, pages 9–14

Unit Tests, pages 15–28

ExamView® Pro, Unit 2

Timesaving Teacher Tools

TeacherWorks
All in One Teacher Planning

TeacherWorks™ is your all in one teacher resource center. Personalize lesson plans, access resources from the Teacher Wraparound Edition, connect to the Internet, or make a to-do list. These are only a few of the many features that can assist you in the planning and organizing of your lessons.

Includes:
- A calendar feature
- Access to all program blackline masters
- Standards correlations and more

Test Bank software for Macintosh and Windows makes creating, editing, customizing, and printing tests quick and easy.

PLEGABLES™
Study Organizer

Manipulatives The foldable activities give students of all learning styles the opportunity to excel in a nontraditional manner. Your students will love these hands-on activities!

Technology Resources

Spanish Online

In the Unit 2 online resources, you and your students will have a chance to learn more about medical services in the Spanish-speaking world.

PuzzleMaker allows you to create crossword puzzles, jumble puzzles, and word searches in minutes or edit a database of key terms and puzzles to review unit vocabulary. You can choose English-Spanish puzzles or Spanish-English puzzles. The puzzles can be printed or played on the computer screen.

Canta con Justo This CD contains songs sung by a young Argentine singer, Justo Lamas, which are specifically geared to review and expand upon the vocabulary learned in each unit. Students will enjoy listening to these songs while they learn from them.

¡En vivo! This music video of Justo Lamas performing his songs live in concert gives your students a chance to experience the songs in a different way while reinforcing the language skills they are learning!

Preview

In this unit, students will learn to talk about routine illnesses and describe their symptoms to a doctor. They will use vocabulary associated with medical exams, prescriptions, and minor illnesses such as colds, flu, and headaches. Students will express characteristics and origin using the verb **ser** and conditions and location using the verb **estar**. They will talk about themselves and others using the pronouns **le** and **les** and reviewing **me, te,** and **nos.**

The cultural focus of the chapter is on medical services in Spanish-speaking countries.

🌸 National Standards

Communication

In Unit 2, students will communicate in spoken and written Spanish on the following topics:
• describing symptoms of minor ailments
• getting a prescription at a pharmacy
• expressing emotions and conditions

Students will obtain and provide information and engage in conversations dealing with health and health services as they fulfill the objectives listed on this page.

Spanish Online

The **Glencoe World Languages Web site** (spanish. glencoe.com) offers options that enable you and your students to experience the Spanish-speaking world via the Internet. For each **Unidad,** there are activities, games, and quizzes. In addition, an *Enrichment* section offers students an opportunity to visit Web sites related to the theme of the unit.

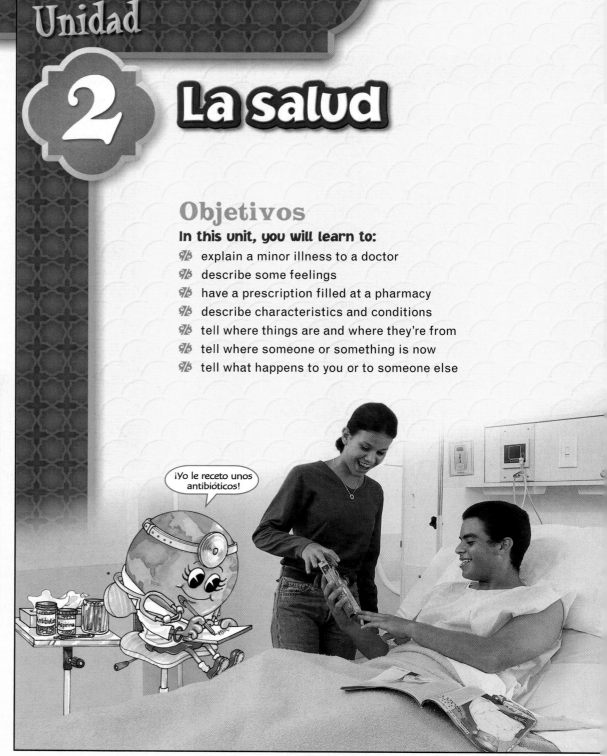

Unidad

2 La salud

Objetivos

In this unit, you will learn to:

- ⁹⁄ₒ explain a minor illness to a doctor
- ⁹⁄ₒ describe some feelings
- ⁹⁄ₒ have a prescription filled at a pharmacy
- ⁹⁄ₒ describe characteristics and conditions
- ⁹⁄ₒ tell where things are and where they're from
- ⁹⁄ₒ tell where someone or something is now
- ⁹⁄ₒ tell what happens to you or to someone else

¡Yo le receto unos antibióticos!

FARMACIA

Spotlight on Culture

Caracas, Venezuela
(page 40) This photo shows a young girl visiting a friend at a hospital in Caracas, Venezuela.

Zafra, Spain
(page 41) This old-style pharmacy is in Zafra, Spain. Zafra is a relatively small town in Extremadura not too far from Mérida.

Learning from Photos

(page 40) Ask the following questions after presenting the new vocabulary on pages 42–43.

¿Quién está en el hospital, Irene o Carlos?
¿A quién visita Irene?
¿Qué opinas? ¿Está muy enfermo Carlos?
¿Tiene Carlos una revista?
¿Lee la revista?
¿Por qué no lee la revista?
¿Qué mira?
¿Es un videocasete?

Palabras

1 PREPARATION

RESOURCE MANAGER

Vocabulary Transparencies 2.1–2.2
Audio Activities TE, pages 21–23
Audio CD 2
Workbook, pages 19–20
Quiz 1, page 9
ExamView® Pro

Bellringer Review

Use BRR Transparency 2.1 or write the following on the board. Answer.

1. **¿Cuántos años tienes?**
2. **¿Tienes una familia grande o pequeña?**
3. **¿Cuántos hermanos tienes?**
4. **¿Tienen Uds. un perro o un gato?**

2 PRESENTATION

STEP 1 Have students close their books. Present the vocabulary using Vocabulary Transparencies 2.1–2.2.

STEP 2 Point to yourself as you teach the words **la garganta, la cabeza, el estómago.**

STEP 3 You can easily use gestures to teach the following words and expressions: **enfermo, cansado, contento, triste, nervioso, toser, estornudar, tener escalofríos, tener dolor de garganta, tener dolor de cabeza, tener dolor de estómago.**

STEP 4 Have students repeat the words and sentences on pages 42–43 after you or Audio CD 2. Then have them open their books and read the new vocabulary aloud.

Palabras   ¿Cómo está?

enfermo

cansada

contento

nervioso

triste

la cama   la fiebre

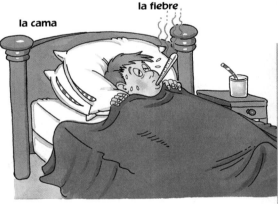

El pobre muchacho está enfermo.
Está en cama.
¿Qué tiene?
Pues, tiene escalofríos y fiebre.
Creo que tiene la gripe.
Tiene que guardar cama.

estornudar

un pañuelo

un kleenex

La muchacha tiene catarro.
Está resfriada.
Estornuda mucho.
Necesita un pañuelo.

Unidad 2: La salud

Total Physical Response

(Student 1), **ven acá, por favor. Imagínate que estás enfermo(a).**
Indícame que estás cansado(a).
Indícame que tienes fiebre.
Indícame que tienes escalofríos.
Indícame que tienes dolor de garganta.
Indícame que tienes dolor de cabeza.

Indícame que tienes dolor de estómago.
Indícame que tienes tos.
Indícame que estás estornudando mucho.
Gracias, *(Student 1).* **Y ahora puedes regresar a tu asiento.**

toser

Enrique tose.
Tiene tos.
Tiene dolor de garganta.

José tiene dolor de estómago.

Charo tiene dolor de cabeza.

José Luis está de mal humor.
No está de buen humor.

Paso 1: Palabras

3 PRACTICE

¿Qué palabra necesito?

¡OJO! When students are doing the **¿Qué palabra necesito?** activities, accept any answer that makes sense. The purpose of these activities is to have students use the new vocabulary. They are not factual recall activities. Thus, it is not necessary for students to remember specific factual information from the vocabulary presentation when answering. If you wish, have students use the illustration on this page as a stimulus, when possible.

Historieta Each time **Historieta** appears, it means that the answers to the activity form a short story. Encourage students to look at the title of the **Historieta,** since it can help them do the activity.

1 and **3** Students can retell the story in Activities 1 and 3 in their own words.

Writing Development
Have students write the answers to Activities 1 and 3 in a paragraph to illustrate how the answers to all the items tell a story.

Universal Access

Ask for volunteers, especially **kinesthetic learners,** to imitate the people in Activity 2. Then have other students, especially **visual learners,** give the appropriate description. Have students do the same using the other words and expressions taught on pages 42–43.

¿Qué palabra necesito?

1 Historieta *¡Qué enferma está!*
Contesten. *(Answer.)*

1. ¿Está enferma la pobre muchacha?
2. ¿Tiene que guardar cama?
3. ¿Está en cama?
4. ¿Tiene tos?
5. ¿Tiene dolor de garganta?
6. ¿Tiene dolor de cabeza también?
7. ¿Tiene fiebre y escalofríos?
8. ¿Está siempre cansada?
9. ¿Qué tiene? ¿Tiene la gripe?

2 ¿Cómo está? Contesten según las fotos.
(Answer based on the photos.)

1. ¿Cómo está el joven? ¿Está triste o contento?

2. Y la joven, ¿cómo está? ¿Está bien o está enferma?

3. Y la señora, ¿está nerviosa o muy tranquila?

4. El señor, ¿está de mal humor o de buen humor?

ANSWERS TO ¿Qué palabra necesito?

1
1. Sí, la pobre muchacha está enferma.
2. Sí, tiene que guardar cama.
3. Sí, está en cama.
4. Sí, tiene tos.
5. Sí, tiene dolor de garganta.
6. Sí, tiene dolor de cabeza también.
7. Sí, tiene fiebre y escalofríos.
8. Sí, siempre está cansada.
9. Sí, tiene la gripe.

2
1. El joven está contento.
2. La joven está enferma.
3. La señora está nerviosa.
4. El señor está de mal humor.

3 Historieta ¿Qué tiene Alicia?

Contesten. (Answer.)

1. ¿Está enferma Alicia?
2. ¿Estornuda mucho?
3. ¿Tiene tos también?
4. ¿Está resfriada?
5. ¿Qué opinión tienes? ¿Está Alicia de buen humor o de mal humor?

4 ¿Cómo estás tú? Contesten. (Answer about yourself.)

1. ¿Cómo estás hoy?
2. Cuando estás enfermo(a), ¿estás de buen humor o estás de mal humor?
3. Cuando tienes dolor de cabeza, ¿estás contento(a) o triste?
4. Cuando tienes catarro, ¿siempre estás cansado(a) o no?
5. Cuando tienes catarro, ¿tienes fiebre y escalofríos?
6. Cuando tienes la gripe, ¿tienes fiebre y escalofríos?
7. ¿Tienes que guardar cama cuando tienes catarro?
8. ¿Tienes que guardar cama cuando tienes fiebre?

5 ¿Qué te pasa?

 Work with a classmate. Ask your partner what's the matter—**¿Qué te pasa?** He or she will tell you. Then suggest something he or she can do to feel better. **¿Por qué no... ?** Take turns.

yo practic o

Use your manipulatives to practice your new vocabulary.

Paso 1: Palabras

cuarenta y cinco ✵ 45

---

4 Activity 4 can be done as an interview or a paired activity.

5 Encourage students to be as creative as possible when doing this activity. They can have a lot of fun with it. Students should use the following model:

—**¿Qué te pasa?**
—**Estoy nervioso(a) porque tengo un examen mañana.**
—**¿Por qué no vas al cine?**

ANSWERS TO ¿Qué palabra necesito?

3

1. Sí, Alicia está enferma.
2. Sí, estornuda mucho.
3. Sí, tiene tos también.
4. Sí, está resfriada.
5. Alicia está de mal humor.

4

1. Estoy ___.
2. Cuando estoy enfermo(a), estoy de mal humor.
3. Cuando tengo dolor de cabeza, estoy triste.
4. Cuando tengo catarro, siempre estoy cansado(a).
5. Sí, cuando tengo catarro, tengo fiebre y escalofríos.

6. Sí, cuando tengo la gripe, tengo fiebre y escalofríos.
7. Sí, (No, no) tengo que guardar cama cuando tengo catarro.
8. Sí, tengo que guardar cama cuando tengo fiebre.

5 Answers will vary; however, students should follow the model.
—¿Qué te pasa?
—(response)
—¿Por qué no ___?

45

Formas

RESOURCE MANAGER

Audio Activities TE, pages 24–27
Audio CD 2
Workbook, pages 21–24
Quizzes 2–3, pages 10–11
ExamView® Pro

Bellringer Review

Use BRR Transparency 2.2 or write the following on the board.
In Spanish, write as many words as you can that describe a person.

2 PRESENTATION

Ser y estar—característica y condición

¡OJO! Explain to students that the verb **ser** comes from the Latin verb **esse,** from which the English word *essence* is derived. Therefore, the verb **ser** is used to describe the essence of something, that which is inherent or characteristic.

On the other hand, the verb **estar** is derived from the Latin **stare,** from which the English word *state* is derived. Therefore, **estar** is used to describe a state or a condition.

STEP 1 Read Items 1 and 2 aloud.
STEP 2 Have students repeat the examples in Items 1 and 2.

3 PRACTICE

¿Cómo lo digo?

6 **Juego** Activity 6 is a recognition activity. This gives students the opportunity to understand the difference between characteristics and conditions before having to produce **ser** or **estar** on their own.

46

Formas **Ser** y **estar**—característica y condición
Characteristics and conditions

1. Spanish has two verbs that mean *to be.* They are **ser** and **estar.** Each of these verbs has very distinct uses. **Ser** expresses a trait or a characteristic that does not change.

   El muchacho es moreno. Él es muy sincero.
   La casa de apartamentos es muy alta.

2. **Estar** expresses a temporary state or condition.

   Juan no está bien hoy. Está enfermo.
   La joven está cansada.
   Está nerviosa también.

¿Cómo lo digo?

6 **Juego** **¿Característica o condición?**

Listen to each sentence. Raise your right hand if it describes a characteristic. Raise your left hand if it describes a condition.

1. Está enfermo.
2. Es muy guapo.
3. Es muy sincera.
4. Está nerviosa.
5. Estoy bien.
6. Son inteligentes.
7. Están cansados.
8. Son simpáticos.

El muchacho está enfermo pero no está de mal humor.

el estrés

7 **Al contrario** Sigan el modelo. *(Follow the model.)*

Roberto es rubio. →
Al contrario. No es rubio. Roberto es moreno.

1. Teresa es morena.
2. Justo es alto.
3. Héctor es feo.
4. Catalina es muy seria.
5. La clase de biología es aburrida.
6. Los cursos son fáciles.
7. Nuestro equipo de fútbol es malo.
8. Su familia es grande.

46 ✷ cuarenta y seis   Unidad 2: La salud

ANSWERS TO ¿Cómo lo digo?

6
1. *Students should raise their left hand.*
2. *Students should raise their right hand.*
3. *Students should raise their right hand.*
4. *Students should raise their left hand.*
5. *Students should raise their left hand.*
6. *Students should raise their right hand.*
7. *Students should raise their left hand.*
8. *Students should raise their right hand.*

7
1. Al contrario. No es morena. Teresa es rubia.
2. Al contrario. No es alto. Justo es bajo.
3. Al contrario. No es feo. Héctor es guapo.
4. Al contrario. No es muy seria. Catalina es muy cómica (graciosa).
5. Al contrario. No es aburrida. La clase de biología es interesante.
6. Al contrario. No son fáciles. Los cursos son difíciles.
7. Al contrario. No es malo. Nuestro equipo de fútbol es bueno.
8. Al contrario. No es grande. Mi familia es pequeña.

8 **Historieta** Mi casa y mi familia

Contesten. *(Answer.)*

1. ¿Es grande o pequeña tu casa?
2. ¿Es bonita tu casa?
3. ¿De qué color es tu casa?
4. ¿Es grande o pequeña tu familia?
5. ¿Son muy cómicos tus primos?
6. ¿Es muy inteligente tu hermano o tu hermana?

Una casa particular. Sitges. España

9 **Historieta** Hoy yo... Contesten. *(Answer.)*

1. Hoy, ¿cómo estás? ¿Estás bien o estás enfermo(a)?
2. ¿Estás contento(a)?
3. ¿Estás triste?
4. ¿Estás nervioso(a)?
5. ¿Estás de mal humor o de buen humor?

10 ¿Cómo está o cómo es? Describan a las personas en el dibujo. *(Describe the people in the picture.)*

11 Yo Give a brief description of yourself.

Paso 1: Formas

cuarenta y siete ❀ 47

---

8 and **9** After going over Activities 8 and 9, have students work in pairs and tell each other as much as they can about their house or one of their family members. Then have students tell each other as much as they can about how they are feeling today.

10 Note that Activity 10 makes students come up with **ser** or **estar** on their own.

11 See who can come up with the most complete description of himself or herself.

Learning from Photos

(page 47) This lovely private home on a residential street of Sitges, Spain, is just two blocks from the Mediterranean Sea. Sitges is very close to the city of Barcelona on the **Costa Dorada,** or in Catalan, **Costa Daurada.** Today Catalan is the language used throughout Cataluña.

ANSWERS TO ¿Cómo lo digo?

8 *Answers will vary but may include:*
1. Mi casa es grande (pequeña).
2. Sí (No), mi casa (no) es bonita.
3. Mi casa es ___.
4. Mi familia es grande (pequeña).
5. Sí (No), mis primos (no) son cómicos.
6. Sí, mi hermano (hermana) es muy inteligente. (No, mi hermano [hermana] no es muy inteligente.)

9 *Answers will vary but may include:*
1. Hoy estoy bien (enfermo[a]).
2. Sí, (No, no) estoy contento(a).
3. Sí, (No, no) estoy triste.
4. Sí, (No, no) estoy nervioso(a).
5. Estoy de buen (mal) humor.

11 *Answers will vary. Students should use the words and expressions taught in this unit as well as adjectives that they learned in ¿Cómo te va? A, Nivel verde.*

1 PREPARATION

Bellringer Review

Use BRR Transparency 2.3 or write the following on the board.
In Spanish, write the names of as many countries as you can.

2 PRESENTATION

 Ser y **estar**—origen y colocación

¡OJO! You may wish to emphasize that **estar** is used with both permanent and temporary locations. For example: **Madrid está en España. Los alumnos de la señora Rivera están en Madrid ahora. Nuestra casa está en la calle quince. Y nuestra escuela está en _____.**

STEP 1 Read Items 1 and 2 with the students and have them read the model sentences aloud.

3 PRACTICE

¿Cómo lo digo?

12 Activity 12 is a recognition activity. This gives students the opportunity to understand the difference between origin and location before having to produce **ser** or **estar** on their own.

Learning from Photos

(page 48) The famous **Gran Vía** of Madrid goes from **Alcalá** to the **Plaza de España.** It is an attractive street with many hotels and all types of theaters, movie houses, shops, cafeterias, jewelers, bookstores, etc. Many of the buildings date from the turn of the twentieth century.

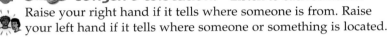 **Ser** y **estar**—origen y colocación
Origin and location

1. You use the verb **ser** to tell where someone or something is from.

   La profesora es de Puerto Rico.
   El café es de Colombia.

2. You use **estar** to express where someone or something is located. **Estar** expresses both temporary and permanent location.

   Los alumnos están en la escuela.
   Madrid está en España.

¿Cómo lo digo?

12 **Juego** **¿Origen o colocación?** Listen to each sentence. Raise your right hand if it tells where someone is from. Raise your left hand if it tells where someone or something is located.

1. Somos de Tejas.
2. Guadalajara está en México.
3. La profesora es de Cuba.
4. Sus abuelos son de España.
5. Su casa está en Miami.
6. Miami está en Florida.

La Gran Vía. Madrid. España

ANSWERS TO ¿Cómo lo digo?

12
1. *Students should raise their right hand.*
2. *Students should raise their left hand.*
3. *Students should raise their right hand.*
4. *Students should raise their right hand.*
5. *Students should raise their left hand.*
6. *Students should raise their left hand.*

¿De dónde es Micaela? Practiquen la conversación.
(Practice the conversation.)

Historieta Micaela Contesten según la conversación.
(Answer based on the conversation.)

1. ¿Es de Nicaragua Micaela?
2. ¿De dónde es?
3. ¿De qué nacionalidad es?
4. ¿Dónde están Teresa y Micaela ahora?
5. ¿Están ellas en la misma clase de inglés?
6. ¿Cómo es Micaela?

Paso 1: Formas

cuarenta y nueve 49

---

13 Have pairs of students practice the conversation together and then have them present the dialogue to the class.

14 You may wish to have students do Activity 14 with books closed as a follow-up activity to the student presentations of the dialogue in Activity 13.

Universal Access

You may wish to allow **students with learning difficulties** and **average students** to read the conversation aloud with as much expression as possible. Then call on **advanced learners** to present the conversation without reading. They do not have to recite it from memory. Permit them to ad-lib and say anything that makes sense.

ANSWERS TO **¿Cómo lo digo?**

14

1. No, Micaela no es de Nicaragua.
2. Es de Guatemala.
3. Es guatemalteca.
4. Teresa y Micaela están en Florida ahora.
5. Sí, ellas están en la misma clase de inglés.
6. Micaela es muy inteligente.

3 PRACTICE (continued)

15 Have students do Activity 15 as an oral paired activity. Be sure they know the meaning of **creo.** Say **Sí, creo que es de Cuba** as you nod your head and give an expression of belief but not absolute certainty. Say the model sentences with the appropriate intonation to indicate the natural-ness of the exchange.

16 The purpose of this activity is to contrast the use of **ser** and **estar** and hopefully make it easy for students to understand the difference between origin and location.

Learning from Photos

(page 50, top) This young indigenous girl is from Arequipa, Perú, a city 7,590 feet above sea level where eternal springtime reigns. When the Spaniards first entered Arequipa it was a small but very important junction in the Incan road system. In 1540 the main square was laid out by the Spaniards, and to this day the city is noted for its gorgeous colonial architecture. Many of the colonial buildings are made from **sillar,** the white volcanic stone that results from the overflow of lava from the several volcanoes that surround the city. Because of the **sillar** material, the city is called **Ciudad Blanca.**

15 **¿De dónde es?** Contesten según el modelo.
(Answer according to the model.)

> **¿Es cubano el muchacho?** →
> **Sí, creo que es de Cuba.**

1. ¿Es colombiana la muchacha?
2. ¿Es guatemalteco?
3. ¿Es puertorriqueña?
4. ¿Es española?
5. ¿Es peruano el médico?
6. ¿Son venezolanos los amigos?
7. ¿Son chilenas las amigas?
8. ¿Son costarricenses los jugadores?

Una niña con su mascota. cerca de Arequipa. Perú

¿Es Bernardo argentino?

16 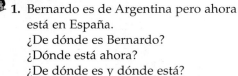 **¿De dónde es y dónde está ahora?**
Contesten. *(Answer.)*

1. Bernardo es de Argentina pero ahora está en España.
   ¿De dónde es Bernardo?
   ¿Dónde está ahora?
   ¿De dónde es y dónde está?
2. Linda es de Estados Unidos pero ahora está en Colombia.
   ¿De dónde es Linda?
   ¿Dónde está ahora?
   ¿De dónde es y dónde está?
3. La señora Martín es de Cuba pero ahora está en Puerto Rico.
   ¿De dónde es la señora Martín?
   ¿Dónde está ella ahora?
   ¿De dónde es y dónde está?

 UN POCO MÁS *For more practice using words and forms from **Paso 1,** do Activity 3 on page H4 at the end of this book.*

50 ✳ cincuenta

Unidad 2: La salud

ANSWERS TO ¿Cómo lo digo?

15

1. Sí, creo que es de Colombia.
2. Sí, creo que es de Guatemala.
3. Sí, creo que es de Puerto Rico.
4. Sí, creo que es de España.
5. Sí, creo que es de Perú.
6. Sí, creo que son de Venezuela.
7. Sí, creo que son de Chile.
8. Sí, creo que son de Costa Rica.

16

1. Bernardo es de Argentina.
   Ahora está en España.
   Es de Argentina y ahora está en España.
2. Linda es de Estados Unidos.
   Ahora está en Colombia.
   Es de Estados Unidos y ahora está en Colombia.
3. La señora Martín es de Cuba.
   Ahora está en Puerto Rico.
   Es de Cuba y ahora está en Puerto Rico.

17 Historieta Una carta a un amigo

Completen la carta. *(Complete the letter with ser or estar.)*

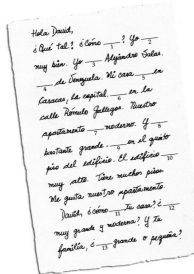

Hola David,

¿Qué tal? ¿Cómo __1__? Yo __2__ muy bien. Yo __3__ Alejandro Salas. __4__ de Venezuela. Mi casa __5__ en Caracas, la capital. __6__ en la calle Rómulo Gallegos. Nuestro apartamento __7__ moderno. Y __8__ bastante grande. __9__ en el quinto piso del edificio. El edificio __10__ muy alto. Tiene muchos pisos. Me gusta nuestro apartamento.

David, ¿cómo __11__ tu casa? ¿ __12__ muy grande y moderna? Y tu familia, ¿ __13__ grande o pequeña?

Caracas, Venezuela

18 Entrevista Contesten. *(Answer about yourself.)*

1. ¿Estás en la escuela ahora?
2. ¿Dónde está la escuela?
3. ¿En qué clase estás?
4. ¿En qué piso está la sala de clase?
5. ¿Está el/la profesor(a) en clase también?
6. ¿De dónde es él/ella?
7. ¿Y de dónde eres tú?
8. ¿Cómo estás hoy?
9. ¿Y el/la profesor(a), ¿cómo está?
10. ¿Y cómo es?

19 Mi familia Talk about your family or friends. Tell where they are from and where they are now.

Un *colegio*, Gaucín, España

cincuenta y uno 51

51

Palabras

1 PREPARATION

RESOURCE MANAGER

Vocabulary Transparencies 2.3–2.4
Audio Activities TE, pages 28–29
Audio CD 2
Workbook, pages 25–27
Quiz 4, page 12
ExamView® Pro

Bellringer Review

Use BRR Transparency 2.4 or write the following on the board.
In Spanish, write some adjectives that describe your family doctor.

2 PRESENTATION

STEP 1 Have students close their books. Present the new words using Vocabulary Transparencies 2.3–2.4. As you point to each item, have students repeat the corresponding word or expression after you two or three times.

STEP 2 Have students keep their books closed. Dramatize the following words or expressions from **Paso 2 Palabras: me duele la cabeza, me duele la garganta, me duele el estómago, abrir la boca, examinar la garganta, dar una receta.**

STEP 3 Ask students to open their books to pages 52–53. Have them read along and repeat the new material after you or Audio CD 2. You may also wish to intersperse questions in your vocabulary presentation.

Palabras   En la consulta del médico

Me duele la cabeza.   Me duele la garganta.   Me duele el estómago.

el médico

la consulta del médico, el consultorio

Unidad 2: La salud

Total Physical Response

(Student 1), **ven acá. Tú vas a ser el/la médico(a).**
(Student 2), **ven acá. Tú vas a ser el/la enfermo(a).**
(Student 2), **siéntate.**
(Student 2), **indica al médico que te duele la garganta.**

(Student 2), **abre la boca.**
(Student 1), **examina la garganta.**
(Student 1), **y ahora examina los ojos.**
(Student 1), **dale una pastilla.**
(Student 2), **toma la pastilla.**

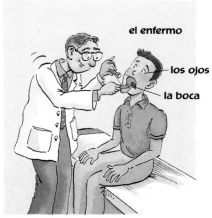

el enfermo

los ojos

la boca

Carlos está en el consultorio.
El médico examina a Carlos.
Carlos abre la boca.
El médico le examina la garganta.

una receta

El médico le da una receta.
El médico le receta unos antibióticos.

la farmacia

la farmacéutica

el farmacéutico

las pastillas, las píldoras

Isabel está en la farmacia.
El farmacéutico le vende (despacha)
   los medicamentos.
Él le da una caja de pastillas.

Nota Study the following cognates
related to health and medicine.

el síntoma	la dosis
la diagnosis	la tableta
la alergia	la aspirina
la inyección	el antibiótico
la medicina	

Paso 2: Palabras

STEP 4 Make sure that students
know the meanings of the cognates listed on page 53.

Learning from Photos

(page 53) This pharmacy is in
Quebradillas, Puerto Rico, a
town in the Northwest.

♻ Recycling

Bring back previously learned
vocabulary by asking: **¿Dónde te
duele?** and point to your arm,
foot, finger, and hand.

About the Spanish Language

- Other words that are used
  often in addition to **las
  pastillas** and **las píldoras** are:
  **los comprimidos, las tabletas,
  las cápsulas.**
- Explain to students that many
  nouns that end in **-ma** come
  from Greek, and they are masculine and take the article **el:
  el problema, el programa, el
  síntoma, el drama.**
- Almost all nouns that end in
  -osis are feminine: **la dosis,
  la diagnosis, la prognosis, la
  tuberculosis.**

Universal Access

The following are examples of categories of
questions:
**(1) ¿Está Carlos en el consultorio?
¿Abre la boca Carlos?**
**(2) ¿Dónde está Carlos, en la farmacia o en el
consultorio?
¿El médico le examina la garganta o los
ojos?**

**(3) ¿Dónde está Carlos?
¿Qué le examina el médico?**
As material is reviewed and reintroduced, **students with learning difficulties** can be called
upon to answer more challenging questions.

53

3 PRACTICE

¿Qué palabra necesito?

1 Have students act out Activity 1 using as much expression as possible.

2 Go over Activity 2 once with the entire class. Then have students retell the story in their own words.

Universal Access

- Have students, especially **visual learners,** draw a picture of someone who isn't feeling well. Then have them describe their pictures to the class or have them write descriptions of their drawings.
- **Kinesthetic learners** will enjoy Activity 3.

¿Qué palabra necesito?

1 **¿Qué te pasa?** Sigan el modelo. (*Follow the model.*)

> **Me duele la garganta.** →
> —¿Qué te pasa? ¿Tienes dolor de garganta?
> —Sí, me duele mucho. ¡Qué enfermo(a) estoy!

1. Me duele el estómago.
2. Me duele la cabeza.

2 **Historieta** **En la consulta del médico**

Contesten. (*Answer.*)

1. ¿Está Ricardo en la consulta del médico?
2. ¿Cómo está Ricardo?
3. ¿Tiene fiebre y escalofríos?
4. ¿Le duele la garganta?
5. ¿Examina el médico a Ricardo?
6. ¿Ricardo abre la boca?
7. ¿Tiene Ricardo la gripe?
8. ¿Le receta unos antibióticos el médico?
9. ¿Va Ricardo a la farmacia con su receta?
10. ¿Le vende los medicamentos el farmacéutico?

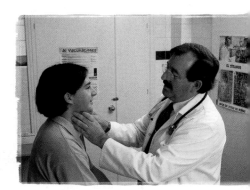

3 **Juego** **¿Qué te pasa?** Work in small groups. Take turns pantomiming different illnesses and emotions. The other group members have to tell what is being pantomimed.

ANSWERS TO **¿Qué palabra necesito?**

1

1. —¿Qué te pasa? ¿Tienes dolor de estómago?
   —Sí, me duele mucho. ¡Qué enfermo(a) estoy!
2. —¿Qué te pasa? ¿Tienes dolor de cabeza?
   —Sí, me duele mucho. ¡Qué enfermo(a) estoy!

2

1. Sí, Ricardo está en la consulta del médico.
2. Ricardo está enfermo.
3. Sí, tiene fiebre y escalofríos.
4. Sí, le duele la garganta.
5. Sí, el médico examina a Ricardo.

6. Sí, Ricardo abre la boca.
7. Sí, Ricardo tiene la gripe.
8. Sí, el médico le receta unos antibióticos.
9. Sí, Ricardo va a la farmacia con su receta.
10. Sí, el farmacéutico le vende los medicamentos.

3 *Answers will vary. Students should pantomime symptoms learned in the unit.*

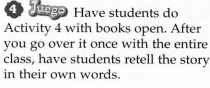

PASO 2

4 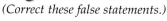 **Todo es falso.** Corrijan estas oraciones falsas.
(Correct these false statements.)

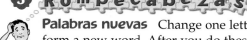
1. El paciente está muy bien.
2. El paciente examina al médico.
3. El paciente está muy tranquilo.
4. El paciente abre la boca y el médico le examina los ojos.
5. La farmacéutica le da una receta.
6. El paciente va al consultorio con su receta.
7. El médico le vende los medicamentos.
8. El farmacéutico le da una lista de píldoras.

5 **R o m p e c a b e z a s**

Palabras nuevas Change one letter in each word to form a new word. After you do these, work with a partner and try to form new words by changing one letter.

1. poco
2. ajo
3. dos
4. bien
5. casa
6. color

6 **Buenos días, doctor López.** Look at this illustration. Pretend you're the patient. Tell the doctor how you're feeling. Give the doctor all your symptoms.

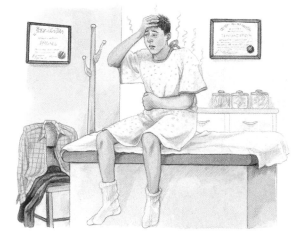

Paso 2: Palabras

cincuenta y cinco 55

4 Have students do Activity 4 with books open. After you go over it once with the entire class, have students retell the story in their own words.

6 You may wish to have pairs of students do Activity 6 as a dialogue. Then have students present their conversations to the class.

EXPANSION In Activity 6 have individual students each come up with a symptom. See how many symptoms the class can come up with.

ANSWERS TO **¿Qué palabra necesito?**

4
1. El paciente está enfermo.
2. El médico examina al paciente.
3. El paciente está muy nervioso.
4. El paciente abre la boca y el médico le examina la garganta.
5. La médica le da una receta.
6. El paciente va a la farmacia con su receta.
7. El farmacéutico le vende los medicamentos.
8. El farmacéutico le da una caja de píldoras.

5
1. toco
2. ojo
3. tos, los
4. buen, cien
5. caja, cama
6. dolor

6 Answers will vary, but students should use the vocabulary from Paso 1 *and* Paso 2. *Answers may include:* Tengo dolor de cabeza, tengo escalofríos, tengo dolor de estómago, etc.

55

PASO 2

1 PREPARATION

RESOURCE MANAGER

Audio Activities TE, pages 29–30
Audio CD 2
Workbook, pages 27–28
Quiz 5, page 13
ExamView® Pro

Bellringer Review

Use BRR Transparency 2.5 or write the following on the board.
In Spanish, write the names for as many parts of the body as you can.

2 PRESENTATION

Los pronombres **me, te, nos**

¡OJO! The pronouns **me, te,** and **nos** were originally presented in Unit 1.

STEP 1 Have students point to themselves as they say **me** and point to or look at a friend as they say **te.**

STEP 2 Have students read the model sentences aloud. You can call on an individual to read them or have the entire class read them in unison.

Formas

Los pronombres **me, te, nos**
Telling what happens to whom

1. You have already learned the pronouns **me, te,** and **nos** with the expressions **me gusta, te interesa,** and **nos aburre.**

   Me gustan los deportes.
   ¿**Te interesa** el arte?
   No **nos aburre** el curso.

2. **Me, te,** and **nos** are called object pronouns. Note that you place the object pronoun right before the verb.

   El médico **me ve. Me examina.**
   ¿**Te habla** el médico?
   Sí, y **me da** una receta.

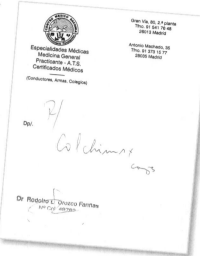

¿Cómo lo digo?

7 Historieta En el consultorio

Contesten. *(Answer.)*

1. ¿Estás enfermo(a)?
2. ¿Vas a la consulta del médico?
3. ¿Te ve el médico?
4. ¿Te examina?
5. ¿Te habla el médico?
6. Según el médico, ¿qué tienes?
7. ¿Te receta unas pastillas?
8. ¿Te despacha los medicamentos la farmacéutica?

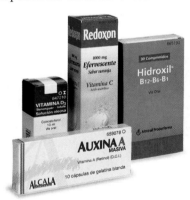

ANSWERS TO ¿Cómo lo digo?

7
1. Sí, (No, no) estoy enfermo(a).
2. Sí, (No, no) voy a la consulta del médico.
3. Sí, (No, no) me ve el médico.
4. Sí, (No, no) me examina.
5. Sí, (No, no) me habla el médico.
6. Según el médico, tengo ___ (la gripe, catarro).
7. Sí, (No, no) me receta unas pastillas.
8. Sí (No), la farmacéutica (no) me despacha los medicamentos.

 8 **Historieta** **El médico** Sigan el modelo.
(Follow the model.)

 ver →
 Cuando estamos enfermos, el médico nos ve.
 1. hablar
 2. examinar
 3. dar una receta
 4. recetar un medicamento

9 **Juego** **Preguntas y más preguntas** Work with a
partner. Have some fun making up silly questions and
giving answers. For example, **¿Te da tu amigo una receta
cuando es tu cumpleaños?** Use as many of the following
words as possible. Be original.

da **tu mamá** te tu amigo(a) **me** enseña

tu profesor(a) **habla** nos **el/la mesero(a)**

 tu abuelo(a) el/la médico(a) **tu papá** invita

compra **el/la farmacéutico(a)** comprende

Una farmacia,
Buenos Aires, Argentina

cincuenta y siete ✸ 57

---

1 PREPARATION

Bellringer Review

Use BRR Transparency 2.6 or write the following on the board.
1. In Spanish, write a list of the sports you know.
2. Write two sentences with **me gusta.**
3. Write two sentences with **me gustan.**

2 PRESENTATION

Los pronombres **le, les**

STEP 1 Have students open their books to page 58. Lead them through Items 1–3.

STEP 2 As you write the sentences from Item 2 on the board, circle **le** and **al enfermo.** Then draw arrows back and forth to indicate that they are the same person. This visual explanation helps many students.

Note: Be sure that students understand that **le** and **les** are both masculine and feminine.

STEP 3 Have students read the model sentences aloud. You can call on an individual to read them or have the entire class read them in unison.

3 PRACTICE

¿Cómo lo digo?

⑩ Have students write the answers to Activity 10 in paragraph form to show how all the answers tell a story.

Los pronombres **le, les**
Telling what happens to others

1. **Le** and **les** are indirect object pronouns. They are the indirect receivers of the action of the verb.

   > **El médico le da una receta a Pablo.**
   > **El médico les habla a sus pacientes.**

   What does the doctor give Pablo?—**una receta. Una receta** is the direct object of the sentence because it is the direct receiver of the action. It tells what was given. Pablo is the indirect object because it indicates to whom the prescription was given.

2. The indirect object pronouns **le** and **les** are both masculine and feminine. **Le** and **les** are often used along with a noun phrase as in the following examples.

   > **El médico le da una receta al enfermo.**
   > **Le da una receta a la enferma.**
   > **El médico les da una receta a sus pacientes.**

3. Since **le** and **les** can refer to more than one person, they are often clarified as follows.

Le hablo	a él.	Les hablo	a ellos.
	a ella.		a ellas.
	a usted.		a ustedes.

¿Cómo lo digo?

⑩ **Historieta En el consultorio**
Contesten. *(Answer.)*
1. ¿Está Pepe en el consultorio?
2. ¿Le habla la médica?
3. ¿Pepe le explica sus síntomas a la médica?
4. ¿La médica le examina los ojos?
5. ¿La médica le da una receta a Pepe?
6. ¿Le receta unos antibióticos?

Médicas Note that the doctor in the blue uniform on page 58 is a woman. In recent years in the United States, more and more women have entered the medical profession. In Spain and Latin America this is not a recent trend. There has always been a large number of both female doctors and female pharmacists.

ANSWERS TO ¿Cómo lo digo?

⑩

1. Sí, Pepe está en el consultorio.
2. Sí, le habla la médica.
3. Sí, Pepe le explica sus síntomas a la médica.
4. Sí, la médica le examina los ojos.
5. Sí, la médica le da una receta a Pepe.
6. Sí, le receta unos antibióticos.

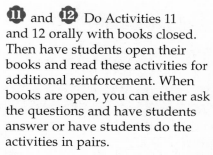
 Sí que... Contesten según el modelo.
(Answer according to the model.)

 ¿Les hablas a tus hermanos? →
Sí que les hablo a mis hermanos.

1. ¿Les hablas a tus amigos?
2. ¿Les hablas por teléfono?
3. ¿Les escribes una carta a tus abuelos?
4. ¿Les envías un correo electrónico?
5. ¿Les das un regalo a tus padres?
6. ¿Les compras un regalo para su cumpleaños?

En el museo del Prado, Madrid, España

 Intereses y gustos Sigan el modelo.
(Follow the model.)

A mí me gusta mucho el arte. →
A mi amigo le gusta mucho también.

1. A mí me gustan mucho los deportes.
2. A mí me gusta mucho la clase de español.
3. A mí me gustan mucho las camisas de mangas cortas.
4. A mí me gustan mucho los blue jeans.
5. A mí me gusta mucho el helado.
6. A mí me gusta mucho la comida mexicana.

 Regalos para todos Work in pairs. Tell what each of the following people is like. Then tell what you buy or give to each one as a gift. If possible, tell where you buy him or her the gift and whether or not he or she likes it.

tu padre   tu madre   tu abuelo(a)

tu amigo(a)   tu hermano(a)

 *For more practice using words and forms from **Paso 2**, do Activity 4 on page H5 at the end of this book.*

Paso 2: Formas

 Andas bien. ¡Adelante!

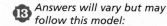

11 and **12** Do Activities 11 and 12 orally with books closed. Then have students open their books and read these activities for additional reinforcement. When books are open, you can either ask the questions and have students answer or have students do the activities in pairs.

13 Students should use **gustar** when telling what each person likes. They will use either **comprar** or **dar** when telling what they buy or give as a gift.

Learning from Photos
(page 59) This gallery is in the famous Prado Museum of Madrid. Shown here is the ***Duquesa de Pontoja*** painting.

 This *InfoGap* activity will allow students to practice in pairs. The activity should be very manageable for them, since all vocabulary and structures are familiar to them.

¡Adelante! At this point, all new material has been presented. Students have learned all the vocabulary and structure necessary to complete the unit. The conversation, cultural readings, and activities in **Paso 3** and **Paso 4** recycle all the material learned up to this point.

ANSWERS TO ¿Cómo lo digo?

11
1. Sí que les hablo a mis amigos.
2. Sí que les hablo por teléfono.
3. Sí que les escribo una carta a mis abuelos.
4. Sí que les envío un correo electrónico.
5. Sí que les doy un regalo a mis padres.
6. Sí que les compro un regalo para su cumpleaños.

12
1. A mi amigo le gustan mucho también.
2. A mi amigo le gusta mucho también.
3. A mi amigo le gustan mucho también.
4. A mi amigo le gustan mucho también.
5. A mi amigo le gusta mucho también.
6. A mi amigo le gusta mucho también.

13 *Answers will vary but may follow this model:*
Mi padre es inteligente. Le gusta mucho leer. Le doy un libro para su cumpleaños. Le compro el libro en la librería García. Le gusta mucho el libro.

Conversación

PASO 3

Conversación

Un muchacho enfermo

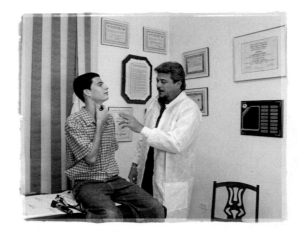

Conversación

1 PREPARATION

RESOURCE MANAGER

Audio Activities TE, pages 31–33
Audio CD 2
Workbook, page 29

Bellringer Review

Use BRR Transparency 2.7 or write the following on the board.
Answer the following questions.

1. **¿Comes mucho cuando estás enfermo(a)?**
2. **¿Tienes mucho apetito cuando estás enfermo(a)?**
3. **¿Tomas muchos líquidos cuando estás enfermo(a)?**
4. **¿Guardas cama cuando estás enfermo(a)?**

2 PRESENTATION

STEP 1 Tell students they will hear a conversation between Ricardo and a doctor. Have students close their books and listen as you read the conversation or play Audio CD 2.

STEP 2 Have students keep their books closed as you reread the conversation to them, stopping after every three sentences to ask simple comprehension questions.

STEP 3 Have students open their books and read the conversation aloud.

STEP 4 Have them dramatize the conversation.

STEP 5 Have a student summarize the visit to the doctor in his or her own words.

Learning from Photos

(page 60) This doctor's office is in Quebradillas, Puerto Rico.

Ricardo Buenos días, doctor Paredes.

Doctor Buenos días, Ricardo. ¿Qué te pasa? ¿Qué tienes?

Ricardo Doctor Paredes, ¡qué enfermo estoy!

Doctor ¿Me puedes explicar tus síntomas?

Ricardo Pues, tengo fiebre. Y tengo escalofríos.

Doctor ¿Te duele la garganta?

Ricardo ¿La garganta? Me duele todo— la garganta, la cabeza.

Doctor Bien, Ricardo. ¿Puedes abrir la boca?
(Después de mirar) Ya veo. Tienes la garganta muy roja.

Ricardo ¿Qué tengo, doctor?

Doctor No es nada serio. Tienes la gripe. Te voy a recetar unos antibióticos. Dentro de dos días vas a estar muy bien.

¿Comprendes?

A. Contesten. *(Answer.)*

1. ¿Dónde está Ricardo?
2. ¿Con quién habla?
3. ¿Cómo está Ricardo?
4. ¿Qué tiene?
5. ¿Tiene dolor de garganta?
6. ¿Tiene dolor de cabeza?
7. ¿Abre la boca Ricardo?
8. ¿Qué examina el médico?
9. ¿Cómo está la garganta?
10. ¿Qué cree el médico que Ricardo tiene?

B. ¿Qué opinas? ¿Va Ricardo a la farmacia? ¿Qué lleva a la farmacia? ¿Qué le da al farmacéutico? ¿Y qué le da el farmacéutico a Ricardo?

---

60 sesenta

Unidad 2: La salud

ANSWERS TO ¿Comprendes?

A.
1. Ricardo está en la consulta (el consultorio) del médico.
2. Habla con el médico (doctor).
3. Ricardo está enfermo.
4. Tiene fiebre y escalofríos.
5. Sí, tiene dolor de garganta.
6. Sí, tiene dolor de cabeza.
7. Sí, Ricardo abre la boca.
8. El médico examina la garganta de Ricardo.
9. La garganta está muy roja.
10. El médico cree que Ricardo tiene la gripe.

B. *Answers will vary but may follow this model:*
Ricardo va a la farmacia. Lleva la receta a la farmacia. Le da la receta al farmacéutico. El farmacéutico le da los antibióticos a Ricardo.

La consonante c

You have already learned that **c** in combination with **e** or **i** (**ce, ci**) is pronounced like an **s**. The consonant **c** in combination with **a, o, u** (**ca, co, cu**) has a hard **k** sound. Since **ce** and **ci** have the soft **s** sound, **c** changes to **qu** when it combines with **e** or **i** (**que, qui**) in order to maintain the hard **k** sound. Repeat the following.

ca	que	qui	co	cu
cama	que	equipo	como	cubano
casa	queso	aquí	médico	cucaracha
catarro	parque	química	cocina	
cansado	pequeño	tranquilo	cola	
cabeza				
boca				

Trabalenguas

Repeat the following.

El médico cubano está en la consulta pequeña.
El queso está en la cocina de la casa.
El cubano come el queso aquí en el parque pequeño.
¿Quién quiere una cola en el café?
¿Qué equipo quiere jugar allí?

Refrán

Can you guess what the following proverb means?

Gallo que no canta, algo tiene en la garganta.

Pronunciación

STEP 1 Remind students that the c sound is somewhat softer in Spanish than it is in English. Have them imitate your pronunciation or the pronunciation of the speaker on Audio CD 2.

STEP 2 You may also use these words and sentences for dictation.

STEP 3 To see if students are grasping this spelling concept, you may also wish to dictate the following words, which they do not know.

queda	quiste
cata	quita
coco	quema
quiosco	coloca
culebra	loco

Career Connection

Hablo español Because the Latino population in the United States is continually growing, Spanish is a very useful tool for communication in all areas of the medical profession. Ask students to think of several positions in the health care field where knowledge of Spanish would be useful or essential. If possible, invite a bilingual health care professional to speak to your class on this topic.

Refrán

If students cannot guess what the proverb means, tell them, "Has the cat got your tongue?"

Universal Access

Call on **students with learning difficulties** to read the conversation with as much expression as possible. Then have **kinesthetic learners** dramatize the conversation. Have **advanced learners** present the conversation without reading. They do not have to recite it from memory. Permit them to ad-lib and say anything that makes sense.

Cultura y lectura

1 PREPARATION

RESOURCE MANAGER

Audio Activities TE, page 34
Audio CD 2
Workbook, page 30

Bellringer Review

Use BRR Transparency 2.8 or write the following on the board. Complete with the correct form of the verb in parentheses. Then rewrite each sentence changing **Teresa** to **nosotros**.

1. Teresa ___ fútbol. (jugar)
2. Ella ___ un partido mañana. (tener)
3. Ella ___ jugar. (querer)
4. Ella no ___ perder el partido. (poder)
5. Si ella ___ el partido, su equipo no ___ ganar. (perder, poder)
6. Desgraciadamente, Teresa ___ un poco enferma. (estar)

National Standards

Cultures

The reading about a visit to the doctor and the related activities on pages 62–63 give students an understanding of daily life in the Spanish-speaking world.

PRESENTATION

PRE-READING

STEP 1 Have students scan the passage to look for cognates.

STEP 2 Give students a brief synopsis of the **Lectura** in Spanish. Ask a few questions based on it.

Cultura y lectura

¿Qué le pasa a Adela?

Reading Strategy

Visualizing As you are reading, try to visualize (or make a mental picture of) exactly what it is you are reading. Allow your mind to freely develop an image. This will help you to remember what you read. It may also help you identify with the subject of the reading.

Hoy la pobre Adela no está bien. Tampoco[1] está muy contenta. Tampoco está de muy buen humor. Ella tiene dolor de garganta y tiene tos. Y siempre está muy cansada. Mañana tiene un partido importante de fútbol y no quiere perder el partido. No hay más remedio. Adela tiene que ir a la consulta del médico.

En el consultorio Adela le habla a la médica. La médica examina a Adela. Ella abre la boca y la médica le examina la garganta. Está un poco roja.

Adela le habla a la médica:

—No puedo guardar cama. Mañana tengo que jugar fútbol y es un partido muy importante.

—No hay problema. No tienes nada serio. Te voy a recetar unos antibióticos. Vas a tomar una pastilla tres veces al día—una pastilla con cada comida. En muy poco tiempo vas a estar mucho mejor[2] y no vas a perder tu partido.

[1] Tampoco *Nor, Neither*   [2] mejor *better*

Una farmacia, Zafra, España

READING

Call on a student to read three or four sentences. Ask several questions to check comprehension before calling on the next student to read. Continue in this way until the selection has been completed.

POST-READING

Assign the reading selection and the ¿Comprendes? activities on page 63 as homework. Go over the homework the next day in class.

¿Comprendes?

A. Contesten. (Answer.)

1. ¿Quién está enferma?
2. ¿Cuáles son sus síntomas?
3. ¿Adónde tiene que ir Adela?
4. ¿Qué examina la médica?
5. ¿Cómo está la garganta?
6. ¿Tiene que guardar cama Adela?
7. ¿Qué le da la médica?
8. ¿Cuántas pastillas tiene que tomar Adela cada día?

9. ¿Cómo va a estar mañana?
10. ¿Va a perder su partido de fútbol?

B. ¿Qué opinas? ¿Por qué le receta la médica unos antibióticos a Adela? ¿Tiene ella catarro o la gripe?

Learning from Photos

(page 63) This lovely old pharmacy with many tile mosaics is in the town of Zafra, Spain, in southern Extremadura.

Universal Access

The Manos a la obra activity will be especially beneficial for visual learners.

Manos a la obra

Read the Reading Strategy again. Draw what you visualized as you were reading this selection. Describe your drawing.

Paso 3: Cultura y lectura

sesenta y tres 63

ANSWERS TO ¿Comprendes?

A.
1. Adela está enferma.
2. Tiene dolor de garganta y tiene tos. Está muy cansada.
3. Adela tiene que ir a la consulta del médico.
4. La médica examina la garganta.
5. La garganta está un poco roja.
6. No, Adela no tiene que guardar cama.
7. La médica le da una receta.

8. Adela tiene que tomar una pastilla tres veces al día—una pastilla con cada comida.
9. Mañana va a estar mucho mejor.
10. No, no va a perder su partido de fútbol.

B. Answers will vary but may include:
La médica le receta unos antibióticos a Adela porque está enferma y su garganta está roja. Ella tiene catarro.

Repaso

This section reviews the salient points from Unit 2. Students will study the uses of **ser** and **estar** and understand the difference between describing characteristics and conditions, origin and location. Students will review the object pronouns **me, te,** and **nos** and the indirect object pronouns **le** and **les.**

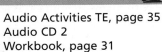

1 PREPARATION

RESOURCE MANAGER

Audio Activities TE, page 35
Audio CD 2
Workbook, page 31
Tests, pages 15–28

2 PRESENTATION

STEP 1 For review purposes, reverse the usual procedure and have students read the Spanish sentences in Item 1 and explain why either **ser** or **estar** is used.

STEP 2 Write **ser** and **estar** on the board and list their uses under the appropriate infinitive as students explain the rules.

STEP 3 Read Items 2 and 3 with students.

STEP 4 When going over Item 3, you may write the sentences on the board. Put a box around the indirect object and draw an arrow from the indirect object to the pronoun as you box in the pronoun.

Repaso

1. In this unit, I learned the uses of the verbs **ser** and **estar.**

   ser

Característica	Ella **es** muy **sincera.**
Origen	Él **es de México.**

   estar

Condición	Ella **está** muy **nerviosa.**
Colocación	Él **está en Venezuela.**

2. I also reviewed the object pronouns **me, te,** and **nos. Me, te,** and **nos** can be either a direct object or an indirect object.

   indirect object
   El médico **me** habla.
   El médico **te** da una receta.

   direct object
   El médico **me** ve.
   El médico **me** examina.

3. In this unit, I learned the indirect object pronouns **le** and **les.**

   Le hablo { a él. / a ella. / a usted.   **Les escribo** { a ellos. / a ellas. / a ustedes.

El señor le da la receta a la farmacéutica.

Unidad 2: La salud

¡Pongo todo junto!

1 **¿Ser o estar?** Completen. *(Complete.)*

1. Él _____ muy simpático pero hoy no _____ muy contento.
2. Yo _____ nervioso(a) porque mañana tengo un examen muy difícil.
3. Nosotros _____ inteligentes y vamos a recibir una nota muy buena.
4. La ciudad de Lima _____ en Perú. La ciudad _____ muy bonita.
5. Los abuelos de Francisco _____ de Galicia pero ahora ellos _____ en Estados Unidos. Galicia _____ en el norte de España.

La Coruña. Galicia. España

2 **En la consulta del médico** Contesten. *(Answer.)*

1. ¿Te habla el médico?
2. ¿Te examina?
3. ¿Te receta un medicamento?
4. ¿Quién te vende los medicamentos?
5. ¿Te da una caja de pastillas?

3 **Una invitación** Completen. *(Complete.)*

—Aquí tienes una carta.
—¿Quién __1__ escribe?
—Carlos __2__ escribe.
—¿Ah, sí?
—Sí, __3__ invita a una fiesta.
—¿__4__ invita a una fiesta?
—Sí, Carlos siempre __5__ invita cuando tiene una fiesta.

4 **En la consulta** Contesten. *(Answer.)*

1. ¿El médico le habla a Alicia?
2. ¿Y Alicia le habla al médico?
3. ¿Alicia le explica sus síntomas?
4. ¿El médico le hace una diagnosis?
5. ¿Los médicos les dan una receta a sus pacientes?
6. ¿Los médicos les despachan los medicamentos a sus pacientes?

Paso 3: Repaso

ANSWERS TO **¡Pongo todo junto!**

1
1. es, está
2. estoy
3. somos
4. está, es
5. son, están, está

2
1. Sí, me habla el médico.
2. Sí, me examina.
3. Sí, me receta un medicamento.
4. El/La farmacéutico(a) me vende los medicamentos.
5. Sí, me da una caja de pastillas.

3
1. me
2. te
3. te
4. Me
5. te

4
1. Sí, el médico le habla a Alicia.
2. Sí, Alicia le habla al médico.
3. Sí, Alicia le explica sus síntomas.
4. Sí, el médico le hace una diagnosis.
5. Sí, los médicos les dan una receta a sus pacientes.
6. No, los médicos no les despachan los medicamentos a sus pacientes.

Recycling

These activities allow students to use the vocabulary and structures from this unit in completely open-ended, real-life situations.

¡OJO! Encourage students to say as much as possible when they do these activities. Tell them not to be afraid to make mistakes, since the goal of the activities is real-life communication. If someone in the group makes an error, allow the others to politely correct him or her. Let students choose the activities they would like to do.

You may wish to divide students into pairs or groups. Encourage students to elaborate on the basic theme and to be creative. They may use props, pictures, or posters if they wish.

1 You may also wish to have one student act out the symptoms for the entire class as another student describes them.

2 You may wish to have some groups present their skits to the entire class.

PASO 3

¡Te toca a ti!

Hablar
1 **Todo el mundo está enfermo.**

✓ *Describe cold symptoms and minor ailments*

Work with a classmate. Choose one of the people in the illustrations. Describe him or her. Your partner will guess which person you're talking about and he or she will say what's the matter with the person. Take turns.

Juan **Isabel**

Federico

Cristina

David

Hablar
2 **Una receta**

✓ *Discuss a prescription with a pharmacist*

You are in a pharmacy in Guanajuato, Mexico. Your classmate will be the pharmacist. Make up a conversation about your prescription. Explain why you have to take the medicine and the pharmacist will tell you how you have to take it.

Hablar
3 **Estoy muy mal hoy.**

✓ *Talk about how you are feeling*

Work with a partner. Make gestures to indicate how you're feeling today. Your partner will ask you why you feel that way. Tell him or her. Be as creative and humorous as possible.

Unidad 2: La salud

ANSWERS TO ¡Te toca a ti!

1 *Answers will vary but may include:*
—Tiene tos. Tiene dolor de garganta.
—Es Isabel. Tiene catarro.

2 *Answers will vary. Students should discuss their symptoms and the proposed treatment, including how often to take the medicine.*

3 *Answers will vary but should include the health-related vocabulary learned in the unit.*

Escribir

4 Perdón

✓ *Write a note describing a minor illness.*

You're supposed to take a Spanish test today but you're not feeling well. Write a note to your Spanish teacher explaining why you can't take the test and mention some symptoms you have.

Writing Strategy

Writing a personal essay When writing a personal essay, you have several options. You can tell a personal story, describe something personal, or encourage your readers to do something or to think a certain way. A personal essay permits you to describe your own experience and express your personal viewpoint. When writing a personal essay in Spanish you will frequently use **yo**. Double check your essay and make sure you have used the correct **yo** form whenever necessary.

Hablar

5 Un voluntario

Escribir Your school has quite a few Spanish-speaking students. Some are new arrivals and speak very little English. Students from the Spanish Club assist the school nurse—**el/la enfermero(a)**—serving as translators for students who speak only Spanish. You are one of the students who takes part in this program. Write a flyer for your Spanish Club. Tell about your experience with one or more "patients." Give your feelings about the work you do.

Quebradillas, Puerto Rico

Paso 3: ¡Te toca a ti!

sesenta y siete 🌸 **67**

Writing Development

Have students keep a notebook or portfolio containing their best written work from each unit. These selected writings can be based on assignments from the Student Textbook and the Writing Activities Workbook. The activities on page 67 are examples of writing assignments that may be included in each student's portfolio.

In the Workbook, students will develop an organized autobiography **(Mi autobiografía)**. These workbook pages may also become a part of their portfolio.

Writing Strategy

Writing a personal essay
Have students read the Writing Strategy on page 67. Then have them refer to the **Vocabulario** on page 77 as they jot down ideas for their essay.

❀ National Standards

Communities
The writing assignment in Activity 5 encourages students to use the language beyond the school setting.

Spanish Online

Encourage students to take advantage of this opportunity to learn more about medical services in the Spanish-speaking world. Perhaps you can do this in class or in a lab if students do not have Internet access at home.

ANSWERS TO ¡Te toca a ti!

4 *Answers will vary but may include:*
No puedo tomar el examen hoy.
Estoy en cama.
Tengo fiebre y escalofríos.
Me duele el estómago.
Creo que tengo la gripe.

5 *Answers will vary. Students should use the health-related vocabulary from the unit, ser, estar, and previously learned structures such as gustar and interesar.*

Learning from Photos

(page 67) Ask students the following questions about this photo: **¿Dónde está el joven? ¿Está enfermo? ¿Con quién habla el joven? ¿Por qué está en el consultorio? ¿Qué le da la médica al joven?**

Assessment

RESOURCE MANAGER

Vocabulary Transparency 2.5
Tests, pages 15–28
ExamView® Pro, Unit 2
Performance Assessment,
   Tasks 3–4

✓ Assessment

This is a pretest for students to take before you administer the unit test. Note that each section is cross-referenced so students can easily find the material they have to review in case they made errors. You may use Assessment Answers Transparency A 2 to do the assessment in class, or you may assign this assessment for homework. You can correct the assessment yourself, or you may prefer to project the answers on the overhead in class.

Assessment
¿Estoy listo(a)?

Palabras

1 Pareen. *(Match.)*

a.   **b.**   **c.**

d.   **e.**   **f.**

*To review words from **Paso 1**, turn to pages 42–43.*

1. Está triste.
2. Está cansado.
3. Está contento.
4. Estornuda.
5. Tose.
6. Tiene dolor de cabeza.

2 Completen. *(Complete.)*

7–8. El enfermo _____ la boca y el médico le examina la _____.
9. El médico examina a sus pacientes en su _____.
10. El médico le _____ unos antibióticos al enfermo.
11. La farmacéutica le da una _____ de pastillas.
12. Vemos con los _____.

*To review words from **Paso 2**, turn to pages 52–53.*

ANSWERS TO Assessment

1
1. c
2. f
3. b
4. d
5. a
6. e

2
7. abre
8. garganta
9. consultorio
10. receta
11. caja
12. ojos

Formas

3 Completen con **ser** o **estar.** *(Complete with* ser *or* estar.*)*

  13. Madrid _____ en España.
  14. El médico _____ muy inteligente.
  15. Le duele la garganta. La garganta _____ muy roja.
  16. Nuestra escuela _____ grande.
  17. Él _____ nervioso porque tiene un examen.
18–19. Ellos _____ de Colombia pero ahora _____ en España.
  20. Su casa _____ muy bonita.

To review **ser** and **estar**, turn to pages 46 and 48.

Learning from Photos

(page 69) This is a typical residential area of San Andrés, Colombia. This type of housing is found on most Caribbean islands and in most coastal areas.

4 Completen. *(Complete.)*

21. ¿_____ va a invitar Juan a la fiesta?
    Sí, siempre me invita.
22. ¿Les habla a Uds. el profesor?
    Sí, _____ habla.
23. A Juan _____ gusta mucho el fútbol.
24. El farmacéutico _____ vende los medicamentos a sus clientes.
25. Elena tiene la gripe y el médico _____ receta unos antibióticos.

To review the pronouns **me, te, nos, le,** and **les** turn to pages 56 and 58.

Un barrio residencial.
San Andrés, Colombia

Paso 3: Assessment

ANSWERS TO *Assessment*

3	**4**
13. está	21. Te
14. es	22. nos
15. está	23. le
16. es	24. les
17. está	25. le
18. son	
19. están	
20. es	

Diversiones

Paso 4 of each **Unidad** includes a **Diversiones** section. As the title indicates, this section contains different types of activities that students in Middle School should enjoy. They also take into account the various learning modalities.

The many types of activities included are:

Canciones This section entitled **Canta con Justo** contains songs performed on the music CD by Justo Lamas, a young singer from Argentina who has written some songs specifically for **¿Cómo te va?**

Teatro These activities provide students the opportunity to get up and perform. They give suggestions for short skits, pantomimes, and dramatizations. These activities are particularly helpful for **kinesthetic learners.**

Manos a la obra

These activities enable students to get involved and use their hands. Some examples are: drawing cards or pictures, preparing ads and brochures, and preparing schedules and announcements.

Rompecabezas

Some units contain riddles or puzzles that reinforce language in a fun way.

Investigaciones

This research section allows those students who like to work on their own to get involved in some research projects that add another dimension to the cultural material of the unit.

Diversiones

Canta con Justo
Siempre por siempre

Ho - jas se - cas que ca - en,_____ el llan - to ha ca - lla - do mi voz._____

Sien - to frí - o en el al - ma_____ y aún guar - do a - que - lla vie - ja can - ción._____

Hoy, mi a - mor,_____ a - ún si - go es - pe - rán - do - te_____ Hey, ¿có - mo es - tás?

___ Cuen - ta con - mi____go, No llo - res más,_____ te ne - ce - si - to._____

___ Siem - pre por siem - pre te a - ma__ ré_____ Y a tu la - do yo es - ta - ré.

___ Siem - pre por siem - pre tú____ se - rás_____ mi a - mor.

Aunque mi vida se apague,
como un mago crearé una ilusión—
Y si el cielo se oculta,
no importa, encontraré mi canción.

Hoy, mi amor, aún sigo esperándote

Hey, ¿cómo estás? Cuenta conmigo.
No llores más, te necesito.
Siempre por siempre te amaré
Y a tu lado yo estaré.
Siempre por siempre tú serás mi amor.

Music Connection

Canta con Justo
The song **Siempre por siempre** will be easy for learners of all ability levels. It will help students practice vocabulary about feelings. You may wish to have students hear the recorded version of **Siempre por siempre**. It can be found on Track 7 of the **Canta con Justo** music CD. In addition, students can watch Justo perform this song on the **Justo Lamas ¡En vivo!** music video that accompanies **¿Cómo te va?** You may also wish to use Song Transparency S 2 to project the music and lyrics on an overhead so students can follow along as they listen or sing.

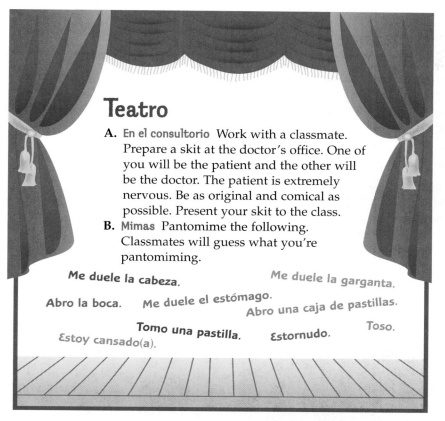

Teatro

A. En el consultorio Work with a classmate. Prepare a skit at the doctor's office. One of you will be the patient and the other will be the doctor. The patient is extremely nervous. Be as original and comical as possible. Present your skit to the class.

B. Mimas Pantomime the following. Classmates will guess what you're pantomiming.

Me duele la cabeza.

Me duele la garganta.

Abro la boca.   Me duele el estómago.

Abro una caja de pastillas.

Tomo una pastilla.   Estornudo.

Toso.

Estoy cansado(a).

Paso 4: Diversiones

Emociones Complete the following statements to explain when you experience certain emotions.

Estoy contento(a) cuando...

Estoy triste cuando...

Estoy nervioso(a) cuando...

Estoy de buen humor cuando...

Estoy de mal humor cuando...

Teatro

- **En el consultorio** You may wish to videotape these skits ahead of time and have a "movie day", complete with popcorn, to watch them.
- **Mimas** Encourage students to have fun with this activity and to be expressive.

EMOCIONES Expand upon this activity by encouraging students to choose emotions from those depicted on the card and to make up similar types of sentences.

Universal Access

The types of activities on this page are very beneficial for **kinesthetic** and **visual learners**.

Manos a la obra

1. Una tira cómica Prepare your own comic strip entitled **En el consultorio.** Do your own drawings and make up the speech bubbles.

2. Caras Draw a series of faces. Indicate in Spanish the emotion, state, condition, or characteristic the expression on the face conveys.

Rompecabezas

 El mensaje secreto Substitute numbers for letters to reveal what the nurse might be saying to Susana. After you solve the puzzle, you may wish to work with a partner to make up **un mensaje secreto** of your own.

1. A	8. H	15. Ñ	22. U
2. B	9. I	16. O	23. V
3. C	10. J	17. P	24. W
4. D	11. K	18. Q	25. X
5. E	12. L	19. R	26. Y
6. F	13. M	20. S	27. Z
7. G	14. N	21. T	

ANSWERS TO Manos a la obra

1–2. *Answers will vary, but students will use vocabulary learned in* Paso 1 Palabras *and* Paso 2 Palabras.

ANSWERS TO Rompecabezas

El mensaje secreto: ¡Sí que vas a ver al médico!

Entrevista

¿Vas al médico cuando tienes (un) catarro?
¿Vas al médico si tienes la gripe?
¿Quién es el médico de tu familia?
¿Dónde está su consultorio?
Si te da una receta, ¿adónde vas?

Las emociones Use this *paper file folder* organizer to keep track of happenings or events that cause you to feel a certain way.

 **Fold** four sheets of paper (8½" x 11") in half like a *hamburger*. Leave one side one inch longer than the other side.

Step 2 On each sheet, **fold** the one-inch tab over the short side, forming an envelopelike fold.

 **Place** the four sheets side-by-side, then move each fold so that the tabs are exposed.

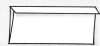 Moving left to right, **cut** staggered tabs in each fold, 2⅛" wide. Fold the tabs upward.

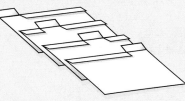

Step 5 **Glue** the ends of the folders together. On each tab, write an emotion you sometimes feel. Pay attention to when it is that you feel happy, sad, nervous, etc. Describe the situation in Spanish and file it in the correct pocket.

Entrevista

The **Entrevista** activity reinforces students' ability to interact with peers in Spanish in a real-life situation. This task recombines material the student has already learned. Students of all ability levels will be able to perform this task.

PLEGABLES Study Organizer

This foldable will help students organize, display, and arrange data as they learn how to talk about how they feel in Spanish. You may wish to encourage them to add information from each unit as they continue to expand upon their ability to describe situations and emotions.

A *paper file folder organizer* foldable is also ideal for having students add information to different categories over a period of time.

73

PASO 4
Más cultura y lectura

 ¡OJO! This reading is optional. You may skip it completely, have the entire class read it, have only several students read it and report to the class, or assign it for extra credit.

✿ National Standards

Cultures
The reading about clinics and the related activities give students an understanding of medical services in the Spanish-speaking world.

Comparisons
In this selection students learn that, unlike clinics in the United States, Spanish and Latin American clinics can be private hospitals.

PRESENTATION

STEP 1 After the students read the selection, ask them to state the main difference between clinics in the United States and those in many Hispanic countries.

STEP 2 You may wish to use the **¿Comprendes?** activities as an informal quiz to find out how well the students understood the reading.

> **Learning from Photos**
> *(page 74)* This art-nouveau-style building, which houses a clinic, is in Palma de Mallorca, Spain.

PASO 4
Más cultura y lectura

Una clínica

Una clínica. Palma de Mallorca

▲ ¿Qué es una clínica en inglés? Pues, una clínica es un establecimiento hospitalario o médico adonde pueden ir los enfermos para recibir asistencia médica gratis o a precio módico. Hay muchas clínicas de este tipo también en España y en los países hispanos.

Pero en español «clínica» tiene otro significado[1]. Una clínica puede ser también un hospital privado. Muchas veces un médico o un grupo de médicos son los dueños o propietarios de la clínica. Algunas clínicas en España y Latinoamérica son muy buenas y muy elegantes.

[1]significado *meaning*

¿Comprendes?

A. In English give a description of the two types of **clínicas** that exist in the Spanish-speaking world.
B. Describe a clinic in the United States.

ANSWERS TO ¿Comprendes?

A. *Answers will vary but may include:*
In Spain and Latin America there are two types of **clínicas.** Some offer patients medical care at reduced prices or at no cost. Others are private hospitals owned by the doctors. They can be very elegant.

B. *Answers will vary but may include:*
Generally, a clinic in the United States is an establishment where patients receive care at a reduced price.

Conexiones

Las ciencias naturales

La nutrición

Good nutrition is very important. What we eat can determine if we will enjoy good or poor health. For this reason, it is important to have a balanced diet and avoid the temptation to eat **chuchería** (junk food).

Comer bien

Si queremos estar de buena salud, es necesario comer una variedad de vegetales, frutas, granos, cereales y carne.

Calorías

El número de calorías que necesita una persona depende de su metabolismo, de su tamaño[1] y de su nivel[2] de actividad física. Los adolescentes, por ejemplo, necesitan más calorías que los ancianos porque son muy activos.

Vitaminas

Las vitaminas son indispensables para el funcionamiento del cuerpo humano. Esta tabla indica algunas fuentes[3] de las vitaminas que necesita el cuerpo humano.

VITAMINA	FUENTE
A	vegetales, leche, algunas frutas
B	carne, huevos, leche, cereales, vegetales verdes
C	frutas cítricas, tomates, lechuga
D	leche, huevos, pescado
E	aceites[4], vegetales, huevos, cereales

[1]tamaño *size*   [3]fuentes *sources*
[2]nivel *level*   [4]aceites *oils*

¿Comprendes?

A. Contesten. *(Answer.)*
1. ¿Qué tenemos que comer cada día?
2. ¿De qué depende el número de calorías que necesita una persona?
3. ¿Quiénes requieren más calorías? ¿Los adolescentes o los ancianos?
4. ¿Por qué necesitan más calorías los adolescentes?
5. ¿Contienen muchas vitaminas las frutas y los vegetales?

B. Make a list of all the cognates in this reading.

C. There are other elements the body needs.

proteínas	grasas o lípidos
carbohidratos	minerales

Can you guess the meanings of these words?

¡OJO! The readings in the **Conexiones** section are optional. They focus on some of the major disciplines taught in schools and universities. The vocabulary is useful for discussing such topics as history, literature, art, economics, business, science, etc. You may choose any of the following ways to do the readings in the **Conexiones** sections.

Independent reading Have students read the selections and do the post-reading activities as homework, which you collect. This option is least intrusive on class time and requires a minimum of teacher involvement.

Homework with in-class follow-up Assign the readings and post-reading activities as homework. Review and discuss the material in class the next day.

Intensive in-class activity This option includes a pre-reading vocabulary presentation, in-class reading and discussion, assignment of the activities for homework, and a discussion of the assignment in class the following day.

ANSWERS TO ¿Comprendes?

A.
1. Cada día tenemos que comer una variedad de vegetales, frutas, granos, cereales y carne.
2. El número de calorías que necesita una persona depende de su metabolismo, de su tamaño y de su nivel de actividad física.
3. Los adolescentes requieren más calorías.
4. Los adolescentes necesitan más calorías porque son muy activos.
5. Sí, las frutas y los vegetales contienen muchas vitaminas.

B. *Answers will vary but may include:*
necesario, variedad, vegetales, frutas, granos, cereales, número, calorías, persona, depende, metabolismo, actividad, física, adolescentes, ejemplo, activos, vitaminas, indispensables, humano, tabla, indica

C.
proteins, carbohydrates, fats or lipids, minerals

¡Hablo como un pro!

This unique section gives students the opportunity to speak freely and say whatever they want on their own. The illustrations serve to remind students of precisely what they know how to say in Spanish. There are no depictions of activities that students do not have the ability to describe or talk about in Spanish. The art in this section recombines all that the students learned in the particular unit and in addition frequently recombines the topic or situation of the particular unit with that of another unit for additional reinforcement.

You can use this section in many ways. Some possibilities are:
1. Have students look at the illustrations and just identify items by giving the correct Spanish words.
2. Have students make up sentences about what they see in the illustrations.
3. Have students make up questions about the illustrations. They can call on another class member to respond if you do this as an entire class activity, or you may prefer to allow students to work in small groups. This activity is extremely beneficial because it enables students to actively use the interrogative words.
4. You may wish to ask questions and call on students to answer.
5. Have students look at the illustrations and give a complete oral review of what they see.
6. Have two students work together and make up a conversation based on the illustrations.
7. Have students look at the illustrations and write a paragraph (or paragraphs) about them in class.

You can also use this section as an assessment or testing tool, taking into account individual differences by having students go from simple to quite complicated tasks.

76

¡Hablo como un pro!

Tell all you can about the following illustration.

The assessment can be either oral or written. You may wish to use the rubrics provided on pages T22–T23 as you give students the following directions.
1. Identify the topic or situation of these illustrations.
2. Identify as many items as you can and give the Spanish words. Don't forget to include actions you see.
3. Give as many sentences as you can to describe the illustrations.
4. Go over your sentences and put them in the best sequence possible.
5. Polish your sentences and sequencing to give a coherent story based on the illustrations.

Universal Access

When talking about the illustration, **students with learning difficulties** may just give random sentences. **Advanced students** will give a coherent story. You may wish to have **advanced students** write a paragraph about the illustration.

Vocabulario

Describing minor health problems

la salud	el catarro	enfermo(a)	toser
la fiebre	el dolor	cansado(a)	
los escalofríos	un pañuelo	estornudar	
la gripe	un kleenex	estar resfriado(a)	

Speaking with the doctor

¿Qué tienes?	el/la médico(a)	abrir la boca
¿Qué te pasa?	el síntoma	guardar cama
la consulta,	la diagnosis	recetar
el consultorio	la alergia	Me duele...
el/la enfermo(a)	la inyección	Tengo dolor de...
el/la paciente	examinar	

Describing some emotions

contento(a)	de buen humor
triste	nervioso(a)
pobre	tranquilo(a)
de mal humor	

Identifying more parts of the body

la garganta	la boca
los ojos	el estómago

Speaking with a pharmacist

la farmacia
el/la farmacéutico(a)
la receta
el medicamento, la medicina
la aspirina
el antibiótico
la pastilla, la píldora, la tableta
la dosis
vender, despachar

Paso 4: Vocabulario

Vocabulario

Vocabulary Review

The words and phrases in the **Vocabulario** have been taught for productive use in this unit. They are summarized here as a resource for both student and teacher. This list also serves as a convenient resource for the **¡Te toca a ti!** activities on pages 66 and 67. There are approximately seventeen cognates in this vocabulary list. Have students find them.

¡OJO! You will notice that the vocabulary list here is not translated. This has been done intentionally, since we feel that by the time students have finished the material in the unit they should be familiar with the meanings of all the words. If there are several words they still do not know, we recommend that they refer to the **Paso 1 Palabras** and **Paso 2 Palabras** sections in the unit or go to the dictionaries at the end of this book to find the meanings. However, if you prefer that your students have the English translations, please refer to Vocabulary Transparency 2.6, where you will find all these words with their translations.

Planning for Unit 3

CORRELATIONS

National Standards

Communication Standard 1.1
pages 82, 83, 85, 88, 92, 93, 94, 97, 98, 104, 109, 110

Communication Standard 1.2
pages 88, 97, 98, 100–101, 112–113, 114, 115

Communication Standard 1.3
pages 89, 93, 97, 105, 110

Cultures Standard 2.1
pages 100–101

Cultures Standard 2.2
pages 108, 112–113

Connections Standard 3.1
pages 100–101, 112–113, 114, 115

Connections Standard 3.2
pages 100–101, 105, 112–113

Comparisons Standard 4.1
pages 94, 99

Comparisons Standard 4.2
page 115

Communities Standard 5.1
page 105

PACING AND PRIORITIES

The unit content is color coded below to assist you in planning.

■ required   ■ recommended   ■ optional

Paso 1 (required)   *Days 1–8*
■ Palabras
  En el aeropuerto
■ Formas
  Hacer, poner, traer y **salir** en el presente
  El presente progresivo

Paso 2 (required)   *Days 9–16*
■ Palabras
  Un vuelo
■ Formas
  Saber y **conocer** en el presente
■ Conversación
  Está saliendo nuestro vuelo.

Paso 3 (recommended)   *Days 17–24*
■ Pronunciación
  Las consonantes **g, j**
■ Cultura y lectura
  El avión en la América del Sur
■ Repaso
■ ¡Te toca a ti!
■ Assessment

Paso 4 (optional)
■ Diversiones
■ Más cultura y lectura
  Un vuelo interesante
  Una astronauta latina
■ Conexiones
  Conversiones

RESOURCE GUIDE

SECTION		PAGES	SECTION RESOURCES

Paso 1

Palabras	En el aeropuerto	80–83	▲ Vocabulary Transparencies 3.1–3.2 ◉ Audio CD 3 ∩ Audio Activities TE, pages 37–39 ▮ Workbook TE, pages 35–36 ▮ Quiz 1, page 15 ◉ ExamView® Pro
Formas	**Hacer, poner, traer** y **salir** en el presente El presente progresivo	84–86 87–89	◉ Audio CD 3 ∩ Audio Activities TE, pages 39–41 ▮ Workbook TE, pages 37–40 ▮ Quizzes 2–3 pages 16–17 ◉ ExamView® Pro

Paso 2

Palabras	Un vuelo	90–93	▲ Vocabulary Transparencies 3.3–3.4 ◉ Audio CD 3 ∩ Audio Activities TE, pages 42–44 ▮ Workbook TE, pages 41–42 ▮ Quiz 4, page 18 ◉ ExamView® Pro
Formas	**Saber** y **conocer** en el presente	94–97	◉ Audio CD 3 ∩ Audio Activities TE, pages 44–45 ▮ Workbook TE, pages 42–44 ▮ Quiz 5, page 19 ◉ ExamView® Pro

Paso 3

Conversación	Está saliendo nuestro vuelo.	98	◉ Audio CD 3 ∩ Audio Activities TE, pages 45–46 ▮ Workbook TE, page 45
Pronunciación	Las consonantes **g, j**	99	▲ Pronunciation Transparency P 3 ◉ Audio CD 3 ∩ Audio Activities TE, page 47 ▮ Workbook TE, page 45
Cultura y lectura	El avión en la América del Sur	100–101	◉ Audio CD 3 ∩ Audio Activities TE, page 48 ▮ Workbook TE, page 46
Repaso		102–103	◉ Audio CD 3 ∩ Audio Activities TE, page 48 ▮ Workbook TE, page 47 ▮ Tests, pages 29–44
¡Te toca a ti!		104–105	◉ Audio CD 3 ∩ Audio Activities TE, pages 49–52 ▮ Workbook TE, pages 48–51
Assessment		106–107	▲ Vocabulary Transparency 3.5 ▮ Tests, pages 29–44 ◉ ExamView® Pro, Unit 3 ▮ Performance Assessment, Tasks 5–6

Paso 4

Diversiones		108–111	▮ Workbook TE, page 52
Más cultura y lectura	Un vuelo interesante Una astronauta latina	112–113 114	▮ Tests, page 35 ▮ Tests, page 35
Conexiones	Conversiones	115	▮ Tests, page 36

Using Your Resources for Unit 3

Transparencies

Bellringer 3.1–3.7

Vocabulary V 3.1–3.6

Assessment A 3

Songs S 3

Workbook

Paso 1 Vocabulary and Structure pages 35–40

Paso 2 Vocabulary and Structure pages 41–44

Conversation and Reading pages 45–46

Repaso, ¡Te toca a ti!, Diversiones pages 47–52

Audio Program and Audio Activities Booklet

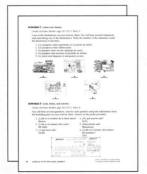

Paso 1 Vocabulary and Structure pages 37–41

Paso 2 Vocabulary and Structure pages 42–45

Conversation, Pronunciation pages 46–48

Repaso, ¡Te toca a ti! pages 48–52

Vocabulary and Structure Quizzes, pages 15–22

Unit Tests, pages 29–44

ExamView® Pro, Unit 3

Timesaving Teacher Tools

TeacherWorks
All in One Teacher Planning

TeacherWorks™ is your all in one teacher resource center. Personalize lesson plans, access resources from the Teacher Wraparound Edition, connect to the Internet, or make a to-do list. These are only a few of the many features that can assist you in the planning and organizing of your lessons.

Includes:
- A calendar feature
- Access to all program blackline masters
- Standards correlations and more

Test Bank software for Macintosh and Windows makes creating, editing, customizing, and printing tests quick and easy.

FOLDABLES™
Study Organizer

Manipulatives The foldable activities give students of all learning styles the opportunity to excel in a nontraditional manner. Your students will love these hands-on activities!

Technology Resources

Spanish Online

In the Unit 3 online resources, you and your students will have a chance to learn more about travel in the Spanish-speaking world.

PuzzleMaker allows you to create crossword puzzles, jumble puzzles, and word searches in minutes or edit a database of key terms and puzzles to review unit vocabulary. You can choose English-Spanish puzzles or Spanish-English puzzles. The puzzles can be printed or played on the computer screen.

Canta con Justo This CD contains songs sung by a young Argentine singer, Justo Lamas, which are specifically geared to review and expand upon the vocabulary learned in each unit. Students will enjoy listening to these songs while they learn from them.

¡En vivo! This music video of Justo Lamas performing his songs live in concert gives your students a chance to experience the songs in a different way while reinforcing the language skills they are learning!

Unidad 3

Preview

In this unit, students will learn vocabulary associated with air travel and airports. In order to describe their travels, students will learn the present tense of verbs with a **g** in the **yo** form, the present progressive, and the verbs **conocer** and **saber**.

Students will also learn about the importance of air travel in South America because of its geographical characteristics.

National Standards

Communication

In Unit 3 students will communicate in Spanish on the following topics:

- checking in at the airport
- going through security and finding their departure gate
- going through customs and passport control
- claiming their bags

Students will obtain and provide information about taking a flight and about procedures at an airport. They will learn to engage in conversations with various types of airline employees.

Spanish Online

The **Glencoe World Languages Web site** (spanish.glencoe.com) offers options that enable you and your students to experience the Spanish-speaking world via the Internet. For each **Unidad,** there are activities, games, and quizzes. In addition, an *Enrichment* section offers students an opportunity to visit Web sites related to the theme of the unit.

Unidad 3 Un viaje en avión

Objetivos

In this unit, you will learn to:

- check in for a flight
- get through the airport after deplaning
- tell what you or others are currently doing
- tell what you know and whom you know
- discuss the importance of air travel in South America

¡Me encanta viajar!

Spotlight on Culture

El Aeropuerto Internacional de las Américas, La República Dominicana *(pages 78–79)*
El Aeropuerto Internacional de las Américas is located east of Santo Domingo, about a 30-minute drive from the heart of the city. **Las Américas** is on the southern coast of the island. The Dominican Republic has more international airports than any other Caribbean island, but **Las Américas** is best when flying to Santo Domingo, Boca Chica, Juan Dolio, and San Pedro de Macorís.

Palabras

1 PREPARATION

RESOURCE MANAGER

Vocabulary Transparencies 3.1–3.2
Audio Activities TE, pages 37–39
Audio CD 3
Workbook, pages 35–36
Quiz 1, page 15
ExamView® Pro

Bellringer Review

Use BRR Transparency 3.1 or write the following on the board.
Write a sentence using each of the following phrases.

en carro (en coche)   **en taxi**
en el bus escolar   **ir a pie**

2 PRESENTATION

STEP 1 Have students close their books. Using Vocabulary Transparencies 3.1–3.2, introduce the words on pages 80–81. Have students repeat after you or Audio CD 3 as you point to the illustrations.

STEP 2 Ask questions such as **¿Es el aeropuerto? ¿Es el taxi? ¿Qué es?**

STEP 3 When presenting the contextualized sentences, you may wish to ask questions that progress from simple to more complex.

Universal Access

The following are examples of categories of questions.
(1) **¿Hace Sandra un viaje?**
(2) **¿Hace un viaje a España o a la América del Sur?**
(3) **¿Quién hace un viaje?**
    ¿Adónde hace un viaje?
As material is reviewed and reintroduced, **students with learning difficulties** can be called upon to answer more challenging questions.

Palabras   En el aeropuerto

el pasaporte

el aeropuerto

el taxi

el billete,
el boleto

la pantalla de
salidas y llegadas

¿Me permite ver su pasaporte, por favor? ¿Y su boleto?

Buenos Aires 10:20

la agente

el agente

el mostrador de
la línea aérea

el equipaje
de mano

la báscula

la maleta

el equipaje

Tomás hace un viaje.
La agente está revisando el pasaporte
 y el boleto.

Sandra hace un viaje a la América del Sur.
Toma un vuelo a Buenos Aires.
Ahora está facturando su equipaje.
Pone su maleta en la báscula.

Unidad 3: Un viaje en avión

Total Physical Response

If students don't already know the meaning of **llámalo, se para,** and **busca,** teach these expressions by using the appropriate gestures as you say each expression. Point to the trunk part of the taxi as you say **maletera.**
(Student 1), **ven acá. Imagínate que vas a hacer un viaje. Tienes que ir al aeropuerto. Aquí viene un taxi. Llámalo.**
El taxi se para. Pon tu maleta en la maletera.

Abre la puerta.
Sube al taxi y siéntate.
Llegas al aeropuerto. Págale al taxista.
Abre la puerta.
Baja (Bájate) del taxi.
Toma tu maleta.
Entra en el aeropuerto.
Mira la pantalla de salidas.
Busca el mostrador de la línea aérea.
Ve al mostrador de la línea aérea.
Pon tu maleta en la báscula.
Gracias, *(Student 1).* **Siéntate.**

la tarjeta de embarque

el número
del vuelo

la puerta
de salida

el número
del asiento

el control de seguridad

Los pasajeros están pasando por el control de seguridad.

el avión

la puerta de salida

Los pasajeros están esperando en la puerta de salida.
El avión sale de la puerta 14.
El vuelo sale a tiempo.

No sale tarde. No sale con una demora.
Los pasajeros están abordando el avión.
Los pasajeros están embarcando.

3 PRACTICE

¿Qué palabra necesito?

¡OJO! When students are doing the **¿Qué palabra necesito?** activities, accept any answer that makes sense. The purpose of these activities is to have students use the new vocabulary. They are not factual recall activities. Thus, it is not necessary for students to remember specific factual information from the vocabulary presentation when answering. If you wish, have students use the photo on this page as a stimulus, when possible.

Historieta Each time **Historieta** appears, it means that the answers to the activity form a short story. Encourage students to look at the title of the **Historieta,** since it can help them do the activity.

Writing Development
Have students write the answers to Activity 1 in paragraph form to illustrate how the answers to all the items tell a story.

Learning from Photos
(page 82) One of Barcelona's most famous streets is the **Ramblas,** a continuous street made up of many sections, each with its own name. It is a bustling street with many kiosks, flower stalls, and people out for a stroll. The **Rambla** seen here is the **Rambla de las Flores** but the street sign today will say **Rambla de les Flors. Catalán** is the language that one hears today throughout Cataluña.

¿Qué palabra necesito?

1 **Historieta** Un viaje a Barcelona

 Contesten con **sí.** *(Answer with sí.)*

1. ¿Hace Mara un viaje a España?
2. ¿Va con su tía?
3. ¿Están en el aeropuerto?
4. ¿Está hablando su tía con la agente en el mostrador?
5. ¿Está facturando su equipaje a Barcelona?
6. ¿Pone su equipaje en la báscula?
7. ¿Tiene que revisar los pasaportes la agente?
8. ¿Le da la agente las tarjetas de embarque a la tía de Mara?

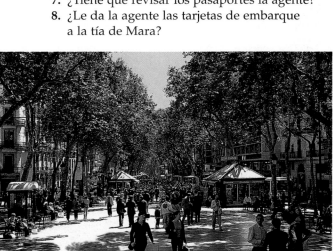

Rambla de las Flores, Barcelona, España

2 **La tarjeta de embarque** Den la información.
(Give the following information.)
1. el nombre de la línea aérea
2. el número del vuelo
3. el destino del vuelo
4. el aeropuerto de salida
5. la hora de embarque
6. la fecha del vuelo, el día que sale

Unidad 3: Un viaje en avión

ANSWERS TO ¿Qué palabra necesito?

1
1. Sí, Mara hace un viaje a España.
2. Sí, va con su tía.
3. Sí, están en el aeropuerto.
4. Sí, su tía está hablando con la agente en el mostrador.
5. Sí, está facturando su equipaje a Barcelona.
6. Sí, pone su equipaje en la báscula.
7. Sí, la agente tiene que revisar los pasaportes.
8. Sí, la agente le da las tarjetas de embarque a la tía de Mara.

2
1. AirEuropa
2. 9002
3. Madrid
4. Palma Mallorca
5. 8:00
6. 20 de agosto

PASO 1

3 **Juego** **El vuelo** ¿Sí o no? *(True or false?)*

1. La pantalla en el aeropuerto indica los vuelos que llegan y los vuelos que salen.

2. Es necesario tener un boleto de avión para tomar un vuelo.

3. Un pasajero puede tomar un taxi o un autobús para ir del aeropuerto al centro de la ciudad.

4. Los pasajeros tienen que facturar su equipaje de mano.

5. El vuelo sale a tiempo. Hay una demora.

4 **En el aeropuerto** Work with a classmate. Discuss all you see in these illustrations of an airport.

Paso 1: Palabras

ochenta y tres 83

ANSWERS TO **¿Qué palabra necesito?**

3
1. Sí
2. Sí
3. Sí
4. No
5. No

4 *Answers will vary. Students will use the vocabulary relating to airports and travel. Students may also incorporate family members in their descriptions.*

Formas

1 PREPARATION

RESOURCE MANAGER

Audio Activities TE, pages 39–41
Audio CD 3
Workbook, pages 37–40
Quizzes 2–3, pages 16–17
ExamView® Pro

Bellringer Review

Use BRR Transparency 3.2 or write the following on the board.
Do the following.
1. Write the names of five things that you have.
2. Write down five things that you and a friend have to do.

2 PRESENTATION

Hacer, poner, traer y salir en el presente

STEP 1 Have students open their books to page 84. You may wish to say the infinitives from Item 1 aloud.

STEP 2 Then point to yourself as you say **hago, pongo, traigo, salgo.**

STEP 3 Write the **yo** forms on the board and ask students what they have in common.

STEP 4 Have students repeat the **yo** forms.

STEP 5 Write the other forms on the board and indicate to students that they are the same as any regular **-er** or **-ir** verb they have already learned. These endings actually serve as a review of **-er** and **-ir** verbs.

Formas

Hacer, poner, traer y salir en el presente
Telling what people do

1. The verbs **hacer** *(to do, to make)*, **poner** *(to put, to place)*, **traer** *(to bring)*, and **salir** *(to leave)* have an irregular **yo** form. The **yo** form has a **g.** All other forms are regular.

	hacer	poner	traer	salir
yo	hago	pongo	traigo	salgo
tú	haces	pones	traes	sales
él, ella, Ud.	hace	pone	trae	sale
nosotros(as)	hacemos	ponemos	traemos	salimos
vosotros(as)	hacéis	ponéis	traéis	salís
ellos, ellas, Uds.	hacen	ponen	traen	salen

2. Remember that the verb **tener** has a **g** in the **yo** form. **Tener** also has a stem change. The verb **venir** *(to come)* follows the same pattern.

tener	venir
tengo	vengo
tienes	vienes
tiene	viene
tenemos	venimos
tenéis	venís
tienen	vienen

Machu Picchu, Perú

STEP 6 For Item 2, have students repeat the forms of the verb **venir.** Point out that it has a **g** in the **yo** form; it also has a stem change. Indicate the similarity between **venir** and **tener,** which they already know.

Learning from Photos

(page 84) Nothing prepares the visitor for the splendor of Machu Picchu in Perú, an imposing architectural complex in a most incredible natural setting. Discovered by U.S. Senator Hiram Bingham in 1911, there are many theories about the city. It could have been part of a fortress chain to protect the Incas from sporadic raids, or it may have been a religious sanctuary or training area for the noble youth of the empire.

¿Cómo lo digo?

5 Historieta **Un viaje en avión**

Contesten. *(Answer.)*

1. ¿Haces un viaje?
2. ¿Haces un viaje a Perú?
3. ¿Haces el viaje con un grupo de alumnos?
4. ¿Sales para el aeropuerto con tus padres?
5. ¿Traes mucho equipaje?
6. En el aeropuerto, ¿pones el equipaje en la báscula?
7. ¿Sales en el vuelo 201?
8. ¿Sales de la puerta número ocho?

Puente sobre el río Rímac,
Lima, Perú

6 **Haciendo la maleta** Haces un viaje. Antes, haces tus maletas.
¿Qué pones en la maleta?

 1.
 2.
 3.
 4.
 5.
 6.
 7.
 8.
 9.
 10.

Paso 1: Formas

ochenta y cinco ✻ 85

3 PRACTICE (continued)

8 Activity 8 has students use all forms.

Universal Access

Have **advanced learners** retell the story from Activity 8 in their own words.

Learning from Photos

(page 86, bottom) This is a beach scene in the world-famous resort of Marbella, on Spain's southern **Costa del Sol.**

7 **Historieta** **Al aeropuerto**

Sigan el modelo. *(Follow the model.)*

> **Ellos hacen un viaje. →**
> **Sí, ellos hacen un viaje y nosotros también hacemos un viaje.**

1. Ellos hacen un viaje a Perú.
2. Ellos salen para el aeropuerto.
3. Ellos traen mucho equipaje.
4. Ellos salen en el mismo vuelo.
5. Ellos vienen al aeropuerto en autobús.

Arequipa, Perú

8 **Historieta** **Un viaje a Marbella** Completen. *(Complete.)*

Yo ___1___ (hacer) un viaje a Marbella. Marbella ___2___ (estar) en la Costa del Sol en el sur de España. Mi amiga Sandra ___3___ (hacer) el viaje también. Nosotros ___4___ (hacer) el viaje en avión hasta Málaga y luego ___5___ (ir) a tomar el autobús a Marbella.

—¡Ay, ay, Sandra! Pero tú ___6___ (traer) mucho equipaje.

—No, yo no ___7___ (traer) mucho. ___8___ (Tener) sólo dos maletas. Tú exageras. Tú también ___9___ (venir) con mucho equipaje.

—¡Oye! ¿A qué hora ___10___ (salir) nuestro vuelo?

—No ___11___ (salir) hasta las seis y media. Nosotros ___12___ (tener) mucho tiempo.

La playa, Marbella, España

ANSWERS TO **¿Cómo lo digo?**

7

1. Sí, ellos hacen un viaje a Perú y nosotros también hacemos un viaje a Perú.
2. Sí, ellos salen para el aeropuerto y nosotros también salimos para el aeropuerto.
3. Sí, ellos traen mucho equipaje y nosotros también traemos mucho equipaje.
4. Sí, ellos salen en el mismo vuelo y nosotros también salimos en el mismo vuelo.
5. Sí, ellos vienen al aeropuerto en autobús y nosotros también venimos al aeropuerto en autobús.

8

1. hago
2. está
3. hace
4. hacemos
5. vamos
6. traes
7. traigo
8. Tengo
9. vienes
10. sale
11. sale
12. tenemos

 El presente progresivo

Describing an action in progress

1. You use the present progressive in Spanish to express an action in progress, an action that is presently taking place.

2. To form the present progressive you use the verb **estar** and the present participle. Study the forms of a present participle.

hablar	comer	vivir	hacer	salir
habl-	com-	viv-	hac-	sal-
hablando	comiendo	viviendo	haciendo	saliendo

The verbs **leer** and **traer** have a **y**.

leyendo	trayendo

Ciudad de México

3. Study the following examples of the present progressive.

José **está haciendo** un viaje a México con su clase de español.
Ahora **está esperando** la salida de su vuelo.
José **está mirando** su tarjeta de embarque.
Sandra **está leyendo** las salidas en la pantalla.

Paso 1: Formas

ochenta y siete 87

1 PREPARATION

Bellringer Review

Use BRR Transparency 3.3 or write the following on the board.
In Spanish, write a list of at least fifteen action words you have learned so far. Then separate them into three columns: **-ar, -er, -ir.**

2 PRESENTATION

 El presente progresivo

STEP 1 Have students open their books to page 87 and lead them through Item 1.

STEP 2 Give students other **-ar, -er,** and **-ir** verbs they know and have them give the present participle after they have seen how it is formed.

STEP 3 Now lead students through Items 2 and 3 on page 87.

STEP 4 Have students take out their Bellringer Review answers from page 87. Ask each student to choose a verb from their list and put it in the present progressive tense. For example: **Estoy bailando.**

3 PRACTICE

¿Cómo lo digo?

9 Have students read the conversation aloud using as much expression as possible.

¿Cómo lo digo?

9 **¿Qué estás haciendo aquí?** Practiquen la conversación.
(Practice the conversation.)

Galicia, España

10 **Historieta Un encuentro en el aeropuerto**
Contesten según la conversación.
(Answer based on the conversation.)

1. ¿Qué está haciendo Anita en el aeropuerto?
2. ¿De dónde está volviendo su padre?
3. ¿Adónde está viajando Sandra?
4. ¿Por qué está haciendo su familia un viaje a España?

Unidad 3: Un viaje en avión

ANSWERS TO **¿Cómo lo digo?**

10
1. Anita está esperando a su padre.
2. Su padre está volviendo de Puerto Rico.
3. Sandra está viajando a España.
4. Su familia está haciendo un viaje a España para visitar a sus abuelos.

11 Historieta Un viaje en avión

Contesten según se indica. *(Answer as indicated.)*

1. ¿Adónde están llegando los pasajeros? (al aeropuerto)
2. ¿Cómo están llegando? (en taxi)
3. ¿Adónde están viajando? (a la América del Sur)
4. ¿Cómo están haciendo el viaje? (en avión)
5. ¿Dónde están facturando el equipaje?
   (en el mostrador de la línea aérea)
6. ¿Qué está mirando el agente?
   (los boletos y los pasaportes)
7. ¿De qué puerta están saliendo los
   pasajeros para Argentina? (número siete)
8. ¿Qué están abordando? (el avión)

Una vista de Ushuaia, Argentina

12 Juego En la clase de español
Look around the room and tell what different students are doing right now in Spanish class.

For more practice using words and forms from **Paso 1,** do Activity 5 on page H6 at the end of this book.

UN POCO MÁS

ochenta y nueve 89

---

11 Have students retell the story from Activity 11 in their own words.

Learning from Photos

(page 89) This is a view of Ushuaia, the southernmost city in the world and the capital of the province of Tierra del Fuego in Argentina. Located 1,450 miles south of Buenos Aires, it was founded some 40 years after Darwin's expedition on the *Beagle*. It was originally a Protestant mission town. Ushuaia is right on the coast of the Straits of Magellan in the midst of waterfalls, glaciers, and snow-capped mountains. It is a rather desolate town, but the houses are painted warm, pastel colors. Industries are sheep raising, timber, fishing, and trapping.

Universal Access

Have **students with learning difficulties** tell one thing that someone is doing in the illustration in Activity 12. Have **average students** provide more information, and have **advanced learners** give a complete summary.

UN POCO MÁS This *InfoGap* activity will allow students to practice in pairs. The activity should be very manageable for them, since all vocabulary and structures are familiar to them.

ANSWERS TO ¿Cómo lo digo?

11

1. Los pasajeros están llegando al aeropuerto.
2. Están llegando en taxi.
3. Están viajando a la América del Sur.
4. Están haciendo el viaje en avión.
5. Están facturando el equipaje en el mostrador de la línea aérea.
6. El agente está mirando los boletos y los pasaportes.
7. Los pasajeros para Argentina están saliendo de la puerta número siete.
8. Están abordando el avión.

12 *Answers will vary. All answers will use the present progressive.*

Palabras

Palabras Un vuelo

1 PREPARATION

RESOURCE MANAGER

Vocabulary Transparencies 3.3–3.4
Audio Activities TE, pages 42–44
Audio CD 3
Workbook, pages 41–43
Quiz 4, page 18
ExamView® Pro

Bellringer Review

Use BRR Transparency 3.4 or write the following on the board.
Answer.
1. **¿Dónde vives?**
2. **¿Tienes parientes que viven en otra ciudad?**
3. **¿Dónde viven?**
4. **¿Visitan ustedes a sus parientes?**
5. **¿Cómo van a su casa?**

2 PRESENTATION

STEP 1 Have students look at Vocabulary Transparencies 3.3–3.4 as they repeat each word or expression after you or Audio CD 3.

STEP 2 As you present the new vocabulary, you may intersperse comprehension questions building from simple to more complex.

About the Spanish Language

The expression *to go through passport control* is expressed as either **pasar por el control de pasaportes** or **pasar por inmigración** in Spanish.

Palabras Un vuelo 🎧

Un avión está despegando.

Otro avión está aterrizando.

el asistente de vuelo   la asistenta de vuelo

¿Sabes a qué hora vamos a aterrizar?

Sí, a las quince veinte.

el comandante

el copiloto

La tripulación trabaja a bordo del avión. Los asistentes de vuelo no conocen a los pasajeros pero saben sus nombres.

IBERIA

Después de aterrizar, los pasajeros desembarcan.

Unidad 3: Un viaje en avión

Total Physical Response

(Student 1), ven acá, por favor.
Tu vuelo está llegando. Vas a desembarcar.
Toma tu equipaje de mano.
Dile «adiós» a la asistenta de vuelo.
Sal o baja del avión.
Aquí estás en el control de pasaportes.
Pasa por el control de pasaportes.
Dale tu pasaporte al agente.

Tienes que reclamar tu equipaje. Está llegando. Tienes dos maletas.
Aquí llega una de tus maletas. Recoge tu maleta.
Aquí viene la otra. Tómala.
Ahora estás en la aduana.
Abre tu maleta para la agente de aduana.
Gracias, *(Student 1).* Siéntate.

Los pasajeros tienen que pasar por el control de pasaportes (la inmigración) cuando llegan de un país extranjero.

Los pasajeros están reclamando (recogiendo) sus maletas.

la aduana

La agente de aduana abre las maletas. Está inspeccionando el equipaje.

3 PRACTICE

¿Qué palabra necesito?

1 After going over Activity 1, have students retell the story in their own words.

Learning from Photos

(page 92) This plane is taking off from the Quito International Airport. Note that the plane must make a steep climb to immediately pass over the Andes.

¿Qué palabra necesito?

1 **Historieta La llegada** Contesten. *(Answer.)*

1. Cuando el avión aterriza, ¿abordan o desembarcan los pasajeros?
2. ¿Tienen que pasar por el control de pasaportes cuando llegan de un país extranjero?
3. ¿Van los pasajeros al reclamo de equipaje?
4. ¿Reclaman su equipaje?
5. ¿Tienen que pasar por la aduana?
6. ¿Abre las maletas el agente?

Un avión despega. Quito, Ecuador

2 Pareo Busquen una palabra relacionada.
(Find the related word.)

1. asistir   a. la llegada
2. controlar   b. la salida
3. reclamar   c. el asistente, la asistenta
4. inspeccionar   d. el despegue
5. despegar   e. el aterrizaje
6. aterrizar   f. el control
7. salir   g. la inspección
8. llegar   h. el reclamo
9. embarcar   i. el vuelo
10. volar   j. el embarque

92 ❀ noventa y dos   Unidad 3: Un viaje en avión

ANSWERS TO ¿Qué palabra necesito?

1
1. Cuando el avión aterriza, los pasajeros desembarcan.
2. Sí, tienen que pasar por el control de pasaportes cuando llegan de un país extranjero.
3. Sí, los pasajeros van al reclamo de equipaje.
4. Sí, reclaman su equipaje.
5. Sí, tienen que pasar por la aduana.
6. Sí, el agente abre las maletas.

2
1. c   6. e
2. f   7. b
3. h   8. a
4. g   9. j
5. d   10. i

San Salvador, El Salvador

3 *Juego* **El viaje** ¿Sí o no? *(True or false?)*

1. El avión aterriza cuando empieza el vuelo.
2. Los pasajeros reclaman su equipaje a bordo del avión.
3. Los asistentes de vuelo conocen muy bien a todos los pasajeros porque son sus amigos.
4. El avión despega cuando llega a su destino.
5. Los agentes de la línea aérea que trabajan en el mostrador en el aeropuerto son miembros de la tripulación.
6. Un vuelo internacional es un vuelo que va a un país extranjero.

4 **Un viaje en avión** Work together in groups of four. Two of you have never flown and two of you are "big shots"—you have flown several times. Take turns asking and answering questions about taking a plane trip.

5 **Rompecabezas**

¡Rimas! How many words can you think of that rhyme with each of the following words?

1. maíz
2. suelo
3. goma
4. carpeta
5. vengo
6. mes

El aeropuerto, Ushuaia, Argentina

Paso 2: Palabras

noventa y tres ✺ 93

Formas

1 PREPARATION

RESOURCE MANAGER

Audio Activities TE, pages 44–45
Audio CD 3
Workbook, pages 42–44
Quiz 5, page 19
ExamView® Pro

Bellringer Review

Use BRR Transparency 3.5 or write the following on the board.
Visualize an airport. In Spanish, write five sentences telling what people are doing there. Use the present progressive.

2 PRESENTATION

Saber y conocer en el presente

¡OJO! These verb forms should be easy for students since only the **yo** form is new. Students will, however, need constant reinforcement with **yo sé.**

STEP 1 Have students repeat **sé** and **conozco** as they point to themselves. Explain to them that once again they are going to learn two verbs that are irregular in the **yo** form only.

STEP 2 Have students open their books to page 94 and repeat all forms of the verbs in Item 1. You may also wish to write the forms on the board.

STEP 3 Lead students through Items 2 and 3 concerning the specific uses of these verbs. Have students read all the model sentences aloud.

 Formas **Saber y conocer en el presente**
Telling what and whom you know

1. The verbs **saber** and **conocer** both mean *to know*. Note that like many Spanish verbs they have an irregular **yo** form in the present tense. All other forms are regular.

	saber	conocer
yo	sé	conozco
tú	sabes	conoces
él, ella, Ud.	sabe	conoce
nosotros(as)	sabemos	conocemos
vosotros(as)	*sabéis*	*conocéis*
ellos, ellas, Uds.	saben	conocen

Nota

Look what happens when **saber** stands alone. **Lo sé.** You must put **lo** before the verb. In the negative you have a choice. **No lo sé.** or **No sé.**

2. The verb **saber** means *to know a fact* or *to have information about something*. It also means *to know how to do something*.

> **Yo sé el número de nuestro vuelo.**
> **Pero no sabemos a qué hora sale.**
> **Yo sé jugar tenis.**

3. The verb **conocer** means *to know* in the sense of *to be acquainted with*. It is used to talk about people and complex or abstract concepts rather than simple facts.

> **Yo conozco a Luis.**
> **Teodoro conoce muy bien la literatura mexicana.**

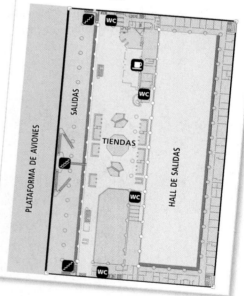

TERMINAL T2
2ª PLANTA
CENTRO COMERCIAL
En las tiendas del aeropuerto hay perfumería, joyería, tienda de ropa deportiva, zapatería y quiosco de periódicos y revistas. También hay tiendas de souvenirs, discos, guías y libros, etc.

Para tomar una cola o un café, puede escoger entre la cafetería o el Café Select.

SALIDAS · WC · TIENDAS · PLATAFORMA DE AVIONES · HALL DE SALIDAS

94 ✿ **noventa y cuatro**   **Unidad 3: Un viaje en avión**

Learning from Realia

(page 94) Have students look at the airport terminal pamphlet shown here. Have them describe as many things as possible that they can do while waiting for their flight.

¿Cómo lo digo?

6 **Mi vuelo** Contesten. *(Answer.)*

1. ¿Sabes el número de tu vuelo?
2. ¿Sabes a qué hora sale?
3. ¿Sabes de qué puerta va a salir?
4. ¿Sabes la hora de tu llegada a Cancún?
5. ¿Conoces al comandante del vuelo?
6. ¿Conoces a mucha gente en Cancún?

7 **Un poco de geografía y cultura**
Contesten. *(Answer.)*

1. ¿Saben ustedes dónde está Madrid?
2. ¿Conocen ustedes a Madrid?
3. ¿Saben ustedes el nombre de un autor español?
4. ¿Conocen ustedes la literatura española?
5. ¿Saben ustedes quién es el presidente de Estados Unidos?
6. ¿Conocen ustedes al presidente?

Don Quijote y Sancho Panza

El oso y el madroño. Madrid

3 **PRACTICE**

¿Cómo lo digo?

6 Activity 6 focuses on the **yo** forms of **saber** and **conocer.**

Learning from Photos

(page 95, top) This statue of Don Quijote and Sancho Panza stands in Madrid, in honor of the famous novel, *El Quijote,* by Miguel de Cervantes Saavedra.
(page 95, bottom) This tile mosaic depicts the bronze statue of Madrid's official symbol, a bear and a strawberry tree—**el oso y el madroño**—found on the **Puerta del Sol.**

ANSWERS TO ¿Cómo lo digo?

6
1. Sí, sé el número de mi vuelo.
2. Sí, sé a qué hora sale.
3. Sí, sé de qué puerta va a salir.
4. Sí, sé la hora de mi llegada a Cancún.
5. Sí, (No, no) conozco al comandante del vuelo.
6. Sí, (No, no) conozco a mucha gente en Cancún.

7
1. Sí, (No, no) sabemos dónde está Madrid.
2. Sí, (No, no) conocemos a Madrid.
3. Sí, (No, no) sabemos el nombre de un autor español.
4. Sí, (No, no) conocemos la literatura española.
5. Sí, sabemos quien es el presidente de Estados Unidos.
6. Sí, (No, no) conocemos al presidente.

③ PRACTICE (continued)

¿Cómo lo digo?

⑧ Since all the other forms of **saber** and **conocer** are the same as those of regular verbs, Activity 8 makes students use all forms of these two verbs.

Universal Access

Have **advanced learners** give a summary of the conversation in their own words. Have **kinesthetic learners** come to the front of the class and act out the conversation with as much expression as possible. You may wish to have students pantomime or speak about the actions that are being discussed in the conversation. For example, one student might play Adela and go purchase a ticket, and another student might play Lola and say, **Soy panameña.**

Learning from Photos

(page 96) Construction of the **Puente de las Américas** began in 1958, and the bridge opened on **el Día de la Raza** in 1962. The bridge is a part of the **Carretera panamericana** that unifies Central and South America. The four-lane bridge is 118 meters above the sea and is 1,670 meters long. It was constructed of steel at a cost of twenty million dollars.

Puente de las Américas. Panamá

⑧ **Historieta** **Adela Del Olmo** Completen con **saber** o **conocer.**
(Complete with saber *or* conocer.*)*

Pepita	Sandra, ¿__1__ tú a Adela Del Olmo?
Sandra	Claro que __2__ a Adela. Ella y yo somos muy buenas amigas.
Pepita	¿__3__ tú que ella va a Panamá?
Sandra	¿Ella va a Panamá? No, yo no __4__ nada de su viaje. ¿Cuándo va a salir?
Pepita	Pues, ella no __5__ exactamente qué día va a salir. Pero __6__ que va a salir en junio. Ella va a hacer su reservación mañana. Yo __7__ que ella quiere tomar un vuelo directo.
Sandra	¿Adela __8__ Panamá?
Pepita	Creo que sí. Pero yo no __9__ definitivamente. Pero yo __10__ que ella __11__ a mucha gente en Panamá.
Sandra	¿Cómo es que ella __12__ a mucha gente allí?
Pepita	Pues, tú __13__ que ella tiene parientes en Panamá, ¿no?
Sandra	Ay, sí, es verdad. Yo __14__ que tiene familia en Panamá porque yo __15__ a su tía Lola. Y __16__ que ella es de Panamá.

 *For more practice using words and forms from **Paso 2**, do Activity 6 on page H7 at the end of this book.*

ANSWERS TO ¿Cómo lo digo? ————

⑧
1. conoces   9. sé
2. conozco   10. sé
3. Sabes   11. conoce
4. sé   12. conoce
5. sabe   13. sabes
6. sabe   14. sé
7. sé   15. conozco
8. conoce   16. sé

 This *InfoGap* activity will allow students to practice in pairs. The activity should be very manageable for them, since all vocabulary and structures are familiar to them.

96

9 🎮 **¿A quién conoces?** Work with a classmate. Think of someone in the class whom you know quite well. Tell your partner some things you know about this person. Don't say who it is. Your partner will guess. Take turns.

10 🎮 **Yo sé hacer muchas cosas.** Work in pairs and compete. In Spanish, tell all the things you know how to do. See who can give more things in two minutes.

11  **R o m p e c a b e z a s**

Unscramble the words below. Then unscramble the circled letters to reveal the name of a famous city.

1. t e l m a a   O _ _ _ _ _
2. u d n a a a   _ _ O _ _
3. x i a t   _ _ O
4. o t d o m s r a r   _ _ _ _ O _ _ _ _
5. a a d e g l l   _ _ _ _ O _
6. e d s g r e a p   O _ _ _ _ _ _
    _ _ _ _ _ _

Palacio Real, Madrid

Paso 2: Formas

Andas bien. ¡Adelante!

9 This is a good activity to use as a warm-up at the beginning of the class period.

Learning from Photos

(page 97) The Royal Palace in Madrid was commissioned in the 1700s by the first Bourbon king of Spain, Felipe V. The palace has 2,800 opulent rooms. The Palace is still used for some state functions but no monarch has lived there since 1931 when Alfonso XIII was forced out of the country by a very unhappy populace.

¡Adelante! At this point, all new material has been presented. Students have learned all the vocabulary and structure necessary to complete the unit. The conversation, cultural readings, and activities in **Paso 3** and **Paso 4** recycle all the material learned up to this point.

ANSWERS TO ¿Cómo lo digo?

9 *Answers will vary. Students should use the vocabulary from previous units in their descriptions.*

10 *Answers will vary. Students will use Yo sé + infinitive, using vocabulary from previous units, to tell the things they know how to do.*

11
1. maleta
2. aduana
3. taxi
4. mostrador
5. llegada
6. despegar
city: Madrid

Conversación

PASO 3

Conversación

1 PREPARATION

RESOURCE MANAGER

Audio Activities TE, pages 45–47
Audio CD 3
Workbook, pages 45–46

Bellringer Review

Use BRR Transparency 3.6 or write the following on the board. Complete with personal information.
Yo quiero hacer un viaje a ___.
Yo quiero visitar a ___.
Yo voy a ir en ___.
Yo voy a salir ___.

2 PRESENTATION

STEP 1 Tell students they are going to hear a conversation at the airport between a girl and her aunt who are about to take a plane trip.

STEP 2 Ask students to open their books to page 98 and follow along as you read the conversation aloud or have them listen to Audio CD 3.

STEP 3 After presenting the conversation, go over the **¿Comprendes?** activity. If students can answer the questions with relative ease, move on. Students should not be expected to memorize the conversation.

Universal Access

Have **students with learning difficulties** role-play the conversation with books open. Let **average students** role-play the conversation making any changes that make sense. Ask questions about their conversations. Have **advanced learners** make up their own conversations.

98

Está saliendo nuestro vuelo.

Señores pasajeros. Su atención, por favor. La compañía de aviación anuncia la salida de su vuelo ciento ocho con destino a San Salvador. Embarque inmediato por la puerta de salida número seis.

Tía Elena ¡Chist, Luisa! Están anunciando la salida de nuestro vuelo.

Luisa Sí, lo sé. ¿Tienes nuestras tarjetas de embarque?

Tía Elena Sí, sí. Ahora estoy buscando la puerta de salida número seis.

Luisa Allí está, tía.

Tía Elena ¡Qué suerte! Estamos saliendo a tiempo. No hay demora.

Luisa Sí, quiero llegar a tiempo. Tengo tantas ganas de ver a abuelita y a abuelito.

Tía Elena Sí, nena. Yo sé que van a estar muy contentos. Pero no te van a conocer—ya que eres una señorita.

¿Comprendes?

Contesten. *(Answer.)*
1. ¿Dónde están Luisa y su tía Elena?
2. ¿Qué están anunciando?
3. ¿Quién tiene las tarjetas de embarque?
4. ¿Qué está buscando la tía Elena?
5. ¿Quién sabe donde está?
6. ¿Están saliendo a tiempo?
7. ¿A quiénes van a visitar Luisa y su tía en San Salvador?
8. ¿Cómo van a estar sus abuelos?
9. ¿Van a conocer a Luisa?
10. ¿Cómo es ella ahora?

         Unidad 3: Un viaje en avión

Career Connection

Because of the popularity of international travel (for business and pleasure) to and from the Spanish-speaking world, Spanish is an important communication tool. Have students make a list of at least four professions in the travel industry for which Spanish would be useful or necessary. Have students try to arrange interviews with some people in these professions.

ANSWERS TO ¿Comprendes?

1. Luisa y su tía Elena están en el aeropuerto.
2. Están anunciando la salida de su vuelo.
3. La tía Elena tiene las tarjetas de embarque.
4. La tía Elena está buscando la puerta de salida número seis.
5. Luisa sabe donde está.
6. Sí, están saliendo a tiempo.
7. Luisa y su tía van a visitar a los abuelos de Luisa en San Salvador.
8. Sus abuelos van a estar muy contentos.
9. No, no van a conocer a Luisa.
10. Ella es una señorita ahora.

Pronunciación

Las consonantes g, j

The consonant **g** has two sounds, hard and soft. In combination with **a, o, u** (**ga, go, gu**), **g** is pronounced somewhat like the *g* in the English word *go*. To maintain this hard **g** sound with **e** or **i**, a **u** is placed after the **g**: **gue, gui**.

ga	*gue*	*gui*	*go*	*gu*
paga	**Rodríguez**	**guisante**	**goma**	**guante**
llega	**despegue**		**estómago**	**seguridad**
despega			**tengo**	

The Spanish **j** sound does not exist in English. In Spain, the **j** sound is very guttural. It comes from the throat. In Latin America, the **j** sound is much softer.

ja	*je*	*ji*	*jo*	*ju*
Jaime	**pasajero**	**Jiménez**	**joven**	**jugar**
hija	**equipaje**		**trabajo**	**junio**
roja	**viaje**		**ojos**	**julio**
trabaja	**tarjeta**			

In combination with **e** or **i**, **g** has the same sound as **j**. For this reason, you must pay particular attention to the spelling of words with **je, ji, ge,** and **gi**.

ge	*gi*
gente	**biología**
agente	**recogiendo**
recoge	**Gijón**

Trabalenguas

Repeat the following.

> **El hijo del viejo general José trabaja en junio en Gijón.**
> **El joven Jiménez trabaja en el garaje.**
> **La gente recoge su equipaje después del aterrizaje.**
> **La hija de Julia viaja con mucho equipaje.**

Refrán

Can you tell what the following proverb means?

Más vale pájaro en mano que cien volando.

Fun Facts

Spaniards and other citizens of the European Union no longer need a passport to travel to nations within the EU. Each country in the European Union does require, however, that its citizens carry a national identification card. In Spain it is called the **Cédula de Identidad.** This ID card can be used for travel within the EU.

Refrán

If students cannot guess what the proverb means, tell them, "A bird in the hand is worth two in the bush."

Pronunciación

STEP 1 Have students carefully repeat **ga, gue, gui, go, gu** after you or Audio CD 3.

Note: English speakers tend to make the **g** sound too hard when speaking Spanish. As students repeat **ga, gue, gui, go, gu,** indicate to them that the sound is produced very softly toward the back of the throat.

STEP 2 Now have students repeat the words after you.

STEP 3 Have students carefully repeat the sounds **ja, je, ji, jo, ju; ge, gi** after you or Audio CD 3.

¡OJO! This is another sound that is radically different in Spain and Latin America. The sound of the letter **j** is quite harsh in Spain, very guttural. It is similar to the German **ach.** In Latin America, however, it is a very soft sound. In many countries it is barely audible. Since the **g** and **j** can present spelling problems, it is recommended that you have students commit to memory the spelling of these words.

STEP 4 Now have them repeat the words after you.

STEP 5 Use Pronunciation Transparency P 3 to model the first sentence: **El hijo del viejo general José trabaja en junio en Gijón.**

STEP 6 Have students open their books to page 99. Call on individuals to read the sentences carefully.

STEP 7 All model sentences on page 99 can be used for dictation.

PASO 3

Cultura y lectura

Cultura y lectura

El avión en la América del Sur

1 PREPARATION

RESOURCE MANAGER

Audio Activities TE, page 48
Audio CD 3
Workbook, page 46

Bellringer Review

Use BRR Transparency 3.7 or write the following on the board.
In Spanish, write a list of the countries in South America that you know. Then list as many of their capitals as you can.

National Standards

Cultures
The reading and the related activities about airline travel in South America on pages 100–101 allow students to understand the importance of this mode of transportation on this continent.

2 PRESENTATION

PRE-READING

STEP 1 Do the Reading Strategy activity on this page. Then have students study the photos. Have them try to imagine what it is like to fly over the landscape they see in these photos.

READING

Present the reading in three segments. Call on an individual to read three sentences. Then ask comprehension questions. For example, questions for the first paragraph may be:
¿Cuál es un medio de transporte importante en la América del Sur?
¿Cómo es el continente sudamericano? ¿Toma mucho tiempo viajar de una ciudad a otra? ¿Por qué?

100

Reading Strategy

Identifying the main idea When reading, it is important to identify the main idea the author is expressing. Each paragraph usually discusses a different idea. The main idea is often found in the first or second sentence of a paragraph. Go through the reading quickly to find the main idea in each paragraph. Do not read every word. Once you know the main idea of the passage, go back and read it again more carefully.

Un pueblo andino en el valle del Urubamba, Perú

El volcán Osorno, Puerto Varas, Chile

100 ✤ **ciento**

El avión es un medio de transporte muy importante en la América del Sur. ¿Por qué? Pues, si ustedes no conocen la geografía de la América del Sur, tienen que mirar un mapa. Es un continente inmenso. Las distancias entre una ciudad y otra son muy largas. Por consiguiente, toma mucho tiempo viajar de una ciudad a otra, sobre todo[1] por tierra.

En muchos casos es imposible viajar de un lugar a otro por tierra. ¿Saben por qué? Pues, vamos a ver.

Aquí vemos los picos altos de los Andes que corren desde el norte hasta el sur del continente. Es imposible cruzar muchos picos andinos en carro o en autobús.

[1] sobre todo *above all*

Universal Access

It may be helpful for students, especially **visual learners**, to look at either the map of South America on page xxiii or Map Transparency M 3 and locate rivers, mountains, cities, and countries.

Geography Connection

The Amazon is the longest river in South America. It flows through Brazil and has many tributaries in Colombia, Ecuador, and Perú. Other important rivers of South America are **el Magdalena** (Colombia), **el Orinoco** (Venezuela), and **el Paraná** (Uruguay, Paraguay, and Argentina).

POST-READING
Have students explain in their own words why air travel is so important in South America.

Y aquí vemos la jungla o selva tropical del río Amazonas. El río Amazonas es el río más grande del mundo en volumen. Y una gran parte de la cuenca[2] del Amazonas es inhóspita e impenetrable.

Por estas razones[3], a todas horas del día y de la noche, muchos aviones sobrevuelan[4] el continente.

[2] cuenca *basin*
[3] estas razones *these reasons*
[4] sobrevuelan *fly over*

La cuenca amazónica, cerca de Iquitos, Perú

¿Comprendes?

A. Digan que **sí** o que **no**. *(Answer sí or no.)*
1. El continente sudamericano es muy pequeño.
2. El tren es un medio de transporte importante en la América del Sur.
3. En muchas partes de la América del Sur, es difícil viajar por tierra.
4. Los picos andinos son muy altos.
5. Las selvas tropicales están en los picos andinos.

B. Escojan la idea principal de esta lectura.
(Choose the main idea of this reading.)
1. Hay muchas montañas en la América del Sur.
2. El río Amazonas es el río más grande del mundo en volumen.
3. El avión es el medio de transporte más importante de la América del Sur porque las distancias son muy largas y muchas áreas son impenetrables.

3 PRACTICE

¿Comprendes?

A. and B. Allow students to refer to the reading to look up the answers, or you may use these activities for informal assessment.

Learning from Photos
(page 100, left) In this photo we see two indigenous women in a small town in the beautiful, fertile valley of the Urubamba River in Perú.
(page 100, bottom) Located in the Chilean lake district, the majestic Osorno Volcano, the largest in the district, is between **el lago Llanquihue** and **el lago de Todos los Santos.**
(page 101) These youngsters are rowing their canoe in one of the many tributaries of the Amazon. This photo was taken not far from Iquitos, Peru's Amazonian port. Canoes, such as this one, serve as the most important means of transportation for the many inhabitants of the small, isolated villages along the river banks. These children belong to the Bora indigenous tribe.

Paso 3: Cultura y lectura   ciento uno 101

Repaso

This section reviews the salient points from Unit 3. Students will review verbs with a **g** in the **yo** form including **venir,** and they will review the present progressive and the verbs **saber** and **conocer.**

1 PREPARATION

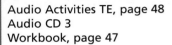
RESOURCE MANAGER

Audio Activities TE, page 48
Audio CD 3
Workbook, page 47

2 PRESENTATION

STEP 1 Have students quickly read aloud the verb forms and other examples given in the review section.

Learning from Photos

(page 102) **El Aeropuerto Internacional de Simón Bolívar** serves Caracas. It is located on the coast in the suburb of **Maiquetía.**

Repaso

1. In this unit, I learned the verbs **poner, hacer, traer,** and **salir** that have a **g** in the **yo** form. All other forms are regular.

> **pongo**   **hago**   **traigo**   **salgo**

2. **Venir,** like the verb **tener,** has a **g** in the **yo** form as well as a stem change.

venir		tener	
vengo	**venimos**	**tengo**	**tenemos**
vienes	*venís*	**tienes**	*tenéis*
viene	**vienen**	**tiene**	**tienen**

3. The present progressive expresses an action that is taking place at the moment. It is formed with the verb **estar** and the present participle.

estoy			
estás			
está	**hablando**	**comiendo**	**saliendo**
estamos			
estáis			
están			

El aeropuerto de Caracas. Venezuela

4. The verb **saber** means *to know a fact* or *to know how to do something.* The verb **conocer** means *to know* in the sense of *to be acquainted with.* **Saber** and **conocer** have an irregular **yo** form. All other forms are regular.

> **Yo sé su nombre y sé donde vive.**
> **Él sabe bailar muy bien.**
> **Conozco a Tomás y él conoce a toda mi familia.**

¡Pongo todo junto!

 1 **¿Qué haces?** Completen. *(Complete.)*

1. Yo _____ un viaje. (hacer)
2. Antes yo _____ la ropa en la maleta. (poner)
3. Nosotros _____ a tiempo. (salir)
4. Ellos _____ en avión y nosotros también _____ en avión. (salir)
5. ¿Adónde _____ (tú) un viaje? (hacer)

Hoyo de Manzanares,
Madrid, España

2 **Un viaje** Escriban las frases en el presente progresivo.
(Write the sentences in the present progressive.)

1. Él sale.
2. Hacemos un viaje.
3. Anuncian la salida de nuestro vuelo.
4. ¿Miras la pantalla?
5. Ella revisa el boleto y el pasaporte.

3 **¿Saber o conocer?** Completen con **saber** o **conocer.**
(Complete with saber *or* conocer.*)*

1. Yo _____ su número de teléfono.
2. Yo _____ a su amigo.
3. Nosotros _____ preparar la comida.
4. ¿_____ tú la hora?
5. Ellos _____ muy bien la cultura latinoamericana.
6. Yo _____ que él tiene muchos amigos pero yo no _____ a sus amigos.

ciento tres 🌼 **103**

---

3 PRACTICE

¡Pongo todo junto!

1 , **2** , and **3** You may go over these activities very quickly with books open or you may wish to have students complete them on their own and then go over them in class orally.

> **Learning from Photos**
>
> *(page 103)* **Hoyo de Manzanares** is a residential area in Madrid, Spain. It takes its name from the Manzanares River that flows through Madrid.

ANSWERS TO ¡Pongo todo junto!

1
1. hago
2. pongo
3. salimos
4. salen, salimos
5. haces

2
1. Él está saliendo.
2. Estamos haciendo un viaje.
3. Están anunciando la salida de nuestro vuelo.
4. ¿Estás mirando la pantalla?
5. Ella está revisando el boleto y el pasaporte.

3
1. sé
2. conozco
3. sabemos
4. Sabes
5. conocen
6. sé, conozco

¡Te toca a ti!

Recycling

These activities allow students to use the vocabulary and structures from this unit in completely open-ended, real-life situations.

 ¡OJO! Encourage students to say as much as possible when they do these activities. Tell them not to be afraid to make mistakes, since the goal of the activities is real-life communication. If someone in the group makes an error, allow the others to politely correct him or her. Let students choose the activities they would like to do.

You may wish to divide students into pairs or groups. Encourage students to elaborate on the basic theme and to be creative. They may use props, pictures, or posters if they wish.

2 Encourage students to be creative regarding their destinations.

Learning from Photos

(page 104) This photo shows the lake in the beautiful **Parque del Retiro** in central Madrid. The rowboats seen here are for rent, and it is a popular family pastime, particularly on Sunday afternoons, to rent a boat and row around the lake.

¡Te toca a ti!

Hablar

1 **Un billete para Madrid**

✓ *Get an airline ticket*

Work with a classmate. You want to fly with your family from somewhere in the United States to Madrid. Call the airline to get a reservation. Your classmate will be the reservation agent. Before you call, think about all the information you will need to provide or get from the airline agent: date of departure, departure time, arrival time in Madrid, flight number, and price.

El Parque del Retiro, Madrid

Hablar

2 **¿Adónde vas?**

✓ *Talk about a plane trip*

You just got to the airport and unexpectedly ran into a friend (your partner). Exchange information about the trip and the flight each of you is about to take.

ANSWERS TO ¡Te toca a ti!

1 *Answers will vary, but students should use the vocabulary from this unit to obtain their flight information.*

2 *Answers will vary, but students should give as many details about their flight as possible using the vocabulary from this unit.*

3 This activity can be done individually, or students may prefer to plan their trip with a partner. Have students tell the class about their trip.

Hablar

3 Voy a hacer un viaje

Escribir ✓ *Plan a plane trip to a Spanish-speaking destination*

Go to a travel agency in your community. Get some travel brochures and prepare a fabulous trip by plane to a Spanish-speaking country. It can be a "make-believe trip." Tell or write all about your trip.

National Standards

Communities

Students who do Activity 3 will find out more about the Spanish-speaking world by using resources in their community.

Writing Strategy

Answering an essay question

When writing an answer to an essay question, first read the question carefully to look for clues to determine how your answer should be structured. Then begin by restating the essay question in a single statement in your introduction. Next, support the statement in the body of your answer with facts, details, and reasons. Finally, close with a conclusion that summarizes your answer.

Writing Development

Have students keep a notebook or portfolio containing their best written work from each unit. These selected writings can be based on assignments from the Student Textbook and the Writing Activities Workbook. Activity 4 on page 105 is an example of a writing assignment that may be included in each student's portfolio. In the Workbook, students will develop an organized autobiography **(Mi autobiografía).** These workbook pages may also become a part of their portfolio.

Escribir

4 Un concurso

A service organization interested in international relations is sponsoring an all-expense-paid trip for an eighth grade student to spend two weeks living with a family in a Spanish-speaking country of his or her choice. In order to win this trip you have to get permission from your parents and then write an essay and send it to the organization sponsoring the trip. Read the following essay questions and then write your answers. You really want to go, so be sure to plan your answers carefully and check your work.

¿Qué país quieres visitar? ¿Cómo quieres viajar? ¿Por qué quieres ir allí? ¿Qué quieres hacer allí? ¿Qué sabes del país? ¿Qué quieres aprender?

Writing Strategy

Answering an essay question

Have students read the Writing Strategy on page 105. Encourage students first to make an outline that includes the elements mentioned in the Writing Strategy. The illustration on page 105 suggests one reason for wanting to go to a Spanish-speaking country. However, students should be encouraged to give other reasons if they wish.

ANSWERS TO ¡Te toca a ti!

3 *Answers will vary, but students should use the vocabulary presented in this unit to describe their trip.*

4 *Answers will vary depending on the students' destinations and their reasons for wanting to go there.*

RESOURCE MANAGER

Vocabulary Transparency 3.5
Tests, pages 29–44
ExamView® Pro, Unit 3
Performance Assessment,
   Tasks 5–6

Assessment

This is a pretest for students to take before you administer the Unit test. Note that each section is cross-referenced so students can easily find the material they have to review in case they made errors. You may use Assessment Answers Transparency A 3 to do the assessment in class, or you may assign this assessment for homework. You can correct the assessment yourself, or you may prefer to project the answers on the overhead in class.

PASO 3

Assessment
¿Estoy listo(a)?

Palabras

1 Completen. (*Complete.*)

To review words from **Paso 1**, turn to pages 80–81.

1–2. El agente trabaja en el _____ de la línea aérea en el _____.

3–4. La tarjeta de embarque indica el número del _____ y el número del _____ del pasajero.

5. Antes de abordar los pasajeros tienen que pasar por el control de _____ con su equipaje de mano.

6. Antes de abordar el avión los pasajeros esperan en la _____.

7. El avión sale a tiempo. No sale _____.

2 Completen. (*Complete.*)

To review words from **Paso 2**, turn to pages 90–91.

8. El avión está _____ porque está llegando a su destino.

9. Los asistentes de vuelo son miembros de la _____ a bordo del avión.

10. Los pasajeros _____ después de aterrizar.

11. Después de un vuelo, los pasajeros _____ su equipaje.

Formas

3 Contesten. (*Answer.*)

To review **hacer**, **poner**, **traer**, **salir**, **tener**, and **venir**, turn to page 84.

12. ¿Adónde haces un viaje?
13. ¿Dónde pones tu ropa?

4 Completen. (*Complete.*)

14. Ellos _____ mañana. (venir)
15. ¿A qué hora _____ tú? (salir)

ANSWERS TO *Assessment*

1
1. mostrador
2. aeropuerto
3. vuelo
4. asiento
5. seguridad
6. puerta de salida
7. tarde (con una demora)

2
8. aterrizando
9. tripulación
10. desembarcan
11. reclaman (recogen)

3
12. Hago un viaje a ___.
13. Pongo mi ropa en la maleta.

4
14. vienen
15. sales

106

5 Escriban en el presente progresivo.
(Write in the present progressive.)

16. El avión aterriza.
17. Salimos a tiempo.
18. Los pasajeros esperan en la puerta de salida.
19. Hago un viaje a México.

To review the present progressive, turn to page 87.

6 Completen con **saber** o **conocer.**
(Complete with saber *or* conocer.*)*

20. Yo _____ que Madrid es la capital de España.
21. Yo _____ a la familia Ureña. Ellos son de Madrid.
22. José _____ jugar muy bien.

To review **saber** and **conocer,** turn to page 94.

Cultura

7 Escojan. *(Choose.)*

23. El continente sudamericano es _____.
   a. pequeño   **b.** alto   **c.** inmenso
24. El Amazonas es _____.
   a. un pico andino   **b.** un río   **c.** un continente

To review this cultural information, turn to pages 100–101.

8 Contesten. *(Answer.)*

25. ¿Por qué es muy difícil viajar por tierra en muchas partes de la América del Sur?

Spanish Online

For additional practice, students may wish to do the online games and quizzes on the **Glencoe Spanish Web site** (spanish.glencoe.com). Quizzes are corrected instantly, and results can be sent via e-mail to you.

Learning from Photos

(page 107) This photo shows how the indigenous peoples of the **altiplano** build their homes on the mountainous slopes. In addition to cultivating crops, they raise sheep.

Casas del altiplano,
cerca de Riobamba, Ecuador

ANSWERS TO *Assessment*

 5
16. El avión está aterrizando.
17. Estamos saliendo a tiempo.
18. Los pasajeros están esperando en la puerta de salida.
19. Estoy haciendo un viaje a México.

 6
20. sé
21. conozco
22. sabe

7
23. c
24. b

 8
25. *Answers will vary but may include:* Es muy difícil viajar por tierra en muchas partes de la América del Sur porque es un continente inmenso, porque es difícil cruzar los picos andinos en carro o en autobús y porque la selva tropical del río Amazonas es inhóspita e impenetrable.

Diversiones

Paso 4 of each Unidad includes a Diversiones section. As the title indicates, this section contains different types of activities that students in Middle School should enjoy. They also take into account the various learning modalities.

The many types of activities included are:

Canciones This section entitled **Canta con Justo** contains songs performed on the music CD by Justo Lamas, a young singer from Argentina who has written some songs specifically for **¿Cómo te va?**

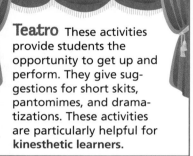

Teatro These activities provide students the opportunity to get up and perform. They give suggestions for short skits, pantomimes, and dramatizations. These activities are particularly helpful for **kinesthetic learners.**

Manos a la obra

These activities enable students to get involved and use their hands. Some examples are: drawing cards or pictures, preparing ads and brochures, and preparing schedules and announcements.

Rompecabezas

Some units contain riddles or puzzles that reinforce language in a fun way.

Investigaciones

This research section allows those students who like to work on their own to get involved in some research projects that add another dimension to the cultural material of the unit.

108

Diversiones

Canta con Justo
Viajando por Latinoamérica

Es-toy pre-pa-ran-do mi e-qui-pa-je, muy con-ten-to de via-jar. Mi pa-dre va a lle-var-me al ae-ro-puer-to, don-de yo voy a em-bar-car. A Ar-gen-ti-na voy a lle-gar, por mu-chos pa-í-ses voy a pa-sar ya mis a-mi-gos voy a vi-si-tar. Via-jan-do es-toy sen-ta-do en el a-vi-ón mi-ran-do las pla-yas de Can-cún. Es-pe-ran-do es-toy, ten-go tan-tas ga-nas de ver las mon-ta-ñas de Pe-rú. Des-pués de Bra-sil pue-do ver la gran ciu-dad, Bue-nos Ai-res te quie-ro co-no-cer.

El avión está llegando a su destino
y estamos por aterrizar.
Mis amigos me esperan en su casa
y una fiesta van a preparar.

Viajando estoy
sentado en el avión
mirando las playas de Cancún.

Esperando estoy,
tengo tantas ganas de ver
las montañas de Perú.
Después de Brasil
puedo ver la gran ciudad,
Buenos Aires
te quiero conocer.

Music Connection

Canta con Justo

The song **Viajando por Latinoamérica** will be easy for learners of all ability levels. It will help students practice the travel vocabulary and the present progressive introduced in this unit. You may wish to have students hear the recorded version of **Viajando por Latinoamérica**. It can be found on Track 6 of the **Canta con Justo** music CD. In addition, students can watch Justo perform this song on the **Justo Lamas ¡En vivo!** music video that accompanies **¿Cómo te va?** You may wish to use Song Transparency S 3 to project the music and lyrics on an overhead so students can follow along as they listen or sing.

Teatro

Work with a classmate. Make up a conversation at a check-in counter at an airport. Following are some words you may want to use.

el boleto   ¿de qué puerta?   ¿a qué hora?

facturar el equipaje   el pasaporte

la tarjeta de embarque

Teatro Encourage students to be as imaginative as possible when making up their skits.

Juego You may wish to do this as a class competition and see who can identify the most things.

Juego **¿De qué color es?** Look at the illustration. List objects and clothing according to color. Include the person **(agente, pasajero, mamá, papá)** to whom the object or clothing belongs.

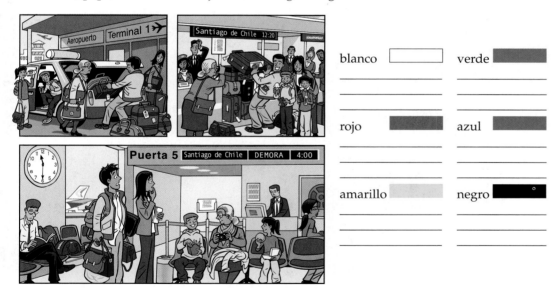

blanco	⬜	verde	🟩
rojo	🟥	azul	🟦
amarillo	🟨	negro	⬛

Manos a la obra

1. Draw and fill in your own boarding pass. Be sure to include the name of the airline, the flight number, the time, the destination, and any continuing flights. Then tell a classmate all about your "trip."

2. Draw a plan of an airport. Use the map below as a guide. Label each section such as **mostrador de las líneas aéreas.** In the margin, write at least one sentence with an arrow to the section telling what passengers or employees do there.

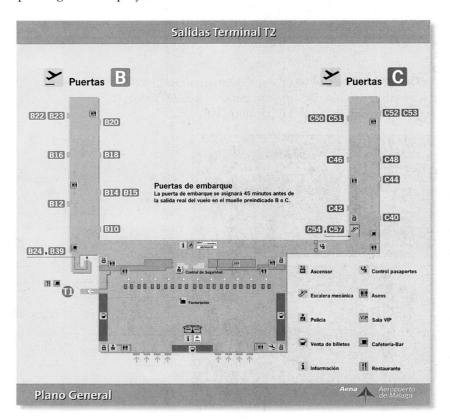

Rompecabezas

Las palabras partidas Join two puzzle pieces to form a word. Use each piece only once. You will have ten words. Form a sentence with these ten words. Write on a separate sheet of paper.

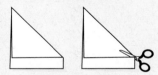

PLEGABLES™
Study Organizer

Un viaje especial Use this *envelope fold* to make a hidden picture or to write secret clues about a city in the Spanish-speaking world you would like to visit.

Step 1 **Fold** a sheet of paper into a *taco* forming a square. Cut off the leftover piece.

Step 2 **Open** the folded *taco* and refold it the oppposite way, forming another *taco* and an X-fold pattern.

Step 3 **Open** the *taco fold* and fold the corners toward the center point of the X, forming a small square.

Step 4 **Trace** this square onto another sheet of paper. Cut and glue it to the inside of the envelope. Pictures can be drawn under the tabs.

Step 5 Use this foldable to draw a picture of the city you would like to visit. Or if you prefer, write clues about the city and have your classmates raise one tab at a time until they can guess what city the picture represents. Number the tabs in the order in which they are to be opened.

ANSWERS TO Rompecabezas

hago, viaje, fantástico, Rico, Puerto, un, a, isla, la, de
Hago un viaje fantástico a la isla de Puerto Rico.

Más cultura y lectura

PASO 4

Más cultura y lectura

 ¡OJO! The reading on pages 112–113 is optional. You may skip it completely, have the entire class read it, have only several students read it and report to the class, or assign it for extra credit.

National Standards

Cultures
The reading about the Nazca lines in Perú and the related activity allow students to learn about one of the unsolved prehistoric mysteries in the Spanish-speaking world.

Un vuelo interesante

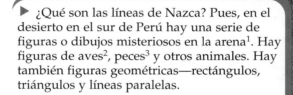

¿Quieres hacer un vuelo interesante? Tienes que tomar una avioneta que sobrevuela las figuras o líneas de Nazca.

▶ ¿Qué son las líneas de Nazca? Pues, en el desierto en el sur de Perú hay una serie de figuras o dibujos misteriosos en la arena[1]. Hay figuras de aves[2], peces[3] y otros animales. Hay también figuras geométricas—rectángulos, triángulos y líneas paralelas.

[1] arena *sand*
[2] aves *birds*
[3] peces *fish*

▲ El origen de las figuras de Nazca es un misterio. No sabemos de dónde vienen. Pero sabemos que tienen unos tres o cuatro mil años de edad. Son muy grandes. Las líneas cubren un territorio tan[4] inmenso que para ver las figuras es necesario tomar un avión. Las avionetas para ver las líneas de Nazca salen del aeropuerto internacional de Lima y del aeropuerto pequeño de Ica, una ciudad en el sur cerca de las líneas.

[4] tan *so*

¿Comprendes?

Contesten. *(Answer.)*

1. ¿Dónde están las figuras de Nazca?
2. ¿Están en un desierto?
3. ¿Sabemos de dónde vienen las líneas de Nazca?
4. ¿Qué formas tienen?
5. ¿Son grandes?
6. ¿Qué es necesario tomar para poder ver las figuras?
7. ¿De dónde salen las avionetas que sobrevuelan las líneas de Nazca?

Teacher's TIP

Use the questions in ¿**Comprendes?** to judge how well students understood the reading.

Learning from Photos

(pages 112–113) No one knows the origin of the Nazca and Paracas groups, but they were presumably nomadic Asian groups who came to the desert valleys of the Pacific coast of Perú. Some of the archaeological treasures they left indicate their cultures existed some 9,000 to 10,000 years ago.

The Nazca lines are believed to have been made some 3,000 to 4,000 years ago. No one is positive of their purpose. Some say they could have served as a calendar. Straight lines, gigantic triangles, spiral forms, and animal figures can be seen over the entire area. They are so large that they must be seen from the air.

Paso 4: Más cultura y lectura   *ciento trece* ❈ 113

ANSWERS TO ¿Comprendes?

1. Las figuras de Nazca están en el sur de Perú.
2. Sí, están en un desierto.
3. No, no sabemos de dónde vienen las líneas de Nazca.
4. Hay figuras de aves, peces y otros animales y figuras geométricas.
5. Sí, son grandes.
6. Es necesario tomar un avión para poder ver las figuras.
7. Las avionetas que sobrevuelan las líneas de Nazca salen del aeropuerto internacional de Lima y del aeropuerto pequeño de Ica.

PASO 4

Más cultura y lectura

Una astronauta latina

◀ Elena Ochoa es de Los Ángeles. Sus padres son de ascendencia mexicana. Cuando Elena está en la escuela intermedia sus padres se divorcian. Su madre siempre les explica a Elena y a sus hermanos que los estudios académicos son muy importantes. Elena les presta mucha atención a los consejos[1] de su mamá.

En la escuela intermedia Elena gana algunos premios[2] porque es una alumna sobresaliente[3] en matemáticas y ciencias. Es valedictoriana de su clase en Grossmont High School.

Elena empieza a trabajar con NASA. En 1990 seleccionan a Elena a tomar parte en la clase para astronautas. La clase consiste en dieciocho hombres y cuatro mujeres.

En abril de 1993 cuando despega la nave espacial *Discovery* de su plataforma de lanzamiento, ¿quién está a bordo?—Elena Ochoa. Ella es la primera astronauta latina que viaja en el espacio.

[1] consejos *advice*
[2] premios *awards*
[3] sobresaliente *outstanding*

¿Comprendes?

A. Contesten. *(Answer.)*
In your own words, say as much as you can about Elena Ochoa.

B. Busquen las palabras. *(In the reading, find the Spanish equivalent for the following.)*
1. astronaut
2. academic studies
3. spaceship
4. launching pad
5. in space

ANSWERS TO ¿Comprendes?

A. *Answers will vary. Students should use vocabulary from the unit to tell as much as they can about Elena Ochoa.*

B.
1. astronauta
2. los estudios académicos
3. la nave espacial
4. plataforma de lanzamiento
5. en el espacio

Conexiones
Las matemáticas

Conversiones

When you travel through many Spanish-speaking countries, you will need to make some mathematical conversions. For example, plane schedules and the time for formal events, radio, and television are given using the twenty-four-hour clock.

La hora

Cuando lees el horario[1] para el avión o un anuncio para un programa cultural, dan la hora usando las veinticuatro horas.

1:00	**La una es la una de la mañana.**
12:00	**Las doce es el mediodía.**
13:00	**Las trece, una hora después del mediodía, es la una de la tarde.**
00:00	**Las veinticuatro horas es la medianoche.**

Nuestros amigos Ángel y Luisa tienen un vuelo que sale de Madrid a las quince veinte. Es decir que sale a las tres y veinte de la tarde. Llega a París a las diecisiete horas—es decir a las cinco de la tarde.

[1] horario *schedule*

Read the timetable. Give the arrival and departure times using the twenty-four-hour clock and the system used in the United States.

SALIDAS

TENERIFE			
Vuelo	Salida	Días	Periodo
AEA9682	330	0030000	02MAY24OCT
FUA7219	915	1000000	26MAR23APR
IB2912	1040	0204060	27MAR27OCT
JKK771	1310	0000060	31MAR27OCT
FUA220P	1315	0004000	12APR12APR
JKK8788	1425	0004000	29MAR29MAR
FUA7271	1525	1000000	02JUL24SEP
FUA7219	1650	1000000	30APR30APR
JKK2420	2215	0200000	03JUL25SEP
AEA9682	2235	0200000	27MAR24APR
AEA9684	2300	0000007	06MAY21OCT

LLEGADAS

TENERIFE			
Vuelo	Llegada	Días	Periodo
AEA9681	230	0030000	02MAY24OCT
AEA9681	230	0000060	05MAY27OCT
FUA806P	335	0004000	12APR12APR
FUA7220	405	0200000	17APR17APR
JKK772	1305	0000007	06MAY21OCT
IB2911	1600	0204060	27MAR27OCT
JKK2419	2115	0200000	03JUL25SEP
AEA9681	2135	0200000	27MAR24APR
FUA7272	2210	1000000	02JUL24SEP
FUA7220	2220	1000000	26MAR09APR
FUA7220	2225	1000000	23APR30APR
JKK772	2225	0000007	25MAR29APR
FUA517P	2455	0030000	28MAR28MAR

Conexiones

National Standards

Connections
This reading about the 24-hour clock establishes a connection with another discipline, allowing students to reinforce and further their knowledge of mathematics through the study of Spanish.

Comparisons
This reading compares the way of telling time in the United States with the method used in many parts of the Spanish-speaking world.

¡OJO! The readings in the **Conexiones** section are optional. They focus on some of the major disciplines taught in schools and universities. The vocabulary is useful for discussing such topics as history, literature, art, economics, business, science, etc. You may choose any of the following ways to do the readings in the **Conexiones** sections.

Independent reading Have students read the selections and do the post-reading activities as homework, which you collect. This option is least intrusive on class time and requires a minimum of teacher involvement.

Homework with in-class follow-up Assign the readings and post-reading activities as homework. Review and discuss the material in class the next day.

Intensive in-class activity This option includes a pre-reading vocabulary presentation, in-class reading and discussion, assignment of the activities for homework, and a discussion of the assignment in class the following day.

¡Hablo como un pro!

This unique section gives students the opportunity to speak freely and say whatever they want on their own. The illustrations serve to remind students of precisely what they know how to say in Spanish. There are no depictions of activities that students do not have the ability to describe or talk about in Spanish. The art in this section recombines all that the students learned in the particular unit and in addition frequently recombines the topic or situation of the particular unit with that of another unit for additional reinforcement.

You can use this section in many ways. Some possibilities are:
1. Have students look at the illustrations and just identify items by giving the correct Spanish words.
2. Have students make up sentences about what they see in the illustrations.
3. Have students make up questions about the illustrations. They can call on another class member to respond if you do this as an entire class activity, or you may prefer to allow students to work in small groups. This activity is extremely beneficial because it enables students to actively use the interrogative words.
4. You may wish to ask questions and call on students to answer.
5. Have students look at the illustrations and give a complete oral review of what they see.
6. Have two students work together and make up a conversation based on the illustrations.
7. Have students look at the illustrations and write a paragraph (or paragraphs) about them in class.

You can also use this section as an assessment or testing tool, taking into account individual differences by having students go from simple to quite complicated tasks.

116

¡Hablo como un pro!   Tell all you can about the following illustration.

VUELO   IB323
DESTINO   BARCELONA
HORA DE SALIDA   14:30

Unidad 3: Un viaje en avión

The assessment can be either oral or written. You may wish to use the rubrics provided on pages T22–T23 as you give students the following directions.
1. Identify the topic or situation of these illustrations.
2. Identify as many items as you can and give the Spanish words. Don't forget to include actions you see.
3. Give as many sentences as you can to describe the illustrations.
4. Go over your sentences and put them in the best sequence possible.
5. Polish your sentences and sequencing to give a coherent story based on the illustrations.

Universal Access

When talking about the illustration, **students with learning difficulties** may just give random sentences. **Advanced learners** will give a coherent story. You may wish to have **advanced learners** write a paragraph about the illustration.

Vocabulario

Getting around an airport

el aeropuerto	el pasaporte	a bordo
el taxi	la pantalla de salidas y	la báscula
la línea aérea	llegadas	la maleta
el avión	la tarjeta de embarque	el equipaje (de mano)
el mostrador	el número del asiento	el control de seguridad
el/la agente	el número del vuelo	el control de pasaportes
el/la pasajero(a)	el destino	la aduana
el billete, el boleto	la puerta de salida	el reclamo de equipaje

Identifying airline personnel

la tripulación	el copiloto
el/la comandante	el/la asistente(a) de vuelo

Describing airport activities

hacer un viaje	despegar
tomar un vuelo	aterrizar
revisar el boleto	desembarcar
facturar el equipaje	reclamar (recoger)
pasar por el control de	el equipaje
seguridad	abrir las maletas
abordar, embarcar	inspeccionar
salir a tiempo	
tarde	
con una demora	

Other useful expressions

el país	poner
extranjero(a)	traer
permitir	saber
venir	conocer

Vocabulario

Vocabulary Review

The words and phrases in the **Vocabulario** have been taught for productive use in this unit. They are summarized here as a resource for both student and teacher. This list also serves as a convenient resource for the **¡Te toca a ti!** activities on pages 104 and 105. There are approximately nineteen cognates in this vocabulary list. Have students find them.

¡OJO! You will notice that the vocabulary list here is not translated. This has been done intentionally, since we feel that by the time students have finished the material in the unit they should be familiar with the meanings of all the words. If there are several words they still do not know, we recommend that they refer to the **Paso 1 Palabras** and **Paso 2 Palabras** sections in the unit or go to the dictionaries at the end of this book to find the meanings. However, if you prefer that your students have the English translations, please refer to Vocabulary Transparency 3.6, where you will find all these words with their translations.

Planning for Unit 4

CORRELATIONS

National Standards

Communication Standard 1.1
pages 122, 123, 125, 126, 127, 131, 133, 134, 136, 137, 138, 144, 149, 151

Communication Standard 1.2
pages 138, 140–141, 149, 152, 153, 154–155

Communication Standard 1.3
pages 125, 130, 136, 144, 145, 150

Cultures Standard 2.1
pages 140–141, 152, 154–155

Cultures Standard 2.2
pages 140–141, 148, 152

Connections Standard 3.1
pages 153, 154–155

Connections Standard 3.2
page 153

Comparisons Standard 4.1
page 139

Comparisons Standard 4.2
pages 154–155

Communities Standard 5.1
page 145

PACING AND PRIORITIES

The unit content is color coded below to assist you in planning.

■ required ■ recommended ■ optional

Paso 1 (required) *Days 1–8*
- ■ Palabras
  El balneario
- ■ Formas
  El pretérito de los verbos en **-ar**

Paso 2 (required) *Days 9–16*
- ■ Palabras
  Una estación de esquí
- ■ Formas
  Los pronombres **lo, la, los, las**
  Ir y **ser** en el pretérito
- ■ Conversación
  ¡A la playa!

Paso 3 (recommended) *Days 17–24*
- ■ Pronunciación
  La consonante **r**
- ■ Cultura y lectura
  Una tarde en la playa
- ■ Repaso
- ■ ¡Te toca a ti!
- ■ Assessment

Paso 4 (optional)
- ■ Diversiones
- ■ Más cultura y lectura
  Playas del mundo hispano
  Un personaje latino famoso
- ■ Conexiones
  El clima y el tiempo

SECTION		PAGES	SECTION RESOURCES
Paso 1			
Palabras	El balneario	120–123	• Vocabulary Transparencies 4.1–4.2 • Audio CD 3 • Audio Activities TE, pages 53–54 • Workbook TE, pages 53–56 • Quiz 1, page 23 • ExamView® Pro
Formas	El pretérito de los verbos en **-ar**	124–127	• Audio CD 3 • Audio Activities TE, pages 55–57 • Workbook TE, pages 56–60 • Quiz 2, page 24 • ExamView® Pro
Paso 2			
Palabras	Una estación de esquí	128–131	• Vocabulary Transparencies 4.3–4.4 • Audio CD 3 • Audio Activities TE, pages 58–59 • Workbook TE, pages 61–62 • Quiz 3, page 25 • ExamView® Pro
Formas	Los pronombres **lo, la, los, las** **Ir** y **ser** en el pretérito	132–134 135–137	• Audio CD 3 • Audio Activities TE, page 60 • Workbook TE, pages 62–64 • Quizzes 4–5, pages 26–27 • ExamView® Pro
Paso 3			
Conversación	¡A la playa!	138	• Audio CD 3 • Audio Activities TE, page 61 • Workbook TE, page 65
Pronunciación	La consonante **r**	139	• Pronunciation Transparency P 4 • Audio CD 3 • Audio Activities TE, page 62
Cultura y lectura	Una tarde en la playa	140–141	• Audio CD 3 • Audio Activities TE, pages 62–63 • Workbook TE, page 66
Repaso		142–143	• Audio CD 3 • Audio Activities TE, page 63 • Workbook TE, pages 67–68 • Tests, pages 45–46
¡Te toca a ti!		144–145	• Audio CD 3 • Audio Activities TE, pages 64–66 • Workbook TE, pages 69–71
Assessment		146–147	• Vocabulary Transparency 4.5 • Tests, pages 45–64 • ExamView® Pro, Unit 4 • Performance Assessment, Tasks 7–8
Paso 4			
Diversiones		148–151	• Workbook TE, page 72
Más cultura y lectura	Playas del mundo hispano Un personaje latino famoso	152 153	• Tests, page 53
Conexiones	El clima y el tiempo	154–155	• Tests, page 53

Using Your Resources for Unit 4

Transparencies

Bellringer 4.1–4.6

Vocabulary V 4.1–4.5

Assessment A 4

Songs S 4

Workbook

**Paso 1 Vocabulary and Structure
pages 53–60**

**Paso 2 Vocabulary and Structure
pages 61–64**

**Conversation and Reading
pages 65–66**

**Repaso, ¡Te toca a ti!, Diversiones
pages 67–72**

Audio Program and Audio Activities Booklet

**Paso 1 Vocabulary and Structure
pages 53–57**

**Paso 2 Vocabulary and Structure
pages 58–60**

**Conversation, Pronunciation
pages 61–63**

**Repaso, ¡Te toca a ti!
pages 63–66**

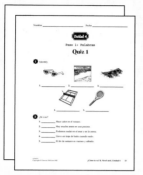

Vocabulary and Structure Quizzes, pages 23–30

Unit Tests, pages 45–64

ExamView® Pro, Unit 4

Timesaving Teacher Tools

TeacherWorks
All in One Teacher Planning

TeacherWorks™ is your all in one teacher resource center. Personalize lesson plans, access resources from the Teacher Wraparound Edition, connect to the Internet, or make a to-do list. These are only a few of the many features that can assist you in the planning and organizing of your lessons.

Includes:
- A calendar feature
- Access to all program blackline masters
- Standards correlations and more

Test Bank software for Macintosh and Windows makes creating, editing, customizing, and printing tests quick and easy.

PLEGABLES™
Study Organizer

Manipulatives The foldable activities give students of all learning styles the opportunity to excel in a nontraditional manner. Your students will love these hands-on activities!

Technology Resources

Spanish Online
In the Unit 4 online resources, you and your students will have a chance to learn more about summer and winter activities in the Spanish-speaking world.

PuzzleMaker allows you to create crossword puzzles, jumble puzzles, and word searches in minutes or edit a database of key terms and puzzles to review unit vocabulary. You can choose English-Spanish puzzles or Spanish-English puzzles. The puzzles can be printed or played on the computer screen.

Canta con Justo This CD contains songs sung by a young Argentine singer, Justo Lamas, which are specifically geared to review and expand upon the vocabulary learned in each unit. Students will enjoy listening to these songs while they learn from them.

¡En vivo! This music video of Justo Lamas performing his songs live in concert gives your students a chance to experience the songs in a different way while reinforcing the language skills they are learning!

Unidad

Preview

In this unit, students will learn to describe summer and winter weather and talk about summer and winter activities. To do this they will learn to use vocabulary associated with the beach, as well as with skiing. Students will also learn to narrate in the past. In order to do this they will learn the preterite of **-ar** verbs and the verbs **ir** and **ser.** In addition they will learn the direct object pronouns **lo, la, los,** and **las.** Students will also learn about the many wonderful summer and winter resorts in the Spanish-speaking world.

National Standards

Communication

In Unit 4, students will communicate in spoken and written Spanish on the following topics:
- summer weather and summer activities
- winter weather and winter activities

Students will also learn to narrate past events. They will obtain and provide information and engage in conversations about beach and ski resorts, water sports, tennis, and skiing as they fulfill the unit objectives listed on this page.

Spanish Online

The **Glencoe World Languages Web site** (spanish. glencoe.com) offers options that enable you and your students to experience the Spanish-speaking world via the Internet. For each **Unidad,** there are activities, games, and quizzes. In addition, an *Enrichment* section offers students an opportunity to visit Web sites related to the theme of the unit.

El verano y el invierno

Objetivos

In this unit, you will learn to:

- describe summer and winter weather
- talk about summer sports and summer activities
- talk about winter sports
- discuss past actions and events
- refer to people and things already mentioned
- talk about resorts in the Spanish-speaking world

¡Ahora me toca a mí!

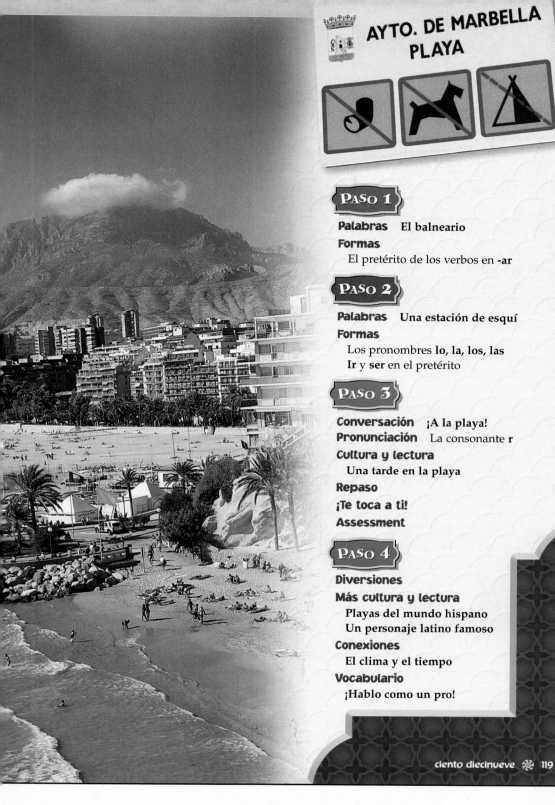

AYTO. DE MARBELLA PLAYA

Spotlight on Culture

Isabela, Puerto Rico
(page 118) These teens are on the beach in Isabela, Puerto Rico. Isabela has several lovely beaches and surfing is a popular sport here.

Benidorm, España
(page 119) The beach resort shown here is in Benidorm, between Valencia and Alicante on the **Costa Blanca**. Benidorm has two crescent-shaped beaches. Like many of the other resorts on the **Costa Blanca**, it has become somewhat overdeveloped.

Learning from Photos

(page 119) Ask the following questions about the photo after presenting the vocabulary on pages 120–121:
¿Es grande o pequeña la playa?
¿Hay mucha gente en la playa?
¿Hay mucha gente en el mar?
¿Son grandes las olas?
¿Qué tiempo hace?

Palabras

RESOURCE MANAGER

Vocabulary Transparencies 4.1–4.2
Audio Activities TE, pages 53–54
Audio CD 3
Workbook, pages 53–56
Quiz 1, page 23
ExamView® Pro

Bellringer Review

Use BRR Transparency 4.1 or write the following on the board.
Complete the following in the present.
1. Yo mir__ un video en casa.
2. Mis amigos y yo (nosotros) escuch__ CDs.
3. Tú siempre habl__ por teléfono.
4. Mis amigos me visit__ en casa.
5. Tomás me invit__ a una fiesta.

2 PRESENTATION

STEP 1 It is recommended that you present the vocabulary initially with books closed as students focus their attention on Vocabulary Transparencies 4.1–4.2. Point to each item and have the class repeat the word two or three times in unison.

STEP 2 When presenting the sentences, intersperse your presentation with questions building from simple to more complex.

STEP 3 Have students repeat the words and sentences after you or Audio CD 3.

Universal Access

Have students look at the illustrations on the transparencies. Call on **students with learning difficulties** to identify each item. Call on **average** and **advanced learners** to say as much as they can about the illustrations.

120

Palabras   El balneario 🎧

¿Qué tiempo hace en el verano?
En el verano hace calor.
Hace buen tiempo.
Hace (Hay) sol.

Hace mal tiempo.
A veces hay nubes en el cielo.
Llueve.

Magalí y sus amigos pasaron el fin de semana en la playa.
Carlos tomó el sol.

120 ✸ **ciento veinte**

Total Physical Response

Do this activity after presenting the new vocabulary. You may wish to bring in the following props to use in this activity: tube of sunscreen, beach towel, tennis ball, tennis racquet. Demonstrate the following verbs using the appropriate gestures: **ponte, tapa, rebota.** (*Student 1*), **ven acá. Aquí tienes un tubo de crema bronceadora.** (*Student 1*), **abre el tubo.**

Ponte la crema bronceadora en el brazo y en la pierna.
Y ahora, tapa el tubo.
Pon el tubo en tu mochila.
Ahora, estás en la playa.
Pon la toalla playera en la arena.
Siéntate.
Toma el sol.
Ahora, levántate.
Ve al agua, al mar.
Nada.
Gracias, (*Student 1*). Siéntate, por favor.

el buceo

la plancha de vela

la tabla hawaiana

esquiar en el agua
el esquí acuático

la piscina, la alberca

nadar

Casandra nadó en la piscina.

Nota

You are already familiar with the following expressions used to talk about things that take place in the present. Look also at time expressions you use to talk about things that took place in the past.

EL PRESENTE	EL PASADO
hoy	ayer
esta noche	anoche
esta tarde	ayer por la tarde
esta mañana	ayer por la mañana
este año	el año pasado
esta semana	la semana pasada

la cancha de tenis
la red
encima
la pelota
la raqueta

Los amigos jugaron (al) tenis.
Jugaron en una cancha al aire libre.
Jugaron singles, no dobles.
Un jugador golpeó la pelota.
La pelota pasó por encima de la red.

ciento veintiuno ✳ 121

STEP 4 Note that the preterite verbs are presented in the third person so students can use them immediately in answering questions without having to change the endings.

STEP 5 You can also use gestures or have students dramatize the following expressions: **usar la loción bronceadora, tomar el sol, esquiar en el agua, nadar, jugar (al) tenis.**

STEP 6 After the oral presentation of the vocabulary, have students open their books and read the material for additional reinforcement.

About the Spanish Language

La piscina is the most commonly used word for swimming pool. **La alberca** is used in Mexico. You will also hear **la pila** which more frequently means *basin* or *trough*.

Learning from Photos

(page 120, top left) Sitges, Spain, is the prettiest and most popular resort easily accessible from Barcelona. *(page 120, bottom left)* This beach scene is in Marbella, a popular resort on Spain's **Costa del Sol.**

Fun Facts

The Welsh privateer Henry Morgan used San Andrés as a harbor during his raids against Spanish strongholds in the seventeenth century. Legend has it that he left over one billion dollars worth of gold bullion in a cave or in one of the island's small cays. The cave in question is open to tourists.

Total Physical Response

(Student 2), **ven acá.**
Toma la pelota.
Rebota la pelota.
Rebota la pelota una vez más.
Toma la raqueta.
Golpea la pelota con la raqueta.
Siéntate, por favor.
Gracias, *(Student 2).*

Vocabulary Expansion

You may wish to teach some additional vocabulary related to the beach.
el malecón *road that parallels the beach*
la silla playera *beach chair*
la sombrilla *umbrella*
correr las olas *to bodysurf*
alquilar (rentar) un barco *to rent a boat*
pescar (ir a la pesca) *to go fishing*

121

3 PRACTICE

¿Qué palabra necesito?

¡OJO! When students are doing the **¿Qué palabra necesito?** activities, accept any answer that makes sense. The purpose of these activities is to have students use the new vocabulary. They are not factual recall activities. Thus, it is not necessary for students to remember specific factual information from the vocabulary presentation when answering. If you wish, have students use the photos on this page as a stimulus, when possible.

Historieta Each time **Historieta** appears, it means that the answers to the activity form a short story. Encourage students to look at the title of the **Historieta,** since it can help them do the activity.

1 Activity 1 can be done first with books closed for oral practice. You may then do it again with books open for additional reinforcement.

2 **EXPANSION** Ask students if they can think of additional items Claudia may have bought. **¿Qué más compró Claudia en la tienda?**

3 Activity 3 should be done with books open.

Learning from Photos

(page 122) Chorrillos is seven miles from downtown Lima and is one of Lima's original beach resorts. The modern six-lane **vía Expresa** unites downtown Lima with Chorrillos and the beaches of the **Costa Verde.**

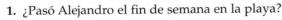

¿Qué palabra necesito?

1 **Historieta** **¡A la playa!** Contesten. *(Answer.)*

1. ¿Pasó Alejandro el fin de semana en la playa?
2. ¿Nadó en el mar?
3. ¿Tomó el sol?
4. ¿Usó una loción bronceadora?
5. ¿Buceó él?
6. ¿Esquió en el agua?

Una playa. Chorrillos. Lima. Perú

2 **¿Qué compró Claudia para ir a la playa?**
Completen. *(Complete.)*

  Claudia compró…

1.   2.

3.   4.

3 **Historieta** *El tiempo en el verano*
Completen. *(Complete.)*

  En el verano __1__ calor. Hay __2__. Pero, a veces, no hace buen tiempo. Hace __3__ tiempo. Hay __4__ y llueve. No me gusta estar en la playa cuando __5__.

Unidad 4: El verano y el invierno

ANSWERS TO **¿Qué palabra necesito?**

1
1. Sí, Alejandro pasó el fin de semana en la playa.
2. Sí, (No, no) nadó en el mar.
3. Sí, (No, no) tomó el sol.
4. Sí, (No, no) usó una loción bronceadora.
5. Sí, (No, no) buceó.
6. Sí, (No, no) esquió en el agua.

2 *Answers should begn with* **Claudia** *compró ...*
1. los anteojos de sol
2. la toalla playera
3. la loción (crema) bronceadora
4. el traje de baño (bañador)

3
1. hace
2. sol
3. mal
4. nubes
5. llueve

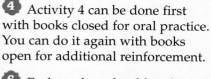
4 Historieta Un juego de tenis

Contesten. *(Answer.)*

1. ¿Dónde jugaron los tenistas (al) tenis?
2. ¿Jugaron singles o dobles?
3. ¿Cuántas personas hay en la cancha cuando juegan singles?
4. ¿Golpearon los tenistas la pelota?
5. ¿La pelota tiene que pasar por encima de la red?

Un juego de tenis. Mazatlán. México

4 Activity 4 can be done first with books closed for oral practice. You can do it again with books open for additional reinforcement.

6 Each student should make a list of the items before beginning the paired activity. Ask several pairs to present their dialogues to the class.

Universal Access

Kinesthetic learners will particularly benefit from Activity 6.

Un hipermercado. Marbella. España

5 Juego En la playa

¿Sí o no? *(True or false?)*

1. Un balneario tiene playas.
2. Hay olas en una piscina.
3. El Mediterráneo es un mar y el Atlántico es un océano.
4. Todo el mundo quiere ir a la playa cuando llueve y hay nubes.
5. Es importante usar una crema protectora cuando uno toma el sol. Da protección contra el sol.
6. Una persona lleva un traje de baño cuando juega al tenis.

6 Vamos a la playa.

Work with a classmate. You are going to spend a day or two at the beach. Go to the store to buy some things you need for your beach trip. One of you will be the clerk and the other will be the shopper. Take turns.

Paso 1: Palabras

ANSWERS TO ¿Qué palabra necesito?

4
1. Los tenistas jugaron (al) tenis en una cancha al aire libre.
2. Jugaron singles.
3. Hay dos personas en la cancha cuando juegan singles.
4. Sí, los tenistas golpearon la pelota.
5. Sí, la pelota tiene que pasar por encima de la red.

5
1. Sí
2. No
3. Sí
4. No
5. Sí
6. No

6 *Answers will vary, but students should use the vocabulary presented on pages 120–121.*

Formas

1 PREPARATION

RESOURCE MANAGER

Audio Activities TE, pages 55–57
Audio CD 3
Workbook, pages 56–60
Quiz 2, page 24
ExamView® Pro

Bellringer Review

Use BRR Transparency 4.2 or write the following on the board.
In Spanish, write at least three words related to each of the following sports.

el fútbol
el béisbol
el básquetbol
el tenis

2 PRESENTATION

 El pretérito de los verbos en **-ar**

STEP 1 Have students open their books to page 124. Read Item 1 aloud. Then have the class repeat the two model sentences after you.

STEP 2 Write the verbs **hablar, nadar,** and **tomar** on the board. Have the class repeat each form after you. After you write the forms for one verb on the board, you may wish to have students provide the forms for the other verbs. For example, under **hablar,** write **hablé.** Underline the ending. Rather than give the endings for **tomar** and/or **nadar,** ask: If it's **hablé** for **hablar,** what's the form for **tomar? nadar?** Have students repeat all forms.

STEP 3 For Item 3, have students look at the examples and point out the spelling changes.

Formas **El pretérito de los verbos en -ar**
Stating past actions

1. To express an action that began and ended at a definite time in the past you use a tense called the preterite. The following sentences are in the preterite.

   Él pasó el viernes pasado en la playa.
   Ella miró la televisión anoche.

2. You form the preterite of regular **-ar** verbs as follows.

infinitive	hablar	nadar	tomar	endings
stem	habl-	nad-	tom-	
yo	hablé	nadé	tomé	-é
tú	hablaste	nadaste	tomaste	-aste
él, ella, Ud.	habló	nadó	tomó	-ó
nosotros(as)	hablamos	nadamos	tomamos	-amos
vosotros(as)	*hablasteis*	*nadasteis*	*tomasteis*	*-asteis*
ellos, ellas, Uds.	hablaron	nadaron	tomaron	-aron

3. Note the spelling of the **yo** form of verbs that end in **-car, -gar,** and **-zar.**

c → qué	g → gué	z → cé

   ¿Marcaste un tanto? Sí, marqué un tanto.
   ¿Llegaste a tiempo? Sí, llegué a tiempo.
   ¿Jugaste (al) baloncesto? Sí, jugué (al) baloncesto.
   ¿Empezaste a jugar? Sí, empecé a jugar.

BRILLA

Unidad 4: El verano y el invierno

Teacher's TIP

While going over Item 3 of the structure explanation, you may wish to review the following sound/spelling correspondences:
   ca, que, qui, co, cu
   ga, gue, gui, go, gu
   za, ce, ci, zo, zu
These explain the spelling of **jugó, jugué, buscó, busqué, empezó, empecé.**

¿Cómo lo digo?

7 Historieta Una tarde en la playa

Contesten. *(Answer.)*

1. Ayer, ¿pasó Rubén la tarde en la playa?
2. ¿Tomó él mucho sol?
3. ¿Usó una crema protectora?
4. ¿Nadó en el mar?
5. ¿Esquió en el agua?

8 Historieta Un partido de tenis

Contesten según se indica. *(Answer as indicated.)*

1. ¿Qué compraron los amigos? (una raqueta)
2. ¿Qué jugaron los jóvenes? (tenis)
3. ¿Jugaron en una cancha cubierta? (no, al aire libre)
4. ¿Golpearon la pelota? (sí)
5. ¿Jugaron singles o dobles? (dobles)
6. ¿Quiénes marcaron el primer tanto? (Alicia y José)
7. ¿Quiénes ganaron el partido? (ellos)

Canchas de tenis.
Buenos Aires, Argentina

9 Historieta En casa Contesten.

(Answer about yourself.)

1. Anoche, ¿a qué hora llegaste a casa?
2. ¿Preparaste la comida?
3. ¿Estudiaste?
4. ¿Miraste la televisión?
5. ¿Escuchaste CDs?
6. ¿Con quién hablaste?
7. ¿Le hablaste por teléfono?

---

3 PRACTICE

¿Cómo lo digo?

¡OJO! The activities on pages 125–127 build from easy to more complex. Some deal with one subject pronoun only. Activity 13 on page 127 combines all subjects.

7, **8**, and **9** It is suggested you go over these activities orally with books closed. You ask the questions and have students answer. Do these activities a second time with books open.

EXPANSION You can have students retell the story in each activity in their own words.

> **Writing Development**
> Students can also write Activities 7, 8, and 9 in paragraph form.

ANSWERS TO ¿Cómo lo digo?

7
1. Sí, Rubén pasó la tarde en la playa ayer.
2. Sí, (No, no) tomó mucho sol.
3. Sí, (No, no) usó una crema protectora.
4. Sí, (No, no) nadó en el mar.
5. Sí, (No, no) esquió en el agua.

8
1. Los amigos compraron una raqueta.
2. Los jóvenes jugaron tenis.
3. No, jugaron al aire libre.
4. Sí, golpearon la pelota.
5. Jugaron dobles.
6. Alicia y José marcaron el primer tanto.
7. Ellos ganaron el partido.

9
1. Anoche llegué a casa a las ___.
2. Sí, (No, no) preparé la comida.
3. Sí, (No, no) estudié.
4. Sí, (No, no) miré la televisión.
5. Sí, (No, no) escuché CDs.
6. Hablé con ___.
7. Sí, (No, no) le hablé por teléfono.

3 PRACTICE (continued)

10 Have pairs of students present Activity 10 as a miniconversation using as much expression as possible.

10 El baloncesto

Sigan el modelo. *(Follow the model.)*

> **¿Jugó Pablo? →**
> **A ver. Pablo, ¿jugaste?**

1. ¿Jugó Pablo (al) baloncesto?
2. ¿Dribló con el balón?
3. ¿Pasó el balón a un amigo?
4. ¿Tiró el balón?
5. ¿Encestó?
6. ¿Marcó un tanto?

11 Historieta Una fiesta

Sigan el modelo. *(Follow the model.)*

> **hablar →**
> **Mis amigos y yo hablamos durante la fiesta.**

1. bailar
2. cantar
3. tomar un refresco
4. tomar fotos
5. escuchar música

12 Historieta Yo llegué al estadio.

Cambien **nosotros** en **yo**.
(Change nosotros *to* yo.*)*

Ayer nosotros llegamos al estadio y empezamos a jugar fútbol. Jugamos muy bien. No tocamos el balón con las manos. Lo lanzamos con el pie o con la cabeza. Marcamos tres tantos.

Estadio Vicente Calderón. Madrid

ANSWERS TO ¿Cómo lo digo?

10
1. A ver. Pablo, ¿jugaste (al) balconcesto?
2. A ver. Pablo, ¿driblaste con el balón?
3. A ver. Pablo, ¿pasaste el balón a un amigo?
4. A ver. Pablo, ¿tiraste el balón?
5. A ver. Pablo, ¿encestaste?
6. A ver. Pablo, ¿marcaste un tanto?

11
1. Mis amigos y yo bailamos durante la fiesta.
2. Mis amigos y yo cantamos durante la fiesta.
3. Mis amigos y yo tomamos un refresco durante la fiesta.
4. Mis amigos y yo tomamos fotos durante la fiesta.
5. Mis amigos y yo escuchamos música durante la fiesta.

12 Ayer yo llegué al estadio y empecé a jugar fútbol. Jugué muy bien. No toqué el balón con las manos. Lo lancé con el pie y con la cabeza. Marqué tres tantos.

126

⑬ Historieta En un balneario Completen. *(Complete.)*

Mis amigos y yo __1__ (pasar) el fin de semana pasado en la playa. Nosotros __2__ (llegar) el viernes por la noche y __3__ (pasar) dos noches en la casa de la familia de nuestro amigo Pablo.

En la playa nosotros __4__ (tomar) el sol. Yo __5__ (nadar) en el mar y __6__ (esquiar) en el agua. Catalina __7__ (bucear).

—José, ¿tú __8__ (llegar) sin traje de baño? ¿__9__ (Dejar) tu bañador en casa?

—Sí. No lo tengo. No lo puedo creer pero (yo) __10__ (dejar) mi bañador en casa.

¿Qué hacer? Pues, José __11__ (comprar) un traje de baño nuevo en una tienda.

Un hotel con alberca y playa. Cancún, México

⑭ Pasaron el fin de semana en la playa. Look at the illustration. Work with a classmate, asking and answering questions about what these Spanish friends did at the beach in Torremolinos.

For more practice using words and forms from Paso 1, do Activity 7 on page H8 at the end of this book.

Paso 1: Formas

ANSWERS TO ¿Cómo lo digo?

⑬
1. pasamos
2. llegamos
3. pasamos
4. tomamos
5. nadé
6. esquié
7. buceó
8. llegaste
9. Dejaste
10. dejé
11. compró

⑭ Answers will vary; however, students should use the vocabulary presented on pages 120–121. Answers should be expressed in the preterite. Answers may include:
—¿Pasaron el día en la playa?
—Sí, pasaron el día en la playa.
—¿Nadaron?
—Sí, nadaron y tomaron el sol.

⑬ Have students retell the story in Activity 13 in their own words.

Universal Access

Have **advanced learners** retell the story in Activity 13 in their own words. Have **students with learning difficulties** answer questions about it.

⑭ This activity encourages students to use the unit vocabulary and structures in an open-ended situation. We have provided a visual with this activity to aid students to speak in the past using the preterite of **-ar** verbs only. It is important that we not give students activities that would force them to use unknown preterite forms or the imperfect.

Before students do this activity, you may want them to quickly review the vocabulary presented on pages 120 and 121. Now have students look at the illustration and ask one another questions about it.

UN POCO MÁS This *InfoGap* activity will allow students to practice in pairs. The activity should be very manageable for them, since all vocabulary and structures are familiar to them.

Learning from Photos

(page 127) Cancún is a very popular tourist destination. Until 1974, this area of the Yucatán Peninsula was jungle. Now luxury hotels line the waterfront. The hotel zone is on a fourteen-mile barrier reef of white sand beaches and crystal clear Caribbean water.

127

1 PREPARATION

Bellringer Review

Use BRR Transparency 4.3 or write the following on the board.
Answer.
1. **¿Compraste un traje de baño nuevo?**
2. **¿Llevaste el traje de baño a la playa?**
3. **¿Nadaste?**
4. **¿Esquiaste en el agua también?**
5. **¿Tomaste el sol?**

2 PRESENTATION

STEP 1 When presenting the sentences, intersperse with questions building from simple to more complex.

STEP 2 Have students close their books. Have them focus their attention on Vocabulary Transparencies 4.3–4.4. Point to each item and have the class repeat the word two or three times in unison. Ask questions such as: **¿Hace frío? ¿Hace calor o hace frío? ¿Qué tiempo hace en el invierno?**

STEP 3 After the oral presentation of the vocabulary, have students open their books and read the material for additional reinforcement. Have them repeat the model sentences after you or Audio CD 3.

Palabras   Una estación de esquí

la esquiadora
el anorak
el esquí
los guantes
la bota   el bastón

¿Qué tiempo hace en el invierno?
Hace frío.
Nieva.
A veces hay mucha nieve.
La temperatura baja a cinco grados bajo cero.

el pico
la montaña
la estación de esquí

Los amigos fueron a una estación de esquí.

Total Physical Response

(Student 1), **levántate y ven acá, por favor.**
Siéntate.
Vamos a hacer gestos.
Ponte las botas.
Ponte los esquís.
Y ahora levántate.
Ponte el anorak.
Toma el bastón.

Pon el bastón en la mano derecha.
Toma el otro bastón.
Pon este bastón en la mano izquierda.
Y ahora, esquía.
Gracias, *(Student 1).* **Ahora puedes regresar a tu asiento.**
Siéntate, por favor.

la ventanilla,
la boletería

el boleto,
el ticket

el telesquí,
el telesilla

Compraron sus boletos para el telesquí.
Los compraron en la ventanilla.

Tomaron el telesilla.
Lo tomaron para subir la montaña.

la pista

Los esquiadores bajaron la pista.
La bajaron sin problema.
Esquiaron bien.
Bajaron la pista para expertos, no la pista
   para principiantes.

x

Paso 2: Palabras

ciento veintinueve ❄ 129

About the Spanish Language

- An airplane or train ticket is called **un billete** in Spain and **un boleto** throughout Latin America. **El ticket** or any of its variations—**el tique, el tiqué, el tiquete**—is commonly used in Spain and throughout Latin America to refer to any small ticket that resembles a stub.
- **La boletería** is used throughout Latin America. It is not used in Spain.
- **El telesilla** is masculine because it is a compound noun.

Vocabulary Expansion

You may wish to present some words related to ice skating.

el hielo	ice
el patinaje	skating
los patines	skates
patinar	to skate
la pista de patinaje, el patinadero	skating rink

Universal Access

As students look at the overhead transparency, call on **kinesthetic learners** and have them point out the following:

La señorita trabaja en la boletería.
Una muchacha mira su boleto.
Un muchacho compra su boleto.
Los amigos bajaron la pista.
Los amigos tomaron el telesilla.

Total Physical Response

Teach the expression **ponte en fila** by putting several students in a line. Also demonstrate **debajo del brazo.**
(Student 1), **levántate y ven acá, por favor.**
Ponte en fila.
Espera el telesquí.
Siéntate en el telesquí.
Pon los bastones debajo del brazo izquierdo.

Adiós. Ahora estás en la parte superior de la montaña.
Bájate del telesquí.
Pon un bastón en la mano izquierda y otro en la mano derecha.
Empieza a esquiar.
Baja la pista.
Gracias, *(Student 1).* **Ahora puedes volver a tu asiento.**

129

PASO 2

3 PRACTICE

¿Qué palabra necesito?

¡OJO! It is recommended that you go over the **¿Qué palabra necesito?** activities before assigning them for homework.

1 Quickly review the weather expressions taught on pages 120 and 128 before doing Activity 1. Students should be able to give at least five or six weather expressions.

Writing Development
Students can write Activities 1 and 3 in paragraph form.

¿Qué palabra necesito?

1 **¿Qué tiempo hace?** Describan.
(Describe the weather in the illustration.)

2 **De compras** Contesten. *(Answer.)*

Anita fue a esquiar. Antes de ir a la estación de esquí, ¿qué compró?
Anita compró...

1. 2. 3.

4. 5.

3 **Historieta** **En una estación de esquí**

Contesten según se indica. *(Answer as indicated.)*

1. ¿Cuándo son populares las estaciones de esquí? (en el invierno cuando hay nieve)
2. ¿Qué compraron los esquiadores en la ventanilla? (los boletos)
3. ¿Qué tomaron los esquiadores para subir la montaña? (el telesilla)
4. ¿Qué bajaron los esquiadores? (la pista para expertos)

Unidad 4: El verano y el invierno

ANSWERS TO **¿Qué palabra necesito?**

1 *Answers will vary but may include:*
Es el invierno. Hace frío. Hay mucha nieve. No hace calor. No es el verano.

2
1. Anita compró los esquís.
2. Anita compró el anorak.
3. Anita compró los guantes.
4. Anita compró las botas.
5. Anita compró los anteojos de sol.

3
1. Las estaciones de esquí son populares en el invierno cuando hay nieve.
2. Los esquiadores compraron los boletos en la ventanilla.
3. Los esquiadores tomaron el telesilla para subir la montaña.
4. Los esquiadores bajaron la pista para expertos.

130

4 **Me gusta esquiar.** Completen. *(Complete.)*

En el __1__ hace frío. A veces nieva. Cuando hay mucha __2__ me gusta ir a una __3__ de esquí. Llevo mis __4__, mis botas y los __5__ y voy a las montañas. Tomo el __6__ para subir la montaña. No soy un esquiador muy bueno. Siempre bajo una __7__ para principiantes.

Villarrica, Chile

5 **¡A esquiar!** You're at a ski resort in Chile and have to rent **(alquilar)** some equipment for a day on the slopes. Tell the clerk (your partner) what you need. Find out whether he or she has what you need and how much it all costs.

Esquís 9.500 pesos
Bastones 3.500 pesos
Botas 5.600 pesos
Guantes 1.500 pesos
Anoraks 8.000 pesos

6 **Rompecabezas**

Change one letter in each of the following to form a new word.

1. plaza
2. color
3. ver
4. son
5. bajo
6. ciento

Paso 2: Palabras

¡OJO! Activity 5 encourages students to use the unit vocabulary and structures in open-ended situations.

5 You may wish to do Activity 5 only with students who are interested in skiing. Determine how much each item will cost in dollars before students begin this activity. You may wish to ask one of the groups doing Activity 5 to volunteer to present the conversation to the entire class.

Universal Access

Have students present their skits in Activity 5 to the class. This activity is especially beneficial for **kinesthetic learners.**

Learning from Photos

(page 131) **Villarrica,** in the Chilean Lake Region, is one of the country's favorite resorts. In addition to water sports on the Villarrica Lake, there are ski slopes on the Villarrica Volcano. There are five runs, some of which are quite easy. The resort has chair and tow lifts.

ANSWERS TO **¿Qué palabra necesito?**

4
1. invierno
2. nieve
3. estación
4. guantes
5. esquís
6. telesquí (telesilla)
7. pista

5 *Answers will vary; however, students should use the vocabulary presented on pages 128–129.*

6
1. playa
2. calor
3. ser, vez
4. sol
5. baño, baja
6. viento

131

Formas

PASO 2

1 PREPARATION

Bellringer Review

Use BRR Transparency 4.4 or write the following on the board. Indicate whether each of the following is associated with **el verano** or **el invierno.**
1. **Bajan la pista.**
2. **Esquían.**
3. **Esquían en el agua.**
4. **Toman el telesilla.**
5. **Usan una toalla playera.**
6. **Bucean.**

2 PRESENTATION

 Los pronombres **lo, la, los, las**

STEP 1 Write several of the model sentences on the board. Draw a box around the direct object (noun). Now circle the direct object pronoun. Then draw a line from the box to the circle. This visual technique helps many students grasp the concept that one word replaces the other.

STEP 2 Have students open their books to page 132. Instead of providing or having students read the information, you may wish to have students come up with the answers for the rest of the model sentences: Does **lo** replace a masculine or feminine noun? What pronoun replaces a feminine noun?

 Formas Los pronombres **lo, la, los, las**
Referring to items already mentioned

Each of the following sentences has a direct object. The direct object is the word in the sentence that receives the action of the verb. It answers the questions *what* or *whom*. The direct object can be either a noun or a pronoun. **Lo, la, los,** and **las** are the direct object pronouns. They can replace either a thing or a person. The pronoun must agree with the noun it replaces and it comes right before the verb.

noun thing

Ella compró el anorak.
Compró los anteojos de sol.
¿Miró Juan la pelota?
¿Miró las raquetas?

pronoun thing

Ella lo compró.
Los compró en la misma tienda.
Sí, la miró.
Sí, las miró.

noun person

¿Invitaste a Juan?
¿Invitaste a María?

pronoun person

Sí, lo invité.
Sí, la invité.

Madrid, España

Learning from Photos

(page 132) Have students take turns describing the photo. This will review vocabulary learned in Unit 4 of **¿Cómo te va? A, Nivel verde.**

¿Cómo lo digo?

7 **Sí, tengo.** Sigan el modelo. *(Follow the model.)*

San Juan, Puerto Rico

   el traje de baño →
   —¿Tienes el traje de baño?
   —Sí, lo tengo.
   —¿Dónde lo compraste?
   —No sé dónde lo compré.

   1. la raqueta
   2. las toallas playeras
   3. el bañador
   4. los anteojos de sol
   5. el anorak

8 **¿Dónde está?** Sigan el modelo. *(Follow the model.)*

   ¿El bañador? →
   Aquí lo tienes.

   1. ¿El traje de baño?   6. ¿Los boletos?
   2. ¿El tubo de crema?   7. ¿Los esquís acuáticos?
   3. ¿La pelota?   8. ¿Las toallas playeras?
   4. ¿La crema bronceadora?   9. ¿Las raquetas?
   5. ¿Los anteojos de sol?   10. ¿Las tablas hawaianas?

Un chiringuito en una playa de Marbella, España

Paso 2: Formas

ciento treinta y tres ✳ 133

---

3 PRACTICE

¿Cómo lo digo?

7 and **8** Have students do Activities 7 and 8 as paired activities as shown in the model.

EXPANSION Have students hold up additional items they know. For example, **¿El lápiz? ¿El cuaderno? ¿El libro?**

Learning from Photos

(page 133, bottom) This **chiringuito** is on one of the beaches of Marbella. A **chiringuito** is a small beach hut or stand that serves food, drinks, and refreshments.

ANSWERS TO ¿Cómo lo digo?

7

1. —¿Tienes la raqueta?
   —Sí, la tengo.
   —¿Dónde la compraste?
   —No sé dónde la compré.

2. —¿Tienes las toallas playeras?
   —Sí, las tengo.
   —¿Dónde las compraste?
   —No sé dónde las compré.

3. —¿Tienes el bañador?
   —Sí, lo tengo.
   —¿Dónde lo compraste?
   —No sé dónde lo compré.

4. —¿Tienes los anteojos de sol?
   —Sí, los tengo.
   —¿Dónde los compraste?
   —No sé dónde los compré.

5. —¿Tienes el anorak?
   —Sí, lo tengo.
   —¿Dónde lo compraste?
   —No sé dónde lo compré.

8

1. Aquí lo tienes.   6. Aquí los tienes.
2. Aquí lo tienes.   7. Aquí los tienes.
3. Aquí la tienes.   8. Aquí las tienes.
4. Aquí la tienes.   9. Aquí las tienes.
5. Aquí los tienes.   10. Aquí las tienes.

133

3 PRACTICE (continued)

9 Have students present each part of Activity 9 as a miniconversation between two people. Have students make up a price for each item in 9.

10 Have students retell the story in Activity 10 in their own words.

11 Students will answer with the appropriate direct object pronoun.

Learning from Photos

(page 134) This Spanish department store with a little park complete with a **tiovivo** *(merry-go-round)* is on **calle Serrano** in Madrid.

9 **De compras** Sigan el modelo. *(Follow the model.)*

—¿Cuándo compraste los bastones?
—Los compré ayer.
—¿Dónde los compraste?
—Los compré en la tienda Solís.
—¿Cuánto te costaron?
—Me costaron ciento cinco pesos.

1.   2.   3.   4.

5.   6.   7.   8.

El Corte Inglés. Calle Serrano. Madrid

10 **Historieta** **Un regalo que le gustó**
Completen. *(Complete.)*

Compré un regalo para Teresa. __1__ compré en la tienda de departamentos Corte Inglés. Compré unos anteojos de sol. A Teresa le gustaron mucho. Ella __2__ llevó el otro día cuando fue a la piscina. Ella tiene algunas fotografías con sus anteojos de sol. Su amigo Miguel __3__ tomó.

11 **Historieta** **Una fiesta** Contesten. *(Answer.)*

1. ¿Invitaste a Juan a la fiesta?
2. ¿Invitaste a Alejandra?
3. ¿Compraste los refrescos?
4. ¿Preparaste la ensalada?
5. ¿Tomó Pepe las fotografías de la fiesta?

ANSWERS TO ¿Cómo lo digo?

9 *Students should make up prices for each item.*

1. —¿Cuándo compraste los esquís?
   —Los compré ayer.
   —¿Dónde los compraste?
   —Los compré en la tienda Solís.
   —¿Cuánto te costaron?
   —Me costaron ___.
2. —¿Cuándo compraste la toalla playera?
   —La compré ayer.
   —¿Dónde la compraste?

—La compré en la tienda Solís.
—¿Cuánto te costó?
—Me costó ___.

3. —¿Cuándo compraste la raqueta?
   —La compré ayer.
   —¿Dónde la compraste?
   —La compré en la tienda Solís.
   —¿Cuánto te costó?
   —Me costó ___.
4. —¿Cuándo compraste el traje de baño (bañador)?
   —Lo compré ayer.

—¿Dónde lo compraste?
—Lo compré en la tienda Solís.
—¿Cuánto te costó?
—Me costó ___.

5. —¿Cuándo compraste las botas?
   —Las compré ayer.
   —¿Dónde las compraste?
   —Las compré en la tienda Solís.
   —¿Cuánto te costaron?
   —Me costaron ___.
6. —¿Cuándo compraste la mochila?
   —La compré ayer.

—¿Dónde la compraste?
—La compré en la tienda Solís.
—¿Cuánto te costó?
—Me costó ___.

7. —¿Cuándo compraste la tabla hawaiana?
   —La compré ayer.
   —¿Dónde la compraste?
   —La compré en la tienda Solís.
   —¿Cuánto te costó?
   —Me costó ___.

134

Ir y ser en el pretérito
Describing past actions

The verbs **ir** and **ser** are irregular in the preterite tense. Note that they have identical forms.

infinitive	ir	ser
yo	fui	fui
tú	fuiste	fuiste
él, ella, Ud.	fue	fue
nosotros(as)	fuimos	fuimos
vosotros(as)	*fuisteis*	*fuisteis*
ellos, ellas, Uds.	fueron	fueron

Una piscina municipal. Fuerte. España

Paso 2: Formas

ciento treinta y cinco 135

1 PREPARATION

Bellringer Review

Use BRR Transparency 4.5 or write the following on the board.
Write the following sentences in the preterite.
1. **Yo busco mi libro.**
2. **Yo juego al tenis.**
3. **Yo llego a las tres.**
4. **Empiezo a hablar.**

2 PRESENTATION

 Ir y ser en el pretérito

STEP 1 Ask students to open their books to page 135. As you go over the explanation, tell students that the meaning of a sentence makes it clear whether the verb is **ir** or **ser**.

STEP 2 Have students repeat the verb forms on page 135 in unison.

Learning from Photos
(page 135) This municipal swimming pool is in the tiny town of Fuerte in Extremadura. Even some of the smallest towns in Spain provide their citizens with a municipal pool.

8. —¿Cuándo compraste los anteojos de sol?
—Los compré ayer.
—¿Dónde los compraste?
—Los compré en la tienda Solís.
—¿Cuánto te costaron?
—Me costaron ___.

10
1. Lo
2. los
3. las

11
1. Sí, (No, no) lo invité a la fiesta.
2. Sí, (No, no) la invité.
3. Sí, (No, no) los compré.
4. Sí, (No, no) la preparé.
5. Sí (No), Pepe (no) las tomó.

135

PASO 2

¿Cómo lo digo?

3 PRACTICE

¿Cómo lo digo?

12 and **13** Students very often confuse **fui** and **fue**. For this reason, Activity 12 gives practice using **fui**. After you finish Activity 12, call on several students to retell the story in their own words. This will assist in evaluating whether they understand the difference between **fui** and **fue**. Activity 13 starts with **fui** and then uses **fue** and **fueron**.

 ¿Y tú? Contesten. *(Answer about yourself.)*

1. Ayer, ¿fuiste a la escuela?
2. ¿Fuiste a las montañas?
3. ¿Fuiste a la estación de esquí?
4. ¿Fuiste a la playa?
5. ¿Fuiste a la piscina?
6. ¿Fuiste al campo de fútbol?

El glaciar Perito Moreno. Patagonia. Argentina

Universal Access

Have **students with learning difficulties** make up an original sentence using **fui,** as they point to themselves. Then have them point to a classmate and make up a sentence using **fue.**

Learning from Photos

(page 136) **El Parque Nacional de los Glaciares** covers 600,000 hectares and is located 50 kilometers from El Calafate, Argentina. The most spectacular of the many glaciers is **El Perito Moreno,** seen here. It is one of the few glaciers in the world that continues growing.

 ¿Quién fue y cómo? Contesten. *(Answer about yourself.)*

1. ¿Fuiste a la escuela ayer?
2. ¿Fue tu amigo también?
3. ¿Fueron ustedes juntos?
4. ¿Fueron en carro?
5. ¿Fue también la hermana de tu amigo?
6. ¿Fue ella en carro o a pie?

ANSWERS TO ¿Cómo lo digo?

12
1. Sí, (No, no) fui a la escuela ayer.
2. Sí, (No, no) fui a las montañas.
3. Sí, (No, no) fui a la estación de esquí.
4. Sí, (No, no) fui a la playa.
5. Sí, (No, no) fui a la piscina.
6. Sí, (No, no) fui al campo de fútbol.

13
1. Sí, (No, no) fui a la escuela ayer.
2. Sí (No), mi amigo (no) fue.
3. Sí, (No, no) fuimos juntos.
4. Sí, (No, no) fuimos en carro.
5. Sí (No), la hermana de mi amigo (no) fue.
6. Ella fue en carro (a pie).

14 **Anteayer** Work with a classmate. Ask whether he or she went to one of the places below the day before yesterday (**anteayer**). Your partner will respond. Take turns asking and answering the questions.

1.   **2.**   **3.**

4.   **5.**

15 **A planear las actividades** Weather has a lot to do with planning our activities. Look at the chart below. Given the weather, decide what you might do with a friend each day.

Día	Tiempo	Temperatura	Actividades
lunes	Hay nubes.	7° C	_____
martes	Hace viento.	15° C	_____
miércoles	Llueve.	26° C	_____
jueves	Hace calor.	33° C	_____
viernes	Hace sol.	35° C	_____
sábado	Hace frío.	22° C	_____
domingo	Nieva.	10° C	_____

 *For more practice using words and forms from **Paso 2**, do Activity 8 on page H9 at the end of this book.*

Andas bien. ¡Adelante!

Paso 2: Formas

14 Make sure students can identify each place illustrated: **la playa, la cancha de tenis, el consultorio (la consulta) del médico, la tienda de ropa, el restaurante.**

EXPANSION After students finish Activity 14, have them look at each illustration and say as much as they can about it.

This *InfoGap* activity will allow students to practice in pairs. The activity should be very manageable for them, since all vocabulary and structures are familiar to them.

¡Adelante! At this point, all new material has been presented. Students have learned all the vocabulary and structure necessary to complete the unit. The conversation, cultural readings, and activities in **Paso 3** and **Paso 4** recycle all the material learned up to this point.

Conversación

1 PREPARATION

RESOURCE MANAGER

Audio Activities TE, page 61
Audio CD 3
Workbook, page 65

Bellringer Review

Use BRR Transparency 4.6 or write the following on the board. Answer.
1. **¿Fuiste a la papelería?**
   ¿Qué compraste allí?
2. **¿Fuiste a la tienda de ropa?**
   ¿Qué compraste?
3. **¿Fuiste al mercado?**
   ¿Qué compraste?

2 PRESENTATION

STEP 1 Tell students they are going to hear a conversation between two young people, José and Anita.

STEP 2 Have students close their books. Read the conversation to them or play Audio CD 3.

STEP 3 Have the class repeat the conversation once or twice in unison.

STEP 4 After presenting the conversation, go over the **¿Comprendes?** activity.

Learning from Photos

(page 138) Have students give a complete description of the beach in this photo, located in Isabela, Puerto Rico.

138

Conversación
¡A la playa!

José	Anita, ¿dónde está tu traje de baño?
Anita	¿Mi traje de baño? No lo tengo. Lo dejé en casa.
José	Aquí estás en la playa y dejaste tu traje de baño en casa. ¡Increíble!
Anita	No importa. Nadé esta mañana.
José	¿Nadaste sin traje de baño? ¡Anita!
Anita	Sí, fui al agua en mi blue jean.

¿Comprendes?

Contesten. *(Answer.)*
1. ¿Tiene Anita su traje de baño?
2. ¿Dónde lo dejó?
3. Y, ¿dónde está ella?
4. ¿Cuándo nadó ella?
5. ¿Cómo fue al agua?

Universal Access

You may wish to allow **students with learning difficulties** to read the conversation aloud. Then change the names of the characters so that José is the one who forgot his swimming trunks. Have **average students** act out the conversation for the class, making any changes necessary. Then call on **advanced learners** to present the conversation to the class without reading. Allow them to make any changes that make sense. Students should not be expected to memorize the conversation.

ANSWERS TO ¿Comprendes?

1. No, Anita no tiene su traje de baño.
2. Lo dejó en casa.
3. Ella está en la playa.
4. Nadó esta mañana.
5. Fue al agua en su blue jean.

La consonante r

When a word begins with an **r** (initial position), the **r** is trilled in Spanish. Within a word, this trilled **r** is spelled **rr.** The Spanish trilled **r** sound does not exist in English. Repeat the following.

ra	re	ri	ro	ru
rápido	reclama	Ricardo	Roberto	Rubén
raqueta	recoger	rico	rojo	rubio
párrafo	corre	perrito	perro	
	red	aterrizar	catarro	

The sound for a single **r** within a word (medial position) does not exist in English either. It is trilled less than the initial **r** or **rr.** Repeat the following.

ra	re	ri	ro	ru
verano	arena	Clarita	número	Perú
para	quiere	boletería	miro	Aruba
playera		consultorio		

Trabalenguas

Repeat the following.

> El mesero recoge los refrescos.
> El perrito de Rubén corre en la arena.
> El pasajero corre rápido por el aeropuerto.
> El avión para Puerto Rico aterriza con una demora de una hora.
> El rico peruano tiene una raqueta de tenis en el carro.

Refrán

Can you guess what the following proverb means?

Después de la lluvia, sale el sol.

Paso 3: Conversación

¡OJO! The following information may help students pronounce the **r** sound correctly. Remember that this is an extremely difficult sound for English speakers to make. Try to have students sound as native as possible. Do not frustrate a student who cannot pronounce perfectly. Many (or most) people cannot, and a bit of an accent can be readily understood. Any native speaker will understand **"el caro"** as **el carro** even if the **rr** sound is mispronounced.

STEP 1 The Spanish **r** sound does not exist in English. A single **r** in medial position is pronounced like a soft **t** in English. The tongue hits the upper part of the mouth in a position similar to when we say "a lot of" *(a lotta)* very quickly in English. Have students practice saying *lotta* and **para** several times.

STEP 2 Have students play a game trying to trill the initial **r** or the **rr.** Let them exaggerate as much as they wish, and they may get it right.

STEP 3 Have students repeat the sounds and words after you or Audio CD 3. Have them imitate very carefully.

STEP 4 Have students open their books to page 139. Call on individuals to read the sentences carefully.

STEP 5 All model sentences on page 139 can be used for dictation.

Universal Access

Give students, especially **auditory learners,** the following directions in order to practice auditory discrimination: Listen to the following. If I am talking about the present, raise one hand. If I am talking about the past, raise both hands:

Hablo.	Miró.
Nadó.	Compro.
Esquío.	Pagó.
Miro.	Esquió.

Refrán

If students cannot guess what the proverb means, tell them, "There's always sunshine after the rain."

Cultura y lectura

PASO 3

Cultura y lectura

Una tarde en la playa

RESOURCE MANAGER

Audio Activities TE, page 63
Audio CD 3
Workbook, page 66

✿ National Standards

Cultures
The reading about Puerto Rico and the related activities allow students to find out more about the beaches and the climate of Puerto Rico. Students also learn how a young Puerto Rican boy spends his Saturdays.

2 PRESENTATION

PRE-READING

STEP 1 Have students scan the **Lectura** for cognates.

STEP 2 Go over the Reading Strategy on page 140.

READING

STEP 1 Have the class read the selection once silently.

STEP 2 Now call on individuals to read about four sentences each.

STEP 3 Ask comprehension questions based on each paragraph. For example, **¿Adónde fueron Iván y algunos amigos el sábado pasado?**

POST-READING

STEP 1 If possible, bring in photos, slides, or videos of Puerto Rico. You may obtain videos from the library. Additional information is available on the Internet.

STEP 2 Have students read the **Cultura y lectura** at home and write the answers to the **¿Comprendes?** activities.

Reading Strategy

Recognizing text organization
Before you read a passage, try to figure out how the text is organized. If you can follow the organization of a text, you will understand the main ideas more quickly and be able to look for certain ideas and information more easily.

Iván es alumno en una escuela intermedia de San Juan, Puerto Rico. El sábado pasado, como muchos sábados, él y algunos de sus amigos fueron a la playa. Pasaron toda la tarde en la playa. Ellos tomaron el sol y nadaron en el Atlántico.

Iván llevó su plancha de vela a la playa. A él le gusta mucho hacer la plancha de vela, sobre todo cuando hay mucho viento.

A eso de[1] las dos de la tarde algunos compraron un hot dog o perro caliente y otros compraron unas empanadas del señor y de la señora Ortiz. Todos los fines de semana los señores Ortiz van a la playa con su carrito. Venden refrescos a los bañistas. La señora Ortiz hace las empanadas en casa y las lleva a la playa en una cesta[2]. ¡Y qué deliciosas están!

[1] A eso de *At about*   [2] cesta *basket*

Learning from Photos

Have students look at this photo of a man selling empanadas. Empanadas can be filled with chicken, chopped meats, crabmeat, or cheese.

Después de comer, los jóvenes jugaron al voleibol. El voleibol es un deporte muy popular en las playas de Puerto Rico.

Los jóvenes puertorriqueños como Iván pueden ir a la playa durante el año entero. Puerto Rico, la isla del encanto[3], es una isla tropical donde el verano es eterno.

[3] encanto *enchantment*

San Juan, Puerto Rico

San Juan, Puerto Rico

¿Comprendes?

A. Contesten. *(Answer.)*
1. ¿De dónde es Iván?
2. ¿Dónde estudia?
3. ¿Cuándo fueron él y algunos amigos a la playa?
4. ¿Qué tomaron?
5. ¿Dónde nadaron?
6. ¿Qué llevó Iván a la playa?
7. ¿Qué compraron los amigos para comer?

8. ¿Dónde los compraron?
9. ¿Qué hacen los señores Ortiz cada fin de semana?
10. ¿Qué jugaron los jóvenes en la playa?

B. Contesten. *(Answer.)*
¿Qué tiempo hace en Puerto Rico? ¿Cuándo? ¿Por qué? ¿Qué es Puerto Rico?

Repaso

This section reviews the salient points from Unit 4. Students will review the preterite of **-ar** verbs, the direct object pronouns **lo, la, los, las,** and the preterite of **ir** and **ser.**

1 PREPARATION

RESOURCE MANAGER

Audio Activities TE, page 63
Audio CD 3
Workbook, pages 67–68

2 PRESENTATION

STEP 1 With books closed, go over the information in Items 1–3 with students.

STEP 2 Write the first column of sentences in Item 2 on the board and have students give you the sentences using **lo, la, los,** and **las.**

STEP 3 Have students make up some original sentences using the preterite forms.

Learning from Photos

(page 142) Ushuaia is the capital of Tierra del Fuego, Argentina, and it is the southernmost city in the world. This coastal town on the Beagle Pass is set in the midst of waterfallls, glaciers, and snow-clad mountains.

PASO 3

Repaso

1. In this unit, I learned the preterite of **-ar** verbs to express actions that began and ended at a specific time in the past.

infinitive	hablar
stem	habl-
hablé	hablamos
hablaste	*hablasteis*
habló	hablaron

2. The direct object pronouns **lo, la, los, las** can replace either a thing or a person. The pronoun comes right before the verb.

Compré el anorak. →	**Lo compré en Argentina.**
Compré los esquís. →	**Los compré en Argentina.**
Compré la crema. →	**La compré en Argentina.**
Compré las botas. →	**Las compré en Argentina.**
Invité a Roberto. →	**Lo invité a la estación de esquí.**
Invité a Teresa. →	**La invité a la estación de esquí.**

3. I also learned the preterite forms of the verbs **ir** and **ser.** They are identical.

fui	**fuimos**
fuiste	**fuisteis**
fue	**fueron**

Ushuaia, Argentina

¡Pongo todo junto!

1 **En el pasado** Escriban en el pretérito.
(Rewrite in the preterite.)

1. Yo paso el fin de semana en la playa.
2. Miramos el juego en la televisión.
3. Ellos juegan voleibol en la playa.
4. ¿Esquías en el agua?
5. Tomo un refresco.
6. Pago en la caja.
7. ¿No compras una crema bronceadora?
8. Ella deja su traje de baño en casa.

Una playa. Marbella, España

2 **Los pronombres** Escriban con pronombres.
(Rewrite with an object pronoun.)

1. Miré *el juego* en la televisión.
2. Él dejó *su bañador* en casa.
3. ¿Dónde compraste *los anteojos de sol?*
4. ¿Quién tomó *las fotografías?*
5. ¿Tienes *la toalla playera?*
6. Compré *los tickets para el telesquí.*
7. Ellos prepararon *la comida* en casa.

3 **¿Adónde?** Completen con el pretérito.
(Complete with the preterite of ir.*)*

1. Él _____ al mercado.
2. Yo _____ al supermercado.
3. Nosotros _____ a la playa.
4. Nuestros amigos _____ a una estación de esquí.
5. ¿Adónde _____ tú?
6. Ustedes _____ en carro, ¿no?

Un hipermercado. Marbella, España

---

3 PRACTICE

¡Pongo todo junto!

1, **2**, and **3** You may wish to go over these activities orally in class, or you may wish to have students prepare them at home and go over them the next day in class.

Learning from Photos
(page 143, top) Here we see a lifeguard **(guardavidas)** tower on one of the larger beaches in Marbella, Spain.

ANSWERS TO ¡Pongo todo junto!

1
1. Yo pasé el fin de semana en la playa.
2. Miramos el juego en la televisión.
3. Ellos jugaron voleibol en la playa.
4. ¿Esquiaste en el agua?
5. Tomé un refresco.
6. Pagué en la caja.
7. ¿No compraste una crema bronceadora?
8. Ella dejó su traje de baño en casa.

2
1. Lo miré en la televisión.
2. Él lo dejó en casa.
3. ¿Dónde los compraste?
4. ¿Quién las tomó?
5. ¿La tienes?
6. Los compré.
7. Ellos la prepararon en casa.

3
1. fue
2. fui
3. fuimos
4. fueron
5. fuiste
6. fueron

143

PASO 3

¡Te toca a ti!

♻ **Recycling**

These activities allow students to use the vocabulary and structure from this unit in completely open-ended, real-life situations.

 Encourage students to say as much as possible when they do these activities. Tell them not to be afraid to make mistakes, since the goal of the activities is real-life communication. If someone in the group makes an error, allow the others to politely correct him or her. Let students choose the activities they would like to do.

You may wish to divide students into pairs or groups. Encourage students to elaborate on the basic theme and to be creative. They may use props, pictures, or posters if they wish.

Learning from Photos

(page 144, right) This photo was taken on the banks of the Tortuguero Canal in the province of Limón, Costa Rica. The road north from Limón goes as far as the airport in Moín. From there one travels on the intricate Tortuguero Canal system, which parallels the sea and goes some eighty miles up the coast to the Nicaraguan border.

The Puerto Limón area is quite different from the rest of Costa Rica. It is a major port, and it has a distinct Caribbean air. Many of its 60,000 inhabitants are descendants of Jamaicans. *(page 144, left)* This photo shows the Fitzroy National Park in Argentina.

¡Te toca a ti!

Hablar

1 **El mar *o* la montaña**

✓ *Talk about summer or winter vacations*

Work with a classmate. Tell him or her where you like to go on vacation. Tell what you do there and some of the reasons why you enjoy it so much. Take turns.

Argentina

A orillas del canal de Tortuguero. Cerca de Puerto Limón, Costa Rica

Hablar

2 **Unas vacaciones estupendas**

✓ *Talk about vacation activities*

Work with a classmate. Pretend you each had a million dollars. You went on a dream vacation. Take turns telling what you did.

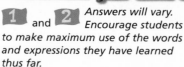

Hablar

3 **El tiempo**

✓ *Describe the weather*

Describe the summer and winter weather where you live.

Unidad 4: El verano y el invierno

ANSWERS TO ¡Te toca a ti!

1 and **2** Answers will vary. Encourage students to make maximum use of the words and expressions they have learned thus far.

3 Answers will vary, but students should use the weather-related vocabulary learned in this Unit.

FUN FACTS

Many people are surprised to learn that there are so many ski resorts in different areas of Spain. There are major ski resorts in the Pyrenees, in the **sierra Nevada** near Granada, and just north of Madrid in the **sierra de Guadarrama** and the **sierra de Gredos.**

Escribir

4 Una tarjeta postal

✓ *Write about a summer or winter vacation destination*

Look at these postcards. Choose one. Pretend you are spending a week there. Write a postcard to a friend.

Vistas, Isla de Providencia, Colombia

Sierra Nevada, España

Writing Development

Have students keep a notebook or portfolio containing their best written work from each unit. These selected writings can be based on assignments from the Student Textbook and the Writing Activities Workbook. The two activities on page 145 are examples of writing assignments that may be included in each student's portfolio.

In the Workbook, students will develop an organized autobiography **(Mi autobiografía).** These workbook pages may also become a part of their portfolio.

Writing Strategy

Comparing and contrasting
Before you begin to write a comparison of people, places, or things, you must be aware of how they are alike or different. When you compare, you are emphasizing similarities; when you contrast, you are emphasizing differences. Making a diagram or a list of similarities and differences is a good way to organize your details before you begin to write.

Escribir

5 En el verano y en el invierno

A summer day in most parts of the world is quite different from a winter day. Write a paragraph comparing how you spend a vacation day in the summer in comparison to the way you spend a vacation day in the winter. Because of the weather, many of your activities are probably quite different. Not everything is different, however. Describe some things you do whether it's summer or winter.

Writing Strategy

Comparing and contrasting
Have students read the Writing Strategy on page 145. Then have students make a diagram or a list of similarities and differences between a summer vacation day and a winter vacation day.

Learning from Photos

(page 145, top right) Providencia is a rural mountainous island that belongs to Colombia. It offers good swimming and a few tourist accommodations. One can fly to Providencia from San Andrés or Cartagena.

(page 145, bottom right) This cross-country skier is in Patagonia, Argentina.

PASO 3

Assessment

RESOURCE MANAGER

Vocabulary Transparency 4.5
Tests, pages 45–64
ExamView® Pro, Unit 4
Performance Assessment,
    Tasks 7–8

✓ Assessment

This is a pretest for students to take before you administer the unit test. Note that each section is cross-referenced so students can easily find the material they have to review in case they made errors. You may use Assessment Answers Transparency A 4 to do the assessment in class, or you may assign this assessment for homework. You can correct the assessment yourself, or you may prefer to project the answers on the overhead in class.

PASO 3

Assessment
¿Estoy listo(a)?

Palabras

1 Completen. (*Complete.*)

To review words from **Paso 1**, *turn to pages 120–121.*

1. En el verano cuando hace calor nos gusta ir a la _____.
2. Es necesario usar una _____ cuando uno toma el sol.
3. Me gusta _____ en el mar y en la piscina.
4. Ellos jugaron (al) tenis en la _____.
5. Muchas veces cuando hace mal tiempo hay _____ en el cielo.

2 Identifiquen. (*Identify.*)

6.

7.

8.

To review words from **Paso 2**, *turn to pages 128–129.*

9.

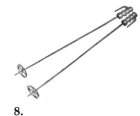

10.

3 Contesten. (*Answer.*)

11. ¿Qué tiempo hace en el invierno?

ANSWERS TO Assessment

1
1. playa
2. loción (crema) bronceadora
3. nadar
4. cancha de tenis
5. nubes

2
6. el anorak
7. las botas
8. los bastones
9. la pista
10. los anteojos de sol

3
11. En el invierno hace frío. Hay mucha nieve.

Formas

4 Completen en el pretérito. *(Complete in the preterite.)*

12. Yo _____ el fin de semana en la playa. (pasar)

13–14. Algunos de mis amigos _____ y otros _____ en el agua. (nadar, esquiar)

15. Todos nosotros _____ el sol. (tomar)

16. ¿Tú _____ tu traje de baño nuevo? (llevar)

17. Ustedes le _____ a Antonio, ¿no? (hablar)

To review the preterite of -ar verbs, turn to page 124.

5 Escriban en el pretérito. *(Write in the preterite.)*

18. Yo pago en la caja.

6 Escriban con un pronombre. *(Write with a pronoun.)*

19. Yo compré *la crema bronceadora* en la farmacia.

20. Él dejó *las toallas* en casa.

21. Aquí tienes *los tickets*.

22. ¿Conoces *a Juan*?

To review lo, la, los, las, turn to page 132.

7 Completen en el pretérito. *(Complete in the preterite.)*

23. Yo _____ a una estación de esquí.

24. José _____ a la boletería para comprar los tickets para el telesilla.

To review the preterite of ir and ser, turn to page 135.

Cultura

8 ¿Sí o no? *(True or false?)*

25. Puerto Rico, la isla del encanto, es una isla tropical donde hace bastante frío.

To review this cultural information, turn to pages 140–141.

Viejo San Juan.
Puerto Rico

Spanish Online

For additional practice, students may wish to do the online games and quizzes on the **Glencoe Spanish Web site** (spanish.glencoe.com). Quizzes are corrected instantly and results can be sent via e-mail to you.

Learning from Photos

(page 147) This parklike setting in **el Viejo San Juan** is near the new piers that accommodate many cruise liners making Caribbean cruises.

ANSWERS TO *Assessment*

4
12. pasé
13. nadaron
14. esquiaron
15. tomamos
16. llevaste
17. hablaron

5
18. Yo pagué en la caja.

6
19. Yo la compré en la farmacia.
20. Él las dejó en casa.
21. Aquí los tienes.
22. ¿Lo conoces?

7
23. fui
24. fue

8
25. No

Diversiones

Paso 4 of each **Unidad** includes a **Diversiones** section. As the title indicates, this section contains different types of activities that students in Middle School should enjoy. They also take into account the various learning modalities.

The many types of activities included are:

Canciones This section entitled **Canta con Justo** contains songs performed on the music CD by Justo Lamas, a young singer from Argentina who has written some songs specifically for **¿Cómo te va?**

Teatro These activities provide students the opportunity to get up and perform. They give suggestions for short skits, pantomimes, and dramatizations. These activities are particularly helpful for **kinesthetic learners.**

Manos a la obra

These activities enable students to get involved and use their hands. Some examples are: drawing cards or pictures, preparing ads and brochures, and preparing schedules and announcements.

Rompecabezas

Some units contain riddles or puzzles that reinforce language in a fun way.

Investigaciones

This research section allows those students who like to work on their own to get involved in some research projects that add another dimension to the cultural material of the unit.

148

Diversiones

Canta con Justo
El verano es lo mejor

De va - ca - cio - nes yo___ me voy. El in - vier - no ya___ lle - gó.___

A mí me gus - ta el___ ca - lor, el mar a - zul__ y mu - cho s-o -l.__

Yo no quie - ro ir___ a es - quiar,__ en la pla - ya quie - ro es - tar___

y al vo - lei-bol__ ju - gar, sal - tar las o - las y__ na - dar.___ El ve - ra-no es lo mejor.

¿Y qué es lo que te gus-ta___ a ti? ¿Y qué es-ta-ción te ha - ce___ fe - liz?__ La pri-ma-ve -

- ra, es la que to-dos___ es - pe - ran.___ Y la tem-pe-ra - tu - ra va a__ su - bir,___ cuan-do el ve-

ra-no lle - gue a-quí. Pla-yas y o - las, te i -nvi-tan a dis-fru-tar.___

En la arena caminé
y al tenis yo jugué.
En las montañas no esquié,
en el mar yo nadé.
Fue este año lo mejor.

¿Y qué es lo que te gusta a ti?
¿Y qué estación te hace feliz?
La primavera,
es la que todos esperan.
Y la temperatura va a subir,
cuando el verano llegue aquí.
Playas y olas,
te invitan a disfrutar.

148 ❀ *ciento cuarenta y ocho*   **Unidad 4: El verano y el invierno**

Music Connection

Canta con Justo

The song **El verano es lo mejor** will be easy for learners of all ability levels. It will help students practice the preterite tense and the weather expressions introduced in this unit. You may wish to have students hear the recorded version of **El verano es lo mejor.** It can be found on Track 2 of the **Canta con Justo** music CD.

In addition, students can watch Justo perform this song on the **Justo Lamas ¡En vivo!** music video that accompanies **¿Cómo te va?** You may wish to use Song Transparency S 4 to project the music and lyrics on an overhead so students can follow along as they listen or sing.

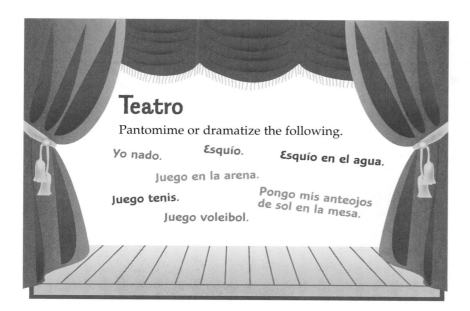

Teatro

Pantomime or dramatize the following.

Yo nado.

Esquío.

Esquío en el agua.

Juego en la arena.

Juego tenis.

Pongo mis anteojos de sol en la mesa.

Juego voleibol.

 Juego Think of an item you need. Your partner will ask you what you're going to do. Use the model as a guide.

—**Necesito crema bronceadora.** →
—**¿Por qué la necesitas? ¿Vas a la playa?**

Investigaciones

Do some research and get some information about the beautiful island of Puerto Rico.

Spanish Online

For more information about Puerto Rico, go to the Glencoe Spanish Web site: spanish.glencoe.com

Humacao, Puerto Rico

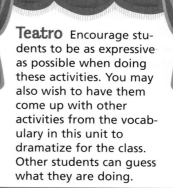

Teatro Encourage students to be as expressive as possible when doing these activities. You may also wish to have them come up with other activities from the vocabulary in this unit to dramatize for the class. Other students can guess what they are doing.

Juego You may wish to have students expand on one of these dialogues and continue the conversation.

Investigaciones

You may wish to encourage students to research this topic via the Internet. This can be done at home or as an in-class activity if your school has a computer lab.

Spanish Online Students will find links dealing with Puerto Rico to help them with their research project should they choose to do one.

Learning from Photos

(page 149) Humacao is an attractive small town a bit inland on the eastern coast of Puerto Rico. Because of its easy access to San Juan it has become one of the capital's residential suburbs. Nearby is the famous **Palmas del Mar** resort.

Universal Access

Activity 1 will be particularly beneficial for **visual learners.** **Kinesthetic learners** will enjoy Activity 2.

Juego After students have completed this activity, have them read their answers aloud as complete sentences in the preterite. For example: **Tomé el sol en la playa.**

Learning from Realia

(page 150) Have students say all they can about the photos from Chile.

Manos a la obra

1. Paint or draw a winter and/or summer scene. Describe your painting or drawing to a classmate.

2. Prepare a brochure for a summer or winter resort. Be sure to mention all the facilities your resort has to offer.

Juego **Cada uno en su sitio** Tell where each of the following might take place. **¡Cuidado!** Some might happen in more than one place.

tomar el sol   tomar un refresco   nadar

mirar un video   hablar por teléfono   usar crema bronceadora

tomar el telesilla   comprar los boletos   esquiar

En la playa	En las montañas	En casa
_____	_____	_____
_____	_____	_____
_____	_____	_____
_____	_____	_____
_____	_____	_____

ANSWERS TO **Juego**

En la playa:
tomar el sol
nadar
usar crema bronceadora
tomar un refresco

En casa:
mirar un video
hablar por teléfono
tomar un refresco

En las montañas:
esquiar
tomar un refresco
tomar el telesilla
comprar los boletos

Entrevista

¿Qué estación te gusta más, el verano o el invierno?
¿Prefieres ir a una estación de esquí o a una playa?
¿Sabes nadar? ¿Adónde vas a nadar?
¿Sabes esquiar? ¿Vas a esquiar con frecuencia?
¿Fuiste a una playa el verano pasado?
¿Nadaste en el mar o en una piscina?
¿Tomaste el sol?
¿Usaste una crema bronceadora?
¿Jugaste voleibol?
¿Lo pasaste bien?

Entrevista

The **Entrevista** activity reinforces students' ability to interact with peers in Spanish in a real-life situation. This task recombines material the student has already learned. Students of all ability levels will be able to perform this task.

PLEGABLES™
Study Organizer

El presente y el pasado Use these *large sentence strips* to help you compare and contrast activities in the past and in the present.

Step 1 Take two sheets of paper (8½ x 11) and **fold** into *hamburgers*. Cut along the fold lines, making four half sheets. (Use as many half sheets as necessary for additional pages to your book.)

Step 2 **Fold** each half sheet in half like a *hot dog*.

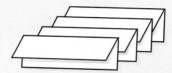

Step 3 Place the folds side-by-side and staple them together on the left side.

Step 4 About one inch from the stapled edge, **cut** the front page of each folded section up to the mountain top. These cuts form flaps that can be raised and lowered.

Step 5 To make a half-cover, use a sheet of construction paper one inch longer than the book. **Glue** the back of the last sheet to the construction paper strip, leaving one inch on the left side to fold over and cover the original staples. Staple this half-cover in place.

Step 6 With a friend, write sentences on the front of the flap, either in the present tense or in the past tense. Then switch your books of sentence strips and write the opposite tense inside under the flaps.

PLEGABLES™
Study Organizer

This foldable will help students organize, display, and arrange data as they learn to use the preterite tense in Spanish. You may wish to encourage them to add pairs of sentences as they continue to expand their understanding of how to use the past and present tenses.

Large sentence strips are also ideal for having students compare and contrast other grammatical structures that they will learn.

PASO 4

Más cultura y lectura

Playas del mundo hispano

National Standards

Cultures

The reading about beach resorts in the Spanish-speaking world and the related activity allow students to find out more about famous tourist destinations in Spain and Latin America.

 ¡OJO! The readings on pages 152–153 are optional. You may skip them completely, have the entire class read them, have only several students read them and report to the class, or assign them for extra credit.

Learning from Photos

(page 152, top left) Nerja is a resort east of Málaga on the Mediterranean coast of Spain. It is home to many British expatriates, especially retirees. Nerja is famous for its beautiful caves, **las cuevas de Nerja.**
(page 152, top right) This beach resort in Acapulco, México, is a sun worshipper's paradise on the Pacific coast, 260 miles south of Mexico City. The temperature is in the 80s year-round. The **bahía de Acapulco** is one of the world's best natural harbors.
(page 152, bottom right) Varadero Beach is one of the largest and most beautiful beaches in the Caribbean. It is known for its 20 km of white, sandy beaches. There have been many hotels built along the beach.
(page 152, bottom left) Punta del Este, a resort city in Uruguay, juts out into the Atlantic Ocean. It has beaches on both sides—**la playa mansa** with calm seas and **la playa brava** with rough seas.

▲ Aquí vemos una playa aislada de la Costa del Sol en España.

Muchos países de habla española tienen playas fabulosas.

▲ La playa de Acapulco en el océano Pacífico en México es muy grande, ¿no?

▲ Punta del Este es un balneario muy elegante en Uruguay. Muchos argentinos y brasileños pasan sus vacaciones en Punta del Este.

▶ Aquí tenemos la playa famosa de Varadero, no muy lejos de La Habana en Cuba.

¿Comprendes?

Mira las fotos de las playas. ¿Qué playa te gusta más?

ANSWERS TO ¿Comprendes?

Answers will vary depending on student preferences. Students will use vocabulary from Paso 1 to say why.

Un personaje latino famoso

▶ ¿Quién es Jennifer Rodríguez? Pues, ella es la primera persona de ascendencia latina que participa en los Juegos Olímpicos de Invierno y es muy interesante porque Jennifer, de ascendencia cubanoamericana, es de Miami. Miami es una ciudad del sur de Florida—lejos del frío, del hielo y de la nieve del invierno.

¿En qué deporte participa Jennifer? Ella es patinadora de velocidad sobre el hielo. Ella es recipiente de muchas medallas. En los Juegos de 2002 Jennifer ganó dos medallas de bronce, la primera en la categoría de 1.000 metros y la segunda en los 1.500 (mil quinientos) metros.

▲ Jennifer patina sobre el hielo.

¿Comprendes?

Contesten. *(Answer.)*

1. ¿En qué Juegos participa Jennifer Rodríguez?
2. ¿Participan muchas latinas en los Juegos Olímpicos de Invierno?
3. ¿Es Jennifer de ascendencia mexicanoamericana?
4. ¿De dónde es ella?
5. ¿Hace frío en Miami en el invierno?
6. ¿Es Jennifer esquiadora?
7. ¿Qué es?
8. ¿Tiene ella muchas medallas?
9. ¿Cuántas medallas ganó en los Juegos de 2002 (dos mil dos)?
10. ¿Ganó medallas de oro, de plata o de bronce?

CONEXIONES

CONEXIONES
Las ciencias sociales

National Standards

Connections
This reading about climate and weather in the Spanish-speaking world establishes a connection with another discipline, allowing students to reinforce and further their knowledge of the social sciences through the study of Spanish.

¡OJO! The readings in the **Conexiones** section are optional. They focus on some of the major disciplines taught in schools and universities. The vocabulary is useful for discussing such topics as history, literature, art, economics, business, science, etc. You may choose any of the following ways to do the readings in the **Conexiones** sections.

Independent reading Have students read the selections and do the post-reading activities as homework, which you collect. This option is least intrusive on class time and requires a minimum of teacher involvement.

Homework with in-class follow-up Assign the readings and post-reading activities as homework. Review and discuss the material in class the next day.

Intensive in-class activity This option includes a pre-reading vocabulary presentation, in-class reading and discussion, assignment of the activities for homework, and a discussion of the assignment in class the following day.

El clima y el tiempo

We often talk about the weather, especially when we are on vacation. When planning a vacation trip, it's a good idea to take into account the climate of the area we are going to visit. When we talk about weather or climate, we must remember, however, that there is a difference between the two. Weather is the condition of the atmosphere for a short period of time. Climate is the term used for the weather that prevails in a region over a long period of time.

El clima y el tiempo

El clima y el tiempo son dos cosas muy diferentes. El tiempo es la condición de la atmósfera durante un período breve o corto. El tiempo que hace puede cambiar[1] de un día al otro. O puede cambiar varias veces en un solo día. Hay sol por la mañana y llueve por la tarde.

El clima es el tiempo que prevalece[2] en una zona o región por un período largo. El clima es el tiempo que hace cada año en el mismo lugar[3].

Estaciones inversas

Es el mes de julio. En España es el verano y la gente va a la playa a nadar.

Pero en julio, los argentinos y los chilenos no van a la playa. Van a las montañas a esquiar. ¿En julio? Sí, en julio, porque es el invierno. En el hemisferio sur las estaciones son inversas de las estaciones del hemisferio norte.

[1] cambiar *change*
[2] prevalece *prevails*
[3] lugar *place*

Learning from Realia

(page 154) This weather map is from the newspaper **El ABC** in Madrid. You may wish to play the following true/false game.

1. Hay sol en Málaga.
2. Llueve en Córdoba.
3. Llueve en Bilbao.
4. Hay nubes (Está nublado) al norte de Madrid.
5. Palma de Mallorca está en una isla.
6. Alicante está en una isla también.
7. Ceuta está en el norte de África.

Un chiringuito, playa de
Casares, España

Las Lenas, Argentina

Aquí vemos unas fotografías de España y Argentina en diferentes estaciones. España y Argentina tienen un clima templado. En una región de clima templado hay cuatro estaciones: el verano, el otoño, el invierno y la primavera. El tiempo cambia con cada estación.

Aquí tenemos una fotografía de Puerto Rico en el mes de febrero. ¿Qué tiempo hace? Hay mucho sol y hace calor aún[4] en febrero. Puerto Rico es una isla tropical. En una región tropical hay solamente dos estaciones—la estación seca y la estación lluviosa cuando llueve mucho.

[4] aún *even*

¿Comprendes?

A. Contesten. *(Answer.)*
1. ¿Qué mes es?
2. ¿Qué estación es en España?
3. ¿Adónde va la gente?
4. ¿Qué estación es en Argentina y Chile?
5. ¿Adónde va la gente?
6. En julio, ¿dónde nada la gente?
7. En julio, ¿dónde esquía la gente?

B. Contesten. *(Answer.)*
1. ¿Viven ustedes en una región de clima templado o de clima tropical?
2. ¿Qué tiempo hace en las varias estaciones donde ustedes viven?

En la selva amazónica, Tambopata, Perú

¡Hablo como un pro!

This unique section gives students the opportunity to speak freely and say whatever they want on their own. The illustrations serve to remind students of precisely what they know how to say in Spanish. There are no depictions of activities that students do not have the ability to describe or talk about in Spanish. The art in this section recombines all that the students learned in the particular unit and in addition frequently recombines the topic or situation of the unit with that of another unit for additional reinforcement.

You can use this section in many ways. Some possibilities are:
1. Have students look at the illustrations and just identify items by giving the correct Spanish words.
2. Have students make up sentences about what they see in the illustrations.
3. Have students make up questions about the illustrations. They can call on another class member to respond if you do this as an entire class activity, or you may prefer to allow students to work in small groups. This activity is extremely beneficial because it enables students to actively use the interrogative words.
4. You may wish to ask questions and call on students to answer.
5. Have students look at the illustrations and give a complete oral review of what they see.
6. Have two students work together and make up a conversation based on the illustrations.
7. Have students look at the illustrations and write a paragraph (or paragraphs) about them in class.

You can also use this section as an assessment or testing tool, taking into account individual differences by having students go from simple to quite complicated tasks.

156

¡Hablo como un pro! Tell all you can about the following illustration.

156 ✹ ciento cincuenta y seis   Unidad 4: El verano y el invierno

The assessment can be either oral or written. You may wish to use the rubrics provided on pages T22–T23 as you give students the following directions.
1. Identify the topic or situation of these illustrations.
2. Identify as many items as you can and give the Spanish words. Don't forget to include actions you see.
3. Give as many sentences as you can to describe the illustrations.
4. Go over your sentences and put them in the best sequence possible.
5. Polish your sentences and sequencing to give a coherent story based on the illustrations.

Universal Access

When talking about the illustration, **students with learning difficulties** may just give random sentences. **Advanced students** will give a coherent story. You may wish to have **advanced students** write a paragraph about the illustration.

Vocabulario

Describing summer weather

el verano	Hace calor.
la nube	Hace buen
el cielo	(mal) tiempo.
Hace (Hay) sol.	Llueve.

Identifying beach gear

el traje de baño, el bañador
la loción (crema) bronceadora
la crema protectora
los anteojos de sol

la toalla playera
el esquí acuático
la tabla hawaiana
la plancha de vela

Describing summer and beach activities

el buceo	esquiar en el agua
nadar	pasar el fin de semana
tomar el sol	

Describing winter weather

el invierno	bajo cero
la nieve	Hace frío.
la temperatura	Nieva.
el grado	

Describing a ski resort

la estación de esquí	la pista
la ventanilla, la boletería	el pico
el boleto, el ticket	el telesquí, el telesilla
el/la esquiador(a)	el/la experto(a)
la montaña	el/la principiante

Describing the beach

el balneario	la ola
la playa	el mar
la arena	la piscina, la alberca

Describing a tennis game

el tenis	la red
la cancha de tenis	singles
(al aire libre)	dobles
la raqueta	jugar (al) tenis
la pelota	golpear la pelota

Identifying ski gear

el esquí	el anorak
la bota	el guante
el bastón	

Describing winter activities

esquiar
tomar (subir en) el telesilla
bajar la pista

Other useful expressions

por encima de	esta noche	esta mañana
a veces	anoche	la semana pasada
hoy	esta tarde	
ayer	por la tarde	

Vocabulario

Vocabulary Review

The words and phrases in the **Vocabulario** have been taught for productive use in this unit. They are summarized here as a resource for both student and teacher. This list also serves as a convenient resource for the **¡Te toca a ti!** activities on pages 144 and 145. There are approximately nineteen cognates in this vocabulary list. Have students find them.

¡OJO! You will notice that the vocabulary list here is not translated. This has been done intentionally, since we feel that by the time students have finished the material in the unit they should be familiar with the meanings of all the words. If there are several words they still do not know, we recommend that they refer to the **Paso 1 Palabras** and **Paso 2 Palabras** sections in the unit or go to the dictionaries at the end of this book to find the meanings. However, if you prefer that your students have the English translations, please refer to Vocabulary Transparency 4.6, where you will find all these words with their translations.

Universal Access

Have students, especially **kinesthetic learners,** prepare brochures for different resorts using information from the library or from the Internet. Use their brochures for a bulletin board display.

Planning for Unit 5

CORRELATIONS

National Standards

Communication Standard 1.1
pages 162, 163, 165, 166, 167, 171, 175, 176, 182, 189

Communication Standard 1.2
pages 176, 178–179, 190–191, 192–193

Communication Standard 1.3
pages 163, 165, 166, 167, 171, 175, 182, 183, 187

Cultures Standard 2.1
pages 178–179, 190–191, 192–193

Cultures Standard 2.2
pages 178–179, 186, 187, 190–191, 192–193

Connections Standard 3.1
pages 171, 178–179, 187, 190–191, 194–195

Connections Standard 3.2
pages 178–179, 190–191, 192–193, 194–195

Comparisons Standard 4.1
pages 177, 188

Comparisons Standard 4.2
page 182

Communities Standard 5.1
page 183

PACING AND PRIORITIES

The unit content is color coded below to assist you in planning.

■ required ■ recommended ■ optional

Paso 1 (required) *Days 1–8*
- ■ Palabras
  Al cine
- ■ Formas
  Pretérito—verbos en **-er, -ir**

Paso 2 (required) *Days 9–16*
- ■ Palabras
  Un concierto, En un museo
- ■ Formas
  Palabras negativas
  Pretérito de **leer, oír**
- ■ Conversación
  ¿Adónde fuiste?

Paso 3 (recommended) *Days 17–24*
- ■ Pronunciación
  La **h**, la **y**, la **ll**
- ■ Cultura y lectura
  Un viernes por la noche
- ■ Repaso
- ■ ¡Te toca a ti!
- ■ Assessment

Paso 4 (optional)
- ■ Diversiones
- ■ Más cultura y lectura
  Artistas hispanos
  Cantantes hispanos
- ■ Conexiones
  La música latina

RESOURCE GUIDE

SECTION		PAGES	SECTION RESOURCES
Paso 1			
Palabras	Al cine	160–163	🎴 Vocabulary Transparencies 5.1–5.2 💿 Audio CD 4 🎧 Audio Activities TE, pages 67–69 📘 Workbook TE, pages 73–74 📘 Quiz 1, page 31 💿 ExamView® Pro
Formas	Pretérito—verbos en **-er, -ir**	164–167	💿 Audio CD 4 🎧 Audio Activities TE, pages 69–70 📘 Workbook TE, pages 75–76 📘 Quiz 2, page 32 💿 ExamView® Pro
Paso 2			
Palabras	Un concierto En un museo	168 169–171	🎴 Vocabulary Transparencies 5.3–5.4 💿 Audio CD 4 🎧 Audio Activities TE, pages 71–72 📘 Workbook TE, pages 77–78 📘 Quiz 3, page 33 💿 ExamView® Pro
Formas	Palabras negativas Pretérito de **leer, oír**	172–173 174–175	💿 Audio CD 4 🎧 Audio Activities TE, pages 72–73 📘 Workbook TE, pages 79–80 📘 Quizzes 4–5, pages 34–35 💿 ExamView® Pro
Paso 3			
Conversación	¿Adónde fuiste?	176	💿 Audio CD 4 🎧 Audio Activities TE, page 74 📘 Workbook TE, page 81
Pronunciación	La **h**, la **y**, la **ll**	177	🎴 Pronunciation Transparency P 5 💿 Audio CD 4 🎧 Audio Activities TE, page 75 📘 Workbook TE, page 81
Cultura y lectura	Un viernes por la noche	178–179	💿 Audio CD 4 🎧 Audio Activities TE, pages 76–77 📘 Workbook TE, pages 82–83
Repaso		180–181	💿 Audio CD 4 🎧 Audio Activities TE, page 78 📘 Workbook TE, pages 83–84 📘 Tests, pages 65–80
¡Te toca a ti!		182–183	💿 Audio CD 4 🎧 Audio Activities TE, pages 79–80 📘 Workbook TE, pages 84–85
Assessment		184–185	🎴 Vocabulary Transparency 5.5 📘 Tests, pages 65–80 💿 ExamView® Pro, Unit 5 📘 Performance Assessment, Tasks 9–10
Paso 4			
Diversiones		186–189	📘 Workbook TE, page 86
Más cultura y lectura	Artistas hispanos Cantantes hispanos	190–191 192–193	📘 Tests, page 71
Conexiones	La música latina	194–195	📘 Tests, page 71

158B

Using Your Resources for Unit 5

Transparencies

Bellringer 5.1–5.5

Vocabulary V 5.1–5.6

Assessment A 5

Songs S 5

Workbook

Paso 1 Vocabulary and Structure pages 73–76

Paso 2 Vocabulary and Structure pages 77–80

Conversation and Reading pages 81–83

Repaso, ¡Te toca a ti!, Diversiones pages 83–86

Audio Program and Audio Activities Booklet

Paso 1 Vocabulary and Structure pages 67–70

Paso 2 Vocabulary and Structure pages 71–73

Conversation, Pronunciation pages 74–77

Repaso, ¡Te toca a ti! pages 78–80

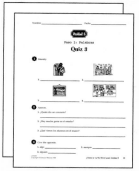

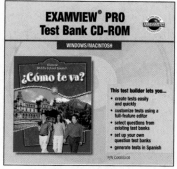

Vocabulary and Structure Quizzes, pages 31–38

Unit Tests, pages 65–80

ExamView® Pro, Unit 5

Timesaving Teacher Tools

TeacherWorks
All in One Teacher Planning

TeacherWorks™ is your all in one teacher resource center. Personalize lesson plans, access resources from the Teacher Wraparound Edition, connect to the Internet, or make a to-do list. These are only a few of the many features that can assist you in the planning and organizing of your lessons.

Includes:
- A calendar feature
- Access to all program blackline masters
- Standards correlations and more

Test Bank software for Macintosh and Windows makes creating, editing, customizing, and printing tests quick and easy.

PLEGABLES™
Study Organizer

Manipulatives The foldable activities give students of all learning styles the opportunity to excel in a nontraditional manner. Your students will love these hands-on activities!

Technology Resources

Spanish Online

In the Unit 5 online resources, you and your students will have a chance to learn more about leisure activities in the Spanish-speaking world.

PuzzleMaker allows you to create crossword puzzles, jumble puzzles, and word searches in minutes or edit a database of key terms and puzzles to review unit vocabulary. You can choose English-Spanish puzzles or Spanish-English puzzles. The puzzles can be printed or played on the computer screen.

Canta con Justo This CD contains songs sung by a young Argentine singer, Justo Lamas, which are specifically geared to review and expand upon the vocabulary learned in each unit. Students will enjoy listening to these songs while they learn from them.

¡En vivo! This music video of Justo Lamas performing his songs live in concert gives your students a chance to experience the songs in a different way while reinforcing the language skills they are learning!

Preview

In this unit, students will learn to discuss several types of cultural activities. To do this they will learn basic vocabulary associated with movies, concerts, and museums. They will also continue to express themselves in the past by learning the preterite of **-er** and **-ir** verbs and the verbs **leer** and **oír.** Students will also learn to express themselves with the negative words **nadie, nada,** and **nunca.** The cultural focus of the chapter will be an exerpt from the famous Spanish novel *Lazarillo de Tormes.*

National Standards

Communication
In Unit 5, students will communicate in spoken and written Spanish on the following topics:
• going to the movies
• going to a concert
• visiting a museum
Students will obtain and provide information about these topics and engage in conversations about their personal exposure to cultural events. They will also continue to learn to express themselves in the past.

Spanish Online

The **Glencoe World Languages Web site** (spanish. glencoe.com) offers options that enable you and your students to experience the Spanish-speaking world via the Internet. For each **Unidad,** there are activities, games, and quizzes. In addition, an *Enrichment* section offers students an opportunity to visit Web sites related to the theme of the unit.

Unidad

5 Pasatiempos y diversiones

Objetivos

In this unit, you will learn to:

% discuss movies, museums, and concerts

% relate more past actions or events

% talk about what doesn't happen

% talk about cultural activities that are popular in the Spanish-speaking world

% discuss a famous Spanish novel

Pero, yo quiero ver la película también.

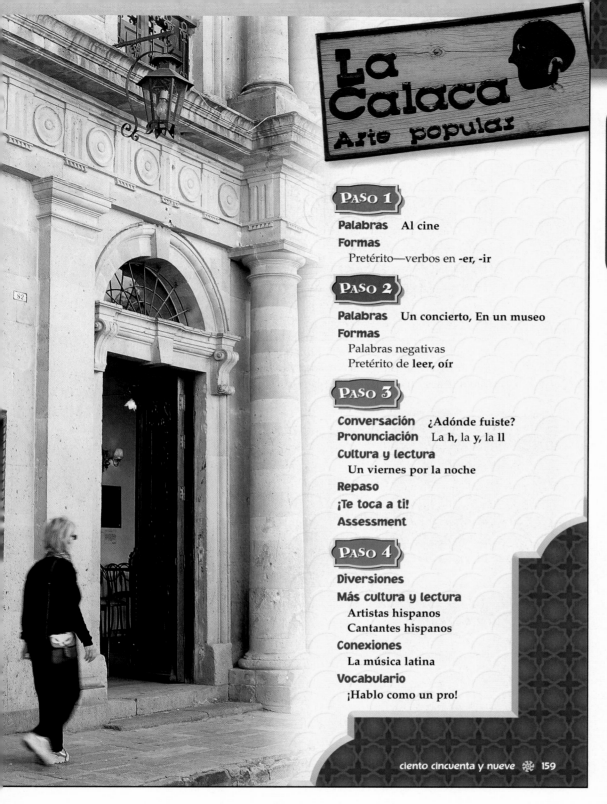

La Calaca
Arte popular

Spotlight on Culture

San Miguel de Allende, México

(page 158) These young people just bought tickets for a performance at the **Teatro Ángela Peralta** in San Miguel de Allende, México.

Palabras

PASO 1

1 PREPARATION

RESOURCE MANAGER

Vocabulary Transparencies 5.1–5.2
Audio Activities TE, pages 67–69
Audio CD 4
Workbook, pages 73–74
Quiz 1, page 31
ExamView® Pro

Bellringer Review

Use BRR Transparency 5.1 or write the following on the board. Complete the following in the past. Then rewrite the sentences changing **yo** to **ella.**

1. Yo ___ un video. (mirar)
2. Y yo ___ unos discos. (escuchar)
3. Luego, yo ___ al café. (ir)
4. En el café yo ___ con el mesero. (hablar)
5. Yo ___ un refresco. (tomar)

2 PRESENTATION

STEP 1 Using Vocabulary Transparencies 5.1–5.2, play the **Paso 1 Palabras** presentation on Audio CD 4. Point to the appropriate illustration as you play the CD.

STEP 2 Have students repeat each word or expression after you two or three times as you point to the corresponding item on the transparency.

STEP 3 Now call on individual students to point to the corresponding illustration on the transparency as you say the word or expression.

Universal Access

You may wish to have **advanced learners** say words or expressions from the vocabulary (with books closed) and have their classmates point to the illustration on the transparency.

Palabras Al cine 🎧

la taquilla,
la boletería

la fila, la cola

la entrada,
el boleto

Cine Apolo

Hay una cola delante de la taquilla.
Los amigos compran sus entradas (boletos).
Van a la sesión de las siete de la tarde.

la película, el film

la pantalla

la butaca

la fila

El joven vio una película.

José salió del cine.
Perdió el autobús (la guagua, el camión).

José decidió tomar el metro.
Subió al metro en la estación Sol.
Volvió a casa en el metro.

Total Physical Response

(Student 1), **levántate, por favor.**
Ven acá. Imagínate que quieres ir al cine.
Ve por el autobús. Allí está.
¡Corre! ¡Anda rápido! Vas a perder el bus.
¡Ay! Perdiste el bus. Pero no hay problema.
Ve a la estación del metro.
Baja al metro.

Espera.
Aquí viene el metro. Sube.
El metro llega a la estación que quieres.
Bájate del metro.
Sube la escalera.
Allí está el cine. Ve a la taquilla.
Ponte en fila.
Indica a la taquillera que quieres una entrada.
Gracias, *(Student 1).* **Y ahora toma tu asiento.**

Carolina y sus amigas decidieron no salir.
Alquilaron (Rentaron) un video en la tienda de videos.

Miraron la película en casa.

Paso 1: Palabras   ciento sesenta y uno ✳ 161

¡**OJO**! Note that only the third person singular forms of the preterite of **-er** and **-ir** verbs are used in the vocabulary presentation so that students can immediately answer questions and use the new vocabulary without having to make ending changes.

Vocabulary Expansion

You may wish to give students the following additional vocabulary.
   **una película en versión
      original**
   una película doblada
   una película con subtítulos

About the Spanish Language

- A ticket to a movie or theater is often referred to as **la entrada** rather than **el boleto** or **el billete. La localidad** is used for both a ticket and a seat in a theater.
- **La taquilla** is the most common word for a movie or theater ticket window. **La boletería** is often used in Latin America, **la taquilla** in Spain. In some areas you also hear **la ventanilla.**
- The word **la fila** or **la cola** can be used for a line of people. **La cola** is heard more in Latin America, **la fila** in Spain.
- In addition to **la película** and **el film,** you will often hear and see **el filme.**
- In addition to **el autobús,** the shortened form **el bus** is more and more frequently heard. In the Caribbean area the word for *bus* is **la guagua;** in Mexico, **el camión.** Other regional terms for *bus* are **el ómnibus, el micro, la góndola,** and **el colectivo.** (In many areas **colectivo** means *public taxi;* in Argentina, however, it means *bus*).
- The subway entrance is called **la boca del metro.**

161

3 PRACTICE

¿Qué palabra necesito?

¡OJO! When students are doing the **¿Qué palabra necesito?** activities, accept any answer that makes sense. The purpose of these activities is to have students use the new vocabulary. They are not factual recall activities. Thus, it is not necessary for students to remember specific factual information from the vocabulary presentation when answering. If you wish, have students use the photos on this page as a stimulus, when possible.

Historieta Each time **Historieta** appears, it means that the answers to the activity form a short story. Encourage students to look at the title of the **Historieta,** since it can help them do the activity.

1 and **3** After going over Activities 1 and 3 have students retell the stories in their own words. It is recommended that you go over all the activities once in class before assigning them for homework.

2 If necessary, have students refer to pages 160 and 161 to find the answers.

Learning from Photos

(page 162, bottom left) This subway station entrance is in downtown Buenos Aires near the **Plaza de Mayo,** where the **catedral Metropolitana** is located. Note than in Argentina the subway or metro is called **el subte**—a shortened form of **el subterráneo.**
(page 163) This theater is on **avenida Corrientes** in central Buenos Aires. This busy street has many theaters and movie houses.

162

¿Qué palabra necesito?

1 **Historieta Al cine** Contesten. *(Answer.)*

1. ¿Decidió Felipe ir al cine?
2. ¿Compró su entrada en la taquilla?
3. ¿Fue a la sesión de las dos de la tarde?
4. ¿A qué hora salió del cine?
5. ¿Perdió el autobús?
6. ¿Volvió a casa en el metro?

2 **¿Cuál es la palabra?** Den un sinónimo. *(Give a synonym.)*

1. la película
2. alquilar
3. el autobús
4. la boletería
5. el boleto

En la taquilla del cine, Barcelona, España

Buenos Aires, Argentina

Madrid, España

Unidad 5: Pasatiempos y diversiones

ANSWERS TO ¿Qué palabra necesito?

1
1. Sí, Felipe decidió ir al cine.
2. Sí, compró su entrada en la taquilla.
3. Sí, (No, no) fue a la sesión de las dos de la tarde.
4. Salió del cine a las ___.
5. Sí, (No, no) perdió el autobús.
6. Sí, (No, no) volvió a casa en el metro.

2
1. el film
2. rentar
3. la guagua, el camión
4. la taquilla
5. la entrada

3 Historieta En la taquilla Escojan. *(Choose.)*

1. La gente hace cola delante de _____.
   a. la pantalla   **b.** la fila   **c.** la taquilla
2. Compran _____ en la taquilla.
   a. butacas   **b.** películas   **c.** entradas
3. En el cine presentan o dan _____ americana.
   a. una entrada   **b.** una película   **c.** una novela
4. Los clientes entran en el cine y toman _____.
   a. una pantalla   **b.** una entrada   **c.** una butaca
5. Proyectan la película en _____.
   a. la pantalla   **b.** la butaca   **c.** la taquilla

4 ¿Quieres ir al cine? Work with a classmate. Make plans to go see a Spanish movie on Saturday afternoon. Discuss your plans together.

León · Mercedes · Víctor

Una boletería. Buenos Aires, Argentina

5 ¿Qué película quieres ver?
You and a friend cannot agree on which movie you want to see. Read the movie ads and try to convince each other which one you should both go to.

STAR WARS

¿SABÍAS QUE?

En los créditos de Episodio I Jabba The Hutt aparece como él mismo.

Burt Reynolds iba a protagonizar originalmente a Han Solo en Star Wars pero decidió no hacerlo.

En "El Regreso del Jedi" el cuerpo de Darth Vader es actuado por David Prowse, la voz por James Earl Jones, y su cara por Shaw Sebastian.

HORMIGUITAZ

ANTZ

¿SABÍAS QUE?

Woody Allen grabó sus diálogos de "Z" en sólo 5 días.

La canción que las hormigas están bailando en el bar es "Guantanamera".

En la última escena del Parque Central, se puede ver en el fondo una figura humana caminando por una vereda. Es un modelo computarizado del actor Martin Short (Viaje Insólito) utilizado en una película anterior.

Writing Development
Have students write the answers to Activities 1 and 3 in a paragraph to illustrate how all of the items tell a story.

4 You may wish to provide students with a list of some Spanish movies they might want to go see.

5 Encourage students to be creative and funny in their conversations. They may enjoy presenting their skits to the class.

Universal Access

You may wish to ask students the following questions:
1. ¿Dónde hay una cola?
2. ¿Qué venden o despachan en la taquilla?
3. ¿Dónde venden (despachan) las entradas?
4. ¿Dónde proyectan la película en el cine?

Have **auditory learners** answer the questions orally. Have **visual learners** write down these answers and then draw a diagram of where each event takes place, labeled with the corresponding sentence. Have **kinesthetic learners** act out each sentence while telling what they are doing. For example: (while standing in line) **Hay una cola delante de la taquilla.**

ANSWERS TO ¿Qué palabra necesito?

3
1. c
2. c
3. b
4. c
5. a

4 Answers will vary. Students should mention the name of the movie, what time it's playing, and how they will get to the movie.

5 Answers will vary. Students should use the information given to convince each other.

163

Formas

1 PREPARATION

RESOURCE MANAGER

Audio Activities TE, pages 69–70
Audio CD 4
Workbook, pages 75–76
Quiz 2, page 32
ExamView® Pro

Bellringer Review

Use BRR Transparency 5.2 or write the following on the board.
Complete in the present.
1. Ellos ___ en una casa de apartamentos. (vivir)
2. Pero nosotros ___ en una casa privada. (vivir)
3. Yo ___ en el comedor. (comer)
4. ¿Dónde ___ tú? ¿En el comedor o en la cocina? (comer)

2 PRESENTATION

Pretérito—verbos en **-er, -ir**

STEP 1 Write the verbs from the first chart on page 164 on the board. Underline the endings and have students repeat each form after you.

STEP 2 After you have written a form for **comer,** for example, **yo comí,** you may wish to have students give you the forms for **volver, vivir,** and **subir.**

STEP 3 Point out to students that the preterite endings for the **-er** and **-ir** verbs are exactly the same.

STEP 4 Have students open their books to page 164 and go over the forms of **dar** and **ver** in Item 2 with them.

STEP 5 Have students read aloud the model sentences in Item 3.

Formas

Pretérito—verbos en -er, -ir
Talking about past actions

1. You have already learned the preterite forms of regular **-ar** verbs. Study the preterite forms of regular **-er** and **-ir** verbs. Note that they also form the preterite by dropping the infinitive ending and adding the appropriate endings to the stem. The preterite endings of regular **-er** and **-ir** verbs are the same.

infinitive	comer	volver	vivir	subir	
stem	com-	volv-	viv-	sub-	endings
yo	comí	volví	viví	subí	-í
tú	comiste	volviste	viviste	subiste	-iste
él, ella, Ud.	comió	volvió	vivió	subió	-ió
nosotros(as)	comimos	volvimos	vivimos	subimos	-imos
vosotros(as)	comisteis	volvisteis	vivisteis	subisteis	-isteis
ellos, ellas, Uds.	comieron	volvieron	vivieron	subieron	-ieron

2. The preterite forms of the verbs **dar** and **ver** are the same as those of regular **-er** and **-ir** verbs.

infinitive	dar	ver
yo	di	vi
tú	diste	viste
él, ella, Ud.	dio	vio
nosotros(as)	dimos	vimos
vosotros(as)	disteis	visteis
ellos, ellas, Uds.	dieron	vieron

3. Remember that the preterite is used to tell about an event that happened at a specific time in the past.

> **Ellos salieron anoche.**
> **Ayer no comí en casa. Comí en el restaurante.**
> **¿Viste una película la semana pasada?**

Un restaurante mexicano en San Isidro, Lima, Perú

Unidad 5: Pasatiempos y diversiones

Universal Access

Give **students with learning difficulties** one of the new verb forms and have them use it in an original sentence. Then indicate a different person or group of people and have them say their sentence again, changing the verb form to refer to that person or group.

Learning from Photos

(page 164) This sign above the entrance to a Mexican restaurant in San Isidro, Lima, Perú, is the title of the popular novel by the Mexican novelist Laura Esquivel. It was also made into a movie.

¿Cómo lo digo?

 Historieta **Una fiesta** Contesten. *(Answer.)*

1. ¿Dio Carlos una fiesta?
2. ¿Dio la fiesta para celebrar el cumpleaños de Teresa?
3. ¿Escribió Carlos las invitaciones?
4. ¿Recibieron las invitaciones los amigos de Teresa?
5. ¿Vio Teresa a todos sus amigos en la fiesta?
6. ¿Le dieron regalos?
7. ¿Recibió Teresa muchos regalos?
8. Durante la fiesta, ¿comieron todos?
9. ¿A qué hora salieron de la fiesta?
10. ¿Volvieron a casa muy tarde?

Historieta **En la escuela** Contesten. *(Answer about yourself.)*

1. ¿A qué hora saliste de casa esta mañana?
2. ¿Perdiste el bus escolar o no?
3. ¿Aprendiste algo nuevo en la clase de español?
4. ¿Escribiste una composición en la clase de inglés?
5. ¿Comprendiste la nueva ecuación en la clase de matemáticas?
6. ¿Viste un video en la clase de español?
7. ¿A qué hora saliste de la escuela?
8. ¿A qué hora volviste a casa?

Alumnos en San Andrés, Colombia

Paso 1: Formas

¿Cómo lo digo?

¡OJO! Note that the activities on pages 165–167 build from simple to more complex. Activity 6 reintroduces the third person forms presented in **Paso 1 Palabras.** Activity 7 enables students to hear the **tú** form as they respond with the **yo** form. Activity 8 makes them use both **tú** and **yo.** Activities 10, 11, and 12 together make them use all forms.

6 This activity recycles vocabulary from earlier units as it practices the preterite.

7 Activity 7 can be done as an interview. Have several students report back to the class after they have finished their interview.

Writing Development
Have students write the answers to Activities 6 and 7 in paragraph form to show how all the answers tell a story.

ANSWERS TO ¿Cómo lo digo?

6

1. Sí, Carlos dio una fiesta.
2. Sí, dio la fiesta para celebrar el cumpleaños de Teresa.
3. Sí, Carlos escribió las invitaciones.
4. Sí (No), los amigos de Teresa (no) recibieron las invitaciones.
5. Sí (No), Teresa (no) vio a todos sus amigos en la fiesta.
6. Sí, (No, no) le dieron regalos.
7. Sí (No), Teresa (no) recibió muchos regalos.
8. Sí (No), todos (no) comieron durante la fiesta.
9. Salieron de la fiesta a las ___.
10. Sí, (No, no) volvieron a casa muy tarde.

7

1. Salí de casa a las ___ esta mañana.
2. Sí, (No, no) perdí el bus escolar.
3. Sí, aprendí algo nuevo en la clase de español.
4. Sí, (No, no) escribí una composición en la clase de inglés.
5. Sí, (No, no) comprendí la nueva ecuación en la clase de matemáticas.
6. Sí, (No, no) vi un video en la clase de español.
7. Salí de la escuela a las ___.
8. Volví a casa a las ___.

165

3 PRACTICE (continued)

8 Activity 8 can be done as a paired activity.

9 Have students present the dialogue to the class.

Writing Development
After going over Activity 10 in class, have students write the information in their own words in paragraph form.

Universal Access

Have **advanced learners** retell the story from Activity 10 in their own words. Have **students with learning difficulties** answer the questions.

Learning from Photos
(page 166, top) The **Gran Rex** is a large theater on the **avenida Corrientes** in Buenos Aires.

---

8 **Al cine** Sigan el modelo. *(Follow the model.)*

ir al cine →
—¿Fuiste al cine?
—Sí, fui al cine.

1. ver una película americana
2. comprender la película
3. salir del cine a qué hora
4. perder el autobús
5. volver a casa en el metro
6. volver a casa un poco tarde

Un cine, Buenos Aires, Argentina

9 **Una experiencia** Work with a classmate. Present the conversation from Activity 8 in its entirety.

10 **Historieta** **Al cine y al restaurante**
Contesten. *(Answer.)*

1. ¿Salieron tú y tus amigos anoche?
2. ¿Vieron una película?
3. ¿Qué vieron?
4. ¿A qué hora salieron del cine?
5. ¿Fueron a un restaurante?
6. ¿Qué comiste?
7. Y tus amigos, ¿qué comieron?
8. ¿A qué hora volviste a casa?

Unos amigos, Caracas, Venezuela

ANSWERS TO **¿Cómo lo digo?**

8
1. —¿Viste una película americana?
   —Sí, vi una película americana.
2. —¿Comprendiste la película?
   —Sí, comprendí la película.
3. —¿Saliste del cine a qué hora?
   —Salí del cine a las ___.

4. —¿Perdiste el autobús?
   —Sí, perdí el autobús.
5. —¿Volviste a casa en el metro?
   —Sí, volví a casa en el metro.
6. —¿Volviste a casa un poco tarde?
   —Sí, volví a casa un poco tarde.

10
1. Sí, mis amigos y yo salimos anoche.
2. Sí, vimos una película.
3. Vimos ___.
4. Salimos del cine a las ___.
5. Sí, fuimos a un restaurante.
6. Comí ___.
7. Mis amigos comieron ___.
8. Volví a casa a las ___.

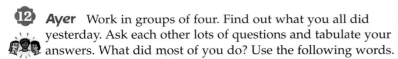

Historieta Ayer en la clase de español

Completen. (Complete.)

—¿__1__ (Aprender) tú una palabra nueva?

—¿Una? __2__ (Aprender) muchas.

—¿Les __3__ (dar) un examen el profesor?

—Sí, nos __4__ (dar) un examen.

—¿__5__ (Salir) ustedes bien en el examen?

—Pues, yo __6__ (salir) bien pero otros
   alumnos no 7____ (salir) muy bien.

—Entonces tú __8__ (recibir) una nota
   buena, ¿no?

12 **Ayer** Work in groups of four. Find out what you all did
yesterday. Ask each other lots of questions and tabulate your
answers. What did most of you do? Use the following words.

| salir | comer | ver | estudiar | mirar | nadar |
| escribir | volver | ir | comprar | tomar |

Después de las clases, fuimos a un café de Internet, Pisco, Perú

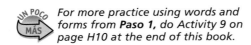

For more practice using words and
forms from **Paso 1,** do Activity 9 on
page H10 at the end of this book.

Paso 1: Formas

ciento sesenta y siete ❀ 167

---

11 Have students do Activity 11
as a miniconversation. Ask several
pairs to present the conversation
to the entire class.

12 Students in the group should
take turns asking someone else a
question, using one of the words
provided.

¡OJO! Activity 12 encourages
students to use the unit
vocabulary and structures in open-
ended situations. However, since
students do not yet know the
preterite of irregular verbs, be sure
that they use the verbs provided
when doing Activity 12. This will
deter them from trying to use
unknown forms.

UN POCO MÁS This *InfoGap* activity will
allow students to practice
in pairs. The activity should be
very manageable for them, since
all vocabulary and structures are
familiar to them.

ANSWERS TO ¿Cómo lo digo?

11
1. Aprendiste
2. Aprendí
3. dio
4. dio
5. Salieron
6. salí
7. salieron
8. recibiste

12 *Answers will vary; however,
students should use the verbs
from the list in the preterite.*

Palabras

1 PREPARATION

RESOURCE MANAGER

Vocabulary Transparencies 5.3–5.4
Audio Activities TE, pages 71–72
Audio CD 4
Workbook, pages 77–78
Quiz 3, page 33
ExamView® Pro

Bellringer Review

Use BRR Transparency 5.3 or write the following on the board.
Rewrite the following in the past.
1. **Yo voy con él.**
2. **Nosotros llegamos.**
3. **Él ve a un amigo.**
4. **Su amigo le habla.**
5. **Ellos me invitan a tomar un refresco.**

2 PRESENTATION

STEP 1 Have students close their books. Show Vocabulary Transparencies 5.3–5.4. Point to each item and have students repeat the corresponding word or expression after you two or three times.

STEP 2 Ask increasingly challenging questions of individual students as you present the vocabulary.

Palabras   Un concierto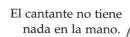

un estadio

la cantante

El estadio está lleno de gente.
La cantante dio un concierto.
El público oyó el concierto.

Al público le gustó mucho el concierto.
Todos aplaudieron.
La cantante recibió muchos aplausos.

Alguien está cantando.

Nadie está cantando.

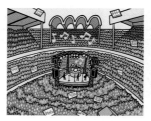

Siempre dan conciertos en el estadio.

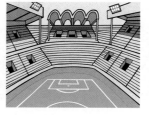

Nunca dan conciertos en el estadio.

El cantante no tiene nada en la mano.

El cantante tiene algo en la mano.

Universal Access

The following are examples of categories of questions: (1) **¿Es el cantante o la cantante? ¿Es un estadio o un cine?** (2) **¿Dio un concierto la cantante? ¿Dio el concierto en el estadio?** (3) **¿Quién dio un concierto? ¿Dónde dio el concierto?**
As material is reviewed and reintroduced, **students with learning difficulties** can be called upon to answer more challenging questions.

En un museo

un museo

un cuadro

una estatua

una artista,
una pintora

un artista,
un pintor

La clase de la Sra. del Río visitó el museo.
Vieron una exposición de arte.

STEP 3 Have students open their books to page 168. Reinforce the new vocabulary by reading the words and sentences on pages 168–169 or play Audio CD 4.

Total Physical Response

(Student 1), **levántate y ven acá, por favor.**
Vas a hacer algunos gestos. ¿De acuerdo?
Muy bien, eres escultor(a). Haz una estatua.
Eres artista. Pinta un cuadro.
Eres director(a) de una orquesta.
Dirige a la orquesta.
Escucha la música de la orquesta.
Gracias, *(Student 1).* **Siéntate.**

About the Spanish Language

El público is the most precise word for audience. **La audiencia,** however, is also taking on this meaning. The actual definition of **audiencia** is: **Admisión de presencia de un príncipe o autoridad; obtener audiencia. Acto de oír los jueces a los litigantes. Tribunal que entiende en los pleitos.**

Learning from Photos

(page 168) This photo of a stadium, full to capacity for a concert, was taken in Buenos Aires.
(page 169) These children on a field trip are about to visit a museum in San José, Costa Rica.

3 PRACTICE

¿Qué palabra necesito?

1 Students should answer in complete sentences. For example, **Felipe y unos amigos salieron anoche.**

2 Ask students to add any additional information as they do Activity 2. For example, for Item 1 they might say, **El cuadro está en el museo.**

¿Qué palabra necesito?

1 **Historieta** **Un concierto** Contesten según se indica. *(Answer as indicated.)*

1. ¿Quiénes salieron anoche? (Felipe y unos amigos)
2. ¿Adónde fueron? (al estadio de fútbol)
3. ¿Vieron un partido de fútbol? (no)
4. ¿Qué oyeron? (un concierto)
5. ¿Les gustó el concierto? (sí, mucho)
6. ¿Quiénes recibieron muchos aplausos? (los cantantes y los músicos)

2 **¿Qué es?** Identifiquen. *(Identify.)*

1.

2.

3.

4.

5.

ANSWERS TO ¿Qué palabra necesito?

1
1. Felipe y unos amigos salieron anoche.
2. Fueron al estadio de fútbol.
3. No, no vieron un partido de fútbol.
4. Oyeron un concierto.
5. Sí, les gustó mucho el concierto.
6. Los cantantes y los músicos recibieron muchos aplausos.

2
1. Es el cuadro.
2. Es la estatua.
3. Es el museo.
4. Es la artista.
5. Es el cantante.

170

Frida Kahlo

3 Historieta **Una excursión escolar**

Contesten según se indica. *(Answer as indicated.)*

1. ¿Qué visitó la clase de la señora Romero?
   (un museo)
2. ¿Qué vieron en el museo?
   (una exposición de arte mexicano)
3. ¿Qué vieron de Diego Rivera?
   (un mural famoso)
4. ¿Vieron muchas estatuas?
   (sí, de los mayas)
5. ¿Vieron algo de Frida Kahlo?
   (sí, un cuadro muy interesante)

4 **Al contrario**

Den lo contrario. *(Give the opposite.)*

1. siempre
2. algo
3. alguien

5 **Una excursión al museo** Using the information below, tell a classmate about a recent visit you made to the Prado Museum in Madrid. Tell how you got there, what it cost to get in, and what you saw. Answer any questions your classmate may have.

MUSEO DEL PRADO
CASON DEL BUEN RETIRO

HORARIO
De martes a domingo de 10.00 a 19.00 horas. Lunes cerrado.
Taquilla cierra a las 18.30 horas

PRECIO DE ENTRADA
General: 4,80 €
Reducida: 3,00 €
           Mayores de 65 años y estudiantes previa acreditación.
Gratuita: Menores de 12 años acompañados.

5 Have students take notes on their partner's trip. Have them report back using the third person preterite verb forms.

Learning from Realia

(page 171) The **Casón del buen retiro** is one of the two buildings of the Museo del Prado. It houses the nineteenth- and twentieth-century works. The other half of the museum is the Villanueva building, which displays Goya's works as well as paintings up to the eighteenth century.

Paso 2: Palabras

ciento setenta y uno 171

ANSWERS TO ¿Qué palabra necesito?

3
1. La clase de la señora Romero visitó un museo.
2. Vieron una exposición de arte mexicano en el museo.
3. Vieron un mural famoso de Diego Rivera.
4. Sí, vieron muchas estatuas de los mayas.
5. Sí, vieron un cuadro muy interesante de Frida Kahlo.

4
1. nunca
2. nada
3. nadie

5 Answers will vary. Students will use the information given as well as preterite verb forms and vocabulary from Paso 2 Palabras.

Formas

1 PREPARATION

RESOURCE MANAGER

Audio Activities TE, pages 72–73
Audio CD 4
Workbook, pages 79–80
Quizzes 4–5, pages 34–35
ExamView® Pro

Bellringer Review

Use BRR Transparency 5.4 or write the following on the board.
Complete.
1. **Ellos están esquiando ahora y ___ ayer también.**
2. **Ahora estoy jugando fútbol y ___ ayer también.**
3. **Ahora estás viendo la misma película que ___ ayer.**
4. **Ahora estamos comiendo la misma cosa que ___ ayer.**

2 PRESENTATION

 Palabras negativas

STEP 1 Have students open their books to page 172. Lead them through Items 1–2 and the accompanying model sentences.

STEP 2 You may wish to write the model sentence from Item 2 on the board and underline the highlighted words.

Universal Access

Advanced learners may enjoy making up as many sentences as they can using all three negative words. These sentences may be serious or silly.

Formas   Palabras negativas
Talking about what doesn't happen

1. Study the following negative words.

Algo está en la mesa.	**Nada** está en la mesa.
Hay **algo** en la mesa.	**No** hay **nada** en la mesa.
Vi **algo** allí.	**No** vi **nada** allí.
Alguien está cantando.	**Nadie** está cantando.
Oí a **alguien**.	**No** oí a **nadie**.
Ellos **siempre** van al cine.	Ellos **nunca** van al cine.
	Ellos **no** van **nunca** al cine.

2. In Spanish, you can use more than one negative word in the same sentence.

   Él **nunca** habla mal de **nada** ni de **nadie**.

Nota

The **a personal** is used with **alguien** and **nadie** when they are objects of the verb.

¿Viste a alguien?
No vi a nadie.

¿Cómo lo digo?

6 **Sí y no** Contesten con **sí** y con **no.**
(Answer with sí and no.)

1. ¿Alguien va al concierto?
2. ¿Está cantando alguien?
3. ¿Hablaste con alguien del concierto?
4. ¿Quieres comer algo?
5. ¿Tienes algo en la mano?
6. ¿Vas siempre al museo?
7. ¿Siempre pierde Juan el autobús?
8. ¿Siempre tienes que ayudar a alguien con algo?

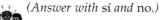

Serie P - 2   Nº 514424
Entrada 3 €

Museo del Prado, Madrid

7 **¿Nada, nunca o nadie?** Contesten con **no.**
(Answer with no.)

1. ¿Hay algo en tu mochila?
2. ¿Tienes algo en la mano?
3. ¿Ves a alguien en la sala?
4. ¿Hay alguien en la cocina?
5. ¿Siempre cantas?
6. ¿Siempre lees algo a alguien?
7. ¿Siempre les escribes algo a tus amigos?

Paso 2: Formas   ciento setenta y tres ✸ **173**

ANSWERS TO ¿Cómo lo digo?

6
1. Sí, alguien va al concierto. No, nadie va al concierto.
2. Sí, alguien está cantando. No, nadie está cantando.
3. Sí, hablé con alguien del concierto. No, no hablé con nadie del concierto.
4. Sí, quiero comer algo. No, no quiero comer nada.
5. Sí, tengo algo en la mano. No, no tengo nada en la mano.

6. Sí, siempre voy al museo. No, no voy al museo nunca. (No, nunca voy al museo.)
7. Sí, Juan siempre pierde el autobús. No, Juan nunca pierde el autobús.
8. Sí, siempre tengo que ayudar a alguien con algo. No, nunca tengo que ayudar a nadie con nada.

7
1. No, no hay nada en mi mochila.
2. No, no tengo nada en la mano.
3. No, no veo a nadie en la sala.
4. No, no hay nadie en la cocina.
5. No, no canto nunca.
6. No, nunca leo nada a nadie.
7. No, nunca les escribo nada a mis amigos.

173

1 PREPARATION

Bellringer Review

Use BRR Transparency 5.5 or write the following on the board.
In Spanish, write six words you could use at an airport.

2 PRESENTATION

Pretérito de **leer**, **oír**

STEP 1 Have students open their books to page 174.

STEP 2 Have the class repeat the verb forms given.

Learning from Photos

(page 174, top) This kiosk is on a street in Madrid. Note that in addition to newspapers and magazines one can also buy bus and metro tickets. *(page 174, bottom)* Mambrú is a group of young, extremely popular singers in Argentina.

Pretérito de **leer**, **oír**
Telling what people did

Note the forms of the verbs **leer** and **oír** in the preterite.

leer		oír	
leí	leímos	oí	oímos
leíste	*leísteis*	oíste	*oísteis*
leyó	leyeron	oyó	oyeron

Un quiosco. Madrid. España

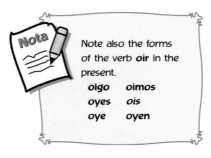

Note also the forms of the verb **oír** in the present.

oigo	oímos
oyes	oís
oye	oyen

¿Oíste al grupo Mambrú?
Buenos Aires. Argentina

174

¿Cómo lo digo?

 8 **Historieta** Juan lo leyó.

Cambien **yo** a **Juan.** (Change yo to Juan.)
1. Yo leí el anuncio del concierto.
2. Yo lo leí en la revista *Tú.*
3. Yo oí el concierto.
4. Yo oí a Alejandro Sanz. Él cantó muy bien.

 9 **¿Qué leíste?** Den el pretérito. (Give the preterite.)
1. Lo leo. No lo oigo.
2. Ella lo lee. No lo oye.
3. Lo leemos. No lo oímos.
4. ¿Lo lees? ¿No lo oyes?

 10 **Ayer** Look at the following illustration. Tell a friend all that your sister and her friends did last weekend. Answer any questions your friend may have.

 UN POCO MÁS *For more practice using words and forms from **Paso 2,** do Activity 10 on page H11 at the end of this book.*

Paso 2: Formas

Andas bien. ¡Adelante!

 3 PRACTICE

¿Cómo lo digo?

8 and **9** These activities can be done with books open.

Universal Access

Have students bring in a book they read recently and a CD they like to listen to. Have them hold up the book or the CD and say they read or listened to it. Then have others in the class tell whether they have read the book or listened to the CD. This activity will be especially beneficial for **kinesthetic learners.**

✓ Assessment

You may wish to give the following dictations.
1. Lo leí.	3. Lo leo.
2. Lo lee.	4. Lo leyó.

or
1. Yo lo leí.	3. Yo lo leo.
2. Ella lo lee.	4. Él lo oyó.

Option 1 strictly tests sound/symbol. Option 2 with the subject pronouns gives grammatical assistance.

UN POCO MÁS This *InfoGap* activity will allow students to practice in pairs. The activity should be very manageable for them, since all vocabulary and structures are familiar to them.

 ¡Adelante! At this point, all new material has been presented. Students have learned all the vocabulary and structure necessary to complete the unit. The conversation, cultural readings, and activities in **Paso 3** and **Paso 4** recycle all the material learned up to this point.

Learning from Realia

(page 175, top left) Have students work in pairs. One student will pretend he or she attended this concert. The other will ask questions about the concert such as who, where, when, and whether he or she enjoyed it.

Conversación

Conversación

¿Adónde fuiste?

1 PREPARATION

RESOURCE MANAGER

Audio Activities TE, pages 74–75
Audio CD 4
Workbook, page 81

2 PRESENTATION

STEP 1 To vary the presentation, have students listen to Audio CD 4 with books closed.

STEP 2 Ask students to tell you in one or two sentences what the conversation is about. This can be done in either Spanish or English.

STEP 3 Have students open their books. Give them two or three minutes to read the conversation silently.

STEP 4 Call on one student to read aloud the part of **Tadeo** and another the part of **Magalí.**

STEP 5 Then go over the **¿Comprendes?** activities that follow.

STEP 6 Call on one student to retell the story of the conversation in narrative form.

Note: If students can answer the **¿Comprendes?** questions with relative ease, move on. Students should not be expected to memorize the conversation.

Tadeo	Hola, Magalí. Te llamé por teléfono anoche y no contestaste.
Magalí	¿A qué hora me llamaste?
Tadeo	A eso de las siete.
Magalí	Volví a casa a las siete.
Tadeo	¿Adónde fuiste?
Magalí	Pues, fui a casa de Andrea. Alquilamos un video.
Tadeo	Ah, ¿sí? ¿Qué vieron?
Magalí	Vimos «Papá por siempre». A mí me gustó mucho pero a Andrea no le gustó nada.

¿Comprendes?

A. Contesten. *(Answer.)*
1. ¿A quién llamó Tadeo por teléfono?
2. ¿Contestó ella o no?
3. ¿A qué hora llamó Tadeo?
4. ¿A qué hora volvió a casa Magalí?
5. ¿Adónde fue Magalí?
6. ¿Qué alquilaron?
7. ¿Qué película vieron?
8. ¿A quién le gustó y a quién no le gustó?

B. Expresen de otra manera.
(Express another way.)
1. Te telefoneé.
2. A las siete o un poco antes.
3. Volví un poco después de las siete.
4. Rentamos.
5. A ella no le gustó en absoluto.

Unidad 5: Pasatiempos y diversiones

Learning from Photos

(page 176) This young couple is on a downtown street in Ponce, Puerto Rico. Ponce, on the southern coast, is the second-largest city on the island after San Juan.

ANSWERS TO ¿Comprendes?

A.
1. Tadeo llamó a Magalí por teléfono.
2. No, ella no contestó.
3. Tadeo llamó a (eso de) las siete.
4. Magalí volvió a casa a las siete.
5. Magalí fue a casa de Andrea.
6. Alquilaron un video.
7. Vieron «Papá por siempre».
8. A Magalí le gustó mucho pero a Andrea no le gustó nada.

B.
1. Te llamé.
2. A eso de las siete.
3. Volví a eso de las siete.
4. Alquilamos.
5. A ella no le gustó nada.

Pronunciación

La h, la y, la ll

The **h** in Spanish is silent. It is never pronounced. Repeat the following.

hijo	**hotel**	**higiénico**	**hola**
hermano	**hace**	**hostal**	**hospital**

Y in Spanish can be either a vowel or a consonant. As a vowel, it is pronounced exactly the same as the vowel **i.** Repeat the following.

> **el hijo y el hermano**
> **el hotel y el hospital**

Y is a consonant when it begins a word or a syllable. As a consonant, **y** is pronounced similarly to the *y* in the English word *yo-yo*. This sound has several variations throughout the Spanish-speaking world. Repeat the following.

ya	**desayuno**	**ayuda**	**playa**
yo	**oye**	**leyó**	

The **ll** is pronounced as a single consonant in Spanish. In many areas of the Spanish-speaking world, it is pronounced the same as the **y.** It too has several variations. Repeat the following.

llama	**botella**	**taquilla**	**toalla**	**lleva**
llega	**pastilla**	**pantalla**	**lluvia**	**lleno**

Trabalenguas

Repeat the following.

> **La hermana habla hoy con su hermano en el hotel.**
> **Está lloviendo cuando ella llega a la calle Hidalgo.**
> **El hombre lleva una botella de agua a la playa hermosa.**
> **Él no lo oyó; lo leyó en la pantalla.**

Refrán

Can you guess what the following proverb means?

Cuando el gato no está, los ratones bailan.

Pronunciación

¡OJO! In all areas of the Spanish-speaking world the **h** is silent. There are no exceptions. The **ll** and **y** have several variations. In most areas they are pronounced somewhat like the *y* in the English word *yoyo* or in the German word **ja.** In Argentina and Uruguay they are pronounced as a **j,** somewhat like the *j* in *Joe.* In Spain you will also hear a **j** sound, similar to the *y* sound Americans make when they pronounce quickly, *Did'ya . . . .*

Tell students that it is not unusual for Spanish speakers to misspell words with **y** and **ll.** Since the two letters sound the same, they often mix them up. They will also omit the **h** in words that should have it. Students may find it reassuring that others sometimes have spelling problems, too.

STEP 1 Have students very carefully repeat the sounds and words after you or Audio CD 4.

STEP 2 Ask students to open their books to page 177. Call on individuals to read the sentences.

STEP 3 All model sentences on this page can be used for dictation.

Refrán

If students cannot guess what the proverb means tell them, "When the cat's away, the mice will play."

Cultura y lectura

1 PREPARATION

RESOURCE MANAGER

Audio Activities TE, pages 76–77
Audio CD 4
Workbook, pages 82–83

National Standards

Cultures/Comparisons
The reading explains what teens in Madrid may possibly do on a Friday night. Students can decide if they would possibly do the same thing.

2 PRESENTATION

PRE-READING

STEP 1 Have students open their books and do the Reading Strategy activity on page 178. Then ask them what they think the reading is about.

STEP 2 Have students discuss things they might do if they have friends visiting on a Friday night.

STEP 3 Ask students about books they have read recently. Ask them to identify the protagonist and then ask some questions about this character. For example: Is the protagonist clearly good or bad, or do students have mixed feelings about this character?

READING

STEP 1 Have students open their books to pages 178–179 and read the selection silently and quickly.

STEP 2 Call on an individual to read approximately half a paragraph. Then stop and ask pertinent comprehension questions.

Cultura y lectura

Un viernes por la noche

Reading Strategy

Drawing conclusions As you read, it is necessary to think about what is taking place in the reading selection and why. You sometimes have to ask yourself why someone is doing something and then draw your own conclusions. It is often interesting to discuss your conclusion with someone else whose conclusion may be quite different from yours.

LAZARILLO DE TORMES

Antonio vive en Aravaca, en las afueras de Madrid. El viernes por la noche los padres de Antonio le dieron permiso para invitar a algunos amigos a su casa. Antonio invitó a algunos amigos muy buenos. Su madre llamó a una pizzería. La pizzería entregó[1] tres pizzas de tomate, queso y salchicha. A todos les gustó la pizza y comieron muy bien.

Después de comer y antes de ver un video, los jóvenes empezaron a hablar un poco de una novela que leyeron en su clase de español. La novela les interesó mucho y no pueden decidir si el protagonista de la novela es una persona mala o no.

Leyeron una parte o un trozo de la famosa novela española *Lazarillo de Tormes*. No sabemos quién escribió la novela. La escribió un autor anónimo en 1554. Es la historia de un muchacho pobre de origen muy humilde—un pícaro. Es Lazarillo.

❋

Lazarillo es de Salamanca. Su madre viuda[2] trabajó en una venta, un tipo de hotel humilde. Un día, un ciego[3] llegó a la venta y la pobre madre dio a su hijo al ciego.

Lazarillo salió de la venta con el ciego.

Lazarillo aprendió muy pronto a no tener confianza[4] en el ciego. Un hombre bastante cruel, el ciego lo trató muy mal.

Un día, el ciego decidió tomar un poco de vino de su jarro. Lazarillo metió una paja[5] en el jarro y él también bebió. En muy poco tiempo no hay más vino.

—Lazarillo, ¿tú también bebiste?

—No, señor. Yo no bebí nada.

—Yo sé que bebiste porque yo no bebí mucho y ahora no hay más vino. Si no lo bebiste tú, ¿quién lo bebió?

Biblioteca, Universidad de Salamanca, España

[1] entregó *delivered*
[2] viuda *widowed*
[3] ciego *blind man*
[4] no tener confianza en *not to trust*
[5] paja *straw*

Literary Connection

This reading familiarizes students with a famous work in Spanish literature, ***Lazarillo de Tormes.***

It was the novel ***Lazarillo de Tormes*** that gave birth to a genre of Spanish literature, **la novela picaresca,** that always has as protagonist a little urchin, or **pícaro,** the likes of Lazarillo.

El ciego tomó el jarro y lo rompió[6] sobre la cabeza de Lazarillo.

Otro día, los dos pasaron por un pueblo pequeño. Alguien le dio al ciego un racimo de uvas[7]. Habla el ciego:

—Lazarillo, yo voy a comer una uva. Cada vez que yo como una, tú también puedes comer una. ¿Me prometes comer solamente una?

—Sí, señor. Prometo comer solamente una.

El ciego tomó el racimo. Empezó a comer. Y, ¿cuántas uvas comió? ¿Una? No, comió dos.

Luego le dio el racimo a Lazarillo. Lazarillo tomó el racimo y él también empezó a comer. Y, ¿cuántas uvas comió? ¿Una? No. ¿Dos? No. Él comió tres.

—Lazarillo, yo sé que tú no comiste solamente una uva. Tú comiste tres.

—No, señor. Comí solamente una.

—Lazarillo. No es verdad. Yo sé que comiste tres porque yo comí dos y tú no dijiste[8] nada. Tú rompiste nuestra promesa.

—Pues, sí, señor. Es verdad que yo rompí nuestra promesa pero usted la rompió primero porque usted comió dos, no solamente una.

Un puente sobre el río Tormes, Salamanca

Los amigos de Antonio están decidiendo si Lazarillo es un muchacho malo o si está haciendo lo que tiene que hacer para poder existir. ¡A ver! ¿Qué opinión tienen ustedes?

[6] rompió *broke*
[7] racimo de uvas *bunch of grapes*
[8] dijiste *said*

¿Comprendes?

A. Contesten. *(Answer.)*
1. ¿Cuál es el título de la novela?
2. ¿Quién la escribió?
3. ¿Quién es el protagonista?
4. ¿De dónde es Lazarillo?
5. ¿Dónde trabajó su madre?
6. ¿Dio la madre a su hijo al ciego?
7. ¿Qué tipo de hombre es el ciego?

B. Expliquen en inglés.
(Explain in English.)
1. ¿Por qué rompió el ciego el jarro sobre la cabeza de Lazarillo?
2. ¿Por qué sabe el ciego que Lazarillo comió tres uvas y no solamente una?

C. ¿Cuál es tu conclusión? ¿Es Lazarillo un muchacho malo o está haciendo lo que tiene que hacer para existir?

Paso 3: Cultura y lectura

ANSWERS TO ¿Comprendes?

A.
1. El título de la novela es *Lazarillo de Tormes*.
2. La escribió un autor anónimo.
3. El protagonista es Lazarillo.
4. Lazarillo es de Salamanca.
5. Su madre trabajó en una venta, un tipo de hotel humilde.
6. Sí, la madre dio a su hijo al ciego.
7. El ciego es un hombre bastante cruel.

B. *Answers will vary but may include:*
1. The blind man hit Lazarillo over the head with his jar because he was angry that Lazarillo had tricked him and had drunk his wine.
2. The blind man knew that Lazarillo ate three grapes because the blind man had eaten two grapes and Lazarillo did not complain.

C. *Answers will vary:*

Repaso

PASO 3

Repaso

This section reviews the salient points from Unit 5. Students will study regular **-er** and **-ir** verbs in the preterite, the irregular verbs **leer** and **oír** in the preterite, as well as negative words such as **nada, nadie,** and **nunca.**

1 PREPARATION

RESOURCE MANAGER

Workbook, pages 83–84
Audio Activities TE, page 78
Audio CD 4
Tests, pages 65–80

2 PRESENTATION

STEP 1 Have students open their books to page 180. Ask them to look at the verbs in Items 1, 2, and 3. You may also have them repeat the verbs aloud. Have students repeat all verb forms of **leer** and **oír** in the preterite.

STEP 2 Have students repeat the words in Item 4, giving the affirmative and then the negative of each to reinforce their opposite meanings.

Learning from Photos

(page 180) The beautiful **Plaza Mayor** of Salamanca was built in the 1730s, and it is one of the largest squares in Spain. The elegant pinkish building is **el ayuntamiento** or Town Hall. No cars are allowed in the square, and it is a popular gathering spot for the local people. Salamanca is famous for its university.

1. In this unit, I learned the preterite of regular **-er** and **-ir** verbs.

comer		escribir	
comí	comimos	escribí	escribimos
comiste	*comisteis*	escribiste	*escribisteis*
comió	comieron	escribió	escribieron

2. The verbs **dar** and **ver** have the same endings as an **-er** and **-ir** verb in the preterite.

dar		ver	
di	dimos	vi	vimos
diste	*disteis*	viste	*visteis*
dio	dieron	vio	vieron

3. The verbs **leer** and **oír** have a change in the **él** and **ellos** forms.

él, ella, Ud.	leyó	oyó
ellos, ellas, Uds.	leyeron	oyeron

4. Important negative words are:

Affirmative	Negative
algo	nada
alguien	nadie
siempre	nunca

Él nunca le dio nada a nadie.
Ella no compró nada en la tienda.

Plaza Mayor. Salamanca. España

¡Pongo todo junto!

1 Ayer Escriban en el pretérito. *(Write in the preterite.)*

1. Yo como mucho.
2. Él no bebe mucho.
3. Aprendemos mucho en la clase de español.
4. ¿Ves el cuadro?
5. Ellos dan una fiesta.
6. Él la escribe.
7. Ellos viven en Salamanca.
8. Yo subo la montaña en el telesilla.
9. ¿Tú recibes el premio?
10. Salimos a las ocho de la mañana.

2 Hoy y ayer Completen.
(Complete in the present and preterite.)

1. Él _____ las novelas de Isabel Allende. (leer)
2. Nosotros las _____ también. (leer)
3. Ellas _____ el concierto. (oír)
4. Pero yo no lo _____. (oír)

3 No, nunca. Cambien en la forma negativa.
(Change to the negative form.)

1. Él siempre está hablando con alguien.
2. Alguien está en la puerta.
3. Yo vi algo allí en la mesa.
4. Él leyó algo sobre el problema.
5. Ellos siempre comen pizza.
6. ¿Llamaste a alguien por teléfono?

ISABEL ALLENDE,
La ciudad de las bestias.

14,90€

Álex se resiste a residir temporalmente en Nueva York con su peculiar abuela. Ella le tiene reservada una expedición a la selva amazónica. Objetivo: encontrar a una criatura misteriosa. Isabel Allende nos transporta a un mundo de escenarios naturales, infundiéndonos la necesidad de preservar la naturaleza.

Un concierto al aire libre. Las Palmas.
Gran Canaria. España

Paso 3: Repaso   **ciento ochenta y uno** ✱ **181**

ANSWERS TO ¡Pongo todo junto!

1
1. Yo comí mucho.
2. Él no bebió mucho.
3. Aprendimos mucho en la clase de español.
4. ¿Viste el cuadro?
5. Ellos dieron una fiesta.
6. Él la escribió.
7. Ellos vivieron en Salamanca.
8. Yo subí la montaña en el telesilla.
9. ¿Tú recibiste el premio?
10. Salimos a las ocho de la mañana.

2
1. lee, leyó
2. leemos, leímos
3. oyen, oyeron
4. oigo, oí

3
1. Él nunca está hablando con nadie.
2. Nadie está en la puerta.
3. Yo no vi nada allí en la mesa.
4. Él no leyó nada sobre el problema.
5. Ellos nunca comen pizza.
6. ¿No llamaste a nadie por teléfono?

Recycling

These activities allow students to use the vocabulary and structure from this unit in completely open-ended, real-life situations.

¡OJO! Encourage students to say as much as possible when they do these activities. Tell them not to be afraid to make mistakes, since the goal of the activities is real-life communication. If someone in the group makes an error, allow the others to politely correct him or her. Let students choose the activities they would like to do. You may wish to divide students into pairs or groups. Encourage students to elaborate on the basic theme and to be creative. They may use props, pictures, or posters if they wish.

PASO 3

¡Te toca a ti!

Hablar

1 ¿Por qué volviste tan tarde?

 ✓ *Tell what you did*

 You got home really late last night. One of your parents (your partner) wants to know why. He or she will ask a lot of questions. You'd better have some good answers.

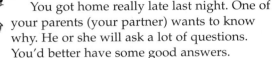

Hablar

2 Diversiones

 ✓ *Talk about leisure time activities*

Work with a classmate. Pretend you're on vacation in Spain. You meet a Spaniard your own age who is interested in knowing what you do in your free time—**cuando tienes tiempo libre.** Tell him or her about all your leisure activities. Then your partner will tell what he or she does.

Pantalla en un hipermercado.
Estepona, España

Hablar

3 Al cine o un video en casa

 ✓ *Talk about going to the movies or seeing a film*

Work with a classmate. Discuss whether or not you like movies. Do you watch them often? Do you prefer to go to the movies or rent a video and watch it at home?

182 ✳ ciento ochenta y dos

Unidad 5: Pasatiempos y diversiones

ANSWERS TO ¡Te toca a ti!

1 *Answers will vary. Students should use the preterite tense and leisure activities presented in this unit.*

2 *Answers will vary. In addition to the leisure activities presented in this unit, students might mention activities they learned to talk about in earlier units, such as listening to music, watching TV, going out to eat, playing sports, etc.*

3 *Answers will vary. Students should use the vocabulary presented in this unit to describe going to the movies or renting a video. Students should also use gustar and interesar to describe their interests.*

Teatro Calderón
Z
ZORRO
EL ESPECTÁCULO
Estreno 2 de Octubre
con *Manuel Bandera*
Entradas ya a la venta
Tel. 902 22 16

Escribir

4 Un anuncio

✓ *Advertise an event*

Prepare a poster in Spanish for a cultural event at your school. It can be a school play, a concert, an exhibit of a student's artwork, etc.

Writing Strategy

Persuasive writing Persuasive writing is writing that encourages a reader to do something or to accept an idea. Newspaper and magazine advertisements, as well as certain articles, are examples of persuasive writing. As you write, present a logical argument to encourage others to follow your line of thinking. Your writing should contain sufficient evidence to persuade readers to "buy into" what you are presenting. Explain how your evidence supports your argument; end by restating your argument.

Escribir

5 Un reportaje

Your local newspaper has asked you to write an article to attract Spanish-speaking readers to a cultural event that is taking place in your hometown. You can write about a real or fictitious event.

You have seen the event and you really liked it. Tell why you liked the event as you try to convince or persuade your readers to go see it.

La Ópera. España

4 Your class can ask students who are performing in the school play and the Theatre Department for information for the posters. Display the best ones.

Writing Development

Have students keep a notebook or portfolio containing their best written work from each unit. These selected writings can be based on assignments from the Student Textbook and the Writing Activities Workbook. The two activities on page 183 are examples of writing assignments that may be included in each student's portfolio.

In the Workbook, students will develop an organized autobiography (**Mi autobiografía**). These workbook pages may also become a part of their portfolio.

Writing Strategy

Persuasive writing Have students read the Writing Strategy on page 183. Before students begin to write their articles, they should make a list of reasons why readers should see the event.

Learning from Photos

(page 183) This photo is of **el Teatro Real**. It was built around 1850 and served as the center of Madrid's cultural society. It had been closed for many years for renovations but is now reopened and serves as Madrid's opera house.

Paso 3: ¡Te toca a ti!

ciento ochenta y tres 🏵 183

ANSWERS TO ¡Te toca a ti!

4 *Posters should include the following information:*
¿Qué es? ¿Cuándo? ¿Dónde es? ¿Cuánto cuestan los boletos?

5 *Answers will vary. Students should use the preterite tense to describe the event. Students may include* gustar *and* interesar *to describe how much they enjoyed it.*

PASO 3

Assessment

✓ **Assessment**

This is a pretest for students to take before you administer the unit test. Note that each section is cross-referenced so students can easily find the material they have to review in case they made errors. You may use Assessment Answers Transparency A 5 to do the assessment in class, or you may assign this assessment for homework. You can correct the assessment yourself, or you may prefer to project the answers on the overhead in class.

Assessment

¿Estoy listo(a)?

Palabras

1 Escojan. *(Choose.)*

1. Presentan o dan una película en _____.
   a. el cine **b.** la taquilla **c.** una tienda de videos
2. Para ir al cine, es necesario comprar _____.
   a. una fila **b.** una entrada **c.** un film
3. Ellos van a _____ de las siete de la tarde.
   a. la película **b.** la taquilla **c.** la sesión
4. Proyectan la película en _____.
   a. la pantalla **b.** la butaca **c.** la fila
5. En cada fila de un cine hay _____.
   a. taquillas **b.** colas **c.** butacas
6. Juan tomó el metro porque _____ el autobús.
   a. subió **b.** perdió **c.** vio

To review words from **Paso 1**, turn to pages 160–161.

2 Identifiquen. *(Identify.)*

To review words from **Paso 2**, turn to pages 168–169.

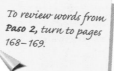
7.

8.

9.

10.

ANSWERS TO Assessment

1

1. a
2. b
3. c
4. a
5. c
6. b

2

7. el cuadro
8. la estatua
9. el museo
10. el cantante

Formas

3 Completen con el pretérito. *(Complete in the preterite.)*
    11. Yo _____ una película muy buena. (ver)
    12. Él público _____ mucho. (aplaudir)
    13. Nosotros _____ ir al concierto. (decidir)
    14. Los cantantes _____ muchos aplausos. (recibir)
    15. ¿A qué hora _____ tú del estadio? (salir)
    16. ¿Quién _____ el autobús? (perder)
    17. Teresa _____ el concierto y le gustó mucho. (oír)
    18. Ellos _____ la novela «Lazarillo de Tormes». (leer)

To review the preterite of -er and -ir verbs, turn to pages 164 and 174.

4 Den la forma negativa. *(Give the negative form.)*
    19. Él tiene algo en la mano.
    20. Ellos van siempre.
    21. Alguien me llamó por teléfono.
    22. Él siempre hace algo.

To review negative words, turn to page 172.

Cultura

5 Identifiquen. *(Identify.)*
    23. el título de una novela española
    24. donde trabajó la madre del joven pobre
    25. el número de uvas que comió el joven

To review this cultural information, turn to pages 178–179.

Spanish Online

For additional practice, students may wish to do the online games and quizzes on the **Glencoe Spanish Web site** (spanish.glencoe.com). Quizzes are corrected instantly and results can be sent via e-mail to you.

ANSWERS TO Assessment

3
11. vi
12. aplaudió
13. decidimos
14. recibieron
15. saliste
16. perdió
17. oyó
18. leyeron

4
19. Él no tiene nada en la mano.
20. Ellos nunca van.
21. Nadie me llamó por teléfono.
22. Él nunca hace nada.

5
23. *Lazarillo de Tormes*
24. una venta (un hotel humilde)
25. tres

Diversiones

Paso 4 of each **Unidad** includes a **Diversiones** section. As the title indicates, this section contains different types of activities that students in Middle School should enjoy. They also take into account the various learning modalities.

The many types of activities included are:

Canciones This section entitled **Canta con Justo** contains songs performed on the music CD by Justo Lamas, a young singer from Argentina who has written some songs specifically for **¿Cómo te va?**

Teatro These activities provide students the opportunity to get up and perform. They give suggestions for short skits, pantomimes, and dramatizations. These activities are particularly helpful for **kinesthetic learners.**

Manos a la obra

These activities enable students to get involved and use their hands. Some examples are: drawing cards or pictures, preparing ads and brochures, and preparing schedules and announcements.

Rompecabezas

Some units contain riddles or puzzles that reinforce language in a fun way.

Investigaciones

This research section allows those students who like to work on their own to get involved in some research projects that add another dimension to the cultural material of the unit.

186

Diversiones

Canta con Justo
Es tiempo de celebrar

Vier-nes por la no - che, hay que ce - le - brar. El fin de se - ma - na va a em-pe-zar. U-nos van al ci - ne, o-tros a bai - lar. en to - do lu - gar tú pue - des ce - leb - rar.___ La gen-te en las ca - lles sa - le a can - tar mú-si-ca la - ti - na sin pa - rar Y si tu es-tás tris-te no lo du - des más y vi - ve la a - le - grí - a y co - mien - za a dan - zar.

Si vas a un concierto
tienes que aplaudir
y con el público saltar.

Unos van al cine,
otros a bailar.
En todo lugar
tú puedes celebrar.

La gente en las calles
sale a cantar
música latina
sin parar.
Y si tú estás triste,
no lo dudes más y
vive la alegría
y comienza a danzar.

baila, canta, salta,
baila, canta, salta sin parar

Music Connection

Canta con Justo

The song **Es tiempo de celebrar** will be easy for learners of all ability levels. It will help students practice the vocabulary introduced in this unit. You may wish to have students hear the recorded version of **Es tiempo de celebrar.** It can be found on Track 11 of the **Canta con Justo** music CD. In addition, students can watch Justo perform this song on the **Justo Lamas ¡En vivo!** music video that accompanies **¿Cómo te va?** You may wish to use Song Transparency S 5 to project the music and lyrics on an overhead so students can follow along as they listen or sing.

Manos a la obra

1. **Lazarillo** Draw a picture of Lazarillo de Tormes. Give a description of your Lazarillo.
2. **Una tira cómica** Make your own comic strip depicting the story of Lazarillo de Tormes.

Teatro

Have a class talent show in Spanish. Some things you can do are:

present a short piece on a musical instrument you play

recite a short Spanish poem

show a drawing or painting you have done

do a pantomime

sing a song in Spanish

Rompecabezas

El intruso Choose the word in each group that does not belong.

1. el autobús	la taquilla	la guagua	el camión
2. el museo	el concierto	la cantante	los aplausos
3. nada	ayer	nunca	nadie
4. la película	el pintor	el cuadro	la estatua
5. bailar	la música	el cuadro	cantar
6. el taxi	el metro	el carro	la entrada

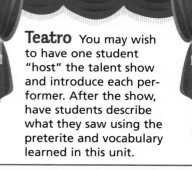
ANSWERS TO **Rompecabezas** ——

1. la taquilla
2. el museo
3. ayer
4. la película
5. el cuadro
6. la entrada

187

PASO 4

Rompecabezas

You may wish to expand upon this activity by having students tell which movies they have seen or have not seen and which movies they liked or did not like. This could be done in small groups or as a whole-class activity.

Learning from Photos

(page 188) This photo is one of the many theaters and movie houses that line the wide, busy **avenida Corrientes** in downtown Buenos Aires.

Rompecabezas

Can you figure out what all the following movie titles are in English? Most of them are movies that you should be familiar with.

Novia fugitiva   Bella y La Bestia   Alicia en el País de las Maravillas

20,000 Leguas de Viaje Submarino   Blanca Nieves   Quédate a Mi Lado

La Gran Estafa   La Ciudadela de los Robinson

La Boda de Mi Mejor Amigo   Juguetes

La Cenicienta   Magnolias de Acero   101 Dalmatas

ANSWERS TO Rompecabezas

Runaway Bride, Beauty and the Beast, Alice in Wonderland, 20,000 Leagues Under the Sea, Snow White, Stand By Me, The Great Escape, Swiss Family Robinson, My Best Friend's Wedding, Toy Story, Cinderella, Steel Magnolias, 101 Dalmatians

Entrevista

¿Te gusta la música?
¿Qué música te gusta más—la música
   popular o la música clásica?
¿Cantas?
¿Tienes una voz bonita?
¿Sabes tocar un instrumento musical?
¿Qué tocas?

 **PLEGABLES** TM
Study Organizer

Diversiones favoritas Use this *project board with tabs* to display a visual about your favorite movie or video. Be sure to make it as attractive as possible to help convince others to see it.

Step 1 **Draw** a large illustration, a series of small illustrations, or write on the front of a sheet of paper.

Step 2 **Pinch** and slightly fold the sheet of paper at the point where a tab is desired on the illustrated piece of paper. Cut into the paper on the fold. Cut straight in, then cut up to form an "L." When the paper is unfolded, it will form a tab with the illustration on the front.

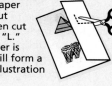

Step 3 After all tabs have been cut, glue this front sheet onto a second sheet of paper. Place glue around all four edges and in the middle, away from tabs.

Step 4 **Write** or draw under the tabs. If the project is made as a bulletin board using butcher paper, tape or glue smaller sheets of paper under the tabs.

Think of favorite scenes from a movie or cultural event that you enjoyed and draw them on the front of the tabs. Underneath the tabs write a description of the scene or tell why you liked that part of the movie. It might be fun to not put a title on the project board and just hang it up and let classmates guess the name of the movie you are describing.

Entrevista

The **Entrevista** activity reinforces students' ability to interact with peers in Spanish in a real-life situation. This task recombines material the student has already learned. Students of all ability levels will be able to perform this task.

PLEGABLES TM
Study Organizer

This foldable will help students organize, display, and arrange data as they learn to describe cultural events in Spanish. You may wish to encourage them to add information from each unit as they continue to watch movies in Spanish.

A *project board with tabs* foldable is also ideal for having students illustrate and describe scenes from other events that they will be learning about.

PASO 4

Más cultura y lectura

Artistas hispanos

National Standards

Cultures
The reading about artists from the Spanish-speaking world and the related activities give students an appreciation of works of art from some of the great artists of the Spanish-speaking world.

¡OJO! This reading is optional. You may skip it completely, have the entire class read it, have only several students read it and report to the class, or assign it for extra credit.

PRESENTATION

STEP 1 Have students read each paragraph silently.

STEP 2 Do the **¿Comprendes?** activities. These activities provide a quick and informal assessment of how well students understood this reading.

Hay muchos artistas españoles y latinoamericanos que son muy famosos.

▲ **Joan Miró (1893–1983)** Joan Miró es un artista español moderno. Es un pintor surrealista. Los sueños[2], la fantasía y la subconciencia inspiran a los artistas surrealistas. Aquí vemos *el Carnaval de Harlequín* de Miró. ¿Te gusta el cuadro o no? ¿Te gustan los colores? ¿Es lógico el cuadro?

▲ **Francisco de Goya (1746–1828)** Un pintor famoso de España es Francisco de Goya. Aquí vemos su cuadro *La marquesa de Pantojas*. Vemos a la señora elegante en un parque. El pintor pinta el traje de la marquesa con mucho detalle. ¿Qué opinas del porte[1] de la marquesa? ¿Es natural o no? ¿Qué expresión tiene la marquesa? ¿Tiene una expresión triste o contenta? O, ¿nos mira sin expresión?

▶ **Frida Kahlo (1910–1954)** Frida Kahlo es también una artista surrealista. Ella es de Coyoacán, México. La vida de Frida Kahlo es una vida bastante triste. Aquí vemos uno de sus autorretratos. ¿Puedes ver la tristeza[3] y el sufrimiento en su cara? A Kahlo le gusta usar muchos colores. ¿Qué colores ves en este cuadro?

[1] porte *poise*
[2] sueños *dreams*
[3] tristeza *sadness*

Art Connection

(page 190, top right) Joan Miró (1893–1983) was a modest man who lived on the island of Mallorca. Because he never lost his childhood curiosity, his house was filled with toys. He loved jack-in-the-boxes and he had hundreds of them. Miró painted a fascinating world of dreams and the subconscious. His *Carnival of Harlequin,* a detail of which is seen here, was among the first paintings to be called "surrealist." This work established him as a major figure in twentieth-century art.

◄ José Clemente Orozco (1883–1949) José Clemente Orozco es uno de los tres muralistas mexicanos famosos. Sus murales tienen motivos políticos y son muy emocionantes. Aquí vemos el cuadro *Zapatistas*. Los zapatistas son los peones o campesinos pobres que tienen como líder Emiliano Zapata durante la Revolución mexicana. En el cuadro los peones caminan (van a pie) de una manera pausada y laboriosa. La inclinación de los cuerpos y la representación de los sombreros y sarapes dan la impresión de una marcha determinada. Van a derrocar[4] a sus opresores.

[4] derrocar *bring down*

¿Comprendes?

A. Contesten. *(Answer.)*
1. ¿Quiénes son dos artistas famosos de España?
2. ¿Quiénes son dos artistas famosos de México?
3. ¿Quiénes son dos artistas surrealistas?
4. ¿Quién pinta murales con motivos políticos?
5. ¿Quién pinta a personas de la familia real española?
6. ¿Quién pinta autorretratos?
7. ¿Qué inspira a los artistas surrealistas?
8. En el mural *Zapatistas*, ¿qué da la impresión de una marcha determinada?

B. Descripciones Describan. *(Describe.)*
1. a la marquesa de Pantojas
2. a Frida Kahlo
3. a los zapatistas

C. Análisis De todos los cuadros que ves aquí, ¿cuál te gusta más? ¿Hay uno que no te gusta? ¿Por qué?

Paso 4: Diversiones

ciento noventa y uno 191

ANSWERS TO ¿Comprendes?

A.
1. Dos artistas famosos de España son Joan Miró y Francisco de Goya.
2. Dos artistas famosos de México son Frida Kahlo y José Clemente Orozco.
3. Dos artistas surrealistas son Joan Miró y Frida Kahlo.
4. José Clemente Orozco pinta murales con motivos políticos.
5. Francisco de Goya pinta a personas de la familia real española.
6. Frida Kahlo pinta autorretratos.
7. Los sueños, la fantasía y la subconciencia inspiran a los artistas surrealistas.
8. La inclinación de los cuerpos y la representación de los sombreros y sarapes dan la impresión de una marcha determinada.

B. *Answers will vary. Students should give as much detail as possible.*

C. *Answers will vary. Students should be able to state and explain their preferences.*

PASO 4

Personajes latinos famosos

National Standards

Cultures/Comparisons

The reading about two famous musicians and the related activities familiarize students with popular culture in the Spanish-speaking world. Students will be able to make comparisons to their own culture, enabling them to understand that some aspects of popular culture may be the same in the United States and in the Spanish-speaking world.

¡OJO! This reading is optional. You may skip it completely, have the entire class read it, have only several students read it and report to the class, or assign it for extra credit.

Learning from Photos

(page 192, top) This photo shows Ricky Martin singing at the German Record Awards in Hamburg, Germany.
(page 192, bottom) In this photo Ricky Martin and Plácido Domingo are acknowledging the orchestra during a rehearsal at the Dorothy Chandler Pavilion in Los Angeles. The two singers sang at the same concert.

Más cultura y lectura

Cantantes hispanos

Dos cantantes latinos que llenan[1] los estadios cuando dan un concierto son Ricky Martin y Plácido Domingo. Los dos son muy populares pero hay muchas diferencias entre estos dos personajes. Ricky Martin es muy joven. Plácido Domingo es un señor mayor. Ricky Martin canta canciones populares y Plácido Domingo canta ópera. Pero cada uno puede llenar de aficionados[2] un gran estadio.

▶Ricky Martin nace en la Víspera del Año Nuevo[3] de 1971 en San Juan, Puerto Rico. Sus padres se divorcian cuando él tiene sólo dos años. Desde muy pequeño, a Ricky le gusta mucho estar delante de un público. Contra[4] los deseos de sus padres, él decide cantar con el popular grupo juvenil de los 80, Menudo.

En 1989 Ricky deja a Menudo y va a vivir en Nueva York. Está muy confundido porque no sabe si quiere ser cantante o carpintero. Pero un año más tarde, va a México para trabajar en películas y en el teatro. Poco después, va a Hollywood.

En 1996, a los 25 años, vuelve a Nueva York donde actúa en el espectáculo fabuloso de Broadway, *Les Miserables*. Pero Ricky sigue[5] cantando. Su álbum *Vuelve* vendió en los millones. Hoy es uno de los artistas latinos de mayor venta[6]. Cuando Ricky da un concierto, el teatro o el estadio está siempre lleno de aficionados.

[1] llenan *fill*
[2] aficionados *fans*
[3] Víspera del Año Nuevo *New Year's Eve*
[4] Contra *Against*
[5] sigue *continues*
[6] de mayor venta *with the greatest sales*

Unidad 5: Pasatiempos y diversiones

▲ Plácido Domingo nace en Madrid en 1941. Sus padres también son cantantes. A Plácido le gustó la música y estudió el piano.

Cuando Plácido tiene sólo ocho años su familia va a vivir en México. En México sus padres fundan una compañía de ópera. El joven Plácido estudia en el famoso Conservatorio Nacional de Música en la Ciudad de México. Aprende a cantar ópera.

Hace su début cuando tiene sólo veinte años. Canta el papel de Alfredo en la ópera *La Traviata* de Verdi. Plácido Domingo sigue cantando en todos los grandes teatros de ópera del mundo. En 2001 es Plácido Domingo que canta la *Ave María* en la ceremonia en el estadio Yankee en memoria de las víctimas del 11 de septiembre.

¿Comprendes?

A. **Contesten.**
1. ¿Dónde y cuándo nace Ricky Martin?
2. ¿Con qué grupo cantó?
3. ¿Adónde va a vivir cuando deja al grupo Menudo?
4. ¿En qué espectáculo de Broadway actuó?
5. Pero, ¿qué sigue haciendo siempre?
6. ¿Qué pasa cuando Ricky da un concierto?

B. **Completen.**
1. _____ nace en Madrid en 1941.
2. Sus padres son _____.
3. Cuando Plácido tiene sólo _____ años su familia va a vivir _____.
4. En el Conservatorio Nacional de Música en la Ciudad de México, Plácido aprende a cantar _____.
5. Plácido Domingo sigue cantando en _____.

C. **Expliquen.**
¿Qué tienen en común Ricky Martin y Plácido Domingo?

ANSWERS TO ¿Comprendes?

A.
1. Ricky Martin nace en la Víspera del Año Nuevo de 1971 en San Juan, Puerto Rico.
2. Cantó con el grupo Menudo.
3. Va a vivir en Nueva York cuando deja al grupo Menudo.
4. Actuó en el espectáculo fabuloso de Broadway, *Les Miserables.*
5. Sigue cantando siempre.
6. Cuando Ricky da un concierto, el teatro o el estadio está siempre lleno de aficionados.

B.
1. Plácido Domingo
2. cantantes
3. ocho, en México
4. ópera
5. todos los grandes teatros de ópera del mundo

C. *Answers will vary but may include:*
Ricky Martin y Plácido Domingo son cantantes. Son muy famosos. Los dos pueden llenar de aficionados un estadio.

CONEXIONES

CONEXIONES
La música

¡OJO! The readings in the **Conexiones** section are optional. They focus on some of the major disciplines taught in schools and universities. The vocabulary is useful for discussing such topics as history, literature, art, economics, business, science, etc. You may choose any of the following ways to do the readings in the **Conexiones** sections.

Independent reading Have students read the selections and do the post-reading activities as homework, which you collect. This option is least intrusive on class time and requires a minimum of teacher involvement.

Homework with in-class follow-up Assign the readings and post-reading activities as homework. Review and discuss the material in class the next day.

Intensive in-class activity This option includes a pre-reading vocabulary presentation, in-class reading and discussion, assignment of the activities for homework, and a discussion of the assignment in class the following day.

PRESENTATION

La música

La música latina

STEP 1 Most students will be familiar with these musical terms in English. Model the terms in Spanish and have students repeat after you.

STEP 2 Ask students to scan the reading on pages 194 and 195 and make a list of words they do not know. Explain the meaning of these words as a whole-class activity.

STEP 3 It is suggested that you play some recordings of the types of Spanish music discussed in this section. Ask a music teacher to help you assemble some selections from the Music Department's library.

La música latina

Music is, and has been, a very integral part of the daily lives of people. Music played an important role in even the most primitive cultures. Can you imagine the world today without music?

The language of music has many cognates. Let's take a look at some of them.

la danza

el coro

la ópera

la orquesta

la banda

In addition, the names of many musical instruments are cognates.

el piano, el órgano, el violín, la viola, la guitarra, la trompeta, el clarinete, el saxofón, la flauta, el trombón

Each culture has its own type of music. The music of Latin America is extremely popular today.

La música latina

En las islas hispanas de las Antillas, Cuba, Puerto Rico y la República Dominicana, hay muchas influencias africanas en la música. Hay también una relación íntima entre el canto (la canción) y la danza (el baile). La salsa y el merengue son canciones y bailes.

Un instrumento muy popular entre los indios andinos es la flauta. El yaraví es una canción popular. En quechua, una lengua[1] de los indios andinos, la palabra «yaraví» significa **lamento.** Es una canción triste. A veces cantan un yaraví. A veces sólo lo tocan en la flauta. No cantan.

Un niño quechua tocando la flauta. Perú

Tocando la marimba. Antigua. Guatemala

Un instrumento popular de los indígenas de Guatemala es la marimba. Hay orquestas de marimba que van de un pueblo a otro para tocar en las fiestas locales.

La banda mariachi es un pequeño grupo de músicos ambulantes. Tocan guitarras, violines y trompetas. La música mariachi tiene su origen en Guadalajara, México, en el estado de Jalisco.

[1] lengua *language*

¿Comprendes?

¿Qué música te gusta?
Listen to samples of the various types of Latin music on the CD program. Decide which are your favorites.

Paso 4: Conexiones

Un grupo mariachi. Xochimilco. México

¡Hablo como un pro!

This unique section gives students the opportunity to speak freely and say whatever they want on their own. The illustrations serve to remind students of precisely what they know how to say in Spanish. There are no depictions of activities that students do not have the ability to describe or talk about in Spanish. The art in this section recombines all that the students learned in the particular unit and in addition frequently recombines the topic or situation of the unit with that of another unit for additional reinforcement.

You can use this section in many ways. Some possibilities are:
1. Have students look at the illustrations and just identify items by giving the correct Spanish words.
2. Have students make up sentences about what they see in the illustrations.
3. Have students make up questions about the illustrations. They can call on another class member to respond if you do this as an entire class activity, or you may prefer to allow students to work in small groups. This activity is extremely beneficial because it enables students to actively use the interrogative words.
4. You may wish to ask questions and call on students to answer.
5. Have students look at the illustrations and give a complete oral review of what they see.
6. Have two students work together and make up a conversation based on the illustrations.
7. Have students look at the illustrations and write a paragraph (or paragraphs) about them in class.

You can also use this section as an assessment or testing tool, taking into account individual differences by having students go from simple to quite complicated tasks.

196

¡Hablo como un pro! Tell all you can about the following illustration.

Unidad 5: Pasatiempos y diversiones

The assessment can be either oral or written. You may wish to use the rubrics provided on pages T22–T23 as you give students the following directions.
1. Identify the topic or situation of these illustrations.
2. Identify as many items as you can and give the Spanish words. Don't forget to include actions you see.
3. Give as many sentences as you can to describe the illustrations.
4. Go over your sentences and put them in the best sequence possible.
5. Polish your sentences and sequencing to give a coherent story based on the illustrations.

Universal Access

When talking about the illustration, **students with learning difficulties** may just give random sentences. **Advanced students** will give a coherent story. You may wish to have **advanced students** write a paragraph about the illustration.

Vocabulario

Discussing a movie theater

el cine	la butaca
la taquilla, la boletería	la fila
la entrada, el boleto	la pantalla
la sesión	la película, el film
la cola	

Describing a museum visit

el museo	la estatua
la exposición	el/la artista
el cuadro	

Describing a concert

el concierto	el público
el estadio	la gente
el/la cantante	lleno(a) de
cantar	

Describing cultural events and activities

dar un concierto	el aplauso
oír un concierto	recibir aplausos
ver una película	alquilar, rentar un video
aplaudir	la tienda de videos

Other useful expressions

nadie	algo	perder el autobús
nunca	el/la joven	(la guagua, el camión)
nada	visitar	la estación del metro
alguien	decidir	
siempre	delante de	

Vocabulario

Vocabulary Review

The words and phrases in the **Vocabulario** have been taught for productive use in this unit. They are summarized here as a resource for both student and teacher. This list also serves as a convenient resource for the **¡Te toca a ti!** activities on pages 182–183. There are approximately nineteen cognates in this unit. Have students find them.

 ¡OJO! You will notice that the vocabulary list here is not translated. This has been done intentionally, since we feel that by the time students have finished the material in the unit they should be familiar with the meanings of all the words. If there are several words they still do not know, we recommend that they refer to the **Paso 1 Palabras** and **Paso 2 Palabras** sections in the unit or go to the dictionaries at the end of this book to find the meanings. However, if you prefer that your students have the English translations, please refer to Vocabulary Transparency 5.6, where you will find all these words with their translations.

Universal Access

Ask the music teacher to come in and teach some of the songs from the Audio Program (Audio CD 1) or from the Music CD featuring Justo Lamas. You may wish to ask students if they would like to perform a Spanish song in the school concert. This will be beneficial for learners of all ability levels, especially those who are musically inclined or who like to perform.

197

Planning for Unit 6

198A

CORRELATIONS

National Standards

Communication Standard 1.1
pages 203, 206, 207, 211, 214, 216, 222, 223, 229

Communication Standard 1.2
pages 216, 218–219, 230–231

Communication Standard 1.3
pages 203, 207, 213, 215, 223, 227, 228

Cultures Standard 2.1
pages 218–219, 230–231

Cultures Standard 2.2
pages 226, 230–231

Connections Standard 3.1
pages 232–233

Connections Standard 3.2
pages 218–219, 230–231

Comparisons Standard 4.1
page 217

Comparisons Standard 4.2
page 230–231

Communities Standard 5.1
page 223

PACING AND PRIORITIES

The unit content is color coded below to assist you in planning.

■ required ■ recommended ■ optional

Paso 1 (required)   *Days 1–8*
■ Palabras
   La rutina
■ Formas
   Verbos reflexivos

Paso 2 (required)   *Days 9–16*
■ Palabras
   El camping
■ Formas
   Verbos reflexivos de cambio radical
■ Conversación
   ¿A qué hora te despertaste?

Paso 3 (recommended)   *Days 17–24*
■ Pronunciación
   Las consonantes ñ, ch, x
■ Cultura y lectura
   El camping
■ Repaso
■ ¡Te toca a ti!
■ Assessment

Paso 4 (optional)
■ Diversiones
■ Más cultura y lectura
   El día empieza con el desayuno.
■ Conexiones
   La ecología

RESOURCE GUIDE

SECTION		PAGES	SECTION RESOURCES
PASO 1			
Palabras	La rutina	200–203	🔲 Vocabulary Transparencies 6.1–6.2 💿 Audio CD 4 🎧 Audio Activities TE, pages 81–82 📘 Workbook TE, pages 87–88 📘 Quiz 1, page 39 💿 ExamView® Pro
Formas	Verbos reflexivos	204–207	💿 Audio CD 4 🎧 Audio Activities TE, page 83 📘 Workbook TE, pages 88–89 📘 Quiz 2, page 40 💿 ExamView® Pro
PASO 2			
Palabras	El camping	208–211	🔲 Vocabulary Transparencies 6.3–6.4 💿 Audio CD 4 🎧 Audio Activities TE, pages 84–86 📘 Workbook TE, pages 90–91 📘 Quiz 3, page 41 💿 ExamView® Pro
Formas	Verbos reflexivos de cambio radical	212–215	💿 Audio CD 4 🎧 Audio Activities TE, page 87 📘 Workbook TE, pages 92–93 📘 Quiz 4, page 42 💿 ExamView® Pro
PASO 3			
Conversación	¿A qué hora te despertaste?	216	💿 Audio CD 4 🎧 Audio Activities TE, pages 88–89 📘 Workbook TE, page 94
Pronunciación	Las consonantes ñ, ch, x	217	🔲 Pronunciation Transparency P 6 💿 Audio CD 4 🎧 Audio Activities TE, page 90
Cultura y lectura	El camping	218–219	💿 Audio CD 4 🎧 Audio Activities TE, page 91 📘 Workbook TE, pages 95–96
Repaso		220–221	💿 Audio CD 4 🎧 Audio Activities TE, page 92 📘 Workbook TE, page 97 📘 Tests, pages 81–96
¡Te toca a ti!		222–223	💿 Audio CD 4 🎧 Audio Activities TE, pages 93–94 📘 Workbook TE, pages 98–99
Assessment		224–225	🔲 Vocabulary Transparency 6.5 📘 Tests, pages 81–86 💿 ExamView® Pro, Unit 6 📘 Performance Assessment, Tasks 11–12
PASO 4			
Diversiones		226–229	📘 Workbook TE, page 100
Más cultura y lectura	El día empieza con el desayuno.	230–231	📘 Tests, page 87
Conexiones	La ecología	232–233	📘 Tests, page 88

Using Your Resources for Unit 6

Transparencies

Bellringer 6.1–6.5   **Vocabulary V 6.1–6.6**   **Assessment A 6**   **Songs S 6**

Workbook

Paso 1 Vocabulary and Structure
pages 87–89

Paso 2 Vocabulary and Structure
pages 90–93

Conversation and Reading
pages 94–96

Repaso, ¡Te toca a ti!, Diversiones
pages 97–100

Audio Program and Audio Activities Booklet

Paso 1 Vocabulary and Structure
pages 81–83

Paso 2 Vocabulary and Structure
pages 84–87

Conversation, Pronunciation
pages 88–91

Repaso, ¡Te toca a ti!
pages 92–94

Vocabulary and Structure Quizzes, pages 39–44

Unit Tests, pages 81–96

ExamView® Pro, Unit 6

Timesaving Teacher Tools

TeacherWorks
All in One Teacher Planning

TeacherWorks™ is your all in one teacher resource center. Personalize lesson plans, access resources from the Teacher Wraparound Edition, connect to the Internet, or make a to-do list. These are only a few of the many features that can assist you in the planning and organizing of your lessons.

Includes:
- A calendar feature
- Access to all program blackline masters
- Standards correlations and more

Test Bank software for Macintosh and Windows makes creating, editing, customizing, and printing tests quick and easy.

PLEGABLES™
Study Organizer

Manipulatives The foldable activities give students of all learning styles the opportunity to excel in a nontraditional manner. Your students will love these hands-on activities!

Technology Resources

Spanish Online
In the Unit 6 online resources, you and your students will have a chance to learn more about daily routines and camping in the Spanish-speaking world.

PuzzleMaker allows you to create crossword puzzles, jumble puzzles, and word searches in minutes or edit a database of key terms and puzzles to review unit vocabulary. You can choose English-Spanish puzzles or Spanish-English puzzles. The puzzles can be printed or played on the computer screen.

Canta con Justo This CD contains songs sung by a young Argentine singer, Justo Lamas, which are specifically geared to review and expand upon the vocabulary learned in each unit. Students will enjoy listening to these songs while they learn from them.

¡En vivo! This music video of Justo Lamas performing his songs live in concert gives your students a chance to experience the songs in a different way while reinforcing the language skills they are learning!

Preview

In this unit, students will learn to discuss their daily routine with particular emphasis on hygiene. To do this they will learn reflexive verbs. The cultural focus is on the popularity of camping in some Spanish-speaking countries.

National Standards

Communication

In Unit 6 students will communicate in spoken and written Spanish on the following topics:
- daily routines
- taking care of oneself
- enjoying a camping trip

Students will obtain and provide information about these topics and engage in conversations about everyday habits, including daily hygiene, as they fulfill the unit objectives listed on this page.

Spanish Online

The **Glencoe World Languages Web site** (spanish. glencoe.com) offers options that enable you and your students to experience the Spanish-speaking world via the Internet. For each **Unidad,** there are activities, games, and quizzes. In addition, an *Enrichment* section offers students an opportunity to visit Web sites related to the theme of the unit.

Unidad

6 La rutina y el camping

Objetivos

In this unit, you will learn to:

- describe your personal grooming habits
- talk about your daily routine
- tell some things you do for yourself
- talk about a camping trip

Más despacio, por favor.

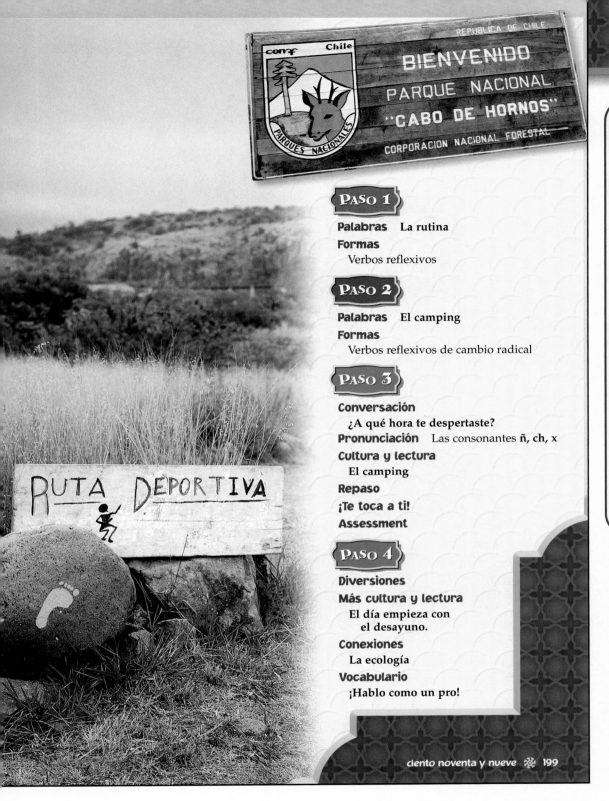

Spotlight on Culture

San Miguel de Allende, México

(page 198) These young girls are jogging up a street in San Miguel de Allende. San Miguel de Allende is situated in Mexico's heartland in the state of Guanajuato at an elevation of 1,870 meters above sea level. It is a very picturesque town with streets paved with rugged cobblestones and many monuments, fountains, and churches. San Miguel has a reputation as a writers' and artists' colony, and it is home to the famous art school **Instituto Allende**.
(page 199) **Parque Juárez** is the largest city park in San Miguel de Allende. It is popular for joggers, hikers, and bicyclists. It is also a favorite spot for bird enthusiasts, as there are many opportunities to observe the many nesting egrets.

Palabras

RESOURCE MANAGER

Vocabulary Transparencies 6.1–6.2
Audio Activities TE, pages 81–82
Audio CD 4
Workbook, pages 87–88
Quiz 1, page 39
ExamView® Pro

Bellringer Review

Use BRR Transparency 6.1 or write the following on the board.
Indicate if the following take place **en el verano, en el invierno,** or **en las dos estaciones.**
1. **Los amigos esquían en el agua.**
2. **Los amigos bucean.**
3. **Los amigos nadan en el mar.**
4. **Los amigos nadan en una piscina cubierta.**
5. **Los amigos juegan tenis en una cancha al aire libre.**
6. **Los amigos bajan la pista para principiantes.**

2 PRESENTATION

STEP 1 Have students close their books. Model the new words using Vocabulary Transparencies 6.1–6.2. Point to each illustration and have the class repeat the corresponding word or expression after you or Audio CD 4.

STEP 2 Now have students open their books and repeat the procedure as they read.

STEP 3 Act out the new words: **despertarse, levantarse, peinarse, lavarse, cepillarse, ponerse la ropa, sentarse.**

Palabras   La rutina

¡Hola! Me llamo José. ¿Y tú? ¿Cómo te llamas?

El muchacho se llama José.

José se acuesta.
Se acuesta a las diez y media de la noche.
Él se duerme enseguida.

El muchacho se lava el pelo.
Toma una ducha.

La muchacha se despierta temprano.
Se levanta enseguida.

La muchacha se lava la cara.

Total Physical Response

You may use a chair for a bed. Bring in a mirror and an alarm clock, or make a buzzing sound when you say **despertador.**
(Student 1), **ven acá, por favor.**
Son las siete de la mañana. Estás durmiendo.
Oyes el despertador. Te despiertas.

Te levantas y vas al cuarto de baño.
Te lavas.
Te miras en el espejo.
Te cepillas los dientes.
Te peinas.
Te pones la ropa.
Sales para la escuela.
Gracias, *(Student 1).* **Y ahora puedes regresar a tu asiento.**

El muchacho se baña.

La muchacha se cepilla
(se lava) los dientes.

el peine   *el espejo*

El muchacho se peina.
Se mira en el espejo cuando
se peina.

Ella se pone la ropa.

La muchacha se sienta a la mesa.
Toma el desayuno.
Se desayuna.

el cereal

pan tostado

*un vaso de jugo
de naranja*

About the Spanish Language

- **Dientes** are *teeth* and **muelas** are *molars.* Both are often used as generic terms for teeth. A *toothache* is a **dolor de muelas.**
- The first meal of the day is breakfast, *to break a fast.* The same concept applies to the Spanish word. Ask students what the word for *a fast* would be in Spanish **(ayuno).** You will hear both **desayunar** and **desayunarse** when referring to having breakfast.

3 PRACTICE

¿Qué palabra necesito?

¡OJO! When students are doing the **¿Qué palabra necesito?** activities, accept any answer that makes sense. The purpose of these activities is to have students use the new vocabulary. They are not factual recall activities. Thus, it is not necessary for students to remember specific factual information from the vocabulary presentation when answering. If you wish, have students use the illustrations on this page as a stimulus, when possible.

Historieta Each time **Historieta** appears, it means that the answers to the activity form a short story. Encourage students to look at the title of the **Historieta,** since it can help them do the activity.

1 Have students look at each illustration on page 202 and describe it in their own words.

2 After going over Activity 2, have students retell the story in their own words.

Writing Development
Have students write the answers to Activity 2 in paragraph form to show how the answers to all the items tell a story.

Learning from Realia
(page 202) Have students prepare a commercial for this toothbrush and present it to the class.

¿Qué palabra necesito?

1 **¿Qué hace el muchacho o la muchacha?**
 Describan. *(Describe.)*

1.

2.

3.

4.

5.

6.

2 **Historieta** **Un día en la vida de...**
Contesten según se indica. *(Answer as indicated.)*
1. ¿Cómo se llama el joven? (Paco)
2. ¿A qué hora se despierta? (a las seis y media)
3. ¿Cuándo se levanta? (enseguida)
4. ¿Adónde va? (al cuarto de baño)
5. ¿Qué hace? (se lava la cara y se cepilla los dientes)
6. Luego, ¿adónde va? (a la cocina)
7. ¿Se sienta a la mesa? (sí)
8. ¿Qué toma? (el desayuno)

Unidad 6: La rutina y el camping

ANSWERS TO ¿Qué palabra necesito?

1
1. La muchacha se levanta.
2. El muchacho se peina.
3. La muchacha se cepilla (se lava) los dientes.
4. La muchacha se lava la cara.
5. El muchacho se lava el pelo. (Toma una ducha.)
6. El muchacho se baña.

2
1. El joven se llama Paco.
2. Se despierta a las seis y media.
3. Se levanta enseguida.
4. Va al cuarto de baño.
5. Se lava la cara y se cepilla los dientes.
6. Luego va a la cocina.
7. Sí, se sienta a la mesa.
8. Toma el desayuno.

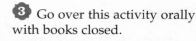

3 **Entrevista** Contesten. *(Answer about yourself.)*

1. ¿Cómo te llamas?
2. ¿Dónde vives?
3. ¿A qué hora tomas el desayuno?
4. ¿Tomas el desayuno en el comedor o en la cocina?
5. ¿Te gusta tomar un desayuno grande?
6. ¿Comes huevos, jamón y pan tostado en el desayuno?
7. ¿Qué comes en el desayuno?
8. ¿Te gustan los cereales?

Desayuno Sana costumbre

superSol   **Hiper**Sol

4 **Juego** **Cada día** ¿Sí o no? *(True or false?)*

1. El joven se acuesta por la mañana.
2. Se cepilla la cara.
3. Se lava la cara.
4. Se duerme cuando se levanta.
5. Se despierta y luego se acuesta.
6. Se despierta y luego se levanta.
7. Se desayuna y después se acuesta.
8. Come y luego se cepilla los dientes.

Una señora con su perro.
Casares, España

5 **La rutina** Work with a classmate. Each of you will choose one family member and tell each other about that person's daily activities.

mi papá   mi prima   **mi gato**
    mi mamá   mi hermana
mi hermano   mi primo   mi perro

6 **Rompecabezas**

 Palabras nuevas Change one letter in each word or add a letter to form a new word.

1. casa
2. mucha
3. noche
4. sopa
5. paso
6. año

Paso 1: Palabras

doscientos tres 203

Formas

1 PREPARATION

RESOURCE MANAGER

Audio Activities TE, page 83
Audio CD 4
Workbook, pages 88–89
Quiz 2, page 40
ExamView® Pro

Bellringer Review

Use BRR Transparency 6.2 or write the following on the board.
Answer.
1. **¿A qué hora sales de casa por la mañana?**
2. **¿Cómo vas a la escuela?**
3. **¿A qué hora llegas a la escuela?**
4. **¿Qué haces en la escuela?**
5. **¿Dónde tomas el almuerzo?**
6. **¿Qué haces después de las clases?**

2 PRESENTATION

 Verbos reflexivos

STEP 1 Have students open their books to page 204 and look at the illustrations.

STEP 2 Ask students in which illustrations someone is doing something to himself or herself and in which illustrations the person is doing something to someone (something) else.

STEP 3 Ask what additional word is used when the person is doing something to himself or herself **(se)**.

STEP 4 Explain to them that **se** is a reflexive pronoun and refers to the subject.

STEP 5 Then read the explanation that follows in Item 1 on page 204.

 Formas   **Verbos reflexivos**
Telling what people do for themselves

1. Read the following sentences as you look at the illustrations.

María baña al bebé.

María se baña.

José lava el carro.

José se lava.

Elena cepilla al perro.

Elena se cepilla.

Pablo mira a su amigo.

Pablo se mira en el espejo.

In the sentences to the left one person performs the action and another person or thing receives the action. In the sentences to the right the same person performs and receives the action of the verb. For this reason the pronoun **se** must be used. **Se** is called a *reflexive pronoun* because it refers back to the subject—**María, José.**

2. Study the forms of a reflexive verb.

infinitive	lavarse	levantarse
yo	me lavo	me levanto
tú	te lavas	te levantas
él, ella, Ud.	se lava	se levanta
nosotros(as)	nos lavamos	nos levantamos
vosotros(as)	*os laváis*	*os levantáis*
ellos, ellas ,Uds.	se lavan	se levantan

3. In the negative form, **no** is placed before the reflexive pronoun.

¿No te lavas las manos?
La familia Martínez no se desayuna en el comedor.

4. In Spanish when you refer to parts of the body and articles of clothing, you often use the definite article, not the possessive adjective.

Me lavo la cara.
Ella se cepilla los dientes.

La familia lava a su mascota en una gasolinera.
Estepona. España

STEP 6 Call on students to read the model sentences under each illustration or have the class read them in unison.

STEP 7 Write the verbs **lavarse** and **levantarse** on the board. After you say **me lavo,** have students supply **me levanto.** Do the same with each subject.

STEP 8 Read Items 3 and 4 and have the class read the model sentences aloud.

STEP 9 You may wish to give additional examples of verbs that can be both reflexive and nonreflexive.
Él se acuesta.   Él acuesta al bebé.
Nos peinamos. Peinamos al gato.

About the Spanish Language

You may wish to explain the following to students:
Ellos se lavan la cara.
Ellos se ponen la chaqueta.
La cara and **la chaqueta** are in the singular because each person has only one face or one jacket. In English the plural forms are used because of the plural subject. Spanish also uses the definite article rather than the possessive adjective.

Learning from Photos

(page 205) This gas station in Estepona, Spain, has a dog wash alongside the self-service car wash. While waiting to wash their car, people can bathe their pet—and it is very popular.

Left margin column

3 PRACTICE

¿Cómo lo digo?

7 You can do Activity 7 with books closed and then with books open. Have students describe in their own words what Antonio does.

8 Activity 8 reinforces the use of the reflexive with both the present and the preterite.

9 Remind students to use the definite article when referring to parts of the body.

Learning from Photos

(page 206) These people are waiting for a bus at a **parada** in Quito, Ecuador. The Ecuadorian students are headed for school, wearing their uniforms and carrying their **mochilas**.

Universal Access

Have **kinesthetic learners** make up a sentence about their daily routine using a reflexive verb. Have them point to themselves as they say the sentence. Then give them a new subject and have them point to the appropriate group as they say the adapted sentence.

Main page

¿Cómo lo digo?

7 **Historieta** **Antonio** Contesten. *(Answer.)*

1. ¿A qué hora se levanta Antonio?
2. ¿Se baña por la mañana o por la noche?
3. ¿Se desayuna en casa?
4. ¿Se lava los dientes después del desayuno?
5. ¿Se pone una chaqueta si sale cuando hace frío?

8 **Mi rutina** Contesten. *(Answer about yourself.)*

1. ¿A qué hora te levantas? ¿Y a qué hora te levantaste esta mañana?
2. ¿Te bañas por la mañana o tomas una ducha? Y esta mañana, ¿te bañaste o tomaste una ducha?
3. ¿Te cepillas los dientes con frecuencia? ¿Cuántas veces te cepillaste los dientes hoy?
4. ¿Te desayunas en casa o en la escuela? Y esta mañana, ¿dónde te desayunaste?
5. ¿Te peinas con frecuencia? ¿Te miras en el espejo cuando te peinas? ¿Cuántas veces te peinaste hoy?

9 **¿Qué haces?** Sigan el modelo. *(Follow the model.)*

—¿Te cepillas? →
—Sí, me cepillo.

1.　　2.　　3.　　4.

10 **¿Y ustedes?** Sigan el modelo. *(Follow the model.)*

Ellos se levantan a las siete. →
—Ah, sí. ¿Y a qué hora se levantan ustedes?
—Nos levantamos a las siete también.

1. Ellos se levantan a las seis y media.
2. Ellos se bañan a las siete menos cuarto.
3. Ellos se desayunan a las siete y media.

Los alumnos se levantan temprano, Quito, Ecuador

Answers section

ANSWERS TO ¿Cómo lo digo?

7

1. Antonio se levanta a las ___.
2. Se baña por la mañana (por la noche).
3. Sí, (No, no) se desayuna en casa.
4. Sí, (No, no) se lava los dientes después del desayuno.
5. Sí, se pone una chaqueta si sale cuando hace frío.

206

8

1. Me levanto a las ___. Esta mañana me levanté a las ___.
2. Me baño (Tomo una ducha) por la mañana. Esta mañana me bañé (tomé una ducha).
3. Sí, (No, no) me cepillo los dientes con frecuencia. Me cepillé los dientes ___ ...
4. Me desayuno en casa (en la escuela). Esta mañana me desayuné en casa (en la escuela).
5. Sí, (No, no) me peino... Sí, (No, no) me miro... cuando me peino. Hoy me peiné...

9

1. ¿Te levantas?
Sí, me levanto.
2. ¿Te lavas la cara?
Sí, me lavo la cara.
3. ¿Te cepillas los dientes?
Sí, me cepillo los dientes.
4. ¿Te peinas?
Sí, me peino.

10

1. —Ah, sí. ¿Y a qué hora se levantan ustedes?
—Nos levantamos a las seis y media también.
2. —Ah, sí. ¿Y a qué hora se bañan ustedes?
—Nos bañamos a las siete menos cuarto también.
3. —Ah, sí. ¿Y a qué hora se desayunan ustedes?
—Nos desayunamos a las siete y media también.

11 **Nombres** Contesten. *(Answer.)*

1. ¿Cómo te llamas?
2. Y tu hermano(a), ¿cómo se llama?
3. ¿Cómo se llama tu profesor(a) de español?
4. ¿Y cómo se llaman tus abuelos?
5. Una vez más, ¿cómo te llamas?

12 **¿Qué hacen todos?** Completen según las fotos. *(Answer based on the photos.)*

1. Yo
   Él
   Tú
   Usted

2. Nosotros
   Ellos
   Ustedes
   Él y yo

13 **Juego** **Me pongo...** Describe some clothing you're putting on. A classmate will guess where you're going and what you're going to do.

 *For more practice using words and forms from **Paso 1**, do Activity 11 on page H12 at the end of this book.*

UN POCO MÁS

Paso 1: Formas

doscientos siete ✹ **207**

---

11 When doing Activity 11, you may wish to go around the room and ask each student **¿Cómo te llamas?** The more times they hear **Me llamo ___**, the better, since students often put **es** after **me llamo.** Up to this point students have identified themselves by using **soy** to avoid this problem.

↻ **Recycling**

Activity 13 gives students the opportunity to use vocabulary and structures from preceding units.

EXPANSION Read this conversation to the class and then ask the questions that follow it.

—¿A qué hora te levantas, Carlos?
—¿Quieres saber a qué hora me levanto o a qué hora me despierto?
—¿A qué hora te levantas?
—Me levanto a las siete.
—¿Y a qué hora sales de la casa?
—Salgo a las siete y media. Me lavo, me cepillo los dientes y tomo el desayuno en media hora.
—¿Y te pones la ropa también?
—Claro que me pongo la ropa.

Now ask the following questions.

1. ¿Cómo se llama el muchacho?
2. ¿A qué hora se levanta?
3. ¿Se cepilla los dientes?
4. ¿Se desayuna?
5. ¿A qué hora sale de casa?
6. ¿Se pone la ropa también?

UN POCO MÁS This *InfoGap* activity will allow students to practice in pairs. The activity should be very manageable for them, since all vocabulary and structures are familiar to them.

ANSWERS TO **¿Cómo lo digo?**

11

1. Me llamo ___.
2. Mi hermano(a) se llama ___. (No tengo un[a] hermano[a]).
3. Mi profesor(a) de español se llama ___.
4. Mis abuelos se llaman ___.
5. Me llamo ___.

12

1. Yo me baño.
   Él se baña.
   Tú te bañas.
   Usted se baña.
2. Nosotros nos peinamos.
   Ellos se peinan.
   Ustedes se peinan.
   Él y yo nos peinamos.

13 *Answers will vary but may include:*
—Me pongo una corbata.
—¿Vas al teatro?
—Me pongo un traje de baño.
—¿Vas a la playa? ¿Vas a nadar?

Palabras

PASO 2

1 PREPARATION

RESOURCE MANAGER

Vocabulary Transparencies 6.3–6.4
Audio Activities TE, pages 84–86
Audio CD 4
Workbook, pages 90–91
Quiz 3, page 41
ExamView® Pro

Bellringer Review

Use BRR Transparency 6.3 or write the following on the board.
Write sentences using the following expressions.
1. **ir a la playa**
2. **tomar el sol**
3. **nadar**
4. **usar una crema bronceadora**

2 PRESENTATION

STEP 1 Have students close their books. Present the vocabulary using Vocabulary Transparencies 6.3–6.4. Have students repeat after you or Audio CD 4.

STEP 2 As you present the vocabulary you may wish to ask the following questions:
¿Quién va de camping?
¿Se divierten los Sánchez?
¿Qué arman los jóvenes?
¿Quiénes arman una tienda de campaña?
¿Dónde se acuestan los jóvenes?
¿Duermen en el saco de dormir?

STEP 3 After you have presented all the vocabulary, have students open their books and read the words and sentences for additional reinforcement.

Palabras El camping 🎧

un camping una caravana

La familia Sánchez va de camping.
Lo están pasando muy bien. Se divierten.

una tienda de campaña, una carpa

Los jóvenes arman una tienda de campaña.

Todos comen en una mesa plegable.

un saco de dormir

Los jóvenes se acuestan en la carpa.
Duermen en un saco de dormir.

Los amigos dan una caminata.
Dan una caminata por un parque nacional.

¿Qué llevan en su mochila?

una botella de
agua mineral

el champú

un cepillo

un cepillo de
dientes

un tubo de pasta
(crema) dentífrica

una barra (una
pastilla) de jabón

un rollo de papel
higiénico

Paso 2: Palabras

doscientos nueve ✹ 209

PASO 2

3 PRACTICE

¿Qué palabra necesito?

1 Activity 1 can be done as a game. Using a stopwatch, see who can identify the most items in the least amount of time.

Writing Development

After going over Activity 2, have students write the story in their own words in paragraph form.

Learning from Photos

(page 210) Cataluña is a beautiful region in northeastern Spain. It has everything from sandy beaches, rocky coasts, foothills, and high sierra, all within easy reach of the cosmopolitan city of Barcelona. The students seen hiking here are in the sierra.

¿Qué palabra necesito?

1 **¿Qué pierde Paco de la mochila?** Identifiquen.
(Tell what is falling out of Paco's backpack.)

Los amigos dan una caminata.
Cataluña. España

2 **Historieta** **De camping**

Contesten con **sí.** *(Answer with yes.)*

1. ¿Va de camping la familia Iglesias?
2. ¿Tienen una caravana?
3. ¿Arman los jóvenes una tienda de campaña al lado de la caravana?
4. ¿Preparan la comida en una barbacoa?
5. ¿Comen en una mesa plegable con sillas plegables?
6. ¿Se divierten todos?
7. ¿Dan una caminata?
8. ¿Duermen los jóvenes en un saco de dormir?

ANSWERS TO **¿Qué palabra necesito?**

1 Pepe pierde un cepillo, un rollo de papel higiénico, un tubo de pasta (crema) dentífrica, una barra (pastilla) de jabón, un peine, un cepillo de dientes.

2
1. Sí, la familia Iglesias va de camping.
2. Sí, tienen una caravana.
3. Sí, los jóvenes arman una tienda de campaña al lado de la caravana.
4. Sí, preparan la comida en una barbacoa.
5. Sí, comen en una mesa plegable con sillas plegables.
6. Sí, todos se divierten.
7. Sí, dan una caminata.
8. Sí, los jóvenes duermen en un saco de dormir.

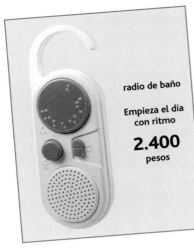

radio de baño

Empieza el día
con ritmo

2.400
pesos

3 En el cuarto de baño
Completen. (*Complete.*)

1. El muchacho va a tomar una ducha. Necesita _____.
2. Su hermana quiere peinarse. Pero, ¿dónde está _____?
3. Joselito quiere lavarse los dientes. ¿Dónde están _____ y _____?
4. No hay más pasta dentífrica. Tiene que comprar otro _____.
5. No hay más jabón. Tiene que comprar otra _____.
6. Se lava el pelo con un _____ especial.

4 En la farmacia
Work with a classmate. One of you is the clerk in a drugstore. The other is a client. Have a conversation about buying the following items.

1.
2.
3.
4.
5.

Una farmacia, Las Palmas, Gran Canaria

4
As a preliminary step for this activity, quickly decide as a class approximately how many **euros** or **pesos** each item will cost. Put the items and prices on the board so students can refer to them during the activity. You can have groups present their conversations to the class.

Universal Access

Write the following list on the board: **el pelo, las manos, los ojos, la cara, los dientes.** Have students write down all the toiletries and verbs from this unit that they associate with each word. For example, **el pelo: lavarse, peinarse, cepillarse, el peine, el champú. Visual learners** may then want to make a chart containing this information.

Learning from Photos

(*page 211, bottom*) This colorful pharmacy is in Las Palmas de Gran Canaria. Have students note the green cross, the symbol for a pharmacy. At night the cross is lit if it is a **farmacia de guardia.** Pharmacies take turns staying open during atypical working hours.

ANSWERS TO ¿Qué palabra necesito?

3
1. una barra (pastilla) de jabón, champú
2. su peine
3. su cepillo de dientes, la pasta (crema) dentífrica
4. tubo
5. barra (pastilla)
6. champú

4
Answers will vary; however, students should begin their conversation with the customary greetings, followed by Quiero (Necesito) comprar...

211

PASO 2

Formas

Bellringer Review

Use BRR Transparency 6.4 or write the following on the board. Complete.

1. Yo ___ (ir) a la playa pero mis amigos ___ (ir) a las montañas. Nosotros no ___ (querer) hacer la misma cosa.
2. Yo ___ (salir) ahora pero mis amigos no ___ (salir) ahora. Nosotros no ___ (poder) salir a la misma hora.
3. Ellos ___ (volver) ahora pero nosotros no ___ (volver). No ___ (poder) volver a la misma hora.

2 PRESENTATION

 Verbos reflexivos de cambio radical

¡OJO! There is actually no new concept here since students are already familiar with the stem-changing verbs and the reflexive pronouns.

STEP 1 Model the forms in the chart on page 212. Have students repeat after you.

STEP 2 Quickly go over the examples in Item 2.

 Formas Verbos reflexivos de cambio radical
Telling what people do for themselves

1. The reflexive verbs **acostarse (o → ue)**, **dormirse (o → ue)**, **sentarse (e → ie)**, and **divertirse (e → ie)** are stem-changing verbs.

infinitive	acostarse	divertirse
yo	me acuesto	me divierto
tú	te acuestas	te diviertes
él, ella, Ud.	se acuesta	se divierte
nosotros(as)	nos acostamos	nos divertimos
vosotros(as)	os acostáis	os divertís
ellos, ellas, Uds.	se acuestan	se divierten

2. Many verbs in Spanish can be used with a reflexive pronoun. Often the reflexive pronoun gives a different meaning to the verb. Study the following examples.

María pone la blusa en la mochila.	*Mary puts the blouse in the backpack.*
María se pone la blusa.	*Mary puts on her blouse.*
María duerme ocho horas.	*Mary sleeps eight hours.*
María se duerme enseguida.	*Mary falls asleep immediately.*
María llama a Carlos.	*Mary calls Carlos.*
Ella se llama María.	*She calls herself Mary. (Her name is Mary.)*
María divierte a sus amigos.	*Mary amuses her friends.*
María se divierte.	*Mary amuses herself. (Mary has a good time.)*

212 ✿ doscientos doce

212

¿Cómo lo digo?

5 **¿Cómo lo haces tú?** Contesten. *(Answer about yourself.)*

1. ¿Duermes en una cama o en un saco de dormir?
2. Cuando te acuestas, ¿te duermes enseguida?
3. Y cuando te despiertas, ¿te levantas enseguida?
4. ¿Te sientas a la mesa para tomar el desayuno?
5. ¿Te diviertes en la escuela?

Una playa, Huanchaco, Perú

6 **Historieta** **¡A la playa!** Completen. *(Complete.)*

1. María _____ su traje de baño en su mochila.
   Cuando llega a la playa _____ el traje de baño.
2. En la playa María ve a un amigo. Ella _____ a su
   amigo. Su amigo _____ Luis.
3. María y sus amigos lo pasan muy bien en la
   playa. Ellos _____ mucho y como María es un
   tipo tan cómico ella también _____ mucho a sus
   amigos.
4. Después de pasar el día en la playa, María está
   muy cansada. Cuando ella se acuesta, _____
   enseguida y _____ más de ocho horas.

Paso 2: Formas

doscientos trece 🌸 213

213

PASO 2

3 PRACTICE (continued)

7 This activity gives students practice using the **yo** and **él** forms of the stem-changing reflexive verbs.

Universal Access

You may wish to allow students a few minutes to prepare some notes before doing Activity 8, especially for **students with learning difficulties.** Encourage all students, especially **advanced learners,** to be creative and to add some twists to their story if they wish, such as whether the trip went well, if there were any problems, whether they forgot to bring a necessary item or other ideas they may come up with.

Learning from Photos

(page 214) Arica is the northernmost city of the Atacama Desert in Chile. It has a constantly sunny climate, and it is called the City of Eternal Spring. Its beaches are good for swimming because unlike most of Chile's beaches, Arica's waters are warm.

The land-locked Bolivians are fond of Arica because it not only serves as their main port but also as a seaside resort.

---

7 **Historieta** **Duermo ocho horas.** Completen. *(Complete.)*

Cuando yo __1__ (acostarse), yo __2__ (dormirse) enseguida. Cada noche yo __3__ (dormir) ocho horas. Yo __4__ (acostarse) a las once y __5__ (levantarse) a las siete de la mañana. Cuando yo __6__ (despertarse), __7__ (levantarse) enseguida. Pero cuando mi hermana __8__ (despertarse), ella no __9__ (levantarse) enseguida. Y mi hermano, cuando él __10__ (acostarse), no __11__ (dormirse) enseguida. Él pasa horas escuchando música en la cama. Así él __12__ (dormir) solamente unas seis horas.

8 **El camping** Work with a classmate. You and your family spent a week camping in Chile. Tell all about it—what you did to prepare for the trip, the plane trip there, renting equipment, and what you did once you got there. Answer any questions your classmate may have.

De camping en Arica. Chile

9 **Una conversación** **Tú y yo**
Work with a classmate. Talk together sharing information about what you usually do when you return home after school. Are your routines somewhat the same?

ANSWERS TO ¿Cómo lo digo?

7

1. me acuesto
2. me duermo
3. duermo
4. me acuesto
5. me levanto
6. me despierto
7. me levanto
8. se despierta

9. se levanta
10. se acuesta
11. se duerme
12. duerme

8 *Answers will vary. Students will use vocabulary learned in this unit as well as in previous units.*

9 *Answers will vary. Students will use vocabulary learned in this unit as well as in previous units.*

  ## Manos a la obra

¿Se divierten o no? Draw some sketches of people doing things you can say in Spanish. Then tell what they're doing. Are they enjoying themselves or not?

 ## Rompecabezas

Cada uno en su sitio Indicate where each of the following might be found. **¡Cuidado!** Some may belong in more than one category.

un libro   **el saco de dormir**   el champú   el cepillo

el perro   **el espejo**   la ropa

la carpa   la cama   una barra de jabón   **la mesa plegable**

En el camping	En el cuarto de baño	En el cuarto de dormir	En una mochila
_____	_____	_____	_____
_____	_____	_____	_____

 *For more practice using words and forms from **Paso 2,** do Activity 12 on page H13 at the end of this book.*

Andas bien. ¡Adelante!

Paso 2: Formas

Manos a la obra

10 You may wish to display some of these drawings and sentences.

This *InfoGap* activity will allow students to practice in pairs. The activity should be very manageable for them, since all vocabulary and structures are familiar to them.

 ¡Adelante! At this point, all new material has been presented. Students have learned all the vocabulary and structure necessary to complete the unit. The conversation, cultural readings, and activities in **Paso 3** and **Paso 4** recycle all the material learned up to this point.

ANSWERS TO ¿Cómo lo digo?

10 *Answers will vary. Students will use vocabulary learned in previous units—going to the beach, watching television, taking a test at school—to create their illustrations. Students should use divertirse to describe the people.*

11 *Answers may vary but may include:*
En el camping: la carpa, el perro, el saco de dormir, la mesa plegable, una barra de jabón, el champú, el cepillo, la ropa
En el cuarto de baño: una barra de jabón, el champú, el espejo, el cepillo
En el cuarto de dormir: un libro, la cama, el espejo, el cepillo, la ropa
En una mochila: una barra de jabón, el champú, un libro, el cepillo, la ropa

PASO 3

Conversación

RESOURCE MANAGER

Audio Activities TE, pages 88–89
Audio CD 4
Workbook, page 94

Bellringer Review

Use BRR Transparency 6.5 or write the following on the board.
In Spanish, write three things you did this morning before leaving your house.

2 PRESENTATION

STEP 1 Have students open their books to page 216 and scan the conversation.

STEP 2 Have them close their books. Read the conversation to them or have them listen to Audio CD 4.

STEP 3 Call on students to read aloud. One takes the part of **Paco,** the other takes the part of **Ana.**

STEP 4 After each third of the conversation, ask some comprehension questions from the **¿Comprendes?** section.

STEP 5 Have students who like to perform read the entire conversation aloud to the class using as much expression as possible.

STEP 6 After presenting the conversation, go over the **¿Comprendes?** activity. If students can answer the questions with relative ease, move on. Students should not be expected to memorize the conversation.

216

Conversación

¿A qué hora te despertaste?

Paco Ana, ¿a qué hora te despertaste esta mañana?

Ana Esta mañana me levanté un poco tarde.

Paco ¿Te levantaste tarde? ¿Por qué?

Ana Porque anoche me acosté muy tarde.

Paco ¿Por qué te acostaste tan tarde? ¿Saliste?

Ana No, no salí. Pasé la noche estudiando. Hoy tengo un examen de matemáticas. Estudié hasta la medianoche.

Paco ¿Estudiaste hasta la medianoche?

Ana Sí, y por lo general me despierto a las seis pero esta mañana no me desperté hasta las seis y media.

Paco ¿Llegaste tarde a la escuela?

Ana No, afortunadamente llegué a tiempo porque la clase de matemáticas es mi primera clase.

Contesten. *(Answer.)*

1. ¿Cuándo se despertó Ana esta mañana?
2. ¿Cuándo se acostó anoche?
3. ¿Salió ella?
4. ¿Cómo pasó la noche?
5. ¿Hasta qué hora estudió?
6. ¿A qué hora se despierta ella por lo general?
7. Y, ¿a qué hora se despertó ella esta mañana?
8. ¿Llegó tarde a la escuela?
9. ¿En qué clase tiene examen?
10. ¿Cuál es su primera clase de la mañana?

Universal Access

You may wish to allow **students with learning difficulties** and **average students** to read the conversation aloud with as much expression as possible. Then call on **advanced learners** to present the conversation without reading. They do not have to recite it from memory. Permit them to ad-lib and say anything that makes sense.

ANSWERS TO ¿Comprendes?

1. Ana se despertó un poco tarde (a las seis y media) esta mañana.
2. Se acostó muy tarde anoche.
3. No, ella no salió.
4. Pasó la noche estudiando.
5. Estudió hasta la medianoche.
6. Por lo general ella se despierta a las seis.
7. Esta mañana se despertó a las seis y media.
8. No, no llegó tarde a la escuela; llegó a tiempo.
9. Tiene examen en la clase de matemáticas.
10. Su primera clase de la mañana es la clase de matemáticas.

Pronunciación

Las consonantes ñ, ch, x

The **ñ** is a separate letter of the Spanish alphabet. The mark over it is called a **tilde.** Note that it is pronounced similarly to the *ny* in the English word *canyon*. Repeat the following.

señor	otoño	España	niño
señora	pequeño	cumpleaños	campaña
año	mañana	baño	

Ch is pronounced much like the *ch* in the English word *church*. Repeat the following.

coche	chaqueta	champú	ducha
chocolate	muchacho	churro	

An **x** between two vowels is pronounced much like the English *x* but a bit softer. It's like a **gs: examen → eg-samen.** Repeat the following.

exacto	examen
éxito	próximo

When **x** is followed by a consonant, it is often pronounced like an **s.** Repeat the following.

extremo	explicar	exclamar

Trabalenguas

Repeat the following.

El señor español compra un coche pequeño cada año en el otoño.
El muchacho de Chinchón come churros y chocolate.
El extranjero exclama que baja en la próxima estación.
Va a tener éxito en su próximo examen.

Cultura y lectura

Cultura y lectura

El camping

De camping a orillas del río Bío Bío. Chile

1 PREPARATION

RESOURCE MANAGER

Audio Activities TE, page 91
Audio CD 4
Workbook TE, pages 95–96

National Standards

Cultures
The reading and the related activities on pages 218–219 allow students to learn about camping trips in the Spanish-speaking world.

2 PRESENTATION

PRE-READING

STEP 1 Students should open their books to page 218.

STEP 2 Have them skim the passage as recommended in the Reading Strategy.

STEP 3 Have students go to the map of Spain on page xxii and the map of South America on page xxiii or project Map Transparencies M 2 and M 3. Indicate the areas described in this reading.

READING

As you go over each paragraph you may wish to call on a student to summarize the paragraph in his or her own words.

Reading Strategy

Skimming There are several ways to read an article or a passage—each one with its own purpose. Skimming means reading quickly in order to find out the general idea of a passage. To skim means to read without paying careful attention to small details, noting only information about the main theme or topic. Sometimes a reader will skim a passage only to decide whether it's interesting enough to then read in detail.

El camping es popular en muchos países hispanos. En Chile y en Ecuador, por ejemplo, el camping es bastante popular—sobre todo con la gente que es muy aficionada a la naturaleza[1]. Una guía ecuatoriana comenta. «Con solamente botas, mochila, carpa y saco de dormir puedes explorar el paisaje espectacular del país.»

De camping en los Andes. cerca de Quito. Ecuador

Los campings en Chile tienen facilidades excelentes—duchas con agua caliente, aseos[2], lavanderías[3], barbacoas para cocinar y tiendas de abarrotes. Algunas tienen piscina (o alberca). La Compañía de Teléfonos de Chile publica cada año una guía de campings con mapas excelentes.

En España, el camping es muy popular. En España hay más de quinientos campings. Como en Chile los campings ofrecen facilidades excelentes—duchas, piscinas, canchas de tenis, restaurantes y discotecas.

[1] naturaleza *nature*
[2] aseos *restrooms, toilets*
[3] lavanderías *laundromats*

Un camping. Sierra de Gredos. España

Sobre todo en agosto los campings están llenos de familias españolas. Cuando van de camping llevan todo consigo[4]. No van a comer ninguna comida rápida. De ninguna manera. En su caravana o en su coche tienen mesas y sillas plegables para poner un comedor. Y no van a comer con platos o utensilios en plástico. Traen de casa los vasos, platos, tenedores, cuchillos y cucharas. Y en la barbacoa preparan una comida deliciosa. Si el camping está cerca del mar, seguro que van a preparar pescado o mariscos. Lo importante es que todos se divierten. Y—a un precio bastante módico, porque el camping no cuesta mucho. Es una manera bastante económica de pasar las vacaciones.

[4] consigo *with them*

Un camping en Burgos, España

¿Comprendes?

A. ¿Sí o no? *(True or false?)*
1. El camping es muy popular en todos los países hispanos.
2. En algunos países de la América del Sur el camping es muy popular entre la gente que es muy aficionada a la naturaleza.
3. A muy pocos españoles les gusta el camping.

B. Contesten. *(Answer.)*
1. ¿Cuáles son algunas facilidades que tienen los campings en Chile y España?
2. ¿Quién publica una guía de campings en Chile?
3. ¿Cuántos campings hay en España?
4. ¿Qué llevan consigo los españoles cuando van de camping?
5. ¿Qué tipo de comida preparan?
6. ¿Cuesta mucho ir de camping?

C. If you and your family go camping, say something about a typical daily routine when camping.

PASO 3

Repaso

This section reviews the salient points from Unit 6. Students will study the conjugations of reflexive verbs, including stem-changing reflexive verbs.

1 PREPARATION

RESOURCE MANAGER

Audio Activities TE, page 92
Audio CD 4
Workbook, page 97
Tests, pages 81–96

2 PRESENTATION

STEP 1 Have students open their books to page 220. Ask them to look at these verbs. You may also have them repeat the verbs aloud.

Repaso

1. In this unit, I learned reflexive verbs. These verbs have an extra pronoun that refers back to the subject because the subject is both the performer (doer) and receiver of the action of the verb.

lavarse

me lavo	nos lavamos
te lavas	*os laváis*
se lava	se lavan

2. Some reflexive verbs have a stem change in the present. Examples are:

sentarse (e → ie)

me siento	nos sentamos
te sientas	*os sentáis*
se sienta	se sientan

dormirse (o → ue)

me duermo	nos dormimos
te duermes	*os dormís*
se duerme	se duermen

Other reflexive verbs you know that have similar stem changes are:

despertarse, divertirse (e → ie)
acostarse (o → ue)

Jogging a orillas del Mediterráneo, Estepona, España

¡Pongo todo junto!

 La rutina Completen. *(Complete.)*

1. **lavarse los dientes**
   Yo
   El niño
   Tú
   Nosotros
   Ellos

2. **levantarse**
   Ellos
   La niña
   Yo
   Nosotros
   Tú
   Ustedes

 ¿Quién? Den la frase de nuevo.
(Form a new sentence.)

1. Yo me despierto a las seis y media.
   Nosotros _____.
2. Ellos se duermen enseguida.
   Yo _____.
3. ¿Ellos se acuestan a qué hora?
   ¿Tú _____?
4. Nosotros nos divertimos.
   Tú _____.

Un hostal para mochileros. Barranco. Lima. Perú

 ¿Y ustedes? Contesten. *(Answer.)*

1. ¿A qué hora se acuestan ustedes?
2. ¿Se duermen enseguida ustedes?
3. ¿Se sientan a la mesa cuando se desayunan?
4. ¿Se divierten ustedes?

PRACTICE

  , , and It is suggested that you go over these activities quickly in class with books closed or open. Students can also write them for homework.

Learning from Photos

(page 221, top) This is the sign at the entranceway to a hostel in Barranco, Lima, Perú. Barranco is on the coast a few miles south of Miraflores. Many houses with fancy balconies, gables, and other unique architectural touches give Barranco an unusual charm.

About the Spanish Language

Note that in some areas **un hostal** is referred to as **un hostel**.

ANSWERS TO ¡Pongo todo junto!

1
1. Yo me lavo los dientes.
El niño se lava los dientes.
Tú te lavas los dientes.
Nosotros nos lavamos los dientes.
Ellos se lavan los dientes.

2. Ellos se levantan.
La niña se levanta.
Yo me levanto.
Nosotros nos levantamos.
Tú te levantas.
Ustedes se levantan.

2
1. Nosotros nos despertamos a las seis y media.
2. Yo me duermo enseguida.
3. ¿Tú te acuestas a qué hora?
4. Tú te diviertes.

3
1. Nosotros nos acostamos a ___.
2. Sí, (No, no) nos dormimos enseguida.
3. Sí, (No, no) nos sentamos a la mesa cuando nos desayunamos.
4. Sí, (No, no) nos divertimos.

¡Te toca a ti!

♻ Recycling

These activities allow students to use the vocabulary and structure from this unit in completely open-ended, real-life situations.

¡OJO! Encourage students to say as much as possible when they do these activities. Tell them not to be afraid to make mistakes, since the goal of the activities is real-life communication. If someone in the group makes an error, allow the others to politely correct him or her. Let students choose the activities they would like to do.

You may wish to divide students into pairs or groups. Encourage students to elaborate on the basic theme and to be creative. They may use props, pictures, or posters if they wish.

2 Students can also tell each other how their own routine changes on the weekend. For example: **Durante la semana me levanto a las seis pero los sábados me levanto a las nueve.**

Learning from Photos

(page 222, top) This young traveler with his backpack is in the lovely, small, mountainous city of Ronda in Andalucía, Spain. Have students note the direction for the campsite. *(page 222, bottom)* The beautiful rapids of the Petrohue River are located near the shore of **el lago Todos los Santos.** The nearby town of Petrohue in the shadow of **el volcán Osorno** is the departure point for the ferry service to Peulla, from which point overland connections can be made to the Argentine Lake District and Bariloche.

PASO 3

¡Te toca a ti!

Hablar

1 **Mi familia**

✓ *Talk about family routines*
Work with a classmate. Compare your family's routine with someone else's. Compare what things you typically do and at what time.

Hablar

2 **No es siempre igual.**

✓ *Talk about your weekday and weekend routines*
Most people like a change of pace on the weekend. Talk with a classmate and compare the things you do or do not do during the week with the things you do or do not do during the weekend.

Hablar

3 **Una excursión de camping**

✓ *Talk about a camping trip*
Work with a classmate. A friend's family invited you to join them on a camping trip. You're going to go. Discuss the things you probably need to take. Also discuss some of the things you'll probably do during the camping trip.

Un joven con sus mochilas. Ronda. España

Saltos de Petrohue. Chile

Unidad 6: La rutina y el camping

Universal Access

Visual learners may wish to make a packing list and a schedule for the camping trip after doing Activity 3.

ANSWERS TO ¡Te toca a ti!

 , **2** , and **3** *Answers will vary.*

Escribir

4 Un día típico

✓ *Write about your daily routine*

You have a Mexican key pal who is curious to know about your daily routine. Write him or her an e-mail describing all the activities you do on a typical day, from the time you wake up until the time you go to bed.

4 Encourage students to describe their routine in as much detail as possible.

Learning from Photos

(page 223) This beautiful view from the tent is of the **volcán Callaquí** in the Biobío Valley in Chile.

Writing Strategy

Keeping a journal There are many kinds of journals you can keep, each having a different purpose. One type of journal is the kind in which you write about daily events and record your thoughts and impressions about these events. It's almost like "thinking out loud." By keeping such a journal, you may find that you discover something new you were not aware of before.

Writing Strategy

Keeping a journal Have students read the Writing Strategy on page 223. Then have them refer to the **Vocabulario** on page 235 as they write about what they do in a typical day.

Una carpa, río Bío Bío, Chile

Escribir

5 Mi agenda

Write down all you do in a typical day. For the next week, keep a diary in Spanish. Write down everything you do in the course of each day.

Writing Development

Have students keep a notebook or portfolio containing their best written work from each unit. These selected writings can be based on assignments from the Student Textbook and the Writing Activities Workbook. Activities 4 and 5 on page 223 are examples of writing assignments that may be included in each student's portfolio. In the Workbook, students will develop an organized autobiography **(Mi autobiografía).** These workbook pages may also become a part of their portfolio.

Paso 3: ¡Te toca a ti!

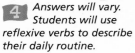

ANSWERS TO ¡Te toca a ti!

4 Answers will vary. Students will use reflexive verbs to describe their daily routine.

5 Answers will vary. Students should use reflexive verbs as they keep track of their week's activities.

PASO 3

Assessment

RESOURCE MANAGER

Vocabulary Transparency 6.5
Tests, pages 81–96
ExamView® Pro, Unit 6
Performance Assessment,
  Tasks 11–12

✓ Assessment

This is a pretest for students to take before you administer the unit test. Note that each section is cross-referenced so students can easily find the material they have to review in case they made errors. You may use Assessment Answers Transparency A 6 to do the assessment in class, or you may assign this assessment for homework. You can correct the assessment yourself, or you may prefer to project the answers on the overhead in class.

PASO 3

Assessment

¿Estoy listo(a)?

Palabras

1 Completen. (*Complete.*)

To review words from **Paso 1,** *turn to pages 200–201.*

1. La muchacha _____ Susana.
2–3. El joven _____ a las once de la noche pero no se duerme _____. Pasa media hora leyendo en la cama.
4–5. Él _____ en el _____ cuando se peina.
6–7. La muchacha _____ en la cocina y luego se lava _____.

2 Contesten. (*Answer.*)

To review words from **Paso 2,** *turn to pages 208–209.*

8. Él va a tomar una ducha. ¿Qué necesita?
9. Ella va a peinarse. ¿Qué necesita?
10. Él tiene que cepillarse los dientes. ¿Qué necesita?
11. Ella va a dormir en una carpa. ¿Qué necesita?
12. Ella quiere lavarse el pelo. ¿Qué necesita?

ANSWERS TO *Assessment*

1

1. se llama
2. se acuesta
3. enseguida
4. se mira
5. espejo
6. se desayuna
7. los dientes

2

8. Necesita una barra (pastilla) de jabón y champú.
9. Necesita un cepillo (o un peine) y un espejo.
10. Necesita un cepillo de dientes y un tubo de pasta (crema) dentífrica.
11. Necesita un saco de dormir.
12. Necesita champú.

224

Formas

3 Completen. *(Complete.)*

13. Yo _____ a la mesa. (sentarse)
14. ¿Tú _____ a qué hora? (acostarse)
15. Ellos _____ José y Magdalena. (llamarse)
16. Nosotros _____ enseguida. (dormirse)
17. Yo _____ los dientes. (lavarse)
18. Ustedes _____ en casa. (desayunarse)
19. Ellos _____ mucho. (divertirse)

To review reflexive verbs, turn to pages 204–205, 212.

4 Completen con un pronombre si es necesario. *(Complete with a pronoun if necessary.)*

20. Ella _____ mira en el espejo cuando se peina.
21. Ella _____ mira a la profesora.
22. Yo _____ lavo a mi perro.
23. Yo _____ lavo antes de ir a la escuela.

To review reflexive pronouns, turn to pages 204–205, 212.

Cultura

5 Escojan. *(Choose.)*

24. ¿A quiénes les gusta ir de camping en la América del Sur?
    a. a muchas familias españolas
    b. a los aficionados a la naturaleza
    c. a los empleados de la Compañía Chilena de Teléfonos
25. ¿Qué usan las familias españolas para comer cuando van de camping?
    a. los vasos y platos que traen de casa
    b. utensilios de plástico
    c. una tienda de campaña

To review this cultural information, turn to pages 218–219.

Spanish Online

For additional practice, students may wish to do the online games and quizzes on the **Glencoe Spanish Web site** (spanish.glencoe.com). Quizzes are corrected instantly and results can be sent via e-mail to you.

ANSWERS TO *Assessment*

3
13. me siento
14. te acuestas
15. se llaman
16. nos dormimos
17. me lavo
18. se desayunan
19. se divierten

4
20. se
21. no pronoun needed
22. no pronoun needed
23. me

5
24. b
25. a

Diversiones

Paso 4 of each **Unidad** includes a **Diversiones** section. As the title indicates, this section contains different types of activities that students in Middle School should enjoy. They also take into account the various learning modalities.

The many types of activities included are:

Canciones This section entitled **Canta con Justo** contains songs performed on the music CD by Justo Lamas, a young singer from Argentina who has written some songs specifically for **¿Cómo te va?**

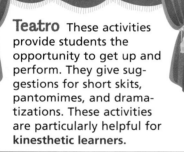

Teatro These activities provide students the opportunity to get up and perform. They give suggestions for short skits, pantomimes, and dramatizations. These activities are particularly helpful for **kinesthetic learners.**

Manos a la obra

These activities enable students to get involved and use their hands. Some examples are: drawing cards or pictures, preparing ads and brochures, and preparing schedules and announcements.

Rompecabezas

Some units contain riddles or puzzles that reinforce language in a fun way.

Investigaciones

This research section allows those students who like to work on their own to get involved in some research projects that add another dimension to the cultural material of the unit.

Diversiones

Canta con Justo
Guantanamera

Guan - ta - na - me - ra, gua-ji - ra, guan-ta-na-me-ra. Guan - ta-na-me - ra,

gua-ji-ra, guan - ta-na-me - ra.___ Guan -ta-na-me - ra, gua-ji-ra,

guan-ta-na-me-ra. Guan-ta-na-me - ra___, gua-ji-ra, guan - ta - na - me - ra.__

Yo soy un hom-bre sin___ ce-ro de don-de cre-ce la

pal - ma. Yo soy un hom-bre sin___ ce-ro de don-de cre-ce la pal - ma.

Y an-tes de mo - rir - me quie___ ro e - char mis ver - sos del al - ma.

Guantanamera, guajira, guantanamera
Guantanamera, guajira, guantanamera
Guantanamera, guajira, guantanamera
Guantanamera, guajira, guantanamera

Mi verso es de un verde claro
y de un carmín encendido.
Mi verso es de un verde claro
y de un carmín encendido.
Mi verso es un ciervo herido
que busca en el monte amparo.

Guantanamera, guajira, guantanamera
Guantanamera, guajira, guantanamera
Guantanamera, guajira, guantanamera
Guantanamera, guajira, guantanamera

Con los pobres de la tierra
quiero yo mi suerte echar.
Con los pobres de la tierra
quiero yo mi suerte echar.
El arroyo de las sierras
me complace más que el mar.

Guantanamera, guajira, guantanamera
Guantanamera, guajira, guantanamera
Guantanamera, guajira, guantanamera
Guantanamera, guajira, guantanamera

Music Connection

Canta con Justo

The song **Guantanamera** will be easy for learners of all ability levels. They will have fun listening to it, and some students may want to make up a dance. Some students may recognize all or part of this song. You may wish to have students hear the recorded version of **Guantanamera.** It can be found on Track 12 of the **Canta con Justo** music CD. You may wish to use Song Transparency S 6 to project the music and lyrics on an overhead so students can follow along as they listen or sing.

Teatro

Mime the following.

Me despierto.   **Me levanto.**   Me lavo la cara.

Me lavo las manos.   **Me lavo el pelo.**

Me cepillo.   Me siento.

Me divierto.   Me lavo los dientes.

 ¿Lo necesito o no? Work in small groups. See who can make the most correct statements in three minutes with **Necesito _____ porque voy a _____.**

Manos a la obra

1. **Un T-shirt** Cut out a pattern for a T-shirt that will fit you. Decorate your T-shirt to tell some things about yourself—who you are, where you are from, all about your family, your school life, your daily routine, and what you like and don't like. When you have finished, it might be fun to have classmates guess which T-shirts belong to which students. Now you'll really find out how well your classmates know you!

2. **Un camping** Prepare the cover of a brochure for a campsite in a Spanish-speaking country.

Camping ARENA BLANCA

ABIERTO 01/01 – 31/12
Tel. (34) 965.861.889
Fax (34) 965.861.107

Distancias
Alicante, 41 km
Parada bus 100 m destino al centro de Benidorm
Estación de ferrocarril 1,2 km
Aeropuerto 40 km

EQUIPAMIENTO Y SERVICIOS

Equipamiento del camping
- Playa 1,2 km
- Totalmente preparado para discapacitados
- Tomas de electricidad
- Agua caliente general gratis
- Calefacción en lavabos

Servicios
- Restaurante
- Platos preparados para llevar
- Supermercado
- Prensa diaria

- Lavadoras automáticas
- Parking y custodia de caravanas
- Información turística
- Cambio de divisas
- Caja de seguridad
- Cajero automático

★★★BENIDORM (ALICANTE)★★★BENIDORM (ALICANTE)★★★BENIDORM (ALICAN

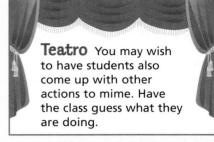

Teatro You may wish to have students also come up with other actions to mime. Have the class guess what they are doing.

 Juego Students may also do this activity in pairs. One student comes up with the first half of the sentence and the other student finishes it. Students take turns beginning and finishing the sentences.

Manos a la obra

The T-shirt also provides a quick review of what students have learned so far in Spanish.

Universal Access

Kinesthetic and **visual learners** will especially enjoy the **Manos a la obra** activities.

MARIO Y MARÍA UNIMUNDO
Encourage students to be as creative as possible when writing their stories. Remind them to look carefully at details in the illustrations if they need help coming up with ideas.

Universal Access

You may wish to advise **students with learning difficulties** to think chronologically, starting with the very first thing Mario and María might do and ending with the last thing they might do. Students may make a list by putting these activities at the top and bottom of the list, adding other main daily activities in the middle, and then using their creativity to fill in the gaps.

Mario y María Unimundo These two new friends you made this year, or perhaps last year, have accompanied you throughout your journey to learn Spanish. By now you have a good idea of the personality that each has. Some of the illustrations below will remind you of some of their adventures. Write a story about a day in the life of Mario and María Unimundo. Illustrate your story and then present it to the class. See who can come up with the most unusual story.

228

Entrevista

¿A qué hora te levantas por la mañana?
¿Te desayunas en casa o en la escuela?
¿A qué hora sales de casa?
¿Cómo vas a la escuela?
¿Dónde tomas el almuerzo?
¿A qué hora terminan tus clases?
¿Adónde vas después de las clases?
¿Qué haces?
¿A qué hora vuelves a casa?
¿Miras la televisión?
¿Cuándo haces tus tareas?
¿A qué hora te acuestas?
¿Te duermes enseguida?

PLEGABLES™ Study Organizer

Para practicar más Use this *sentence strip* holder to practice your vocabulary, your verbs, or anything else you might feel you need extra help with.

Step 1 **Fold** a sheet of paper (8½" x 11") in half like a *hamburger*.

Step 2 **Open** the *hamburger* and fold the two outer edges toward the valley. This forms a shutter fold.

Step 3 **Fold** one of the inside edges of the shutter back to the outside fold. This fold forms a floppy L.

Step 4 **Glue** the floppy L tab down to the base so that it forms a strong straight L tab.

Step 5 **Glue** the other shutter side to the front of this L tab. This forms a tent that is the backboard for the flashcards or student work to be displayed.

Step 6 **Fold** the edge of the L up ¼" to ½" to form a lip that will keep the sentence strips from slipping off the holder.

Vocabulary and spelling words can be stored inside the "tent" formed by this fold.

Entrevista

The **Entrevista** activity reinforces students' ability to interact with peers in Spanish in a real-life situation. This task recombines material the student has already learned. Students of all ability levels will be able to perform this task.

PLEGABLES™ Study Organizer

This foldable will help students organize, display, and arrange data as they review the vocabulary, verbs, and verb forms they know in Spanish. You may wish to encourage them to add information from each unit as they continue to expand their vocabulary.

A *sentence strip holder* foldable is also ideal as students continue their study of Spanish and learn more and more words.

Más cultura y lectura

El día empieza con el desayuno.

Por la mañana nos despertamos, nos levantamos, nos lavamos las manos y la cara y luego, ¿qué? Nos desayunamos, ¿no?

◄ El desayuno que tomamos no es el mismo en todas partes del mundo. En Estados Unidos muchos de nosotros comemos huevos—huevos fritos, huevos revueltos[1] o huevos pasados por agua[2]. Los huevos vienen acompañados de tocino[3], jamón o salchicha y, a veces, papas. Pero hoy en día mucha gente no tiene el tiempo para preparar un desayuno tan grande. Muchos comemos solamente fruta, cereales, pan tostado o un pan dulce con jugo de naranja y café o chocolate.

[1] revueltos *scrambled*
[2] pasados por agua *soft-boiled*
[3] tocino *bacon*

► En la gran mayoría de los países hispanos el desayuno es una comida muy pequeña. Los españoles, por ejemplo, comen pan o un bolillo con mantequilla y mermelada. Un desayuno típico es churros, un tipo de «doughnut» frito y una taza grande de café o, en el caso de los más jóvenes, chocolate caliente.

National Standards

Cultures
This reading about breakfast introduces students to breakfast foods that are eaten in the Spanish-speaking world.

Comparisons
This reading makes comparisons between breakfast foods in the Spanish-speaking world and in the United States.

 ¡OJO! This reading is optional. You may skip it completely, have the entire class read it, have only several students read it and report to the class, or assign it for extra credit.

PRESENTATION

STEP 1 Have students look at the photos on these two pages as they read about typical breakfasts in the Spanish-speaking world.

STEP 2 Have students discuss what information they find interesting.

Churros are fried in olive oil and coated with sugar. Ideally they are served hot. People dunk them in either **café con leche** or **chocolate.**

◀ En muchas ciudades latinoamericanas el desayuno es muy parecido[4] al desayuno en España. Pero en los pueblos del campo el desayuno tiene influencias indígenas y puede ser un poco más grande. Por ejemplo, en un pueblo de Guatemala, el desayuno puede incluir un tipo de *oatmeal* que se llama **mosh** servido con canela[5], o un cereal de maíz servido con leche caliente. Comen también huevos fritos con frijoles y un queso blanco, tortillas y unas tazas grandes de café muy caliente.

[4] parecido *similar*
[5] canela *cinnamon*

¿Comprendes?

A. Contesten. *(Answer.)*
1. En España, ¿es el desayuno una comida grande o pequeña?
2. ¿Qué comen los españoles en el desayuno?
3. ¿Qué es un churro?
4. ¿Qué beben los españoles con el desayuno?

B. ¿Sí o no? *(True or false?)*
1. En las ciudades latinoamericanas el desayuno es parecido al desayuno norteamericano.
2. En los pueblos pequeños del campo hay influencias indígenas en la comida.

C. Describan. *(Describe.)*
1. un desayuno típico en Estados Unidos
2. un desayuno típico en un pueblo pequeño de Guatemala o México, por ejemplo

¿Comprendes?

A. You may use these activities to assess how well your students understood the reading.

Universal Access

Time permitting, you may wish to have a Latin American breakfast where you prepare a breakfast typical of a small town in Guatemala (or another part of the Spanish-speaking world) for students. In Spanish, discuss with students what they are eating. This may be especially beneficial for **kinesthetic learners**.

ANSWERS TO ¿Comprendes?

A.
1. En España el desayuno es una comida pequeña.
2. Los españoles comen pan o un bolillo con mantequilla y mermelada.
3. Un churro es un tipo de «doughnut» frito.
4. Los españoles beben café o chocolate caliente con el desayuno.

B.
1. No
2. Sí

C. *Answers will vary but may include:*
1. huevos, tocino, jamón, salchicha, fruta, cereal, pan tostado, pan dulce, jugo de naranja, café, chocolate caliente
2. mosh con canela, cereal de maíz servido con leche caliente, huevos fritos, frijoles, queso blanco, tortillas, café

231

Conexiones

PASO 4

Conexiones
Las ciencias naturales

 ¡OJO! The readings in the **Conexiones** section are optional. They focus on some of the major disciplines taught in schools and universities. The vocabulary is useful for discussing such topics as history, literature, art, economics, business, science, etc. You may choose any of the following ways to do the readings in the **Conexiones** sections.

Independent reading Have students read the selections and do the post-reading activities as homework, which you collect. This option is least intrusive on class time and requires a minimum of teacher involvement.

Homework with in-class follow-up Assign the readings and post-reading activities as homework. Review and discuss the material in class the next day.

Intensive in-class activity This option includes a pre-reading vocabulary presentation, in-class reading and discussion, assignment of the activities for homework, and a discussion of the assignment in class the following day.

La ecología

Ecology is a subject of great interest to young people around the world. No one wants to wake up each morning and breathe polluted air. No one wants to see the countryside loaded with debris from campers and picnickers. Nor does anyone want to swim in a polluted ocean or lake. We are all aware that urgent and dramatic steps must be taken to clean up our environment.

La ecología

El término «ecología» significa el equilibrio entre los seres vivientes—los seres humanos—y la naturaleza[1].

La contaminación del aire

La contaminación del medio ambiente[2] es el problema ecológico número uno. El aire que respiramos en muchas partes del mundo está contaminado.

Las emisiones de gases que se escapan de los automóviles, autobuses y camiones[3] contaminan el aire.

El humo que emiten las chimeneas de las fábricas[4] contaminan el aire.

[1] naturaleza *nature*   [2] medio ambiente *environment*   [3] camiones *trucks*   [4] fábricas *factories*

Contaminación del aire. Ciudad de México

Learning from Photos

(pages 232–233) Have students choose one sentence from the reading that best describes each photo. For example, they might say: **Las emisiones de gases que se escapan de los automóviles, autobuses y camiones contaminan el aire.**

Vocabulary Expansion

You may wish to give students a few extra words and phrases that are useful when talking about ecology and the environment:

el aumento de la temperatura global	*global warming*
la lluvia ácida	*acid rain*
la erosión	*erosion*
la energía solar	*solar energy*
la extinción	*extinction*
la conservación	*conservation*

El agua

Nuestras aguas están contaminadas también. Los buques petroleros derraman[4] cantidades de petróleo en nuestros mares y océanos.

Las fábricas echan los desechos[5] industriales en los mares y en los ríos. Y muchos de los desechos son tóxicos.

El reciclaje

Hoy en día hay grandes campañas de reciclaje. En las ciudades grandes y en los pueblos pequeños hay receptáculos para recoger los desechos como papel, vidrio[6] (cristal) y metal.

[4] derraman *dump*
[5] desechos *wastes*
[6] vidrio *glass*

Cerca del río Grande en la frontera entre México y Texas

¿Comprendes?

Contesten. (*Answer.*)

1. ¿Está contaminado el aire donde ustedes viven?
2. ¿Hay mucha industria donde viven?
3. ¿Hay muchas fábricas?
4. ¿Hay muchos automóviles y camiones?
5. ¿Se escapan gases de los automóviles?
6. ¿Hay campañas de reciclaje donde viven?

233

¡Hablo como un pro!

This unique section gives students the opportunity to speak freely and say whatever they want on their own. The illustrations serve to remind students of precisely what they know how to say in Spanish. There are no depictions of activities that students do not have the ability to describe or talk about in Spanish. The art in this section recombines all that the students learned in the particular unit and in addition frequently recombines the topic or situation of the unit with that of another unit for additional reinforcement.

You can use this section in many ways. Some possibilities are:
1. Have students look at the illustrations and just identify items by giving the correct Spanish words.
2. Have students make up sentences about what they see in the illustrations.
3. Have students make up questions about the illustrations. They can call on another class member to respond if you do this as an entire class activity, or you may prefer to allow students to work in small groups. This activity is extremely beneficial because it enables students to actively use the interrogative words.
4. You may wish to ask questions and call on students to answer.
5. Have students look at the illustrations and give a complete oral review of what they see.
6. Have two students work together and make up a conversation based on the illustrations.
7. Have students look at the illustrations and write a paragraph (or paragraphs) about them in class.

You can also use this section as an assessment or testing tool, taking into account individual differences by having students go from simple to quite complicated tasks.

234

Say as much as you can about the illustration.

¡Hablo como un pro!

The assessment can be either oral or written. You may wish to use the rubrics provided on pages T22–T23 as you give students the following directions.
1. Identify the topic or situation of these illustrations.
2. Identify as many items as you can and give the Spanish words. Don't forget to include actions you see.
3. Give as many sentences as you can to describe the illustrations.
4. Go over your sentences and put them in the best sequence possible.
5. Polish your sentences and sequencing to give a coherent story based on the illustrations.

Universal Access

When talking about the illustration, **students with learning difficulties** may just give random sentences. **Advanced students** will give a coherent story. You may wish to have **advanced students** write a paragraph about the illustration.

Vocabulario

Stating daily activities

la rutina	ponerse la ropa	acostarse
despertarse	mirarse	dormirse
levantarse	cepillarse	llamarse
lavarse	peinarse	divertirse
bañarse	sentarse	
tomar una ducha	desayunarse	

Identifying more parts of the body

la cara   los dientes   el pelo

Identifying articles for grooming and hygiene

el cepillo	el tubo de pasta (crema)
el peine	dentífrica
el cepillo de dientes	un rollo de papel higiénico
el espejo	el champú
una barra (una pastilla) de jabón	

Identifying more breakfast foods

una botella de agua mineral
un vaso de jugo de naranja
el cereal
el pan tostado

Describing camping

el camping	la caravana	dar una caminata
un parque nacional	la carpa, la tienda de	armar
la mochila	campaña	llevar
el saco de dormir	la mesa plegable	

Other useful expressions

enseguida
temprano

Vocabulario

Vocabulary Review

The words and phrases in the **Vocabulario** have been taught for productive use in this unit. They are summarized here as a resource for both student and teacher. This list also serves as a convenient resource for the **¡Te toca a ti!** activities on pages 222–223. There are approximately seventeen cognates in this vocabulary list. Have students find them.

¡OJO! You will notice that the vocabulary list here is not translated. This has been done intentionally, since we feel that by the time students have finished the material in the unit they should be familiar with the meanings of all the words. If there are several words they still do not know, we recommend that they refer to the **Paso 1 Palabras** and **Paso 2 Palabras** sections in the unit or go to the dictionaries at the end of this book to find the meanings. However, if you prefer that your students have the English translations, please refer to Vocabulary Transparency 6.6, where you will find all these words with their translations.

El Quijote

Literary Companion

National Standards

Cultures
Students experience, discuss, and analyze an adapted excerpt from the novel *El Quijote* by Miguel de Cervantes Saavedra.

¡OJO! This literary selection is optional. You may present the piece thoroughly as a class activity or you may have some or all students read it on their own. If you present it as a class activity, you may wish to vary presentation procedures from section to section. Some options are:

- Students read silently.
- Students read after you in unison.
- When dialogue appears in the story, call on students to take parts.

With any of the above procedures, intersperse some comprehension questions. Call on a student or students to give a brief synopsis of a section in Spanish.

Introducción

STEP 1 You may go over the **Introducción** with the class or you may decide to omit it and just have them read the story.

STEP 2 You may wish to ask the following questions about the **Introducción:**

¿Cuál es el nombre de una novela española muy famosa?

¿Quién es el autor?

¿Cómo se llaman los personajes principales?

¿Cómo es don Quijote?

¿Cómo es Sancho Panza?

El Quijote
Miguel de Cervantes Saavedra

Introducción
La obra más famosa de todas las letras hispanas es la novela *El ingenioso hidalgo don Quijote de la Mancha* de Miguel de Cervantes Saavedra.

Los dos personajes principales de la novela son don Quijote y Sancho Panza. Don Quijote, un hombre alto y delgado, es un caballero andante. Es un idealista que quiere conquistar todos los males[1] del mundo. Su escudero, Sancho Panza, es un hombre bajo y gordo. Él es un realista puro. Siempre trata de desviar[2] a don Quijote de sus ilusiones y aventuras.

[1] males *evils*   [2] trata de desviar *tries to dissuade*

236

¡OJO! The exposure to literature early in one's study of another language should be a pleasant experience. As students read the selection, it is not necessary for them to understand every word. Explain to them that they should try to enjoy the experience of reading literature in a new language. As they read they should look for the following:

• who the main characters are
• what they are like
• what they are doing—the plot
• what happens to them—the outcome of the story

Learning from Photos

(pages 236–237) This photo shows the **Biblioteca Central** of the **Universidad Nacional Autónoma de México.** It is the most spectacular building on the campus. The beautiful mosaics depicting different periods of Mexican history and scientific achievements were done by Juan O'Gorman.

Note: The following teaching suggestions are for a thorough presentation of *El Quijote*.

Teaching Vocabulary

 Students merely need to be familiar with the vocabulary to help them understand the story. This vocabulary does not have to be a part of their active, productive vocabulary.

STEP 1 Have students open their books to pages 238–239. Have them repeat the new vocabulary words after you.

El Quijote   Miguel de Cervantes Saavedra

Palabras

la lanza

don Quijote

un caballero andante

delgado

el caballo

el asno

gordo

Sancho Panza

un escudero

238

el molino de viento   **el aspa**

el campo

un(a) vecino(a) una persona que vive cerca, en la misma calle, por ejemplo
sabio(a) inteligente, astuto(a)
espantoso(a) horrible, terrible
a toda prisa muy rápido
de nuevo otra vez
socorrer ayudar, dar auxilio o ayuda
no les hace caso no les presta atención
una tontería una cosa estúpida

¿Qué palabra necesito?

1 Contesten. (*Answer.*)

1. ¿Es don Quijote delgado o gordo?
2. ¿Quién es gordo?
3. ¿Quién es un caballero andante?
4. ¿Quién es su escudero?
5. ¿Quién tiene una lanza?
6. ¿Quién tiene un caballo?
7. Y Sancho Panza, ¿qué tiene él?
8. ¿Tiene aspas un molino de viento?

2 Describan a don Quijote y a Sancho Panza.
(*Describe Don Quijote and Sancho Panza.*)

3 Expresen de otra manera.
(*Express in a different way.*)

1. Ellos viven en *una región rural*.
2. Fue una aventura *horrible*.
3. Él salió *rápido*.
4. No le *presta atención* a su vecino.
5. Él es un señor *inteligente y astuto*.
6. Él lo hace *otra vez*.
7. Quiere pero no puede *ayudar* a su vecino.
8. Él siempre habla de *cosas estúpidas*.

STEP 2 Quickly go over the activities on page 239 orally to ascertain that the students can recognize the vocabulary for receptive purposes.

¿Qué palabra necesito?

2 EXPANSION If any of your students are artistic, ask them to draw a picture of don Quijote and/or Sancho Panza. Have them describe their picture either orally or in written form. This will be especially helpful for **visual learners.**

FUN FACTS

It is claimed that after the Bible, *El Quijote* is the most widely read book in the world.

Universal Access

You may have students work in groups and prepare a play entitled **Don Quijote y los molinos de viento.** This windmill episode lends itself to some very funny skits. Students can present their play to the entire class, other Spanish classes, or to the Spanish Club. This should be very helpful for **visual** and **kinesthetic learners.**

Discussing Literature
El Quijote

STEP 1 Tell students that this reading is an excerpt from the novel written in the early 1600s. The novel was written as a parody to poke fun at the idealistic adventure novels of the time.

STEP 2 You may wish to have students take a few minutes to read each section silently before going over it orally in class.

STEP 3 Since this reading is rather long you may wish to go over only certain sections orally and just have students read the others silently.

STEP 4 Call on **advanced learners** to give a synopsis of each section. This helps **students with learning difficulties** better understand the selection.

STEP 5 Here are some additional hints to help you teach the various sections of the reading:

SECTION 1 Ask students what **la categoría de don Quijote** might refer to.

SECTION 2
A. Have students discuss the difference between idealistic and realistic points of view.

B. Tell students that **Vuestra Merced** is a form of address to show respect for someone in a position of power or authority.

El Quijote
Miguel de Cervantes Saavedra

En su casa don Quijote tiene una biblioteca. En la biblioteca tiene muchos libros de caballeros andantes. Don Quijote los lee todos y se vuelve loco°. Decide que quiere tener aventuras como los caballeros andantes en sus libros. Quiere conquistar todo el mal que existe en el mundo.

Un día don Quijote decidió salir de su pueblo en la región de la Mancha. Salió en busca de aventuras. Es el trabajo de un buen caballero andante. Pero después de unos pocos días don Quijote volvió a casa. ¿Por qué? Porque un caballero andante de la categoría de don Quijote no puede viajar solo. Tiene que tener un escudero.

Cuando volvió a su pueblo, empezó enseguida a buscar un escudero. Por fin, encontró° a un vecino, Sancho Panza, un hombre bajo y gordo. Don Quijote salió por segunda vez, esta vez acompañado de su escudero. Don Quijote montó a su caballo, Rocinante, y Sancho montó en su asno.

se vuelve loco *goes crazy*

encontró *he met*

Los dos hacen muchas expediciones por la región de la Mancha. El idealista don Quijote hace muchas cosas que no quiere hacer el realista Sancho Panza. Más de una vez Sancho le dice°:

—Pero, don Quijote, noble caballero y fiel° compañero. Vuestra Merced está loco. ¿Por qué no dejamos° con estas tonterías? ¿Por qué no volvemos a casa? Yo quiero comer. Y quiero dormir en mi cama.

Pero don Quijote no le presta atención a Sancho. No le hace caso y las aventuras continúan.

dice *says*
fiel *faithful*
dejamos *put an end to*

Un día, en un lugar de la Mancha don Quijote ve algo misterioso.

—Sancho, Sancho. ¿Tú ves lo que veo yo?

—No, Vuestra Merced. No veo nada.

—Amigo Sancho, ¿no ves allí unos treinta o más gigantes que vienen hacia nosotros para hacer batalla?

—¿Qué gigantes?

—Los gigantes de los brazos largos que ves allí.

—Don Quijote. No son gigantes que ves. Son simples molinos de viento. Y lo que parecen° ser brazos, son aspas.

—Sancho, yo sé que tú no sabes nada de aventuras. Son gigantes y sí tú tienes miedo°...

—¡Don Quijote! ¿A – d – ó – n –d – e va Vuestra Merced?

parecen *seem, appear*

tienes miedo *you are scared*

¿Adónde fue don Quijote? Fue a hacer batalla contra los terribles gigantes. Gigantes como estos no deben ni pueden existir en el mundo. Don Quijote los tiene que atacar. No hay otro remedio.

Don Quijote ataca. Pone su lanza en el aspa de uno de los molinos. En el mismo instante viene (sopla) un viento fuerte. El viento mueve el

Molinos de viento, La Mancha, España

SECTION 3 Ask students what they think the symbolism is behind don Quijote seeing the **molinos de viento** as **gigantes que vienen a hacer batalla.**

SECTION 4 As you present this reading there are many opportunities to use gestures to assist students with comprehension. Some examples are:

Don Quijote los tiene que atacar. (Attack two chairs.)

Pone su lanza en el aspa. (Put a long ruler or pointer through the space in the back of a chair.)

Viene un viento fuerte. (Make a howling sound.)

El viento mueve el aspa. (Move your hand in a circular motion.)

El Quijote   **doscientos cuarenta y uno** ✺ **241**

Discussing Literature

Universal Access

Some students may enjoy drawing don Quijote attacking the windmills. Using their drawing, they can describe the episode in their own words, either orally or in writing. **Visual** and **kinesthetic learners** will especially enjoy this activity.

CLASS MOTIVATOR

¡Vamos a cantar! After reading this passage, you may wish to play some songs from the show *Man of La Mancha*.

aspa. La revuelve° con tanta furia que hace pedazos° de la lanza de don Quijote y levanta al pobre don Quijote en el aire.

A toda prisa Sancho fue a socorrer a su caballero andante. Lo encontró en el suelo muy mal herido°.

—¡Don Quijote! Nunca me haces caso. ¿Por qué quiere Vuestra Merced atacar unos molinos de viento? ¿No ves ahora que son simples molinos de viento y no gigantes?

—Sancho, tienes razón. Ahora son molinos. Pero tú no comprendes. No sabes nada de aventuras. Yo tengo un enemigo muy malo. Mi enemigo se llama Frestón. Es un monstruo horrible pero muy sabio y muy inteligente. Él siempre me hace cosas malas y ahora convierte a los gigantes en molinos de viento.

—Pues, don Quijote. Yo no sé lo que te hace el enemigo Frestón. Pero yo sé lo que te han hecho° estos molinos de viento.

Sancho levantó a don Quijote del suelo. Don Quijote subió de nuevo sobre Rocinante. Sancho subió sobre su asno. Don Quijote habló más de la pasada aventura pero Sancho no le prestó atención.

Los dos siguieron° el camino hacia Puerto Lápice en busca de otras aventuras.

revuelve turns
pedazos pieces

herido injured

han hecho have done

siguieron continued

Plaza de España, Madrid

¿Comprendes?

A. Escojan. (Choose.)

1. En su casa don Quijote tiene _____.
   a. caballeros andantes   b. una biblioteca   c. muchos males
2. Don Quijote salió de su pueblo _____.
   a. en busca de la Mancha   b. en busca de un escudero   c. en busca de aventuras
3. Don Quijote volvió a casa para _____.
   a. comenzar otra expedición   b. buscar un escudero   c. conocer a su vecino
4. Sancho Panza es _____.
   a. un caballero andante   b. un idealista sin par   c. un vecino de don Quijote
5. Sancho Panza tiene _____.
   a. un asno   b. un caballo   c. una lanza

B. ¿Sí o no? (True or false?)

1. Sancho Panza y don Quijote hacen sólo dos expediciones.
2. Sancho quiere hacer todo lo que don Quijote quiere hacer.
3. Sancho le dice a don Quijote que está loco.
4. Don Quijote siempre quiere volver a casa.
5. Sancho quiere dormir en su cama.

C. Completen. (Complete.)

1. Un día don Quijote ve algo muy _____.
2. Pero Sancho no ve _____.
3. Don Quijote ve unos treinta o más _____.
4. Según don Quijote, los gigantes tienen _____.
5. Sancho dice que no son _____; son _____.
6. Los brazos son las _____ de _____.

D. Contesten. (Answer.)

1. ¿Contra quiénes fue a hacer batalla don Quijote?
2. ¿Dónde pone don Quijote su lanza?
3. ¿Qué hace revolver el aspa?
4. ¿Adónde levanta a don Quijote?
5. ¿Quién fue a socorrer a don Quijote?
6. ¿Dónde lo encontró?
7. ¿Quién convierte los gigantes en molinos?
8. ¿Cómo se llama el enemigo de don Quijote?
9. Cuando Sancho levanta a don Quijote del suelo y lo pone sobre Rocinante, ¿vuelven a casa?
10. ¿Admite don Quijote que los gigantes son molinos de viento?

El Quijote

Note: Each of the four **¿Comprendes?** activities corresponds to a different section of the reading. Activity A corresponds to Section 1, B to Section 2, C to Section 3, and D to Section 4. As you finish each section of the story you can go over the corresponding activity.

ANSWERS TO ¿Comprendes?

A.
1. b
2. c
3. b
4. c
5. a

B.
1. No
2. No
3. Sí
4. No
5. Sí

C.
1. misterioso
2. nada
3. gigantes
4. brazos largos
5. gigantes, molinos de viento (brazos, aspas)
6. aspas, los molinos de viento

D.
1. Don Quijote fue a hacer batalla contra los terribles gigantes.
2. Don Quijote pone su lanza en el aspa de uno de los molinos.
3. Un viento fuerte hace revolver el aspa.
4. Levanta a don Quijote en el aire.
5. Sancho fue a socorrer a don Quijote.
6. Lo encontró en el suelo.
7. Su enemigo convierte los gigantes en molinos.
8. El enemigo de don Quijote se llama Frestón.
9. No, van en busca de otras aventuras.
10. No, don Quijote no admite que los gigantes son molinos de viento.

Handbook

La tiendita

FIUGGI

Alta Moda en P

InfoGap

Activity 1

Unidad 1, Paso 1, pages 2-3

Alumno A

Ask your partner the following questions. Correct answers are in parentheses.

1. ¿Qué juega Antonio?
   (*Antonio juega [al] fútbol.*)
2. ¿Qué quiere el portero?
   (*El portero quiere bloquear el balón.*)
3. ¿Qué prefieren Luisa y Carlos?
   (*Luisa y Carlos prefieren el fútbol.*)
4. ¿Prefieres ser espectador(a) o jugador(a)?
   (*Yo prefiero ser _____.*)
5. ¿Qué lanza la jugadora?
   (*La jugadora lanza el balón.*)

Alumno A

Now use the chart below to answer your partner's questions. Reminder: **tú** is you.

Tomás y Sara	fútbol
Marco	ser espectador
Los jugadores	marcar muchos tantos
Tú	?
Los equipos	al campo

Alumno B

Use the chart below to answer your partner's questions. Reminder: **tú** is you.

Antonio	fútbol
El portero	bloquear el balón
Luisa y Carlos	el fútbol
Tú	?
La jugadora	el balón

Alumno B

Now ask your partner the following questions. Correct answers are in parentheses.

1. ¿Adónde vuelven los equipos?
   (*Los equipos vuelven al campo.*)
2. ¿Prefieres ser espectador(a) o jugador(a)? (*Yo prefiero ser _____.*)
3. ¿Qué quieren los jugadores? (*Los jugadores quieren marcar muchos tantos.*)
4. ¿Qué prefiere Marco?
   (*Marco prefiere ser espectador.*)
5. ¿Qué juegan Tomás y Sara?
   (*Tomás y Sara juegan [al] fútbol.*)

H2 Handbook

Activity 2

Alumno A
Ask your partner the following questions. Correct answers are in parentheses.

1. ¿Qué deporte es?
   (Es el básquetbol. / Es el baloncesto.)
2. ¿Quiénes están en la cancha de básquetbol, los espectadores o los jugadores? (Los jugadores están en la cancha de básquetbol.)
3. ¿Driblan los jugadores con el balón? (No, los jugadores no driblan con el balón.)
4. ¿Ganan o pierden el partido los jugadores? (Los jugadores ganan.)
5. ¿Qué ganan? (Ganan un trofeo.)

Alumno A
Now answer your partner's questions based on the illustration.

Alumno B
Answer your partner's questions based on the illustration.

Alumno B
Now ask your partner the following questions. Correct answers are in parentheses.

1. ¿Qué deporte es? *(Es el béisbol.)*
2. ¿Adónde vuelven los jugadores, al campo o a casa?
   (Los jugadores vuelven al campo.)
3. ¿Queda empatado el tanto?
   (Sí, el tanto queda empatado.)
4. ¿Qué continúa, el tanto o el partido?
   (El partido continúa.)
5. ¿Hay muchos espectadores?
   (Sí, hay muchos espectadores.)

Activity 3

Unidad 2, Paso 1, pages 42–51

Antonio

Ramón

Alicia

Alumno A

Now answer your partner's questions based on the illustrations below.

Alumno A

Ask your partner the following questions. Correct answers are in parentheses.

1. ¿Cómo está Beatriz, cansada o contenta? *(Beatriz está cansada.)*

2. ¿Cómo es Beatriz, rubia o morena? *(Beatriz es morena.)*

3. ¿Es rubio o moreno Rafael? *(Rafael es moreno.)*

4. ¿Rafael está cansado o nervioso? *(Rafael está nervioso.)*

5. ¿Dónde está Amanda, en casa o en la escuela? *(Amanda está en casa.)*

6. ¿Cómo está Amanda, contenta o enferma? *(Amanda está enferma.)*

Alumno B

Answer your partner's questions based on the illustrations below.

Beatriz

Rafael

Amanda

Alumno B

Now ask your partner the following questions. Correct answers are in parentheses.

1. ¿Cómo está Alicia, contenta o triste? *(Alicia está triste.)*

2. ¿Cómo es Alicia, rubia o morena? *(Alicia es rubia.)*

3. ¿Está nervioso o contento Ramón? *(Ramón está contento.)*

4. ¿Ramón es moreno o pelirrojo? *(Ramón es moreno.)*

5. ¿Está enfermo Antonio? *(Sí, Antonio está enfermo.)*

6. ¿Dónde está Antonio, en su dormitorio o en la sala? *(Antonio está en su dormitorio.)*

Alumno A
Now answer your partner's questions based on the picture below.

Alumno A
Ask your partner the following questions. Correct answers are in parentheses.

1. ¿Dónde está el joven, en el consultorio o en la farmacia?
(El joven está en el consultorio.)

2. ¿Quién examina al joven, un médico o una médica?
(Un médico examina al joven.)

3. ¿El médico le examina la garganta o los ojos?
(El médico le examina la garganta.)

4. ¿Tiene el joven dolor de estómago?
(No, el joven no tiene dolor de estómago.)

5. ¿Abre la boca el joven?
(Sí, el joven abre la boca.)

Alumno B
Answer your partner's questions based on the illustration below.

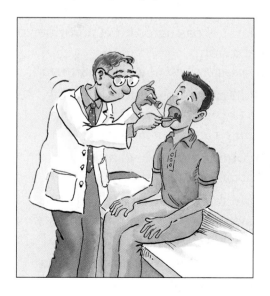

Alumno B
Now ask your partner the following questions. Correct answers are in parentheses.

1. ¿Dónde está el joven, en el consultorio o en casa? *(El joven está en el consultorio.)*

2. ¿Quién examina al joven, un médico o una médica?
(Una médica examina al joven.)

3. ¿La médica le examina la garganta o los ojos? *(La médica le examina los ojos.)*

4. ¿Tiene el joven dolor de garganta?
(No, el joven no tiene dolor de garganta.)

5. ¿Abre la boca el joven?
(No, el joven no abre la boca.)

Activity 5

Alumno A

Ask your partner the following questions. Correct answers are in parentheses.

1. ¿Están los pasajeros en el mostrador de la línea aérea? *(Sí, los pasajeros están en el mostrador de la línea aérea.)*

2. ¿Hacen un viaje a la América del Sur o a Europa? *(Hacen un viaje a la América del Sur.)*

3. ¿Qué pone la señora en la báscula? *(La señora pone su equipaje [maleta] en la báscula.)*

4. ¿Quién está revisando el pasaporte, el agente o la agente? *(La agente está revisando el pasaporte.)*

5. ¿A qué hora sale el vuelo? *(El vuelo sale a las diez y veinte.)*

Alumno A

Now answer your partner's questions based on the illustration below.

Alumno B

Answer your partner's questions based on the illustration below.

Alumno B

Now ask your partner the following questions. Correct answers are in parentheses.

1. ¿Están los pasajeros en el aeropuerto o en el avión?
   (Los pasajeros están en el aeropuerto.)

2. ¿Están en el mostrador de la línea aérea o en la puerta de salida?
   (Están en la puerta de salida.)

3. ¿De qué puerta sale el avión?
   (El avión sale de la puerta catorce.)

4. ¿Están facturando el equipaje los pasajeros? *(No, los pasajeros no están facturando el equipaje.)*

5. ¿Sale el vuelo a tiempo o con una demora? *(El vuelo sale a tiempo.)*

Alumno A

Now answer your partner's questions based on the picture below.

Alumno A

Ask your partner the following questions. Correct answers are in parentheses.

1. ¿Dónde están los pasajeros, en el aeropuerto o en el avión?
   (Los pasajeros están en el avión.)

2. ¿Cuántos asistentes de vuelo hay?
   (Hay dos asistentes de vuelo.)

3. ¿Están desembarcando los pasajeros?
   (No, los pasajeros no están desembarcando.)

4. ¿Cuántos miembros de la tripulación hay en el avión?
   (Hay cuatro miembros de la tripulación en el avión.)

Alumno B

Answer your partner's questions based on the illustration below.

Alumno B

Now ask your partner the following questions. Correct answers are in parentheses.

1. ¿Dónde están los pasajeros, en el avión o en el aeropuerto?
   (Los pasajeros están en el aeropuerto.)

2. ¿Están reclamando sus maletas o pasando por el control de pasaportes?
   (Están pasando por el control de pasaportes.)

3. ¿Quién trabaja en el control, un agente de la línea aérea o un policía?
   (Un policía trabaja en el control.)

4. ¿El policía está inspeccionando el equipaje o revisando el pasaporte?
   (El policía está revisando el pasaporte.)

InfoGap

Activity 7

Unidad 4, Paso 1, pages 120–127

Alumno A

Now answer your partner's questions based on the illustration below.

Alumno A

Ask your partner the following questions. Correct answers are in parentheses.

1. ¿Qué jugaron los jóvenes, tenis o baloncesto? *(Los jóvenes jugaron tenis.)*

2. ¿Jugaron singles o dobles? *(Jugaron singles.)*

3. ¿Jugaron en una cancha al aire libre? *(Sí, jugaron en una cancha al aire libre.)*

4. ¿Qué golpeó el jugador con la raqueta? *(El jugador golpeó la pelota con la raqueta.)*

5. ¿Pasó la pelota por encima de la red? *(Sí, la pelota pasó por encima de la red.)*

Alumno B

Answer your partner's questions based on the illustration below.

Alumno B

Now ask your partner the following questions. Correct answers are in parentheses.

1. ¿Dónde pasó el día la joven, en la cancha de tenis o en la playa? *(La joven pasó el día en la playa.)*

2. ¿Hace sol o llueve? *(Hace sol.)*

3. ¿Tomó el sol o nadó en el mar? *(Tomó el sol.)*

4. ¿Llevó anteojos de sol? *(Sí, llevó anteojos de sol.)*

5. ¿Llevó loción bronceadora a la playa? *(Sí, llevó loción bronceadora a la playa.)*

Activity 8

Alumno A

Ask your partner the following questions. Correct answers are in parentheses.

1. ¿Adónde fueron los jóvenes, a la playa o a las montañas?
   (Los jóvenes fueron a las montañas.)
2. ¿Fueron a una estación de esquí?
   (Sí, fueron a una estación de esquí.)
3. ¿Qué bajaron? *(Bajaron la pista.)*
4. ¿Bajaron la pista para principiantes o para expertos?
   (Bajaron la pista para expertos.)
5. ¿Llevaron guantes los esquiadores?
   (Sí, los esquiadores llevaron guantes.)

Alumno A

Now answer your partner's questions based on the illustration below.

Alumno B

Answer your partner's questions based on the illustration below.

Alumno B

Now ask your partner the following questions. Correct answers are in parentheses.

1. ¿Hace frío o hace calor? *(Hace frío.)*
2. ¿Fueron los amigos a la estación de esquí o a la playa?
   (Los amigos fueron a la estación de esquí.)
3. ¿Qué compraron los amigos, un café o boletos para el telesilla?
   (Compraron boletos para el telesilla.)
4. ¿Dónde compraron los boletos, en la ventanilla o en la tienda?
   (Compraron los boletos en la ventanilla.)
5. ¿Llevaron anoraks los amigos?
   (Sí, los amigos llevaron anoraks.)

Alumno A

Now answer your partner's questions based on the illustrations below.

Alumno A

Ask your partner the following questions. Correct answers are in parentheses.

1. ¿Fueron al cine las amigas o alquilaron una película?
   (Las amigas alquilaron una película.)
2. ¿Dónde miraron la película, en la sala o en el dormitorio?
   (Miraron la película en la sala.)
3. ¿Comieron algo? *(Sí, comieron algo.)*
4. ¿Bebieron un refresco?
   (Sí, bebieron un refresco.)

Alumno B

Answer your partner's questions based on the illustration below.

Alumno B

Now ask your partner the following questions. Correct answers are in parentheses.

1. ¿El joven decidió ir a la tienda de videos o al cine?
   (El joven decidió ir al cine.)

2. ¿Qué vio? *(Vio una película.)*

3. ¿Fue al cine solo o con unos amigos?
   (Fue al cine solo.)

4. ¿Tomó el autobús el joven?
   (No, el joven perdió el autobús.) /
   (No, el joven no tomó el autobús.)

Activity 10

Alumno A

Ask your partner the following questions. Correct answers are in parentheses.

1. ¿Oyó un concierto el público?
   (Sí, el público oyó un concierto.)

2. ¿Está cantando alguien ahora?
   (No, nadie está cantando ahora.)

3. ¿Recibió muchos aplausos la cantante?
   (Sí, la cantante recibió muchos aplausos.)

4. ¿Tiene el cantante algo en la mano?
   (No, el cantante no tiene nada en la mano.)

Alumno A

Now answer your partner's questions based on the illustration below.

Alumno B

Answer your partner's questions based on the illustrations below.

1–3.

4.

Alumno B

Now ask your partner the following questions. Correct answers are in parentheses.

1. ¿Dónde está la gente?
   (La gente está en el museo.)

2. ¿Qué mira la joven, un cuadro o una estatua? (La joven mira un cuadro.)

3. ¿Vio la joven una exposición de arte o un concierto de música?
   (La joven vio una exposición de arte.)

4. ¿Tiene algo en la mano la artista?
   (Sí, la artista tiene algo en la mano.)

InfoGap

Activity 11

Unidad 6, Paso 1, pages 198–205

Alumno A

Ask your partner the following questions. Correct answers are in parentheses.

1. ¿Cómo se llama el muchacho?
   (El muchacho se llama Armando.)

2. ¿Armando se lava el pelo o la cara?
   (Armando se lava el pelo.)

3. ¿Cómo se llaman las muchachas?
   (Las muchachas se llaman Teresa y Gabriela.)

4. ¿Quién se pone la ropa?
   (Teresa se pone la ropa.)

5. ¿Quién se cepilla el pelo?
   (Gabriela se cepilla el pelo.)

Alumno A

Now answer your partner's questions based on the illustrations below.

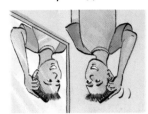

Manuel

Pablo

Cristina

Alumno B

Answer your partner's questions based on the illustrations below.

Armando

Teresa

Gabriela

Alumno B

Now ask your partner the following questions. Correct answers are in parentheses.

1. ¿Cómo se llama la muchacha?
   (La muchacha se llama Cristina.)

2. ¿Cristina se cepilla los dientes o se peina? *(Cristina se cepilla los dientes.)*

3. ¿Se levanta o se acuesta Pablo?
   (Pablo se levanta.)

4. ¿Quién se mira en el espejo?
   (Manuel se mira en el espejo.)

5. ¿Cómo se llaman los muchachos?
   (Los muchachos se llaman Pablo y Manuel.)

InfoGap

Activity 12

Unidad 6, Paso 2, pages 206–213

Alumno A

Now answer your partner's questions based on the illustrations below.

Alumno A

Ask your partner the following questions. Correct answers are in parentheses.

1. ¿Qué hace la familia, va de camping o va de compras?
   (La familia va de camping.)

2. ¿Ellos comen en la caravana o en una mesa plegable?
   (Ellos comen en una mesa plegable.)

3. ¿Tiene la familia una carpa?
   (Sí, la familia tiene una carpa.)

Alumno B

Answer your partner's questions based on the illustration below.

Alumno B

Now ask your partner the following questions. Correct answers are in parentheses.

1. ¿Qué arman los jóvenes?
   (Los jóvenes arman una tienda de campaña [una carpa].)

2. ¿Duermen los jóvenes en una cama o en un saco de dormir? *(Los jóvenes duermen en un saco de dormir.)*

3. ¿Se acuestan en la carpa?
   (Sí, se acuestan en la carpa.)

Verb Charts

Regular Verbs			
INFINITIVO	**hablar** *to speak*	**comer** *to eat*	**vivir** *to live*
PRESENTE	hablo	como	vivo
	hablas	comes	vives
	habla	come	vive
	hablamos	comemos	vivimos
	habláis	*coméis*	*vivís*
	hablan	comen	viven
PRETÉRITO	hablé	comí	viví
	hablaste	comiste	viviste
	habló	comió	vivió
	hablamos	comimos	vivimos
	hablasteis	*comisteis*	*vivisteis*
	hablaron	comieron	vivieron

Verbs with a Spelling Change in the Preterite (-car, -gar, -zar)			
INFINITIVO	**marcar** *to score*	**llegar** *to arrive*	**empezar** *to begin*
PRETÉRITO	marqué	llegué	empecé
	marcaste	llegaste	empezaste
	marcó	llegó	empezó
	marcamos	llegamos	empezamos
	marcasteis	*llegasteis*	*empezasteis*
	marcaron	llegaron	empezaron

Verb Charts

Stem-Changing Verbs*			
INFINITIVO	**empezar[1] (e ⟶ ie)** *to begin*	**perder[2] (e ⟶ ie)** *to lose*	**volver[3] (o ⟶ ue)** *to return*
PRESENTE	empiezo	pierdo	vuelvo
	empiezas	pierdes	vuelves
	empieza	pierde	vuelve
	empezamos	perdemos	volvemos
	empezáis	*perdéis*	*volvéis*
	empiezan	pierden	vuelven

INFINITIVO	**preferir[4, 5] (e ⟶ ie)** *to prefer*	**dormir[5] (o ⟶ ue)** *to sleep*	
PRESENTE	prefiero	duermo	
	prefieres	duermes	
	prefiere	duerme	
	preferimos	dormimos	
	preferís	*dormís*	
	prefieren	duermen	

*Note that the **u** in **jugar** *(to play)* changes to **ue**.
juego   juegas   juega   jugamos   jugáis   juegan

[1] **Comenzar** and **sentarse** are similar.

[2] **Querer** and **entender** are similar.

[3] **Poder, devolver,** and **acostarse** are similar.

[4] **Divertirse** is similar.

[5] Note that these verbs also have a stem change in the preterite which you will learn later.

Verb Charts

Irregular Verbs				
INFINITIVO	**conocer** *to know*	**dar** *to give*	**estar** *to be*	**hacer** *to do*
PRESENTE	conozco conoces conoce conocemos *conocéis* conocen	doy das da damos *dais* dan	estoy estás está estamos *estáis* están	hago haces hace hacemos *hacéis* hacen
PRETÉRITO	[regular]	di diste dio dimos *disteis* dieron	▬▬▬	▬▬▬

INFINITIVO	**ir** *to go*	**poner** *to put*	**saber** *to know*
PRESENTE	voy vas va vamos *vais* van	pongo pones pone ponemos *ponéis* ponen	sé sabes sabe sabemos *sabéis* saben
PRETÉRITO	fui fuiste fue fuimos *fuisteis* fueron	▬▬▬	▬▬▬

Note that the irregular preterite forms given here are taught in
¿Como te va? B, Nivel azul. The shaded boxes represent verbs that
have an irregular preterite that has not yet been taught.

Verb Charts

Irregular Verbs			
INFINITIVO	**salir** *to leave*	**ser** *to be*	**tener** *to have*
PRESENTE	salgo sales sale salimos *salís* salen	soy eres es somos *sois* son	tengo tienes tiene tenemos *tenéis* tienen
PRETÉRITO	[regular]	fui fuiste fue fuimos *fuisteis* fueron	�

INFINITIVO	**traer** *to bring*	**venir** *to come*	**ver** *to see*
PRESENTE	traigo traes trae traemos *traéis* traen	vengo vienes viene venimos *venís* vienen	veo ves ve vemos *veis* ven
PRETÉRITO	▬	▬	[regular]

Spanish-English Dictionary

This Spanish-English Dictionary contains all productive and receptive vocabulary from ¿Cómo te va? A, Nivel verde and B, Nivel azul. The numbers following each productive entry indicate the unit and vocabulary section in which the word is introduced. For example, 3.2 in dark print means that the word is taught in this textbook Unidad 3, Paso 2. A light print number means that the word was introduced in ¿Cómo te va? A, Nivel verde. BV refers to the introductory Bienvenidos lessons in A, Nivel verde. If there is no number following an entry, this means that the word or expression is included for receptive purposes only.

a at
   a bordo on board, **3.2**
   ¿A cuánto está(n)... ? How much is (are) …?
   a eso de at about
   a la una (las dos...) at one o'clock (two o'clock . . .), BV
   a pie on foot, 3.2
   ¿a qué hora? at what time?, BV
   a tiempo on time, **3.1**
   a toda prisa as quickly as possible
   a veces at times, sometimes, 3.1; **4.1**
   a ver let's see
el **abarrote** grocery
   la tienda de abarrotes grocery store
  abordar to board, **3.1**
  abril April, BV
  abrir to open, **2.2**
   abrir la boca to open one's mouth, **2.2**
   abrir las maletas to open the suitcases, **3.2**
  absoluto(a): en absoluto not at all
la **abuela** grandmother, 2.1
la **abuelita** grandma
el **abuelito** grandpa
el **abuelo** grandfather, 2.1
los **abuelos** grandparents, 2.1
  aburrido(a) boring, bored
  aburrir to bore, 6.2; **1.2**
la **academia** academy, school
  académico(a) academic
  acariciar to caress
el **aceite** oil
  aceptar to accept
  acompañado(a) accompanied
  acostarse (ue) to go to bed, **6.1**
la **actividad** activity
  activo(a) active
  actuar to act
  acuático(a) (related to) water
   el esquí acuático waterskiing, **4.1**
   los esquís acuáticos water skis, **4.1**
  ¡Adelante! Let's go ahead!

  además (de) besides
  adiós good-bye, BV
  adivinar to guess
  admitir to admit
el/la **adolescente** adolescent
  ¿adónde? where?, 3.2
  adorable adorable
la **aduana** customs, **3.2**
   el/la agente de aduana customs agent, **3.2**
  adverso(a) opposing, opposite
  aéreo(a): la línea aérea airline, **3.1**
el **aeropuerto** airport, **3.1**
  aficionado(a) fond of
el/la **aficionado(a)** fan
  afortunadamente fortunately
  africano(a) African
las **afueras** outskirts
el/la **agente** agent, **3.1**
   el/la agente de aduana customs agent, **3.2**
  agosto August, BV
  agradable pleasant
el **agua** water, 5.2
   el agua mineral mineral water, 5.2; **6.2**
   la botella de agua mineral bottle of mineral water, **6.2**
   esquiar en el agua to water-ski, **4.1**
   los huevos pasados por agua *(pl.)* soft-boiled eggs
el **agujero** hole
  ahora now
  ahorrar to save
el **ahorro** saving
   la cuenta de ahorros savings account
el **aire** air
   el aire libre outdoor, **4.1**
   la contaminación del aire air pollution
  aislado(a) isolated
la **alberca** pool, **4.1**
el **álbum** album
  alegre happy
la **alergia** allergy, **2.2**
la **alfombrilla** (mouse) pad
el **álgebra** algebra
  algo something, **5.2**

algo más something (anything) else

alguien someone, **5.2**

algunos(as) some

el **alimento** food

allí there

el **almuerzo** lunch, 3.2

    tomar el almuerzo to have lunch

alquilar to rent, **5.1**

    alquilar (rentar) un video to rent a video, **5.1**

alrededor de around

alto(a) tall, 1.1; high, 4.2

el/la **alumno(a)** student, 1.2

    amarillo(a) yellow, 4.2

el **Amazonas** Amazon

    el río Amazonas Amazon River

el **ambiente** atmosphere

    el medio ambiente environment

ambulante traveling

la **América Central** Central America

la **América del Sur** South America

    americano(a) American, 1.1

el/la **amigo(a)** friend, 1.1

el **análisis** analysis

la **anatomía** anatomy

el/la **anciano(a)** old person

    andante: el caballero andante knight errant

    andar to go, to walk

    andino(a) Andean

el **animal** animal

    anoche last night, **4.1**

    anónimo(a) anonymous

el **anorak** parka, **4.2**

    anteayer day before yesterday

los **anteojos** glasses

    los anteojos de (para el) sol sunglasses, **4.1**

    antes (de) before

el **antibiótico** antibiotic, **2.2**

    anunciar to announce

el **año** year

    el año pasado last year

    ¿Cuántos años tiene? How old is he (she)?

    tener... años to be . . . years old, 2.1

el **aparato** system

    el aparato respiratorio respiratory system

el **apartamento** apartment, 2.2

    la casa de apartamentos apartment house

    aplaudir to applaud, **5.2**

el **aplauso** applause, **5.2**

    recibir aplausos to receive applause, **5.2**

el **apodo** nickname

    aprender to learn, 5.1

el **apunte** note

    tomar apuntes to take notes, 3.2

aquí here

el **árbol** tree

    el árbol genealógico family tree

el **área** area

la **arena** sand, **4.1**

    argentino(a) Argentine, 1.1

la **aritmética** arithmetic

    armar: armar una tienda de campaña to pitch a tent, **6.2**

el **arroz** rice, 5.2

el **arte** art, 1.2

    la exposición de arte art exhibition, **5.2**

la **arteria** artery

el/la **artista** artist, 5.2

la **ascendencia** ancestry

    así so

el **asiento** seat, 3.1

    el número del asiento seat number, **3.1**

la **asignatura** subject (school)

la **asistencia** help, assistance

el/la **asistente(a)** assistant

    el/la asistente(a) de vuelo flight attendant, **3.2**

    asistir to attend; to help

el **asno** donkey

el **aspa** sail (of a windmill)

la **aspirina** aspirin, **2.2**

el/la **astronauta** astronaut

    astuto(a) astute

    atacar to attack

la **atención** attention

    prestar atención to pay attention, 3.2

el **aterrizaje** landing

    aterrizar to land, **3.2**

la **atmósfera** atmosphere

    atrapar to catch, 6.2; **1.2**

el **atún** tuna, 5.2

    aún even

el **autobús** bus

    en autobús by bus

    perder el autobús to miss the bus, **5.1**

el **automóvil** car, automobile

el/la **autor(a)** author

el **autorretrato** self-portrait

el **auxilio** help

el **ave** bird

la **avenida** avenue

la **aventura** adventure

la **aviación** aviation

    la compañía de aviación airline company, air carrier

el **avión** airplane, 3.1

    el boleto de avión plane ticket

    en avión by plane

la **avioneta** light aircraft (plane)
ayer yesterday, **4.1**
   ayer por la mañana yesterday morning
la **ayuda** help
ayudar to help
azul blue, 4.2

bailar to dance, 3.1
el **baile** dance
bajar to go down, **4.2;** to lower
bajo under, below, **4.2**
   bajo cero below zero, **4.2**
bajo(a) short, 1.1; low, 4.2
   la nota baja low grade (mark), 3.2
   la planta baja ground floor, 2.2
el **balcón** balcony, 2.2
el **balneario** beach resort, **4.1**
el **balón** ball, 6.1; **1.1**
el **baloncesto** basketball, 6.2; **1.2**
el **banco** bank
la **banda** band
el **bañador** bathing suit, **4.1**
bañar to bathe
bañarse to take a bath, **6.1**
el/la **bañista** bather
el **baño** bath, bathroom, 2.2
   el cuarto de baño bathroom, 2.2
   el traje de baño bathing suit, **4.1**
barato(a) cheap, inexpensive, 4.2
la **barra** bar
   la barra (pastilla) de jabón bar of soap, **6.2**
el **barrio** district, area, region
basado(a) based
la **báscula** scale, **3.1**
la **base** base, 6.2; **1.2**
el **básquetbol** basketball, 6.2; **1.2**
   la cancha de básquetbol basketball court, 6.2; **1.2**
bastante enough, rather, quite, 1.2
el **bastón** ski pole, **4.2**
la **batalla** battle
   hacer batalla to do battle
el **bate** bat, 6.2; **1.2**
el/la **bateador(a)** batter, 6.2; **1.2**
batear to bat, 6.2; **1.2**
el/la **bebé** baby
beber to drink, 5.1
el **béisbol** baseball, 6.2; **1.2**
   el campo de béisbol baseball field, 6.2; **1.2**
   el/la jugador(a) de béisbol baseball player, 6.2; **1.2**
la **biblioteca** library

la **bicicleta** bicycle
bien well, fine
   muy bien very well, BV
   pasarlo bien to have a good time
   salir bien (en un examen) to do well (on an exam)
el **biftec** steak
el **billete** ticket, **3.1**
la **biología** biology
blanco(a) white, 4.2
blando(a) short
el **bloc** notebook, writing pad, 4.1
   bloquear to block, 6.1; **1.1**
el **blue jean** jeans, 4.2
los **blue jeans** jeans, 4.2
la **blusa** blouse, 4.2
la **boca** mouth, **2.2**
   abrir la boca to open one's mouth, **2.2**
el **bocadillo** sandwich, 5.1
la **bodega** grocery store
la **boletería** ticket window, **4.2**
el **boleto** ticket, **3.1**
   el boleto de avión plane ticket
   revisar el boleto to check a ticket, **3.1**
el **bolígrafo** pen, 4.1
el **bolillo** bread roll
el **bolívar** currency of Venezuela
la **bolsa** bag, 5.2
el **bolsillo** pocket
bonito(a) pretty, 1.1
el **borrador** eraser, 4.1
borrar to erase
   la goma (de borrar) eraser, 4.1
la **bota** boot, **4.2**
el **bote** can, 5.2
la **botella** bottle, 5.2
brasileño(a) Brazilian
el **brazo** arm, 6.1; **1.1**
breve short
brillante bright
bronceador(a): la crema (loción) bronceadora suntan cream (lotion), **4.1**
el **bronquio** bronchial tube
bucear to swim underwater
el **buceo** diving, underwater swimming, **4.1**
buen good
   estar de buen humor to be in a good mood, **2.1**
   Hace buen tiempo. The weather's nice., **4.1**
bueno(a) good, 1.1
   Buenas noches. Good evening., BV
   Buenas tardes. Good afternoon., BV
   Buenos días. Good morning., BV
   de buena salud in good health
el **buque** boat, ship

el **bus** bus, 3.2

    el bus escolar school bus, 3.2

    tomar el bus to take the bus

la **busca** search

    en busca de in search of

    buscar to look for, to search 4.1

la **butaca** seat, **5.1**

el **caballero** knight

    el caballero andante knight errant

el **caballete** easel

el **caballo** horse

la **cabeza** head, 6.1; **1.1**

    el dolor de cabeza headache, **2.1**

    Me duele la cabeza. I have a headache., **2.1**

  cada each, every

    cada día every day

    cada vez every time

el **café** café, coffee, 5.1

la **cafetería** cafeteria, 3.1

la **caja** cash register, 4.1; box, **2.2**

el **calcetín** sock, 4.2

    los calcetines socks, 4.2

la **calculadora** calculator, 4.1

  caliente hot

    el perro caliente hot dog

la **calle** street

el **calor** heat

    Hace calor. It's hot (weather).

la **caloría** calorie

  calzar to take, to wear (shoe size)

la **cama** bed, **2.1**

    en cama in bed

    guardar cama to stay in bed, **2.1**

la **cámara** camera

la **camarera** waitress, 5.1

el **camarero** waiter, 5.1

  cambiar to change

  caminar to walk

la **caminata** long walk, hike, **6.2**

    dar una caminata to take a long walk, to hike, **6.2**

el **camino** way, road

el **camión** bus (Mex.), **5.1** truck

    perder el camión to miss the bus, **5.1**

la **camisa** shirt, 4.2

    la camisa de mangas cortas short-sleeved shirt, 4.2

la **camiseta** T-shirt, undershirt, 4.2

la **campaña** camp, countryside; campaign

    armar una tienda de campaña to pitch a tent, **6.2**

    la tienda de campaña tent, **6.2**

el/la **campeón(ona)** champion, 6.2; **1.2**

  el **campesino(a)** peasant, farmer

  el **camping** camping; campsite, **6.2**

    la excursión de camping camping trip

    la guía de campings camping guide(book)

    ir de camping to go camping

  el **campo** field, 6.1; **1.1**; country

    el campo de béisbol baseball field, 6.2; **1.2**

    el campo de fútbol soccer field, 6.1; **1.1**

  la **canasta** basket, 6.2; **1.2**

  el **canasto** basket

  la **cancha** court, field, 6.2; **1.2**

    la cancha de básquetbol basketball court, 6.2; **1.2**

    la cancha de tenis tennis court, 4.1

    la cancha cubierta enclosed (covered) court

  la **canción** song

  la **canela** cinnamon

    cansado(a) tired, **2.1**

el/la **cantante** singer, 5.2

    cantar to sing, 3.1; **5.2**

  la **cantidad** quantity

  la **cantina** cafeteria

  el **canto** song

  la **capital** capital

  la **cara** face, **6.1**

  la **caravana** trailer, **6.2**

  el **carbohidrato** carbohydrate

  el **carbono** carbon

    el dióxido de carbono carbon dioxide

    cargado(a) full

    caribe Caribbean

    el mar Caribe Caribbean Sea

  la **carne** meat, 5.2

    caro(a) expensive, 4.2

  la **carpa** tent (camping), **6.2**

  la **carpeta** folder, 4.1

el/la **carpintero(a)** carpenter

  el **carrito** cart

  el **carro** car, 2.2

    en carro by car, 3.2

    ir en carro to go by car

  la **carta** letter

  el **cartel** poster

  la **casa** house, 2.2

    la casa de apartamentos apartment house

    la casa privada private house

    en casa at home

  el **caso** case

    hacer caso to pay attention

  el **catálogo** catalogue

  el **catarro** cold (illness), **2.1**

el/la **cátcher** catcher, 6.2; **1.2**

Spanish-English Dictionary

la **categoría** category
catorce fourteen, 1.1
el **CD** compact disc (CD), 3.2
la **cebolla** onion
la **celebración** celebration
celebrar to celebrate, 3.1
la **cena** dinner, 3.1
cenar to have dinner, 3.1
el **centro** center
cepillar to brush
cepillarse to brush one's hair, **6.1**
cepillarse los dientes to brush one's teeth, **6.1**
el **cepillo** brush, **6.2**
el cepillo de dientes toothbrush, **6.2**
cerca de near
el **cereal** cereal, **6.1**
la **ceremonia** ceremony
cero zero
bajo cero below zero, **4.2**
cerrado(a) closed, shut
la **cesta** basket
el **cesto** basket, 6.2; **1.2**
el **chaleco** vest
el **champú** shampoo, **6.2**
¡Chao! Good-bye!, BV
la **chaqueta** jacket, 4.2
chileno(a) Chilean, 1.1
la **chimenea** chimney
el **chocolate** chocolate, 5.1
el helado de chocolate chocolate ice cream, 5.1
la **chuchería** junk food, tidbits, sweets
el **churro** (type of) doughnut
ciego(a) blind
el/la **ciego(a)** blind person
el **cielo** sky, **4.1**
la **ciencia** science, 1.2
las ciencias naturales natural sciences
cien(to) one hundred, 2.1
cinco five, 1.1
cincuenta fifty, 2.1
el **cine** movie theater, **5.1**
la **circulación** circulation
la **ciudad** city
el **clarinete** clarinet
claro(a) clear
¡claro! sure!, of course!
claro que of course
la **clase** class, 1.2
la sala de clase classroom
clásico(a) classical, classic
el/la **cliente** customer, client
el **clima** climate
la **clínica** clinic

el **club** club
el Club de español Spanish Club
el **coche** car
la **cocina** kitchen, 2.2
cocinar to cook
la **coincidencia** coincidence
la **cola** cola, 5.1; line (queue), **5.1**
hacer cola to form a line, to line up
la **colección** collection
el **colegio** school, 1.3
colgado(a) hung
colgar (ue) to hang
colombiano(a) Colombian, 1.1
el **color** color, 4.2
¿de qué color? what color?, 4.2
el/la **comandante** captain, **3.2**
el **comedor** dining room, 2.2
comentar to comment
comenzar (ie) to begin
comer to eat, 5.1
comercial commercial
el **comestible** food
cómico(a) funny, comical, 1.1
la **comida** meal, food, 3.1
la comida rápida fast food
como like, as
¿cómo? what? how?, 1.1
¿Cómo es él (ella)? What is he (she) like?
¿Cómo está(s)? How are you?
compacto(a) compact
el disco compacto compact disc (CD)
el/la **compañero(a)** friend, companion
la **compañía** company
la compañía de aviación airline company, air carrier
la compañía de teléfonos telephone company
la **competencia** competition
la **composición** composition
la **compra** purchase
ir de compras to go shopping, to shop, 5.2
comprar to buy, 4.1
comprender to understand, 5.1
la **computadora** computer
con with
con frecuencia frequently
el **concierto** concert, **5.2**
dar un concierto to give (have) a concert, **5.2**
oír un concierto to attend a concert, **5.2**
la **conclusión** conclusion
el **concurso** contest
la **condición** condition
conectado(a) connected
conectar to connect

Spanish-English Dictionary

la **conexión** connection

la **confianza** trust

    tener confianza en to trust

confundido(a) confused

congelado(a) frozen

    los productos congelados frozen foods, 5.2

conocer to know, to be familiar with, **3.2;** to recognize

conquistar to conquer

consecutivo(a) consecutive

el **consejo** advice

el **conservatorio** conservatory

    el Conservatorio Nacional de Música National Conservatory of Music

consigo with himself, with herself, with themselves

consiguiente resulting

    por consiguiente therefore, consequently

consistir (en) to consist of

la **consonante** consonant

la **consulta** office, **2.2**

    la consulta del médico doctor's office, **2.2**

el **consultorio** medical office, **2.2**

el **contacto** contact

la **contaminación** pollution

    la contaminación del aire air pollution

contaminado polluted

contaminar to pollute

contar (ue) to count

    contar (ue) con to rely on

contener to contain

contento(a) happy, **2.1**

contestar to answer

    contestar (a) la pregunta to answer the question, 3.2

el **continente** continent

continuar to continue, 6.2; **1.2**

contra against, 6.1; **1.1**

el **contrario** contrary

    al contrario on the contrary

el **contrato** contract

el **control** control

    el control de pasaportes passport control, **3.2**

    el control de seguridad security (checkpoint), **3.1**

la **conversación** conversation

la **conversión** conversion

convertir to convert

la **copa** cup

    la Copa mundial World Cup

el/la **copiloto** copilot, **3.2**

el **corazón** heart

la **corbata** tie, 4.2

el **coro** choir

el **correo** mail

el **correo electrónico** e-mail

correr to run, 6.2; **1.2**

la **cortesía** courtesy

corto(a) short

    la manga corta short sleeve, 4.2

    el pantalón corto shorts, 4.2

la **cosa** thing

coser to sew

la **costa** coast

costar (ue) to cost

    ¿Cuánto cuesta? How much does it cost?

    Cuesta mucho (poco). It costs a lot (little)., 4.1

costarricense Costa Rican

la **costura** sewing

creer to believe, to think

    Creo que sí. I think so.

la **crema** cream

    la crema (loción) bronceadora suntan cream (lotion), **4.1**

    la crema dentífrica toothpaste, **6.2**

    la crema protectora sunblock, **4.1**

el **cristal** crystal

cruel cruel

cruzar to cross

el **cuaderno** notebook, 4.1

el **cuadro** painting, **5.2**

¿cuál? which?, what?

    ¿Cuál es la fecha de hoy? What is today's date?

cualquier(a) any

    cualquier otro any other

cuando when

¿cuándo? when?, 3.1

¿cuánto? how much?

    ¿A cuánto está(n)... ? How much is (are) . . . ?, 5.2

    ¿Cuánto cuesta? How much does it cost?, 4.1

    ¿Cuánto es? How much does it cost?, 4.1

¿cuántos(as)? how much?, how many?, 2.1

    ¿Cuántos años tiene? How old is he (she)?, 2.1

cuarenta forty, 2.1

el **cuarto** room, 2.2; quarter

    el cuarto de baño bathroom, 2.2

    el cuarto de dormir bedroom, 2.2

    menos cuarto quarter to (the hour)

    y cuarto quarter past (the hour)

cuatro four, 1.1

cuatrocientos(as) four hundred, 3.1

cubano(a) Cuban, 1.1

cubanoamericano(a) Cuban American

cubierto(a) covered

    la cancha cubierta enclosed (covered) court

cubrir to cover

Spanish-English Dictionary

la **cuchara** spoon
el **cuchillo** knife
la **cuenca** basin
la **cuenta** bill, check, 5.1; account
    la **cuenta de ahorros** savings account
el/la **cuentista** short-story writer
el **cuento** story
el **cuerpo** body
    el **cuerpo humano** human body
la **cultura** culture
el **cumpleaños** birthday, 2.2
el **curso** course, 1.2

D

la **dama** lady-in-waiting
la **danza** dance
  dar to give, 3.1
    dar una caminata to take a long walk, to hike, 6.2
    dar un concierto to have (give) a concert, 5.2
    dar permiso to give permission
los **datos** data
  de of, from
    de buena salud in good health
    de compras shopping
    de día en día from day to day
    ¿de dónde? from where?, 1.1
    de habla española Spanish-speaking
    de mangas cortas short-sleeved
    de la mañana A.M. (time)
    de moda in style
    De nada. You're welcome., BV
    de ninguna manera not at all, by no means
    de nuevo again
    ¿de qué color? what color?, 4.2
    ¿de qué nacionalidad? what nationality?, 1.1
    ¿de quién? whose?
    No hay de qué. You're welcome., BV
  debajo (de) under
  deber must, should; to owe
  débil weak
el **début** debut
  decidir to decide, 5.1
  decimal decimal
  decir to say
    es decir that is (to say)
el **dedo** finger
  definitivamente definitely
  dejar to leave
  delante de in front of, 5.1
  delgado(a) thin
  delicioso(a) delicious
  demás rest

la **demora** delay, 3.1
  con una demora with a delay, 3.1
  dentífrica: la pasta (crema) dentífrica toothpaste, 6.2
  dentro (de) within
el **departamento** apartment
  la tienda de departamentos department store
  depender (de) to depend (on)
el/la **dependiente(a)** employee, 4.1
el **deporte** sport, 6.1; **1.1**
  el deporte de equipo team sport
  el deporte individual individual sport
  deportivo(a) (related to) sports
  la emisión deportiva sports program
  depositar to deposit
  derecho(a) right, 6.1; **1.1**
  derramar to dump
  derrocar to bring down, to overthrow
  desayunarse to have breakfast, 6.1
el **desayuno** breakfast, 3.1
  tomar el desayuno to have breakfast, 3.1
  describir to describe
la **descripción** description
  desde from, since
  desear to wish, to want
el **desecho** waste
  desembarcar to disembark, 3.2
el **desembarque** unloading, landing
el **deseo** wish
el **desierto** desert
  despachar to dispense, 2.2
  despegar to take off, 3.2
el **despegue** takeoff
  despertarse (ie) to wake up, 6.1
  después de after, 3.1
el **destino** destination, 3.1
  con destino a bound for, to
  desviar to dissuade
el **detalle** detail
  determinado(a) determined, definite
  devolver (ue) to return (something), 6.1; **1.1**
el **día** day
  al día per day
  Buenos días. Good morning., BV
  cada día every day
  de día en día from day to day
  el Día de los Muertos All Souls' Day, Day of the Dead
  hoy en día nowadays
  ¿Qué día es (hoy)? What day is it (today)?
la **diagnosis** diagnosis, 2.2
  hacer una diagnosis to make a diagnosis
el **dibujo** picture, drawing, 1.2
  diciembre December, 1.1

diecinueve nineteen, 1.1
dieciocho eighteen, 1.1
dieciséis sixteen, 1.1
diecisiete seventeen, 1.1
el **diente** tooth, **6.1**
    cepillarse los dientes to brush one's teeth, **6.1**
    el cepillo de dientes toothbrush, **6.2**
    lavarse los dientes to brush one's teeth
diez ten, 1.1
    de diez en diez by tens
la **diferencia** difference
diferente different
difícil hard, difficult, 1.2
el **dinero** money
directamente directly
directo(a) direct
el **disco** record, disc
    el disco compacto compact disc (CD)
la **discoteca** discotheque
la **distancia** distance
distinto(a) different
la **diversión** amusement, pastime
divertido(a) fun, amusing
divertir (ie) to amuse
divertirse (ie) to enjoy oneself, to have a good
    time, **6.2**
divino(a) divine
divorciarse to get divorced
doblado(a) dubbed
los **dobles** doubles (tennis), **4.1**
doce twelve, 1.1
el/la **doctor(a)** doctor
doler (ue) to ache, to hurt
    Me duele(n)... My . . . hurt(s) me, **2.2**
el **dolor** pain, ache, **2.1**
    el dolor de cabeza headache, **2.1**
    el dolor de estómago stomachache, **2.1**
    el dolor de garganta sore throat, **2.1**
el **domingo** Sunday, BV
dominicano(a) Dominican
    La República Dominicana Dominican
        Republic
¿dónde? where?, 1.1
    ¿de dónde? from where?, 1.1
dormido(a) asleep
dormir (ue) to sleep, 6.1; **1.1**
    el cuarto de dormir bedroom, 2.2
    el saco de dormir sleeping bag, **6.2**
dormirse (ue) to fall asleep, **6.1**
el **dormitorio** bedroom, 2.2
dos two, 1.1
doscientos(as) two hundred, 3.1
la **dosis** dose, **2.2**
el/la **dramaturgo(a)** playwright
    driblar to dribble, 6.2; **1.2**

la **ducha** shower, **6.1**
    tomar una ducha to take a shower, **6.1**
la **duda** doubt
el/la **dueño(a)** owner
dulce sweet
    el pan dulce sweet roll
durante during, 3.1
duro(a) hard, difficult, 1.2
el **DVD** digital video disc (DVD), 3.2

echar to throw
la **ecología** ecology
ecológico(a) ecological
la **ecuación** equation
ecuatoriano(a) Ecuadorean
la **edad** age
el **edificio** building, 2.2
la **educación** education
    la educación física physical education, 1.2
el **ejemplar** copy
el **ejemplo** example
    por ejemplo for example
el **ejote** string bean, 5.2
el the
él he
electrónico(a) electronic
    el correo electrónico e-mail
elegante elegant
ella she
ellos(as) they
embarcar to board, **3.1**
el **embarque** boarding
    la hora de embarque boarding time
    la tarjeta de embarque boarding pass, **3.1**
la **emisión** program, 3.1; emission
    la emisión deportiva sports program
emitir to emit
emocionante emotional
empatado(a) tied (score), 6.1; **1.1**
empezar (ie) to begin, 6.1; **1.1**
el/la **empleado(a)** employee, 4.1
en in, on
    en absoluto absolutely not, not at all
    en autobús by bus
    en avión by plane
    en busca de in search of
    en cama in bed,
    en carro by car, 3.2
    en casa at home
    en cuanto a as for
el **encanto** enchantment
    la isla del encanto island of enchantment
encender (ie) to light

Spanish-English Dictionary

el **encestado** basket
  encestar to make a basket, 6.2; **1.2**
la **enchilada** enchilada
  encima de over, on top of
    por encima de on top of, **4.1**
  encontrar (ue) to find
el **encuentro** encounter, meeting
el/la **enemigo(a)** enemy
  enero January, BV
el/la **enfermero(a)** nurse
  enfermo(a) sick, **2.1**
el/la **enfermo(a)** ill person, patient, **2.2**
  enrollado(a) rolled up
la **ensalada** salad, 5.1
  enseguida right away, immediately, **6.1**
  enseñar to teach
  entero(a) entire
  entonces then
la **entrada** inning, 6.2; **1.2;** admission ticket, **5.1**
  entrar to enter, 3.2
  entre between, among
  entregar to deliver
el/la **entrenador(a)** trainer, coach
la **entrevista** interview
el **envase** container, 5.2
  enviar to send, to mail
el **equilibrio** equilibrium
el **equipaje** baggage, luggage, 3.1
    el equipaje de mano carry-on luggage, **3.1**
    facturar el equipaje to check luggage, **3.1**
    reclamar (recoger) el equipaje to pick up one's luggage, **3.2**
    el reclamo de equipaje baggage claim, **3.2**
el **equipo** team, 6.1; **1.1;** equipment
    el deporte de equipo team sport, 6.2; **1.2**
    el equipo de fútbol soccer team
  equivaler to be equivalent
los **escalofríos** chills, **2.1**
  escamotear to secretly take out
  escaparse to escape
  escoger to choose
  escolar (related to) school
    el bus escolar school bus, 3.2
    los materiales escolares school supplies, 4.1
  esconder to hide
  escribir to write, 5.1
  escuchar to listen (to), 3.2
el **escudero** squire
la **escuela** school, 1.2
    la escuela intermedia middle school
    la escuela primaria elementary school
    la escuela superior high school
el/la **escultor(a)** sculptor

la **escultura** sculpture
  espacial (related to) space
    la nave espacial spaceship
el **espacio** space
la **espalda** back
  espantoso(a) frightful
  España Spain
  español(a) Spanish *(adj.)*
    de habla española Spanish-speaking
el **español** Spanish, 1.2
    el Club de español Spanish club
  especial special
  especialmente especially
  espectacular spectacular
el **espectáculo** show
el/la **espectador(a)** spectator, 6.1; **1.1**
el **espejo** mirror, **6.1**
  esperar to wait for, 5.1
la **esposa** wife
el **esposo** husband
  esquelético(a) skeletal
el **esqueleto** skeleton
el **esquí** skiing, **4.1,** ski, **4.2**
    el esquí acuático waterskiing, **4.1**
    los esquís acuáticos water skis, **4.2**
    la estación de esquí ski resort, **4.2**
el/la **esquiador(a)** skier, **4.2**
  esquiar to ski, **4.2**
    esquiar en el agua to water-ski, **4.1**
  esta this
    esta mañana this morning, **4.1**
    esta noche tonight, **4.1**
    esta tarde this afternoon, **4.1**
  establecer to establish
el **establecimiento** establishment
la **estación** resort, 4.2; season; station
    la estación de esquí ski resort, **4.2**
    la estación del metro subway station, **5.1**
el **estadio** stadium, 6.1; **1.1**
    el estadio de fútbol soccer stadium
el **estado** state
  Estados Unidos United States
  estar to be, 3.1
    ¿A cuánto está(n)? How much is it (are they)?
    ¿Cómo está(s)? How are you?
    estar de buen humor to be in a good mood, **2.1**
    estar de buena salud to be in good health
    estar de mal humor to be in a bad mood, **2.1**
    estar en clase to be in class, 3.2
    estar mal to feel sick (ill)
    estar resfriado(a) to have a cold, **2.1**
la **estatua** statue, **5.2**
  este(a) this *(adj.)*

Spanish-English Dictionary

el **estilo** style
el **estómago** stomach, **2.1**
    el dolor de estómago stomachache, **2.1**
  estornudar to sneeze, **2.1**
  estos(as) these
la **estrella** star
  estudiar to study, 3.1
el **estudio** study
    los estudios sociales social studies, 1.2
  estupendo(a) stupendous
  estúpido(a) stupid
  eterno(a) eternal
el **euro** euro (currency of all countries of the European Common Market)
  exactamente exactly
  exagerar to exaggerate
el **examen** test, exam
  examinar to examine, **2.2**
  excelente excellent
  exclamar to exclaim
la **excursión** trip, excursion
    la excursión de camping camping trip
  existir to exist
el **éxito** success
    tener éxito to be successful
la **expedición** expedition
la **experiencia** experience
el/la **experto(a)** expert, **4.2**
    la pista para expertos expert slope, **4.2**
  explicar to explain
  explorar to explore
la **exposición** exhibition, **5.2**
    la exposición de arte art exhibition, **5.2**
la **expresión** expression
  extranjero(a) foreign, **3.2**
el/la **extranjero(a)** foreigner, stranger
  extraordinario(a) extraordinary
  extremo(a) extreme

la **fábrica** factory
  fabuloso(a) fabulous
  fácil easy, 1.2
la **facilidad** facility
  facturar to check in
    facturar el equipaje to check luggage, **3.1**
la **falda** skirt, 4.2
  falso(a) false
la **familia** family, 2.1
  familiar (related to) family
  famoso(a) famous

la **fantasía** fantasy
  fantástico(a) fantastic
el/la **farmacéutico(a)** pharmacist, **2.2**
la **farmacia** pharmacy, **2.2**
el **favor** favor
    por favor please, BV
  favorito(a) favorite
  febrero February, BV
la **fecha** date
    ¿Cuál es la fecha de hoy? What is today's date?, BV
  feo(a) ugly, 1.1
la **fiebre** fever, **2.1**
  fiel faithful
la **fiesta** party, 2.2; holiday
la **figura** figure
la **fila** line (queue); row (of seats), **5.1**
el **film** film, **5.1**
el **fin** end
    el fin de semana weekend
    el fin de semana pasado last weekend
    pasar el fin de semana to spend the weekend, **4.1**
    por fin finally
  firmar to sign
  físico(a) physical, 1.2
    la educación física physical education, 1.2
la **flauta** flute
la **flor** flower
la **forma** form
  formal formal
  formar to form
la **foto** photo
la **fotografía** photograph
el **francés** French
la **frecuencia** frequency
  frecuentemente frequently
  fresco(a) fresh (food), 5.2; cool
    Hace fresco. It's cool (weather).
el **frijol** bean, 5.2
el **frío** cold
    Hace frío. It's cold (weather)., **4.2**
  frito fried
    los huevos fritos *(pl.)* fried eggs
    las papas (patatas) fritas *(pl.)* French fries, 5.1
la **fruta** fruit, 5.2
la **fuente** source; fountain
  fuerte strong
el **funcionamiento** functioning, operation
  funcionar to operate
la **fundación** foundation
  fundar to found, to establish
la **furia** fury

Spanish-English Dictionary

el **fútbol** soccer, 6.1; **1.1**
    el campo de fútbol soccer field, 6.1; **1.1**
    el equipo de fútbol soccer team
    el estadio de fútbol soccer stadium
    jugar (ue) (al) fútbol to play soccer

G

el **gallo** rooster
el **galón** gallon
la **gana** desire, wish
  ganar to win, 6.1; **1.1;** to earn
el **garabato** scribble
el **garaje** garage, 2.2
la **garganta** throat, **2.1**
    el dolor de garganta sore throat, **2.1**
el **gas** gas
la **gaseosa** carbonated drink, 5.1
  gastar to spend
el **gasto** expense
el/la **gato(a)** cat, 2.1
  genealógico(a) genealogical
    el árbol genealógico family tree
  general general
    en general generally
    por lo general generally
  generoso(a) generous
la **gente** people, **5.2**
la **geografía** geography
  geométrico(a) geometrical
el **gigante** giant
el/la **gobernador(a)** governor
el **gol** goal, 6.1; **1.1**
    meter un gol to score a goal, 6.1; **1.1**
el **golf** golf, 6.2; **1.2**
  golpear to hit, **4.1**
la **goma (de borrar)** eraser, 4.1
  gordo(a) fat
la **gorra** cap, 4.2
  gozar (de) to enjoy
  Gracias. Thank you., BV
  gracioso(a) funny, 1.1
el **grado** degree, **4.2**
el **gramo** gram
  gran, grande big, large, great, 1.2
    las Grandes Ligas Major Leagues
el **grano** grain
la **grasa** fat
  gratis free
la **gripe** flu, **2.1**
  gris gray, 4.2
el **grupo** group
la **guagua** bus (P.R., Cuba), **5.1**
    perder la guagua to miss the bus, **5.1**

el **guante** glove, 6.2; **1.2**
  guapo(a) handsome, good-looking, 1.1
  guardar to guard, 6.1; **1.1;** to keep
    guardar cama to stay in bed, **2.1**
  guatemalteco(a) Guatemalan
el/la **guía** guide
    la guía de campings camping guide (book)
el **guisante** pea, 5.2
la **guitarra** guitar
  gustar to please; to like, 6.2; **1.2**
el **gusto** pleasure; like; taste
    Mucho gusto. Nice to meet you.

H

la **habichuela** bean, 5.2
el **habla** speech, language
    de habla española Spanish-speaking
  hablar to talk, to speak, 3.1
    hablar por teléfono to speak on the phone, 3.1
  hacer to do, to make
    Hace buen tiempo. The weather is nice., **4.1**
    Hace calor. It's hot (weather)., **4.1**
    Hace fresco. It's cool (weather).
    Hace frío. It's cold (weather)., **4.2**
    Hace mal tiempo. The weather is bad., **4.1**
    Hace sol. It's sunny., **4.1**
    Hace viento. It's windy.
    hacer batalla to do battle
    hacer caso to pay attention
    hacer cola to form a line, to line up
    hacer una diagnosis to make a diagnosis
    hacer la maleta to pack one's suitcase
    hacer pedazos to tear (break) to pieces
    hacer la plancha de vela to windsurf
    hacer un viaje to take a trip, 3.1
    ¿Qué tiempo hace? What is the weather (like)?, **4.1**
  hacia toward
  hallar to find
el **hambre** hunger
    tener hambre to be hungry, 5.1
la **hamburguesa** hamburger, 5.1
el **hardware** hardware
la **harina** flour
  hasta until, up to, as far as
    ¡Hasta luego! See you later!, BV
    ¡Hasta mañana! See you tomorrow!, BV
    ¡Hasta pronto! See you soon!, BV
  hawaiana: la tabla hawaiana surfboard, **4.1**
  hay there is, there are, 2.2
    Hay nubes. It's cloudy.
    Hay sol. It's sunny., **4.1**
    Hay viento. It's windy.

No hay de qué. You're welcome., BV
No hay más remedio. There is nothing more we can do.
¿Qué hay? What's new (up)?
helado(a) frozen, iced
  el té helado iced tea, 5.1
el **helado** ice cream, 5.1
  el helado de chocolate chocolate ice cream, 5.1
  el helado de vainilla vanilla ice cream, 5.1
el **hemisferio** hemisphere
  el hemisferio norte northern hemisphere
  el hemisferio sur southern hemisphere
herido(a) wounded, injured
la **hermana** sister, 2.1
la **hermanastra** stepsister, 2.1
el **hermanastro** stepbrother, 2.1
el **hermano** brother, 2.1
el **héroe** hero
la **heroína** heroine
higiénico(a) hygienic
  el papel higiénico(a) toilet paper, **6.2**
la **hija** daughter, 2.1
el **hijo** son, 2.1
  los hijos children
el **hipermercado** (wholesale) supermarket
hispano(a) Hispanic
  las letras hispanas Spanish literature
la **historia** history, 1.2; story
la **historieta** short story
la **hoja** leaf, sheet
  la hoja de papel sheet of paper, 4.1
¡Hola! Hello!, BV
el **hombre** man
el **honor** honor
la **hora** hour, time
  ¿A qué hora? At what time?, BV
  la hora de embarque boarding time
  las veinticuatro horas midnight
  ¿Qué hora es? What time is it?, BV
el **horario** timetable, schedule
horrible horrible
el **hospital** hospital
hospitalario(a) (related to) hospital
el **hostal** hostelry, inn
el **hotel** hotel
hoy today, BV; **4.1**
  ¿Cuál es la fecha de hoy? What is today's date?
  hoy en día nowadays
  ¿Qué día es (hoy)? What day is it (today)?
el **hueso** bone
el **huevo** egg, 5.2
  los huevos fritos (*pl.*) fried eggs

  los huevos pasados por agua (*pl.*) soft-boiled eggs
  los huevos revueltos (*pl.*) scrambled eggs
humano(a) human
  el cuerpo humano human body
  el ser humano human being
humilde humble
el **humo** smoke
el **humor** mood
  estar de buen humor to be in a good mood, **2.1**
  estar de mal humor to be in a bad mood, **2.1**

la **idea** idea
el/la **idealista** idealist
igual equal
la **igualdad** equality
la **ilusión** illusion
impenetrable impenetrable
importante important
importar to matter
  No importa. It doesn't matter.
imposible impossible
la **impresión** impression
la **impresora** printer
la **inclinación** inclination, slant
incluir to include
increíble incredible
la **independencia** independence
el **indicador** indicator
  el tablero indicador scoreboard, 6.1; **1.1**
  indicar to indicate, 6.1; **1.1**
  indígena native, indigenous
el/la **indígena** native person
indio(a) Indian
el/la **indio(a)** Indian
indispensable indispensable
individual individual
  el deporte individual individual sport
la **industria** industry
industrial industrial
la **influencia** influence
el **inglés** English, 1.2
inhóspito(a) inhospitable
inmediato(a) immediate
la **inspección** inspection
inspeccionar to inspect, **3.2**
inspirar to inspire
el **instante** instant
el **instituto** high school, secondary school, institute
la **instrucción** instruction
el **instrumento** instrument

Spanish-English Dictionary

inteligente intelligent, 1.2
el **interés** interest
interesante interesting, 1.2
interesar to interest, 6.2; **1.2**
intermedio(a) intermediate, 1.2
   la **escuela intermedia** middle school
internacional international
el/la **Internet** Internet
interno(a) internal
íntimo(a) close, intimate
la **introducción** introduction
el/la **intruso(a)** intruder
la **invención** invention
inverso(a) reverse
la **investigación** research, investigation
el **invierno** winter, BV; **4.2**
la **invitación** invitation
invitar to invite, 3.1
la **inyección** injection, **2.2**
ir to go, 3.1
   ir a pie to walk, 3.2
   ir de camping to go camping
   ir de compras to go shopping, 5.2
   ir en carro to go by car
   irse por to go (fall) through
la **isla** island
   la **isla del encanto** island of enchantment
italiano(a) Italian
izquierdo(a) left, 6.1; **1.1**

el **jabón** soap, **6.2**
   la **pastilla (barra) de jabón** bar of soap, **6.2**
el **jamón** ham, 5.1
   el **sándwich de jamón y queso** ham and cheese sandwich, 5.1
el **jardín** garden, 2.2
el/la **jardinero(a)** outfielder, 6.2; **1.2**
el **jarro** jug, jar
el **jean** jeans, 4.2
el **jonrón** home run, 6.2; **1.2**
joven young
el/la **joven** young person, **5.1**
la **judía** bean
   la **judía verde** green bean, 5.2
el **juego** game
   el **juego de tenis** tennis game, **4.1**
el **jueves** Thursday, BV
el/la **jugador(a)** player, 6.1; **1.1**
   el/la **jugador(a) de béisbol** baseball player, 6.2; **1.2**
   jugar (ue) to play, 6.1; **1.1**
   jugar (al) tenis to play tennis, **4.1**

el **jugo** juice, **6.1**
   el **jugo de naranja** orange juice, **6.1**
el **juguete** toy
julio July, BV
la **jungla** jungle
junio June, BV
junto(a) together
juvenil juvenile

el **kilo** kilo, 5.2
el **kilogramo** kilogram
el **kleenex** tissue, **2.1**

la the; it, her
el **laboratorio** laboratory
laborioso(a) laborious
lacustre (related to) lake
el **lado** side
   al lado de beside, next to
ladrar to bark
el **lamento** lament
la **lana** wool
la **lanza** lance
el/la **lanzador(a)** pitcher, 6.2; **1.2**
el **lanzamiento** throw, launching
   la **plataforma de lanzamiento** launchpad
lanzar to throw, to kick, 6.1; **1.1**
el **lápiz** pencil, 4.1
largo(a) long
   la **manga larga** long sleeve, 4.2
   el **pantalón largo** long pants, 4.2
las them *(f. pl. pron.)*
la **lata** can, 5.2
el **latín** Latin (language)
latino(a) Latin
Latinoamérica Latin America
latinoamericano(a) Latin American
la **lavandería** laundromat
lavar to wash
lavarse to wash oneself, **6.1**
   lavarse los dientes to brush one's teeth, **6.1**
le to him, to her, to you *(pron.)*
la **lección** lesson, 3.1
la **leche** milk, 5.2
la **lechuga** lettuce, 5.2
la **lectura** reading
leer to read, 5.1
la **legumbre** vegetable, 5.2
lejos far
la **lengua** language, tongue

Spanish-English Dictionary

les to them; to you *(pl. pron.)*

las **letras** letters (literature)

    las letras hispanas Spanish literature

levantar to raise, to lift

    levantar la mano to raise your hand, 3.2

levantarse to get up, **6.1**

el/la **libertador(a)** liberator

la **libra** pound

libre free, unoccupied, 5.1

    al aire libre outdoor, **4.1**

el **libro** book, 4.1

el **liceo** high school

el **líder** leader

la **liga** league

    las Grandes Ligas Major Leagues

la **limonada** lemonade

la **línea** line

    la línea aérea airline, 3.1

el **lípido** lipid

la **liquidación** sale, 4.2

el **líquido** liquid

la **lista** list

listo(a) ready

la **literatura** literature

el **litro** liter

llamar to call

    llamar por teléfono to call on the phone

llamarse to call oneself, to be called, **6.1**

la **llegada** arrival

    la pantalla de salidas y llegadas arrival and departure screen (board), **3.1**

llegar to arrive, 5.1

llenar to fill

lleno(a) full, **5.2**

llevar to wear, 3.2; to carry, 4.1; **6.2**

    llevar subtítulos to have subtitles

llover (ue) to rain, it's raining

    Llueve. It's raining., **4.1**

la **lluvia** rain

lluvioso(a) rainy

lo it; him *(m. sing. pron.)*

    lo que what, that which

local local

la **loción** lotion

    la loción (crema) bronceadora suntan lotion, **4.2**

loco(a) crazy

    volverse (ue) loco(a) to go mad

lógico(a) logical

los them *(m. pl. pron.)*

luchar to fight

luego later; then

    ¡Hasta luego! See you later!, BV

el **lugar** place

la **luna** moon

el **lunes** Monday, BV

la **luz** light

la **madrastra** stepmother, 2.1

la **madre** mother, 2.1

madrileño(a) native of Madrid

el/la **maestro(a)** teacher

el **maíz** corn, 5.2

mal ill, sick, bad

    estar de mal humor to be in a bad mood, **2.1**

    estar mal to feel sick (ill)

    Hace mal tiempo. The weather is bad., **4.1**

el **mal** evil

malagueño(a) native of Málaga, Spain

la **maleta** suitcase, 3.1

    abrir las maletas to open the suitcases, **3.2**

    hacer la maleta to pack one's suitcase, **3.1**

    reclamar (recoger) las maletas to pick up one's suitcases, **3.2**

malhumorado(a) bad-tempered

malo(a) bad, 1.2

    la nota mala bad grade (mark), 3.2

la **mamá** mom

el **mambo** mambo

la **manera** manner

    de ninguna manera not at all, by no means, no way

la **manga** sleeve

    la manga corta short sleeve, 4.2

    la manga larga long sleeve, 4.2

la **mano** hand, 6.1

    el equipaje de mano carry-on luggage, **3.1**

    ¡Manos a la obra! Let's get to work!

el **mantel** tablecloth

la **mantequilla** butter

la **manzana** apple, 5.2

mañana tomorrow, BV

    ¡Hasta mañana! See you tomorrow!, BV

la **mañana** morning

    ayer por la mañana yesterday morning

    de la mañana A.M. (time)

    esta mañana this morning, **4.1**

    por la mañana in the morning, 5.2

el **mapa** map

la **máquina** machine

el **mar** sea, **4.1**

    el mar Caribe Caribbean Sea

    el mar Mediterráneo Mediterranean Sea

el **marcador** marker, 4.1

marcar to score

    marcar un tanto to score a point, 6.1; **1.1**

Spanish-English Dictionary

la **marcha** march
el **marido** husband
los **mariscos** shellfish, 5.2
el **marqués** marquis
la **marquesa** marquise
marrón brown, 4.2
martes Tuesday, BV
marzo March, BV
más more
  más de (que) more than
  un poco más a little more
  ¡Qué... más... ! What a . . . !
  una vez más one more time
las **matemáticas** mathematics, 1.2
la **materia** matter, subject (school)
el **material** material
  los materiales escolares school supplies, 4.1
el/la **maya** Maya
mayo May, BV
mayor older, 2.1
el/la **mayor** oldest, 2.1
la **mayoría** majority
me me
la **medalla** medal
la **medianoche** midnight
el **medicamento** medication, medicine, **2.2**
la **medicina** medicine, **2.2**
médico(a) medical
el/la **médico(a)** doctor, **2.2**
  la consulta del médico doctor's office, **2.2**
la **medida** measure
medio(a) half
el **medio** means; medium
  el medio ambiente environment
  el medio de transporte means of transportation
  por medio de by means of
el **mediodía** noon
mejor better
el/la **mejor** best
melancólico(a) sad, melancholic
la **memoria** memory
el/la **menino(a)** young page of a royal family
menor younger, 2.1
el/la **menor** youngest, 2.1
menos less; minus
  menos cuarto quarter to (the hour)
el **menú** menu, 5.1
el **mercado** market, 5.2
la **merced** mercy
el **merengue** merengue
la **mermelada** marmalade
el **mes** month

la **mesa** table, 5.1
  la mesa plegable folding table, **6.2**
la **mesera** waitress, 5.1
el **mesero** waiter, 5.1
el **metabolismo** metabolism
el **metal** metal
meter to put, to place
  meter un gol to score a goal, 6.1; **1.1**
métrico(a) metric
el **metro** subway, **5.1**
  la estación del metro subway station, **5.1**
mexicano(a) Mexican, 1.1
mi my
mí me
el **miedo** fear
  tener miedo to be afraid
el **miembro** member
mientras while
el **miércoles** Wednesday, BV
mil one thousand, 3.1
el **millón** million, 4.1
mineral mineral
  el agua mineral mineral water, 5.2, **6.2**
mirar to watch, to look at, 3.1
mirarse to look at oneself, **6.1**
mismo(a) same, 1.2; himself, herself
el **misterio** mystery
misterioso(a) mysterious
la **mochila** knapsack, backpack, 4.1, **6.2**
la **moda** style
  de moda in style
el/la **modelo** model
moderno(a) modern
módico(a) moderate, reasonable
  al precio módico(a) at a reasonable price
el **molino** mill
  el molino de viento windmill
el **momento** moment
la **moneda** coin
  la moneda de oro gold coin
el **monitor** monitor
el **monstruo** monster
la **montaña** mountain, 4.2
montar (a caballo) to mount, to get on (a horse)
  montar en un asno to ride a donkey
el **monto** sum, total
morder (ue) to bite
moreno(a) dark, brunette, 1.1
la **mosca** fly
el **mostrador** counter, **3.1**
mostrar (ue) to show
el **motivo** motive

Spanish-English Dictionary

mover (ue) to move
la **muchacha** girl, 1.1
el **muchacho** boy, 1.1
mucho(a) a lot, many, much, 2.1
    Mucho gusto. Nice to meet you.
el/la **muerto(a)** dead (person)
    el Día de los Muertos All Souls' Day, Day of the Dead
la **mujer** woman, wife
mundial (related to) world
    la Copa mundial World Cup
    la Serie mundial World Series
el **mundo** world
    todo el mundo everyone
municipal municipal
el **mural** mural
el/la **muralista** mural painter
muscular muscular
el **músculo** muscle
el **museo** museum, 5.2
la **música** music, 1.2
    el Conservatorio Nacional de Música National Conservatory of Music
el/la **músico(a)** musician
muy very, 1.2
    muy bien very well, BV

N

nacer to be born
nacional national
    el Conservatorio Nacional de Música National Conservatory of Music
    el parque nacional national park, 6.2
la **nacionalidad** nationality
    ¿de qué nacionalidad? what nationality?, 1.1
nada nothing, 5.2
    De nada. You're welcome., BV
    nada más nothing else, 5.2
    Por nada. You're welcome., BV
nadar to swim, 4.1
nadie no one, 5.2
naranja orange (color), 4.2
la **naranja** orange (fruit), 5.1
    el jugo de naranja orange juice, 6.1
natal native
natural natural
la **naturaleza** nature
la **nave** ship
    la nave espacial spaceship
navegar to navigate
    navegar la red to surf the Net
la **Navidad** Christmas

necesario(a) necessary
necesitado(a) needy
necesitar to need, 4.1
negro(a) black, 4.2
la **nene(a)** baby
    nene(a) dear, darling (term of endearment)
nervioso(a) nervous, 2.1
nevar (ie) to snow, it's snowing
    Nieva. It's snowing., 4.2
la **nieta** granddaughter, 2.1
el **nieto** grandson, 2.1
la **nieve** snow, 4.2
ninguno(a) no, not any
    de ninguna manera not at all, by no means, no way
el/la **niño(a)** child
el **nivel** level
no no, not
    No hay de qué. You're welcome., BV
la **noche** night, evening
    anoche last night, 4.1
    Buenas noches. Good evening., BV
    esta noche tonight, 4.1
    por la noche at night
la **Nochebuena** Christmas Eve
nombrar to name
el **nombre** name
el **norte** north
nos us
nosotros(as) we, 1.2
la **nota** grade, mark
    sacar notas altas (bajas) to get high (low) grades, 3.2
    sacar notas buenas (malas) to get good (bad) grades, 3.2
notar to note, to notice
novecientos(as) nine hundred, 3.1
la **novela** novel
el/la **novelista** novelist
noveno(a) ninth
noventa ninety, 2.1
noviembre November, BV
la **nube** cloud, 4.1
    Hay nubes. It's cloudy.
nuestro(a) our
nueve nine, 1.1
nuevo(a) new, 1.2
    de nuevo again
el **número** number, size, 4.2
    el número de teléfono telephone number
    el número del asiento seat number, 3.1
    el número del vuelo flight number, 3.1
nunca never, 5.2
la **nutrición** nutrition

Spanish-English Dictionary

o or
objetivo objective
obligatorio(a) required, obligatory
la **obra** work
    la **obra de teatro** play, theatrical work
    ¡**Manos a la obra!** Let's get to work!
el **océano** ocean
    el **océano Atlántico** Atlantic ocean
    el **océano Pacífico** Pacific ocean
ochenta eighty, 2.1
ocho eight, 1.1
ochocientos(as) eight hundred, 3.1
octubre October, BV
ocupado(a) occupied, 5.1
ofrecer to offer
oír to hear
    oír un concierto to attend a concert, **5.2**
el **ojo** eye, **2.2**
la **ola** wave, **4.1**
    once eleven, 1.1
la **onza** ounce
opcional optional
la **ópera** opera
opinar to think, to have an opinion
la **opinión** opinion
el/la **opresor(a)** oppressor
la **oración** sentence
el **orden** order (sequential)
la **orden** order (restaurant), 5.1
el **ordenador** computer
el **órgano** organ
el **origen** origin
original original
    en versión original in the original version
el **oro** gold
    la **moneda de oro** gold coin
la **orquestra** orchestra
oscuro(a) dark
el **otoño** fall, BV
otro(a) other, another
    cualquier otro any other
    otra vez again
¡**Oye!** Listen!

el/la **paciente** patient, **2.2**
el **padrastro** stepfather, 2.1
el **padre** father, 2.1
los **padres** parents, 2.1
pagar to pay, 4.1

la **página** page
    la **página Web** Web page
el **país** country, **3.2**
    los **países de habla española** Spanish-speaking
        countries
el **paisaje** countryside
la **paja** straw
la **palabra** word
el **palo** pole
el **pan** bread, 5.1
    el **pan dulce** sweet roll
    el **pan tostado** toast, 5.1; **6.1**
el **panqueque** pancake
la **pantalla** screen (movie theater), 5.1
    la **pantalla de salidas y llegadas** arrival and
        departure screen (board), **3.1**
el **pantalón** pants, 4.2
    el **pantalón corto** shorts, 4.2
    el **pantalón largo** long pants, 4.2
el **pañuelo** handkerchief, **2.1**
el **papa** dad, 3.1
la **papa** potato, 5.2
    las **papas fritas** French fries, 5.1
el **papel** paper, 4.1; role
    la **hoja de papel** sheet of paper, 4.1
    el **papel higiénico** toilet paper, **6.2**
la **papelería** stationery store, 4.1
el **paquete** package, 5.2
el **par** pair; equal
    el **par de tenis** pair of tennis shoes
        (sneakers), 4.2
    sin par without equal, matchless
para for
paralelo(a) parallel
parar to stop, 6.1; **1.1**
parecer to seem, to look like
parecido(a) similar
el/la **pariente(a)** relative, 2.1
el **parque** park
    el **parque nacional** national park, **6.2**
el **párrafo** paragraph
la **parte** part
    tomar parte to take part
participar to participate
particular private
el **partido** game, 6.1; **1.1**
    el **partido de tenis** tennis game
pasado(a) passed
    el **año pasado** last year
    el **fin de semana pasado** last weekend
    los **huevos pasados por agua** soft-boiled eggs
    la **semana pasada** last week, **4.1**
    el **viernes pasado** last Friday
el/la **pasajero(a)** passenger, **3.1**

el **pasaporte** passport, **3.1**

    el control de pasaportes passport control, **3.2**

  pasar to pass, 6.2; **1.2;** to occur, to happen; to spend (time)

    pasar el fin de semana to spend the weekend, **4.1**

    pasar por to pass (walk) through

    pasar las vacaciones to spend one's vacation

    pasarlo bien to have a good time

    ¿Qué te pasa? What's the matter (with you)?, **2.1**

el **paso** step

la **pasta: la pasta (crema) dentífrica** toothpaste, **6.2**

el **pastel** cake, 2.2

la **pastilla** pill, tablet, **2.2;** bar

    la pastilla de jabón bar of soap, **6.2**

la **patata** potato, 5.2

    las patatas fritas French fries, 5.1

  pausado(a) slow, calm

el **pecho** chest

el **pedazo** piece

    hacer pedazos to tear (break) to pieces

  peinarse to comb one's hair, **6.1**

el **peine** comb, **6.1**

la **película** film, **5.1**

    ver una película to see a film, **5.1**

  pelirrojo(a) redheaded, 1.1

el **pelo** hair, **6.1**

la **pelota** ball, 6.2; **1.2**

la **pena** pain

    ¡Qué pena! What a shame!

el **peón** farmer, laborer

  pequeño(a) small, 1.2

  perder (ie) to lose, 6.1; **1.1**

    perder el autobús (la guagua, el camión) to miss the bus, **5.1**

  ¡Perdón! Excuse me!

  perfecto(a) perfect

el **periódico** newspaper

el **período** period

el **permiso** permission

    dar permiso to give permission

  permitir to permit, **3.1**

  pero but

el **perrito** puppy, 2.1

el/la **perro(a)** dog, 2.1

la **persona** person

el **personaje** character

  personalmente personally

  peruano(a) Peruvian, 1.1

  pesar to weigh

el **pescado** fish, 5.2

el **peso** peso; weight

el **petróleo** oil

  petrolero (related to) oil

el **pez** fish

el **piano** piano

  picado(a) chopped, ground

el/la **pícaro(a)** rogue, rascal

el/la **pícher** pitcher, 6.2; **1.2**

el **pico** peak, **4.2**

el **pie** foot, 6.1; **1.1**

    a pie on foot, 3.2

    ir a pie to walk, 3.2

la **piedra** stone

la **pierna** leg, 6.1; **1.1**

la **pieza** room

la **píldora** pill, **2.2**

la **pinta** pint

  pintar to paint

el/la **pintor(a)** painter

la **pintura** painting

la **piscina** pool, **4.1**

el **piso** floor, 2.2; apartment

la **pista** slope, **4.2**

    la pista para expertos expert slope, **4.2**

    la pista para principiantes beginners' slope, **4.2**

la **pizza** pizza

la **pizzería** pizzeria

el **plan** plan

la **plancha** board

    hacer la plancha de vela to windsurf

    la plancha de vela sailboard, **4.1**

la **planta** floor

    la planta baja ground floor, 2.2

  plástico(a) plastic

    el utensilio de plástico plastic utensil

la **plataforma** platform, pad

    la plataforma de lanzamiento launchpad

el **plátano** banana, 5.2

el **platillo** home plate, 6.2; **1.2**

el **plato** plate, dish

la **playa** beach, **4.1**

  playera (related to) beach

    la toalla playera beach towel, **4.1**

  plegable folding

    la mesa plegable folding table, **6.2**

    la silla plegable folding chair

la **pluma** pen, 4.1

la **población** population

  pobre poor, **2.1**

  poco(a) a little, few, 2.1

    un poco más a little more

  poder (ue) to be able, 6.1; **1.1**

el/la **poeta** poet

  político(a) political

el **pollo** chicken, 5.2

Spanish-English Dictionary

ponceño(a) of or from Ponce, Puerto Rico
el **poncho** poncho
poner to put, to place, **3.1**
ponerse to put on, **6.1**
    ponerse la ropa to put on one's clothes, **6.1**
popular popular
la **popularidad** popularity
por for, by
    irse por to go (fall) through
    por consiguiente therefore, consequently
    por ejemplo for example
    por encima de on top of, **4.1**
    por favor please, BV
    por fin finally
    por lo general generally
    por la mañana in the morning, 5.2
    por medio de by means of
    Por nada. You're welcome., BV
    por la noche at night
    por la tarde in the afternoon, **4.1**
    ¿por qué? why?
    por tierra overland
porque because
el **porte** poise
la **portería** goal, 6.1; **1.1**
el/la **portero(a)** goalie, 6.1; **1.1**
posible possible
postal postal
    la tarjeta postal postcard
el **postre** dessert, 5.1
practicar to practice
el **precio** price, 4.2
    a precio módico at a reasonable price
preferir (ie) to prefer, 6.1; **1.1**
la **pregunta** question, 3.2
    contestar (a) la pregunta to answer the question, 3.2
preguntar to ask
el **premio** award
preparar to prepare, 3.1
presentar to present
el/la **presidente(a)** president
prestar to lend
    prestar atención to pay attention, 3.2
el **presupuesto** budget
prevalecer to prevail
primario(a) primary, elementary
    la escuela primaria elementary school
la **primavera** spring, BV
primero(a) first
el/la **primo(a)** cousin, 2.1
la **princesa** princess
principal main, principal
el/la **principiante** beginner, **4.2**

la pista para principiantes beginners' slope, **4.2**
la **prisa** rush, hurry, haste
    a toda prisa as quickly as possible
privado(a) private, 2.2
    la casa privada private house
el **problema** problem
procesar to process
producir to produce
el **producto** product
    los productos congelados frozen foods, 5.2
la **profesión** occupation, profession
profesional professional
el/la **profesor(a)** teacher, 1.2
el **programa** program
la **promesa** promise
prometer to promise
pronto soon, quickly
    ¡Hasta pronto! See you soon!, BV
el/la **propietario(a)** owner
el/la **protagonista** protagonist
la **protección** protection
    protector(a): la crema protectora sunblock, **4.1**
publicar to publish
el **público** public, **5.2**
el **pueblo** town
la **puerta** gate, **3.1;** door
    la puerta de salida departure gate, **3.1**
el **puerto** port
puertorriqueño(a) Puerto Rican, 1.1
pues well
el **pulmón** lung
pulmonar pulmonary
el **punto** point
purificado(a) purified
puro(a) pure

que that
    lo que what, that which
¿qué? what?, how?, 3.1
    ¿A qué hora? At what time?, BV
    ¿de qué color? what color?, 4.2
    ¿de qué nacionalidad? what nationality?, 1.1
    No hay de qué. You're welcome., BV
    ¿por qué? why?
    ¿Qué desea Ud.?, May I help you? (in a store), 4.2
    ¿Qué día es (hoy)? What day is it (today)?
    ¿Qué hay? What's new (up)?
    ¿Qué hora es? What time is it?, BV
    ¡Qué... más... ! What a . . . !
    ¿Qué número usa Ud.?, What size do you wear?, 4.2

Spanish-English Dictionary

¡Qué pena! What a shame!

¡Qué suerte! What luck!

¿Qué tal? How are you?, BV

¿Qué talla usa Ud.? What size do you wear?, 4.2

¿Qué te pasa? What's the matter (with you)?, **2.1**

¿Qué tiempo hace? What is the weather (like)?, **4.1**

¿Qué tienes? What's the matter (with you)?, **2.1**

quechua Quechuan

quedar to remain, 6.1; **1.1**

querer (ie) to want, to wish

querido(a) dear

el **queso** cheese, 5.1

el sándwich de jamón y queso ham and cheese sandwich, 5.1

el **quetzal** currency of Guatemala

¿quién? who?, whom? 1.1

¿de quién? whose?

¿quiénes? who?, 1.1

la **química** chemistry

quince fifteen, 1.1

la **quinceañera** fifteen-year-old (girl), 2.2

quinientos(as) five hundred, 3.1

quinto(a) fifth

quitarse to take off

Ⓡ

racial racial

el **racimo** bunch

el racimo de uvas bunch of grapes

rápido(a) fast, quick

la comida rápida fast food

la **raqueta** racket, **4.1**

el **rato** while

el **ratón** mouse

la **razón** reason

tener razón to be right

real royal

el/la **realista** realist

realmente really

la **recámara** bedroom, 2.2

el **receptáculo** receptacle

el/la **receptor(a)** catcher, 6.2; **1.2**

la **receta** prescription, **2.2**

recetar to prescribe, **2.2**

recibir to receive, 5.1

recibir aplausos to receive applause, **5.2**

el **reciclaje** recycling

reclamar to claim, 3.2

reclamar el equipaje to pick up one's luggage, 3.2

reclamar las maletas to pick up one's suitcases, 3.2

el **reclamo** claim

el reclamo de equipaje baggage claim, 3.2

recoger to pick up, 3.2

recoger el equipaje to pick up one's luggage, 3.2

recoger las maletas to pick up one's suitcases, 3.2

el **rectángulo** rectangle

la **red** net, **4.1;** network

navegar la red to surf the Net

reducido(a) reduced

reflejar to reflect

el **reflejo** reflection

reflexionar to reflect

el **refresco** refreshment, drink, 5.1

tomar un refresco to have a drink

el **regalo** gift, 2.2

la **región** region

la **reina** queen

la **relación** relationship

relleno(a) full, stuffed

relleno de stuffed with

el **remedio** recourse

No hay más remedio. There is nothing more we can do.

rentar to rent, **5.1**

rentar un video to rent a video, **5.1**

el **repaso** review

la **representación** representation

la **república** republic

la República Dominicana Dominican Republic

requerir (ie) to require

la **reservación** reservation

resfriado(a): estar resfriado(a) to have a cold, **2.1**

respirar to breathe

respiratorio(a) respiratory

el aparato respiratorio respiratory system

el **restaurante** restaurant

el **resto** rest, remainder

el **retintín** jingle

el **retrato** portrait

revisar to check

revisar el boleto to check a ticket, **3.1**

la **revista** magazine

la **revolución** revolution

revolver (ue) to turn around

revuelto(a) scrambled, jumbled

los huevos revueltos scrambled eggs

el **rey** king

rico(a) rich

el **río** river

el río Amazonas Amazon River

la **rodilla** knee, 6.1; **1.1**

rojo(a) red, 4.2

el **rollo** roll, **6.2**

Spanish-English Dictionary

el rollo de papel higiénico roll of toilet paper, **6.2**

el rompecabezas puzzle

romper to break

la ropa clothing, 4.2
  ponerse la ropa to put on one's clothes, **6.1**
  la tienda de ropa clothing store, 4.2

rosado(a) pink, 4.2

rubio(a) blond(e), 1.1

rural rural

la rutina routine, **6.1**

S

el sábado Saturday, BV

saber to know, **3.2**

sabio(a) wise

sacar to get, 3.2
  sacar notas altas (bajas) to get high (low) grades, 3.2
  sacar notas buenas (malas) to get good (bad) grades, 3.2

el saco bag, sack; jacket
  el saco de dormir sleeping bag, **6.2**

la sala room; living room, 2.2
  la sala de clase classroom

la salchicha sausage

la salida departure
  la pantalla de llegadas y salidas arrival and departure screen (board), **3.1**
  la puerta de salida departure gate, **3.1**

salir to leave, to depart, **3.1**
  salir a tiempo to leave on time, **3.1**
  salir bien (en un examen) to do well (on an exam)
  salir tarde to leave late, **3.1**

la salsa salsa

saltar to jump

la salud health, **2.1**
  de buena salud in good health

el sándwich sandwich, 5.1
  el sándwich de jamón y queso ham and cheese sandwich, 5.1

la sangre blood

el sarape serape

el saxofón saxophone

la sección section

seco(a) dry

secundario(a) secondary

la sed thirst
  tener sed to be thirsty, 5.1

seguir (i) to continue, to follow

según according to

segundo(a) second

el segundo tiempo second half (soccer), 6.1; **1.1**

la seguridad security
  la control de seguridad security (checkpoint), **3.1**

seguro(a) sure, certain

seis six, 1.1

seiscientos(as) six hundred, 3.1

seleccionar to pick, to select

la selva forest

la semana week, BV
  el fin de semana weekend
  el fin de semana pasado last weekend
  pasar el fin de semana to spend the weekend, **4.1**
  la semana pasada last week, **4.1**

sencillo(a) simple

sentarse (ie) to sit down, **6.1**

el señor sir, Mr., gentleman, BV
  los señores ladies and gentlemen; Mr. and Mrs.

la señora Ms., Mrs., madam, BV

la señorita Miss, Ms., BV

septiembre September, BV

ser to be, 1.1
  ¿Cómo es él (ella)? What is he (she) like?
  ¿Cuánto es? How much does it cost (is it)?
  es decir that is (to say)
  Es verdad. That's true.

el ser: el ser humano human being
  el ser viviente living creature, being

la serie series
  la Serie mundial World Series

serio(a) serious, 1.1

servido(a) served

sesenta sixty, 2.1

la sesión performance, show (movies), **5.1**

setecientos(as) seven hundred, 3.1

setenta seventy, 2.1

si if

sí yes
  Creo que sí. I think so.

siempre always, **5.2**

siete seven, 1.1

el siglo century

el significado meaning

significar to mean

la silla chair, 5.1

similar similar

simpático(a) nice, 1.1

simple simple

sin without
  sin par without equal, matchless

sincero(a) sincere, 1.1

los singles singles (tennis), **4.1**

el síntoma symptom, **2.2**

el sistema system

situado(a) situated
sobre on, on top of, about
    sobre todo especially, above all
sobresaltar to jump up
sobrevolar (ue) to fly over
la **sobrina** niece, 2.1
el **sobrino** nephew, 2.1
social social
    los estudios sociales social studies, 1.2
socorrer to help
la **soda** soda
el **software** software
el **sol** sun
    Hace (Hay) sol. It's sunny.
    los anteojos de (para el) sol sunglasses, **4.1**
    tomar el sol to sunbathe, **4.1**
solamente only
solo(a) alone
sólo only
el **sombrero** hat
la **sopa** soup, 5.1
    soplar to blow
la **sorpresa** surprise
    su his, her, their, your
la **subconciencia** subconscious
    subir to go up
    subir en el telesilla to ride the ski lift, **4.2**
el **subtítulo** subtitle
    llevar subtítulos to have subtitles
el **suburbio** suburb
    sudamericano(a) South American
el **suelo** ground
el **sueño** dream
la **suerte** luck
    ¡Qué suerte! What luck!
    tener suerte to be lucky
el **sufrimiento** suffering
    superior superior, high
    la escuela superior high school
el **supermercado** supermarket, 5.2
el **sur** south
    la América del Sur South America
    surrealista surrealist
    sus their, your *(pl.)*
    suspirar to sigh

T

el **T-shirt** T-shirt, 4.2
la **tabla** board; table
    la tabla hawaiana surfboard; **4.1**
el **tablero** board
    el tablero indicador scoreboard, 6.1; **1.1**

la **tableta** tablet, **2.2**
el **taco** taco
    tal such (a thing)
        ¿Qué tal? How are things?, How are you?, BV
la **talla** size, 4.2
el **tamaño** size
    también also, too, 1.1
    tampoco neither, nor
    tan so
    tanto(a) so much
el **tanto** point, score, 6.1; **1.1**
    marcar un tanto to score a point, 6.1; **1.1**
la **taquilla** box office, **5.1**
    tarde late, **3.1**
la **tarde** afternoon
    ayer por la tarde yesterday afternoon, **4.1**
    Buenas tardes. Good afternoon., BV
    de la tarde in the afternoon, P.M. (time)
    esta tarde this afternoon, **4.1**
    por la tarde in the afternoon, **4.1**
la **tarea** homework, chore
la **tarjeta** card
    la tarjeta de embarque boarding pass, **3.1**
    la tarjeta postal postcard
el **taxi** taxi, **3.1**
la **taza** cup
    te you
el **té** tea, 5.1
    el té helado iced tea, 5.1
el **teatro** theater
    la obra de teatro play, theatrical work
el **techo** roof
el **teclado** keyboard
la **tecnología** technology
la **tele** TV, television
    telefonear to telephone, to call on the phone
el **teléfono** telephone, 3.1
    la compañía de teléfonos telephone company
    hablar por teléfono to speak on the phone, 3.1
    llamar por teléfono to call on the phone
    el número de teléfono telephone number
el **telesilla** chairlift, **4.2**
    tomar (subir en) el telesilla to ride the chairlift, **4.2**
el **telesquí** ski lift, **4.2**
la **televisión** television, 3.1
la **temperatura** temperature, **4.2**
    templado(a) temperate, mild
    temprano early, **6.1**
el **tendón** tendon
el **tenedor** fork
    tener to have, 2.1
    ¿Qué tienes? What's the matter (with you)?, **2.1**
    tener... años to be . . . years old, 2.1

tener confianza en to trust
tener éxito to be successful
tener ganas de to be longing to, to want
tener hambre to be hungry, 5.1
tener miedo to be afraid
tener que to have to, 4.1
tener razón to be right
tener sed to be thirsty, 5.1
tener suerte to be lucky
el **tenis** tennis, **4.1**
  la cancha de tenis tennis court, **4.1**
  el juego (partido) de tenis tennis game
  jugar (ue) (al) tenis to play tennis, **4.1**
  el par de tenis pair of tennis shoes (sneakers), 4.2
  los tenis tennis shoes, sneakers, 4.2
el/la **tenista** tennis player
la **terminal** terminal
  terminar to end
el **término** word, term
la **terraza** terrace, 2.2
  terrible terrible
el **territorio** territory
el **terror** fear, terror
el **tesoro** treasure
  ti you, 6.2; **1.2**
la **tía** aunt, 2.1
el **ticket** ticket, **4.2**
el **tiempo** half (soccer), 6.1; **1.1;** time; weather
  a tiempo on time, 3.1
  Hace buen tiempo. The weather is nice., **4.1**
  Hace mal tiempo. The weather is bad., **4.1**
  ¿Qué tiempo hace? What is the weather (like)?, **4.1**
  el segundo tiempo second half (soccer), 6.1; **1.1**
la **tienda** store, 4.2
  la tienda de abarrotes grocery store
  la tienda de campaña tent, **6.2**
  la tienda de departamentos department store
  la tienda de ropa clothing store, 4.2
  la tienda de videos video store, **5.1**
  tierno(a) tender
la **tierra** land, earth
  por tierra overland
las **tijeras** scissors, 4.1
  tímido(a) timid, shy, 1.1
el **tío** uncle, 2.1
  típico(a) typical
el **tipo** type
la **tira** strip
  la tira cómica comic strip
  tirar to throw, 6.2; **1.2**
el **título** title

la **toalla** towel, **4.1**
  la toalla playera beach towel, **4.1**
tocar to touch, **1.3;** to play (instrument)
  ¡Te toca a ti! It's your turn!
el **tocino** bacon
  todo(a) all, everything, 2.1
  a toda prisa as quickly as possible
  sobre todo above all, especially
  todo el mundo everyone
  todos(as) everyone, everything, all
  tomar to take, 3.1
  tomar el almuerzo to have lunch, 3.2
  tomar apuntes to take notes, 3.2
  tomar el bus to take the bus
  tomar el desayuno to have breakfast, 3.1
  tomar una ducha to take a shower, **6.1**
  tomar parte to take part
  tomar un refresco to have a drink
  tomar el telesilla to ride the ski lift, **4.2**
  tomar el sol to sunbathe, **4.1**
  tomar un vuelo to take a flight, **3.1**
el **tomate** tomato, 5.2
la **tonelada** ton
la **tontería** foolishness, stupidity
la **torta** cake, 2.2
la **tortilla** tortilla
la **tos** cough, **2.1**
  toser to cough, **2.1**
la **tostada** toast
  tostado(a) toasted
  el pan tostado toast, 5.1; **6.1**
el **total** total
  tóxico(a) toxic
  trabajar to work, 4.2
el **trabajo** work
el **trabalenguas** tongue twister
  tradicional traditional
  traer to bring, **3.1**
el **traje** suit, 4.2
  el traje de baño bathing suit, **4.1**
  tranquilo(a) calm, **2.1**
el **transporte** transportation
  el medio de transporte means of transportation
  tratar to treat; to try
  trece thirteen, 1.1
  treinta thirty, 1.1
  treinta y cinco thirty-five, 2.1
  treinta y cuatro thirty-four, 2.1
  treinta y dos thirty-two, 2.1
  treinta y nueve thirty-nine, 2.1
  treinta y ocho thirty-eight, 2.1
  treinta y seis thirty-six, 2.1

treinta y siete thirty-seven, 2.1
treinta y tres thiry-three, 2.1
treinta y uno thirty-one, 1.1
el **tren** train
la **trenza** braid
tres three, 1.1
trescientos(as) three hundred, 3.1
el **triángulo** triangle
la **tripulación** flight crew, **3.2**
triste sad, **2.1**
la **tristeza** sadness
el **trofeo** trophy, 6.2; **1.2**
el **trombón** trombone
el **trompeta** trumpet
tropical tropical
el **trozo** piece
tu your
tú you
el **tubo** tube
    el **tubo de crema** tube of cream
    el **tubo de pasta (crema) dentífrica** tube of
      toothpaste, **6.2**

Ud., usted you (*sing.*)
Uds., ustedes you (*pl.*)
un a, an
el **uniforme** uniform, 3.2
la **universidad** university
uno(a) one, a, 1.1
unos(as) some
usar to use, 4.2
el **utensilio** utensil
    el **utensilio de plástico** plastic utensil
la **uva** grape
    el **racimo de uvas** bunch of grapes

la **vacación** vacation
    pasar las vacaciones to spend one's vacation
la **vainilla** vanilla
    el **helado de vainilla** vanilla ice cream, 5.1
valedictoriano(a) valedictorian
valer to be worth
variar to vary, to change
la **variedad** variety
vario(a) various
el **vaso** glass, **6.1**
    el **vaso de jugo de naranja** glass of orange
      juice, **6.1**

el/la **vecino(a)** neighbor
el **vegetal** vegetable
veinte twenty, 1.1
veinticinco twenty-five, 1.1
veinticuatro twenty-four, 1.1
    las **veinticuatro horas** midnight
veintidós twenty-two, 1.1
veintinueve twenty-nine, 1.1
veintiocho twenty-eight, 1.1
veintiséis twenty-six, 1.1
veintisiete twenty-seven, 1.1
veintitrés twenty-three, 1.1
veintiuno twenty-one, 1.1
la **vela** candle, 2.2; sail
    hacer la plancha de vela to windsurf
    la **plancha de vela** sailboard, **4.1**
la **vena** vein
vender to sell, 5.2; **2.2**
venezolano(a) Venezuelan, 1.1
venir (ie) to come, **3.1**
la **venta** inn
la **ventanilla** ticket window, **4.2**
ver to see, 5.1; to look at, **3.1;** to watch
    a ver let's see
    ver una película to watch a film, **5.1**
el **verano** summer, BV; **4.1**
la **verdad** truth
    Es verdad. That's true.
    ¡verdad! that's right (true)!
verde green, 4.2
    la **judía verde** green bean, 5.2
    verde olivo olive green, 4.2
la **versión** version
    en versión original in the original version
la **vez** time
    a veces at times, sometimes, 3.1; **4.1**
    cada vez every time
    otra vez again
    una vez más one more time
viajar to travel
el **viaje** trip, **3.1**
    hacer un viaje to take a trip, **3.1**
la **víctima** victim
la **vida** life
el **video** video, 3.2
    alquilar (rentar) un video to rent a video, **5.1**
    la **tienda de videos** video store, **5.1**
el **vidrio** glass
viejo(a) old, 2.2
el/la **viejo(a)** old person
el **viento** wind
    Hace viento. It's windy.
    el **molino de viento** windmill

Spanish-English Dictionary

el **viernes** Friday, BV

el **vino** wine

la **viola** viola

   violeta violet, purple, 4.2

el **violín** violin

   visitar to visit, **5.2**

la **vista** view

   vital vital

la **vitamina** vitamin

   viudo(a) widowed

   viviente: el ser viviente living being

   vivir to live, 5.2

la **vocal** vowel

   volar (ue) to fly

el **voleibol** volleyball

el **volumen** volume

   volver (ue) to return, 6.1; **1.1**

   volverse (ue) to become

     volverse (ue) loco(a) to go mad

   vosotros(as) you

la **voz** voice

el **vuelo** flight, 3.1

   el/la asistente(a) de vuelo flight attendant, **3.2**

   el número del vuelo flight number, **3.1**

   tomar un vuelo to take a flight, **3.1**

   vuestro(a) your

   y and

   ya now, already

el **yaraví** melancholic Incan song

   yo I

la **zanahoria** carrot, 5.2

el/la **zapatista** follower of Emiliano Zapata

el **zapato** shoe, 4.2

la **zona** zone

el **zumo** juice

English-Spanish Dictionary

This English-Spanish Dictionary contains all productive and receptive vocabulary from ¿**Cómo te va? A, Nivel verde** and **B, Nivel azul.** *The numbers following each productive entry indicate the unit and vocabulary section in which the word is introduced. For example,* **3.2** *in dark print means that the word is taught in this textbook* **Unidad 3, Paso 2.** *A light print number means that the word was introduced in* ¿**Cómo te va? A, Nivel verde.** *BV refers to the introductory* **Bienvenidos** *lessons in* **A, Nivel verde.** *If there is no number following an entry, this means that the word or expression is included for receptive purposes only.*

a un(a)
  a day al día
  a lot mucho(a)
able: to be able poder (ue), 6.1; **1.1**
above sobre
  above all sobre todo
academic académico(a)
academy la academia
to **accept** aceptar
accompanied acompañado(a)
according to según
account la cuenta
  savings account la cuenta de ahorros
ache el dolor, **2.1**
to **ache** dolor (ue)
  My . . . ache(s), Me duele(n)... , **2.2**
to **act** actuar
active activo(a)
activity la actividad
to **admit** admitir
adolescent el/la adolescente
adorable adorable
adventure la aventura
advice el consejo
afraid: to be afraid tener miedo
African africano(a)
after después de, 3.1
afternoon la tarde
  Good afternoon. Buenas tardes., BV
  in the afternoon por la tarde, **4.1**
  in the afternoon (P.M.) (time) de la tarde
  this afternoon esta tarde, **4.1**
  yesterday afternoon ayer por la tarde, **4.1**
again de nuevo, otra vez
against contra, 6.1; **1.1**
age la edad
agent el/la agente, **3.1**
  customs agent el/la agente de aduana, **3.2**
ahead: Let's go ahead! ¡Adelante!
air el aire
  air carrier la compañía de aviación
  air pollution la contaminación del aire
aircraft (light plane) la avioneta

airline la línea aérea, **3.1**
  airline company la compañía de aviación
airplane el avión, **3.1**
  airplane ticket el boleto de avión
  by airplane en avión
  light aircraft la avioneta
airport el aeropuerto, **3.1**
album el álbum
algebra el álgebra
all todo(a), 2.1; todos(as)
  above all sobre todo
All Souls' Day el Día de los Muertos
allergy la alergia, **2.2**
alone solo(a)
already ya
also también, 1.1
always siempre, **5.2**
Amazon el Amazonas
  Amazon River el río Amazonas
American americano(a), 1.1
among entre
to **amuse** divertir (ie)
amusement la diversión
amusing divertido(a)
analysis el análisis
anatomy la anatomía
ancestry la ascendencia
and y
Andean andino(a)
animal el animal
to **announce** anunciar
announcement el anuncio
anonymous anónimo
another otro(a)
to **answer** contestar
  to answer the question contestar (a) la pregunta, 3.2
antibiotic el antibiótico, **2.2**
any other cualquier otro
apartment el apartamento, 2.2; el departamento; el piso
apartment house la casa de apartamentos
to **applaud** aplaudir, **5.2**
applause el aplauso, **5.2**
  to receive applause recibir aplausos, **5.2**
apple la manzana, 5.2

English-Spanish Dictionary

April abril, BV
area el área
Argentine argentino(a), 1.1
arithmetic la aritmética
arm el brazo, 6.1; **1.1**
around alrededor de
arrival la llegada
    arrival and departure screen (board) la pantalla de salidas y llegadas, **3.1**
to **arrive** llegar, 5.1
art el arte, 1.2
    art exhibition la exposición de arte, **5.2**
artery la arteria
artist el/la artista, **5.2**
as como
to **ask (a question)** preguntar
asleep dormido(a)
    to fall asleep dormirse (ue), **6.1**
aspirin la aspirina, **2.2**
assistance la asistencia
assistant el/la asistente(a)
astronaut el/la astronauta
astute astuto(a)
at a
    at about a eso de
    at home en casa
    at the movies al cine
    at night por la noche
    at one o'clock (two o'clock . . .) a la una (las dos...), BV
    at a reasonable price a precio módico
    at times a veces, 3.1; **4.1**
    At what time? ¿A qué hora?, BV
atmosphere la atmósfera, el ambiente
to **attack** atacar
to **attend** asistir
    to attend a concert oír un concierto, **5.2**
attendant el/la asistente(a)
    flight attendant el/la asistente(a) de vuelo, **3.2**
attention la atención
    to pay attention prestar atención, 3.2; hacer caso
August agosto, BV
aunt la tía, 2.1
author el/la autor(a)
automobile el automóvil
avenue la avenida
aviation la aviación
award el premio

baby el/la bebé, el/la nene(a)
back la espalda
backpack la mochila, 4.1; **6.2**
bacon el tocino

bad malo(a), 1.2; mal
    bad grade (mark) la nota mala, 3.2
    to be in a bad mood estar de mal humor, **2.1**
    The weather is bad. Hace mal tiempo., **4.1**
bad-tempered malhumorado(a)
bag la bolsa, 5.2; el saco
    sleeping bag el saco de dormir, **6.2**
baggage el equipaje, 3.1
    baggage claim el reclamo de equipaje, **3.2**
balcony el balcón, 2.2
ball el balón, 6.1; **1.1**; la pelota, 6.2; **1.2**
banana el plátano, 5.2
band la banda
bank el banco
bar of soap la barra (pastilla) de jabón, **6.2**
barbecue la barbacoa
to **bark** ladrar
base la base, 6.2; **1.2**
baseball el béisbol, 6.2; **1.2**
    baseball field el campo de béisbol, 6.2; **1.2**
    baseball player el/la jugador(a) de béisbol, 6.2; **1.2**
based basado(a)
basin la cuenca
basket el cesto, la canasta, 6.2; **1.2**; el canasto, el encestado
    to make a basket encestar, 6.2; **1.2**
basketball el baloncesto, el básquetbol, 6.2; **1.2**
    basketball court la cancha de básquetbol, 6.2; **1.2**
bat el bate, 6.2; **1.2**
to **bat** batear, 6.2; **1.2**
bath el baño, 2.2
    to take a bath bañarse, **6.1**
to **bathe** bañar
bather el/la bañista
bathing suit el bañador, el traje de baño, **4.1**
bathroom el cuarto de baño, 2.2; el baño
batter el/la bateador(a), 6.2; **1.2**
battle la batalla
    to do battle hacer batalla
to **be** ser, 1.1; estar, 3.1
    to be able poder (ue), 6.1; **1.1**
    to be afraid tener miedo
    to be born nacer
    to be called llamarse, **6.1**
    to be equivalent equivaler
    to be hungry tener hambre, 5.1
    to be in class estar en clase, 3.2
    to be in good health estar de buena salud
    to be in a good (bad) mood estar de buen (mal) humor, **2.1**
    to be longing to tener ganas de
    to be lucky tener suerte
    to be pleasing gustar, 6.2; **1.2**
    to be right tener razón
    to be sick (ill) estar mal

English-Spanish Dictionary

to be successful tener éxito
to be thirsty tener sed, 5.1
to be worth valer
to be . . . years old tener... años, 2.1
How are you? ¿Qué tal?, BV; ¿Cómo estas?
How is the weather? ¿Qué tiempo hace?, **4.1**
that is (to say) es decir
That's true. Es verdad.
What is he (she) like? ¿Cómo es él (ella)?
beach la playa, **4.1**
  beach resort el balneario, **4.1**
beach (related to) playero(a)
  beach towel la toalla playera, **4.1**
bean la habichuela, el frijol, 5.2; la judía
  green bean la judía verde, 5.2
  string bean el ejote, 5.2
beautiful hermoso(a)
because porque
to **become** volverse (ue)
  to become (go) crazy (mad) volverse (ue) loco(a)
bed la cama, **2.1**
  in bed en cama
  to go to bed acostarse (ue), **6.1**
  to stay in bed guardar cama, **2.1**
bedroom el cuarto de dormir, el dormitorio, la recámara, 2.2
before antes (de)
to **begin** empezar (ie), 6.1; **1.1**; comenzar (ie)
beginner el/la principiante, **4.2**
  beginners' slope la pista para principiantes, **4.2**
being el ser
  living being (creature) el ser viviente
below bajo, **4.2**
  below zero bajo cero, **4.2**
beside al lado de
besides además (de)
best el/la mejor
better mejor
between entre
bicycle la bicicleta
big gran, grande, 1.2
bill la cuenta, 5.1
biology la biología
bird el ave
birthday el cumpleaños, 2.2
to **bite** morder (ue)
black negro(a), 4.2
blind ciego(a)
  blind person el/la ciego(a)
block bloquear, 6.1; **1.1**
blond(e) rubio(a), 1.1
blood la sangre
blouse la blusa, 4.2
to **blow** soplar
blue azul, 4.2
board el tablero, 6.1; **1.1**; la plancha, la tabla

arrival and departure board la pantalla de salidas y llegadas, **3.1**
  on board a bordo, **3.2**
  scoreboard el tablero indicador, 6.1; **1.1**
to **board** abordar; embarcar, **3.1**
  boarding el embarque
  boarding pass la tarjeta de embarque, **3.1**
  boarding time la hora de embarque
boat el buque
body el cuerpo
  human body el cuerpo humano
bone el hueso
book el libro, 4.1
boot la bota, **4.2**
to **bore** aburrir, 6.2; **1.2**
bored aburrido(a)
boring aburrido(a)
born: to be born nacer
bottle la botella, 5.2
bound for con destino a
box la caja
box office la taquilla, 5.1
boy el muchacho, 1.1
braid la trenza
Brazilian brasileño(a)
bread el pan, 5.1
to **break** romper
  to break (tear) to pieces hacer pedazos
breakfast el desayuno, 3.1
  to have breakfast tomar el desayuno, 3.1; desayunarse, **6.1**
to **breathe** respirar
brief breve
bright brillante
to **bring** traer, **3.1**
bronchial tube el bronquio
brother el hermano, 2.1
brown marrón, 4.2
brunette moreno(a), 1.1
brush el cepillo, **6.2**
to **brush** cepillar
  to brush one's hair cepillarse, **6.1**
  to brush one's teeth cepillarse los dientes, **6.1**; lavarse los dientes
budget el presupuesto
building el edificio, 2.2
bunch el racimo
  bunch of grapes el racimo de uvas
bus el bus, 3.2; el autobús; el camión *(Mex.)*, la guagua *(P.R., Cuba)*, **5.1**
  by bus en autobús
  to miss the bus perder el autobús (el camión, la guagua), **5.1**
  school bus el bus escolar, 3.2
  to take the bus tomar el bus
but pero

English-Spanish Dictionary

butter la mantequilla
to **buy** comprar, 4.1
  by por
    by bus en autobús, **3.1**
    by car en carro, 3.2
    by means of por medio de
    by plane en avión
    by tens de diez en diez

C

café el café, 5.1
cafeteria la cafetería, 3.1; la cantina
cake la torta, el pastel, 2.2
calculator la calculadora, 4.1
to **call** llamar
    to call on the phone llamar por teléfono, telefonear
to **call oneself** llamarse, 6.1
  calm tranquilo(a), **2.1;** pausado(a)
  calorie la caloría
  camera la cámara
  camp la campaña
  campaign la campaña
  camping el camping, **6.2**
    camping guide(book) la guía de campings
    camping trip la excursión de camping
    to go camping ir de camping
  campsite el camping, **6.2**
  can la lata, el bote, 5.2
  candle la vela, 2.2
  cap la gorra, 4.2
  capital la capital
  captain (airplane) el/la comandante, **3.2**
  car el carro, 2.2; el coche
    by car en carro, 3.2
    to go by car ir en carro
  carbohydrate el carbohidrato
  carbon dioxide el dióxido de carbono
  carbonated drink la gaseosa, 5.1
  card la tarjeta
to **caress** acariciar
  Caribbean caribe
    Caribbean Sea el mar Caribe
  carpenter el/la carpintero(a)
  carrot la zanahoria, 5.2
to **carry** llevar, 4.1; **6.2**
    to carry (have) subtitles llevar subtítulos
  carry-on luggage el equipaje de mano, **3.1**
  cart el carrito
  case el caso
  cash register la caja, 4.1
  cat el/la gato(a), 2.1
  catalogue el catálogo
to **catch** atrapar, 6.2; **1.2**
  catcher el/la cátcher, el/la receptor(a), 6.2; **1.2**

category la categoría
CD (compact disc) el CD, 3.2
to **celebrate** celebrar, 3.1
  celebration la celebración
  center el centro
  Central America la América Central
  century el siglo
  cereal el cereal, **6.1**
  chair la silla, 5.1
    folding chair la silla plegable
  chairlift el telesilla, **4.2**
    to ride the chairlift tomar (subir en) el telesilla, **4.2**
  champion el/la campeón(ona), 6.2; **1.2**
to **change** cambiar, variar
  character el personaje
  cheap barato(a), 4.2
  check la cuenta, 5.1
to **check** revisar
    to check luggage facturar el equipaje, **3.1**
    to check a ticket revisar el boleto, **3.1**
  checkpoint: security checkpoint el control de seguridad, **3.1**
  cheese el queso, 5.1
    ham and cheese sandwich el sándwich de jamón y queso, 5.1
  chest el pecho
  chicken el pollo, 5.2
  child el/la niño(a)
  Chilean chileno(a), 1.1
  chills los escalofríos, **2.1**
  chocolate el chocolate, 5.1
    chocolate ice cream el helado de chocolate, 5.1
to **choose** escoger
  chopped picado(a)
  Christmas la Navidad
  Christmas Eve la Nochebuena
  circulation la circulación
  city la ciudad
  claim: baggage claim el reclamo de equipaje, **3.2**
to **claim** reclamar, **3.2**
  class la clase, 1.2
  classic clásico(a)
  classical clásico(a)
  classroom la sala de clase
  clear claro(a)
  client el/la cliente, 5.1
  climate el clima
  clinic la clínica
  close íntimo(a)
  closed cerrado(a)
  clothing la ropa, 4.2
    clothing store la tienda de ropa, 4.2
    to put on one's clothes ponerse la ropa, **6.1**
  cloud la nube, **4.1**
  cloudy: It's cloudy. Hay nubes.

English-Spanish Dictionary

club el club
   Spanish Club el Club de español
coach el/la entrenador(a)
coast la costa
coffee el café, 5.1
coin la moneda
   gold coin la moneda de oro
coincidence la coincidencia
cola la cola, 5.1
cold el frío; **(illness)** el catarro, **2.1**
   to have a cold estar resfriado(a), **2.1**
   It's cold (weather). Hace frío., **4.2**
collection la colección
Colombian colombiano(a), 1.1
color el color, 4.2
   what color? ¿de qué color?, 4.2
comb el peine, **6.1**
to **comb one's hair** peinarse, **6.1**
to **come** venir (ie), **3.1**
comic cómico(a), 1.1
   comic strip la tira cómica
comical cómico(a), 1.1
to **comment** comentar
commercial comercial
compact compacto(a)
   compact disc (CD) el CD, 3.2; el disco
      compacto
companion el/la compañero(a)
company la compañía
   airline company la compañía de aviación
   telephone company la compañía de teléfonos
competition la competencia
composition la composición
computer la computadora, el ordenador
concert el concierto, 5.2
   to attend a concert oír un concierto, 5.2
   to give (have) a concert dar un concierto, 5.2
conclusion la conclusión
condition la condición
confused confundido(a)
to **connect** conectar
connected conectado(a)
connection la conexión
to **conquer** conquistar
consecutive consecutivo(a)
consequently por consiguiente
conservatory el conservatorio
   National Conservatory of Music el
      Conservatorio Nacional de Música
to **consist of** consistir (en)
consonant la consonante
contact el contacto
to **contain** contener
container el envase, 5.2
contest el concurso
continent el continente

to **continue** continuar, 6.2; **1.2;** seguir (i,i)
contract el contrato
contrary el contrario
   on the contrary al contrario
control el control
   passport control el control de pasaportes, **3.2**
to **control** controlar
conversation la conversación
to **convert** convertir (ie)
to **cook** cocinar
cool fresco
   It's cool (weather). Hace fresco.
copilot el/la copiloto(a), **3.2**
copy el ejemplar
corn el maíz, 5.2
to **cost** costar (ue)
   How much does it cost? ¿Cuánto cuesta?
Costa Rican costarricense
cough la tos, **2.1**
to **cough** toser, **2.1**
to **count** contar (ue)
counter el mostrador, **3.1**
country el país, **3.2;** el campo
   Spanish-speaking countries los países de
      habla española
countryside la campaña, el paisaje
course el curso, 1.2
   of course! ¡claro!
court la cancha, 6.2; **1.2**
   basketball court la cancha de básquetbol,
      6.2; **1.2**
   enclosed court la cancha cubierta
   tennis court la cancha de tenis, **4.1**
courtesy la cortesía
cousin el/la primo(a), 2.1
to **cover** cubrir
covered cubierto(a)
   covered (enclosed) court la cancha cubierta
crazy loco(a)
   to go crazy (mad) volverse (ue) loco(a)
cream la crema
   suntan cream (lotion) la crema (loción)
      bronceadora, **4.1**
   tube of cream el tubo de crema
crew (flight) la tripulación, **3.2**
to **cross** cruzar
cruel cruel
crystal el cristal
Cuban cubano(a), 1.1
Cuban American cubanoamericano(a)
culture la cultura
cup la copa
   World Cup la Copa mundial
customer el/la cliente, 5.1
customs la aduana, **3.2**
   customs agent el/la agente de aduana, **3.2**

English-Spanish Dictionary

dad el papá, 3.1
dance el baile, la danza
to **dance** bailar, 3.1
dark moreno(a), 1.1; oscuro(a)
darling (term of endearment) nene(a)
data los datos
date la fecha
   What is today's date? ¿Cuál es la fecha de hoy?
daughter la hija, 2.1
day el día
   All Souls' Day el Día de los Muertos
   day before yesterday anteayer
   every day cada día
   from day to day de día en día
   nowadays hoy en día
   per day al día
   What day is it (today)? ¿Qué día es (hoy)?
dead (person) el/la muerto(a)
dear querido(a)
dear (term of endearment) nene(a)
debut el début
December diciembre, BV
to **decide** decidir, 5.1
decimal decimal
definite determinado(a)
definitely definitivamente
degree el grado, 4.2
delay la demora, 3.1
   with a delay con una demora, 3.1
delicious delicioso(a)
to **deliver** entregar
to **depart** salir, 3.1
department el departamento
   department store la tienda de departamentos
departure la salida
   arrival and departure board (screen) la pantalla de salidas y llegadas, 3.1
   departure gate la puerta de salida, 3.1
to **depend (on)** depender (de)
to **deposit** depositar
to **describe** describir
description la descripción
desert el desierto
desire la gana
dessert el postre, 5.1
destination el destino, 3.1
detail el detalle
determined determinado(a)
diagnosis la diagnosis, 2.2
   to make a diagnosis hacer una diagnosis, 2.2
difference la diferencia
different diferente, distinto(a)
difficult difícil, duro(a), 1.2

dining room el comedor, 2.2
dinner la cena, 3.1
   to have dinner cenar, 3.1
direct directo(a)
directly directamente
disc el disco
   compact disc (CD) el CD, 3.2; el disco compacto
discoteque la discoteca
disembark desembarcar, 3.2
dish el plato
to **dispense** despachar, 2.2
to **dissuade** desviar
distance la distancia
district el barrio
divine divino(a)
diving el buceo, 4.1
divorce: to get divorced divorciarse
to **do** hacer
   to do battle hacer batalla
   to do well (on an exam) salir bien (en un examen)
doctor el/la médico(a), 2.2, el/la doctor(a)
   doctor's office la consulta del médico, 2.2
dog el/la perro(a), 2.1
   hot dog el perro caliente
Dominican dominicano(a)
   Dominican Republic la República Dominicana
donkey el asno
   to ride a donkey montar en un asno
door la puerta
dose la dosis, 2.2
doubles (tennis) los dobles, 4.1
doubt la duda
doughnut (type of) el churro
down: to go down bajar, 4.2
drawing el dibujo, 1.2
dream el sueño
to **dribble** driblar, 6.2; 1.2
drink el refresco, 5.1
   to have a drink tomar un refresco
to **drink** beber, 5.1
dry seco(a)
dubbed doblado(a)
to **dump** derramar
during durante, 3.1
DVD el DVD, 3.2

each cada, 2.2
early temprano, 6.1
to **earn** ganar
earth la tierra
easel el caballete

easy fácil, 1.2
to **eat** comer, 5.1
ecological ecológico(a)
ecology la ecología
Ecuadorean ecuatoriano(a)
education la educación
   physical education la educación física, 1.2
egg el huevo, 5.2
   fried eggs los huevos fritos
   scrambled eggs los huevos revueltos
   soft-boiled eggs los huevos pasados por agua
eight ocho, 1.1
eight hundred ochocientos(as), 3.1
eighteen dieciocho, 1.1
eighty ochenta, 2.1
electronic electrónico(a)
elegant elegante
elementary primario(a)
   elementary school la escuela primaria
eleven once, 1.1
e-mail el correo electrónico
emission la emisión
to **emit** emitir
emotional emocionante
employee el/la empleado(a), el/la
   dependiente(a), 4.1
enchantment el encanto
   island of enchantment la isla del encanto
enchilada la enchilada
encounter el encuentro
end el fin
to **end** terminar
enemy el enemigo
English el inglés
to **enjoy** gozar (de)
to **enjoy oneself** divertirse (ie), **6.2**
   enough bastante, 1.2
to **enter** entrar, 3.2
   entire entero(a)
   environment el medio ambiente
   equal igual
   equality la igualdad
   equation la ecuación
   equilibrium el equilibrio
   equipment el equipo
   equivalent: to be equivalent equivaler
to **erase** borrar
   eraser la goma (de borrar), el borrador, 4.1
to **escape** escaparse
   especially sobre todo, especialmente
to **establish** establecer, fundar
   establishment el establecimiento
   eternal eterno(a)
   even aún
   evening la noche
      Good evening. Buenas noches., BV

every cada
   every day cada día
   every time cada vez
everyone todos
everything todo(a), 2.1; todos(as)
evil el mal
exactly exactamente
to **exaggerate** exagerar
exam el examen
   to do well (on an exam) salir bien (en un examen)
to **examine** examinar, **2.2**
example el ejemplo
   for example por ejemplo
excellent excelente
to **exclaim** exclamar
excursion la excursión
Excuse (me)! ¡Perdón!
exhibition la exposición, **5.2**
   art exhibition la exposición de arte, **5.2**
to **exist** existir
expedition la expedición
expense el gasto
expensive caro(a), 4.2
experience la experiencia
expert el/la experto(a), **4.2**
   expert slope la pista para expertos, **4.2**
to **explain** explicar
to **explore** explorar
expression la expresión
extraordinary extraordinario(a)
extreme extremo(a)
eye el ojo, **2.2**
eyeglasses los anteojos

fabulous fabuloso(a)
face la cara, **6.1**
facility la facilidad
factory la fábrica
faithful fiel
fall el otoño, BV
to **fall: to fall asleep** dormirse (ue), **6.1**
   false falso(a)
   familiar: to be familiar with conocer, **3.2**
   family la familia, 2.1
   family (related to) familiar
      family tree el árbol genealógico
   famous famoso(a)
   fan el/la aficionado(a)
   fantastic fantástico(a)
   fantasy la fantasía
   far lejos
   farmer el/la campesino(a), el peón

English-Spanish Dictionary

fast rápido(a)
    fast food la comida rápida
fat gordo(a)
fat la grasa
father el padre, 2.1
favor el favor
favorite favorito(a)
fear el miedo, el terror
February febrero, BV
fever la fiebre, **2.1**
few poco(a), 2.1; pocos(as)
field el campo, 6.1; **1.1**
    baseball field el campo de béisbol, 6.2; **1.2**
    soccer field el campo de fútbol, 6.1; **1.1**
fifteen quince, 1.1
fifteen-year-old (girl) la quinceañera, 2.2
fifth quinto(a)
fifty cincuenta, 2.1
to **fight** luchar
figure la figura
to **fill** llenar
    film el film, la película, **5.1**
    to see a film ver una película, **5.1**
finally por fin
to **find** encontrar (ue), hallar
fine bien
finger el dedo
first primero(a)
fish el pescado, 5.2; el pez
five cinco, 1.1
five hundred quinientos(as), 3.1
flight el vuelo, **3.1**
    flight attendant el/la asistente(a) de vuelo, **3.2**
    flight crew la tripulación, **3.2**
    flight number el número del vuelo, **3.1**
    to take a flight tomar un vuelo, **3.1**
floor el piso, 2.2; la planta
    ground floor la planta baja, 2.2
flour la harina
flower la flor
flu la gripe, **2.1**
flute la flauta
fly la mosca
to **fly** volar (ue)
    to fly over sobrevolar (ue)
folder la carpeta, 4.1
folding plegable
    folding chair la silla plegable
    folding table la mesa plegable, **6.2**
to **follow** seguir (i,i)
food la comida, 3.1; el alimento; el comestible
    fast food la comida rápida
    frozen foods los productos congelados, 5.2
    junk food la chuchería
foolishness la tontería
foot el pie, 6.1

on foot a pie, 3.2
for por; para
    for example por ejemplo
foreign extranjero(a), **3.2**
foreigner el/la extranjero(a)
forest la selva
fork el tenedor
form la forma
to **form** formar
    to form a line hacer cola
formal formal
fortunately afortunadamente
forty cuarenta, 2.1
to **found** fundar
foundation la fundación
fountain la fuente
four cuatro, 1.1
four hundred cuatrocientos(as), 3.1
fourteen catorce, 1.1
free (unoccupied) libre, 5.1; **(of charge)** gratis
French el francés
frequently frecuentemente, con frecuencia
fresh (food) fresco, 5.2
Friday el viernes, BV
    Friday night el viernes por la noche
    last Friday el viernes pasado
fried frito(a)
    French fries las papas (patatas) fritas, 5.1
    fried eggs los huevos fritos
friend el/la amigo(a), 1.1; el/la compañero(a)
frightful espantoso(a)
from de; desde
    from day to day de día en día
    from where? ¿de dónde?, 1.1
front: in front of delante de, **5.1**
frozen helado(a), congelado(a)
    frozen foods los productos congelados, 5.2
fruit la fruta, 5.2
full lleno(a), **5.2;** cargado(a); relleno(a)
fun divertido(a)
functioning el funcionamiento
funny gracioso(a), 1.1; cómico(a), 1.1
fury la furia

gallon el galón
game el partido, 6.1; **1.1**; el juego
    tennis game el juego (partido) de tenis, **4.1**
garage el garaje, 2.2
garden el jardín, 2.2
gas el gas
gate la puerta, **3.1**
    departure gate la puerta de salida, **3.1**
genealogical genealógico(a)
general general

English-Spanish Dictionary

general el general
generally en general, por lo general
generous generoso(a)
gentleman el señor, BV
geography la geografía
geometrical geométrico(a)
to **get** sacar, 3.2
    to get divorced divorciarse
    to get good (bad) grades (marks) sacar notas buenas (malas), 3.2
    to get high (low) grades (marks) sacar notas altas (bajas), 3.2
    to get on (ride) a donkey montar en un asno
    to get on (ride) a horse montar a caballo
to **get up** levantarse, **6.1**
    giant el gigante
    gift el regalo, 2.2
    girl la muchacha, 1.1
to **give** dar, 3.1
    to give a concert dar un concierto, **5.2**
    to give permission dar permiso
    glass (drinking) el vaso, **6.1**; (pane) el vidrio
    glasses los anteojos
    glove el guante, 6.2; **1.2**
to **go** ir, 3.1; andar
    to go to bed acostarse (ue), **6.1**
    to go by car ir en carro
    to go camping ir de camping
    to go down bajar, **4.2**
    to go (fall) through irse por
    to go mad (crazy) volverse (ue) loco(a)
    to go (pass) through pasar por
    to go shopping ir de compras, 5.2
    to go up subir
    Let's go ahead! ¡Adelante!
    goal el gol, 6.1; **1.1**
    goal (box) la portería, 6.1; **1.1**
    to score a goal meter un gol, 6.1; **1.1**
    goalie el/la portero(a), 6.1; **1.1**
    gold el oro
    gold coin la moneda de oro
    golf el golf, 6.2; **1.2**
    good bueno(a), 1.1
    to be in good health estar de buena salud
    to be in a good mood estar de buen humor, **2.1**
    Good afternoon. Buenas tardes., BV
    Good evening. Buenas noches., BV
    good grade (mark) la nota buena, 3.2
    Good morning. Buenos días., BV
    to have a good time divertirse (ie), **6.2**; pasarlo bien
    It's good weather. Hace buen tiempo.
    good-bye adiós, ¡chao!, BV
    good-looking guapo(a), 1.1
    governor el/la gobernador(a)
    grade (mark) la nota

    to get good (bad) grades sacar notas buenas (malas), 3.2
    to get high (low) grades (marks) sacar notas altas (bajas), 3.2
    good (bad) grade (mark) la nota buena (mala), 3.2
    high (low) grade (mark) la nota alta (baja), 3.2
grain el grano
gram el gramo
granddaughter la nieta, 2.1
grandfather el abuelo, 2.1
grandma la abuelita
grandmother la abuela, 2.1
grandpa el abuelito
grandparents los abuelos, 2.1
grandson el nieto, 2.1
grape la uva
    bunch of grapes el racimo de uvas
gray gris, 4.2
great gran, grande, 1.2
green verde, 4.2
    green bean la judía verde, 5.2
    olive green verde olivo, 4.2
grocery el abarrote
    grocery store la tienda de abarrotes, la bodega
ground el suelo
group el grupo
to **guard** guardar, 6.1; **1.1**
    Guatemalan guatemalteco(a)
to **guess** adivinar
    guide el/la guía
    guidebook la guía
    camping guidebook la guía de campings

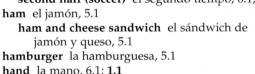

hair el pelo, **6.1**
    to brush one's hair cepillarse, **6.1**
    to comb one's hair peinarse, **6.1**
half medio(a)
    half (soccer) el tiempo, 6.1; **1.1**
    second half (soccer) el segundo tiempo, 6.1; **1.1**
ham el jamón, 5.1
    ham and cheese sandwich el sándwich de jamón y queso, 5.1
hamburger la hamburguesa, 5.1
hand la mano, 6.1; **1.1**
handkerchief el pañuelo, **2.1**
handsome guapo(a), 1.1
to **hang** colgar (ue)
to **happen** pasar
    happy contento(a), **2.1**; alegre
    hard duro(a), difícil, 1.2
    hardware el hardware
    haste la prisa
    hat el sombrero

English-Spanish Dictionary

to **have** tener, 2.1
    to have a cold estar resfriado(a), **2.1**
    to have a concert dar un concierto, **5.2**
    to have a drink tomar un refresco
    to have a good time divertirse (ie), **6.2;** pasarlo
        bien
    to have a party dar una fiesta
    to have an opinion opinar
    to have breakfast tomar el desayuno, 3.1;
        desayunarse, **6.1**
    to have dinner cenar, 3.1
    to have lunch tomar el almuerzo, 3.2
    to have subtitles llevar subtítulos
    to have to tener que, 4.1
    I have a headache. Me duele la cabeza., **2.1**
he él
head la cabeza, 6.1; **1.1**
headache el dolor de cabeza, **2.1**
    I have a headache. Me duele la cabeza., **2.1**
health la salud, **2.1**
    to be in good health estar de buena salud
    in good health de buena salud
to **hear** oír
heart el corazón
heat el calor
Hello! ¡Hola!, BV
help la ayuda, la asistencia, el auxilio
to **help** asistir, ayudar, socorrer
hemisphere el hemisferio
    northern hemisphere el hemisferio norte
    southern hemisphere el hemisferio sur
her la; su(s)
    to her le
here aquí
hero el héroe
heroine la heroína
to **hide** esconder
high alto(a), 4.2; superior
    to get high grades (marks) sacar notas altas, 3.2
    high grade (mark) la nota alta, 3.2
    high school el colegio, la escuela superior, la
        escuela secundaria
hike la caminata, **6.2**
to **hike** dar una caminata, **6.2**
him lo
    to him le
his su(s)
Hispanic hispano(a)
history la historia
to **hit** golpear, **4.1**
hole el agujero
holiday la fiesta
home la casa, 2.2
    at home en casa
    home plate el platillo, 6.2; **1.2**
    home run el jonrón, 6.2; **1.2**

homework la tarea
honor el honor
horrible horrible
horse el caballo
    to ride a horse montar a caballo
hospital el hospital
hospital (related to) hospitalario(a)
hostelry el hostal
hot caliente
    hot dog el perro caliente
    It's hot (weather). Hace calor., **4.1**
hotel el hotel
hour la hora
house la casa, 2.2
    apartment house la casa de apartamentos
    private house la casa privada
how? ¿cómo?, 1.1; ¿qué?
    How are you? ¿Qué tal?, BV; ¿Cómo estás?
    How is the weather? ¿Qué tiempo hace?, **4.1**
    how much? ¿cuánto?
    how many? ¿cuántos(as)?
    How much does it cost? ¿Cuánto cuesta?
    How much is (are) . . . ? ¿A cuánto está(n)... ?, 5.2
human humano(a)
    human being el ser humano
    human body el cuerpo humano
humble humilde
hunger hambre
hungry: to be hungry tener hambre, 5.1
hurry la prisa
to **hurt** doler (ue)
    My . . . hurt(s) me Me duele(n)... , **2.2**
husband el esposo, el marido
hygienic higiénico(a)

I

I yo
ice cream el helado, 5.1
    chocolate ice cream el helado de chocolate, 5.1
    vanilla ice cream el helado de vainilla, 5.1
idea la idea
idealist el/la idealista
if si
ill enfermo(a), **2.1,** mal
    to feel ill estar mal
    ill person el/la enfermo(a), **2.2**
illusion la ilusión
immediate inmediato(a)
immediately enseguida, **6.1**
immense inmenso(a)
impenetrable impenetrable
important importante
impossible imposible
in en
    to be in good health estar de buena salud

in bed en cama
in front of delante de, **5.1**
in good health de buena salud
in order to para
in search of en busca de
in style de moda
in the afternoon por la tarde, **4.1**
in the afternoon (P.M.) (time) de la tarde
in the morning por la mañana, 5.2
in the morning (A.M.) (time) de la mañana
in the original version en versión original
to stay in bed guardar cama, **2.1**
inclination la inclinación
to **include** incluir
incredible increíble
independence la independencia
Indian indio(a)
Indian el indio(a)
to **indicate** indicar, 6.1; **1.1**
indicator el indicador
indigenous indígena
indispensable indispensable
individual individual
individual sport el deporte individual
industrial industrial
industry la industria
inexpensive barato(a), 4.2
injection la inyección, **2.2**
inn el hostal, la venta
inning la entrada, 6.2; **1.2**
to **inspect** inspeccionar, **3.2**
inspection la inspección
to **inspire** inspirar
instant el instante
institute el instituto
instruction la instrucción
instrument el instrumento
intelligent inteligente, 1.2
interest el interés
to **interest** interesar, 6.2; **1.2**
interesting interesante, 1.2
intermediate intermedio(a)
intermediate (middle) school la escuela
intermedia
internal interno(a)
international internacional
Internet el/la Internet
interview la entrevista
introduction la introducción
intruder el/la intruso(a)
invention la invención
investigation la investigación
invitation la invitación
to **invite** invitar, 3.1
island la isla
island of enchantment la isla del encanto

isolated aislado(a)
it la; lo
Italian italiano(a)

jacket la chaqueta, 4.2; el saco
jam la mermelada
January enero, BV
jar el jarro
jeans el jean, el blue jean, los blue jeans, 4.2
jingle el retintín
jug el jarro
juice el jugo, **6.1;** el zumo
orange juice el jugo de naranja, **6.1**
July julio, BV
jumbled revuelto(a)
to **jump** saltar
to jump up sobresaltar
June junio, BV
jungle la jungla
juvenile juvenil

to **keep** guardar
keyboard el teclado
to **kick** lanzar, 6.1; **1.1**
kilo el kilo, 5.2
kilogram el kilogramo
king el rey
kitchen la cocina, 2.2
knapsack la mochila, 4.1; **6.2**
knee la rodilla, 6.1; **1.1**
knife el cuchillo
knight el caballero
knight errant el caballero andante
to **know** conocer, saber, **3.2**

laboratory el laboratorio
laborer el peón
laborious laborioso(a)
lady-in-waiting la dama
lake (related to) lacustre
lament el lamento
lance la lanza
land la tierra
overland por tierra
to **land** aterrizar, **3.2**
landing el desembarque; el aterrizaje
language la lengua, el habla
large gran, grande, 1.2
late tarde, **3.1**

English-Spanish Dictionary

later luego
    See you later! ¡Hasta luego!, BV
Latin el latín
Latin latino(a)
Latin America Latinoamérica
Latin American latinoamericano(a)
launching el lanzamiento
    launchpad el lanzamiento
laundromat la lavandería
leader el líder
leaf la hoja
league la liga
    Major Leagues las Grandes Ligas
to **learn** aprender, 5.1
to **leave** salir, **3.1;** dejar
    left izquierdo(a), 6.1; **1.1**
    leg la pierna, 6.1; **1.1**
    lemonade la limonada
to **lend** prestar
    less menos
    lesson la lección
    letter la carta
    letters (literature) las letras
    lettuce la lechuga, 5.2
    level el nivel
    liberator el/la libertador(a)
    library la biblioteca
    life la vida
    lift: ski lift el telesquí, **4.2**
    to ride the ski lift subir en el telesilla, **4.2**
to **lift** levantar
    light la luz
to **light** encender (ie)
    like el gusto
to **like** gustar, 6.2; **1.2**
    line la línea
    line (queue) la cola, la fila, **5.1**
    to form a line hacer cola
    to line up hacer cola
    lipid el lípido
    liquid el líquido
    list la lista
to **listen (to)** escuchar, 3.2
    Listen! ¡Oye!
    liter el litro
    literature la literatura; las letras
    Spanish literature las letras hispanas
    little poco(a)
    a little more un poco más
to **live** vivir, 5.2
    living creature el ser viviente
    living room la sala, 2.2
    local local
    logical lógico(a)
    long largo(a)
    long pants el pantalón largo, 4.2

    long sleeve la manga larga, 4.2
    long walk la caminata, **6.2**
to **look at** mirar, 3.1; ver
    to look at oneself mirarse, **6.1**
to **look for** buscar, 4.1
to **look like** parecer
to **lose** perder (ie), 6.1; **1.1**
  lot: a lot mucho(a), 2.1
  lotion la loción
    suntan lotion la loción bronceadora, **4.1**
  low bajo(a), 4.2
    to get low grades (marks) sacar notas bajas, 3.2
    low grade (mark) la nota baja, 3.2
to **lower** bajar
  luck la suerte
    to be lucky tener suerte
    What luck! ¡Qué suerte!
  luggage el equipaje, **3.1**
    carry-on luggage el equipaje de mano, **3.1**
    to check luggage facturar el equipaje, **3.1**
    to pick up one's luggage reclamar (recoger) el equipaje, **3.2**
  lunch el almuerzo, 3.2
    to have lunch tomar el almuerzo
  lung el pulmón

machine la máquina
mad (crazy) loco(a)
    to go mad (crazy) volverse (ue) loco(a)
madam la señora, BV
mail el correo
    e-mail el correo electrónico
main principal
Major Leagues las Grandes Ligas
majority la mayoría
to **make** hacer
    to make a basket encestar, 6.2; **1.2**
    to make a diagnosis hacer una diagnosis, **2.2**
mambo el mambo
man el hombre
manner la manera
many muchos(as)
map el mapa
March marzo, BV
march la marcha
mark (grade) la nota, 3.2
    to get good (bad) marks sacar notas buenas (malas), 3.2
    to get high (low) marks sacar notas altas (bajas), 3.2
    good (bad) mark la nota buena (mala), 3.2
    high (low) mark la nota alta (baja), 3.2
marker el marcador, 4.1

English-Spanish Dictionary

market el mercado, 5.2
marmalade la mermelada
marquis el marqués
marquise la marquesa
matchless sin par
material el material
mathematics las matemáticas
matter (subject) la materia
matter: What's the matter (with you)? ¿Qué te pasa?, **2.1**; ¿Qué tienes?
to **matter** importar
   It doesn't matter. No importa.
May mayo, BV
Maya el/la maya
me me
   (to) me (a) mí
meal la comida, 3.1
to **mean** significar
meaning el significado
means el medio
   by means of por medio de
   means of transportation el medio de transporte
measure la medida
meat la carne, 5.2
medal la medalla
medical médico(a)
   medical office el consultorio, **2.2**
medicine el medicamento, la medicina, **2.2**; **(discipline)** la medicina
meeting el encuentro
melancholic melancólico(a)
member el/la miembro
memory la memoria
menu el menú, 5.1
mercy la merced
merengue el merengue
metabolism el metabolismo
metal el metal
metric métrico(a)
Mexican mexicano(a)
middle: middle school la escuela intermedia
midnight la medianoche; las veinticuatro horas
mild templado(a)
milk la leche, 5.2
mill el molino
million el millón
mineral mineral
   mineral water el agua mineral, 5.2; **6.2**
minus menos
mirror el espejo, **6.1**
to **miss** perder (ie)
   to miss the bus perder el autobús (el camión, la guagua), 5.1
Miss la señorita, BV
model el/la modelo

moderate módico(a)
modern moderno(a)
mom la mamá
moment el momento
Monday el lunes, BV
money el dinero
monitor el monitor
monster el monstruo
month el mes
mood el humor
   to be in a good (bad) mood estar de buen (mal) humor, **2.1**
moon la luna
more más
   a little more un poco más
   one more time una vez más
   There is nothing more we can do. No hay más remedio.
morning la mañana
   Good morning. Buenos días., BV
   in the morning por la mañana, 5.2
   in the morning (A.M.) (time) de la mañana
   this morning esta mañana, **4.1**
   yesterday morning ayer por la mañana
mother la madre, 2.1
motive el motivo
mountain la montaña; **4.2**
mouse el ratón
   (mouse) pad la alfombrilla
mouth la boca, 2.2
   to open one's mouth abrir la boca, 2.2
to **move** mover (ue)
movie theater el cine, 5.1
   at the movies al cine
Mr. el señor, BV
Mrs. la señora, BV
Ms. la señorita, la señora, BV
much mucho(a), 2.1
   How much? ¿Cuánto?
   How much does it cost? ¿Cuánto es?, 4.1
   How much is (are) . . . ? ¿A cuánto está(n)... ?, 5.2
municipal municipal
mural el mural
muralist el/la muralista
muscle el músculo
muscular muscular
museum el museo, **5.2**
music la música, 1.2
   National Conservatory of Music el Conservatorio Nacional de Música
musical musical
musician el/la músico(a)
must deber
my mi
mysterious misterioso(a)
mystery el misterio

English-Spanish Dictionary

name el nombre
to name nombrar
national nacional
    National Conservatory of Music el Conservatorio Nacional de Música
    national park el parque nacional, **6.2**
nationality la nacionalidad
    what nationality? ¿de qué nacionalidad?, 1.1
native indígena
native person el/la indígena
natural natural
nature naturaleza
to navigate navegar
near cerca de
necessary necesario(a)
to need necesitar, 4.1
needy necesitado(a)
neighbor el/la vecino(a)
neither tampoco
nephew el sobrino, 2.1
nervous nervioso(a), **2.1**
net la red, **4.1**
    Net (Internet) la red
    to surf the Net navegar la red
network la red
never nunca, **5.2**
new nuevo(a), 1.2
newspaper el periódico
next próximo(a)
next to al lado de
nice simpático(a), 1.1
    The weather is nice. Hace buen tiempo., **4.1**
nickname el apodo
niece la sobrina, 2.1
night la noche
    at night por la noche
    Friday night el viernes por la noche
    last night anoche, **4.1**
nine nueve, 1.1
nine hundred novecientos(as), 3.1
nineteen diecinueve, 1.1
ninety noventa, 2.1
ninth noveno(a)
no no
    by no means, no way de ninguna manera
no one nadie; **5.2**
noble noble
none ninguno(a)
nor tampoco
north el norte
    northern hemisphere el hemisferio norte
not no, 1.1
    absolutely not en absoluto

not any, none ninguno(a)
    not at all de ninguna manera
note el apunte
    to take notes tomar apuntes, 3.2
to note notar
notebook el bloc, el cuaderno, 4.1
nothing nada, **5.2**
    nothing else nada más, 5.2
    There is nothing more we can do. No hay más remedio.
to notice notar
novel la novela
novelist el/la novelista
November noviembre, BV
now ahora; ya
nowadays hoy en día
number el número
    flight number el número del vuelo, **3.1**
    seat number el número del asiento, **3.1**
    telephone number el número de teléfono
nurse el/la enfermero(a)
nutrition la nutrición

objective el objetivo
obligatory obligatorio(a)
occupation la profesión
occupied ocupado(a), 5.1
to occur pasar
ocean el océano
    Atlantic ocean el océano Atlántico
    Pacific ocean el océano Pacífico
October octubre, BV
of de
    of course! ¡claro!
to offer ofrecer
office la consulta, **2.2**
    box office la taquilla, **5.1**
    doctor's office la consulta del médico, **2.2**
    medical office el consultorio, **2.2**
oil el aceite; el petróleo
oil (related to) petrolero(a)
old viejo(a), 2.2
    How old is he (she)? ¿Cuántos años tiene?, 2.1
    old person el/la viejo(a), el/la anciano(a)
older mayor, 2.1
oldest el/la mayor, 2.1
olive green verde olivo, 4.2
on en, sobre
    on board a bordo, **3.2**
    on the contrary al contrario
    on foot a pie, 3.2
    on time a tiempo, **3.1**
    on top of (por) encima de, **4.1;** sobre

English-Spanish Dictionary

one uno(a), 1.1
 no one nadie; **5.2**
 one more time una vez más
one hundred cien(to), 2.1
one thousand mil, 3.1
onion la cebolla
only solamente, sólo
to **open** abrir, **2.2**
 to open the suitcases abrir las maletas, **3.2**
opera la operá
to **operate** funcionar
operation el funcionamiento
opinion la opinión
 to have an opinion opinar
opposing adverso(a)
opposite adverso(a)
oppressor el/la opresor(a)
optional opcional
or o
orange (color) naranja, 4.2
orange (fruit) la naranja, 5.2
 orange juice el jugo de naranja, **6.1**
orchestra la orquesta
order (restaurant) la orden, 5.1; **(sequential)**
 el orden
organ el órgano
origin el origen
original original
 in the original version en versión
  original
other otro(a)
 any other cualquier otro
ounce la onza
our nuestro(a)
outdoor al aire libre, **4.1**
outfielder el/la jardinero(a), 6.2; **1.2**
overland por tierra
to **overthrow** derrocar
to **owe** deber
 owner el/la dueño(a), el/la propietario(a)

to **pack** hacer la maleta, **3.1**
 package el paquete, 5.2
 pad (writing) el bloc, 4.1
  launchpad el lanzamiento; la plataforma de
   lanzamiento
  (mouse) pad la alfombrilla
 page la página
  Web page la página Web
 pain el dolor, **2.1**; la pena
to **paint** pintar
 painter el/la pintor(a)
  mural painter el/la muralista
 painting el cuadro, **5.2**; la pintura

pair el par
 pair of tennis shoes (sneakers) el par de
  tenis, 4.2
pancake el panqueque
pants el pantalón, 4.2
 long pants el pantalón largo, 4.2
 short pants el pantalón corto, 4.2
paper el papel, 4.1
 sheet of paper la hoja de papel, 4.1
 toilet paper el papel higiénico, **6.2**
paragraph el párrafo
parallel paralelo(a)
parents los padres, 2.1
park el parque
 national park el parque nacional, **6.2**
parka el anorak, **4.2**
part la parte
 to take part tomar parte
to **participate** participar
party la fiesta, 2.2
 to have (give) a party dar una fiesta
pass: boarding pass la tarjeta de embarque, **3.1**
to **pass** pasar, 6.2; **1.2**
 to pass (walk) through pasar por, **3.2**
passenger el/la pasajero(a), **3.1**
passport el pasaporte, **3.1**
 passport control el control de pasaportes, **3.2**
pastime la diversión
patient el/la enfermo(a), el/la paciente, **2.2**
to **pay** pagar, 4.1
 to pay attention prestar atención, 3.2; hacer caso
pea el guisante, 5.2
peak el pico, **4.2**
peasant el/la campesino(a)
pen el bolígrafo, la pluma, 4.1
pencil el lápiz, 4.1
people la gente, **5.2**
perfect perfecto(a)
performance la sesión, **5.1**
period el período
permission el permiso
 to give permission dar permiso
to **permit** permitir, **3.1**
person la persona
 young person el/la joven
personally personalmente
Peruvian peruano(a), 1.1
peso el peso
pharmacist el/la farmacéutico(a), **2.2**
pharmacy la farmacia, **2.2**
phone el teléfono
 to call on the phone llamar por teléfono,
  telefonear
 phone company la compañía de teléfonos
 phone number el número de teléfono
 to speak on the phone hablar por teléfono, 3.1

English-Spanish Dictionary

photo la foto
photograph la fotografía
physical físico(a)
    physical education la educación física, 1.2
piano el piano
to **pick** seleccionar
to **pick up** recoger, reclamar, **3.2**
    to pick up one's luggage reclamar (recoger) el equipaje, **3.2**
    to pick up one's suitcases reclamar (recoger) las maletas, **3.2**
picture el dibujo
piece el pedazo, el trozo
    to tear (break) to pieces hacer pedazos
pill la píldora, la pastilla, **2.2**
pink rosado(a), 4.2
pint la pinta
to **pitch: to pitch a tent** armar una tienda de campaña (carpa), **6.2**
pitcher el/la lanzador(a), el/la pícher, 6.2; **1.2**
pizza la pizza
pizzeria la pizzería
place el lugar
to **place** poner, **3.1;** meter
plan el plan, 3.1
plane el avión, **3.1**
    by plane en avión
    light aircraft (plane) la avioneta
    plane ticket el boleto de avión
plastic plástico(a)
    plastic utensil el utensilio de plástico
plate el plato
platform la plataforma
play (theatrical) la obra de teatro
to **play** jugar (ue), 6.1; **1.1**
    to play soccer jugar (ue) (al) fútbol
    to play tennis jugar (ue) (al) tenis, **4.1**
to **play (musical instrument)** tocar
player el/la jugador(a), 6.1; **1.1**
    baseball player el/la jugador(a) de béisbol, 6.2; **1.2**
playwright el/la dramaturgo(a)
pleasant agradable
please por favor, BV
to **please** gustar, 6.2; **1.2**
pleasure el gusto
    It's a pleasure to meet you. (Nice to meet you.) Mucho gusto.
pocket el bolsillo
poet el/la poeta
point el tanto, 6.1; **1.1;** el punto
    to score a point marcar un tanto, 6.1; **1.1**
poise el porte
pole el palo
    ski pole el bastón, **4.2**
political político(a)

to **pollute** contaminar
    polluted contaminado(a)
    pollution la contaminación
        air pollution la contaminación del aire
Ponce (of or from) ponceño(a)
poncho el poncho
pool la alberca, la piscina, **4.1**
poor pobre, **2.1**
popular popular
popularity la popularidad
population la población
port el puerto
portrait el retrato
possible posible
postal postal
postcard la tarjeta postal
poster el cartel
potato la papa, la patata, 5.2
    French fried potatoes las papas (patatas) fritas, 5.1
pound la libra
to **practice** practicar
to **prefer** preferir (ie), 6.1; **1.1**
to **prepare** preparar, 3.1
to **prescribe** recetar, **2.2**
    prescription la receta, **2.2**
to **present** presentar
    president el/la presidente(a)
    pretty bonito(a), 1.1
to **prevail** prevalecer
    price el precio, 4.2
        at a reasonable price a precio módico
    primary primario(a)
    princess la princesa
    principal principal
    printer la impresora
    private privado(a), 2.2
        private house la casa privada
    problem el problema
to **process** procesar
to **produce** producir
    product el producto
        frozen products (foods) los productos congelados, 5.2
    profession la profesión
    professional profesional
    program la emisión, 3.1; el programa
        sports program la emisión deportiva
to **project** proyectar
    promise la promesa
to **promise** prometer
    protagonist el/la protagonista
    protection la protección
    protein la proteína
    public el público, **5.2**
to **publish** publicar

English-Spanish Dictionary

Puerto Rican puertorriqueño(a), 1.1
pulmonary pulmonar
puppy el perrito, 2.1
purchase la compra
pure puro(a)
purified purificado(a)
purple violeta, 4.2
to **put** poner, **3.1;** meter
    to put on one's clothes ponerse la ropa, **6.1**
puzzle el rompecabezas

quantity la cantidad
quarter el cuarto
    quarter past (the hour) y cuarto
    quarter to (the hour) menos cuarto
Quechuan quechua
queen la reina
question la pregunta, 3.2
    to answer the question contestar (a) la
        pregunta, 3.2
queue la cola, la fila, **5.1**
quickly pronto, rápido
    as quickly as possible a toda prisa
quite bastante, 1.2

racial racial
racket la raqueta, **4.1**
rain la lluvia
    It's raining. Llueve., **4.1**
to **rain** llover (ue)
rainy lluvioso(a)
to **raise** levantar
    to raise one's hand levantar la mano, 3.2
rascal el/la pícaro(a)
rather bastante, 1.2
to **read** leer, 5.1
reading la lectura
ready listo(a)
realist el/la realista
really realmente
reason la razón
reasonable módico(a)
    at a reasonable price a precio módico
to **receive** recibir, 5.1
receptacle el receptáculo
record el disco
recourse el remedio
rectangle el rectángulo
recycling el reciclaje
red rojo(a), 4.2
redheaded pelirrojo(a), 1.1
reduced reducido(a)

to **reflect** reflexionar, reflejar
reflection el reflejo
refreshment el refresco, 5.1
region el barrio, la región
relationship la relación
relative el/la pariente(a), 2.1
to **rely on** contar (ue) con
to **remain** quedar, 6.1; **1.1**
remainder el resto
to **rent** alquilar, rentar, 5.1
    to rent a video alquilar (rentar) un video, **5.1**
representation la repesentación
republic la república
    Dominican Republic la República Dominicana
to **require** requerir (ie)
required obligatorio(a)
research la investigación
reservation la reservación
resort la estación
    beach resort el balneario, **4.1**
    ski resort la estación de esquí, **4.2**
respiratory respiratorio(a)
    respiratory system el aparato respiratorio
rest lo demás; el resto
restaurant el restaurante
restroom el aseo
resulting consiguiente
to **return** volver (ue), 6.1; **1.1**
    to return something devolver (ue), 6.1; **1.1**
reverse inverso(a)
review el repaso
revolution la revolución
rice el arroz, 5.2
rich rico(a)
to **ride** montar
    to ride the chairlift tomar (subir en) el
        telesilla, **4.2**
    to ride a donkey montar en un asno
    to ride a horse montar a caballo
    to ride the ski lift subir en el telesilla, **4.2**
right derecho(a), 6.1; **1.1**
right away enseguida, **6.1**
right: to be right tener razón
river el río
    Amazon River el río Amazonas
road el camino
rogue el/la pícaro(a)
role el papel
roll el rollo, 6.2
    roll of toilet paper el rollo de papel higiénico, **6.2**
roll (bread) el bolillo
roll (sweet) el pan dulce
rolled up enrollado(a)
roof el techo
room el cuarto, 2.2; la pieza; la sala
    classroom la sala de clase

English-Spanish Dictionary

dining room el comedor, 2.2
living room la sala, 2.2
rooster el gallo
routine la rutina, **6.1**
row (of seats) la fila, **5.1**
royal real
to **run** correr, 6.2; **1.2**
rural rural
rush la prisa

sad triste, **2.2;** melancólico(a)
sadness la tristeza
sail la vela
sail (of a windmill) el aspa
sailboard la plancha de vela, **4.1**
salad la ensalada, 5.1
sale la liquidación, 4.2
salsa la salsa
same mismo(a), 1.2
sand la arena, **4.1**
sandwich el sándwich, 5.1; el bocadillo, 5.1
ham and cheese sandwich el sándwich de jamón y queso, 5.1
Saturday el sábado, BV
sausage la salchicha
to **save** ahorrar
saving el ahorro
savings account la cuenta de ahorros
saxophone el saxofón
to **say** decir
that is (to say) es decir
scale la básucula, **3.1**
schedule el horario
school la escuela, 1.2; el colegio, 1.3; la academia
elementary school la escuela primaria
high school el colegio, la escuela superior, la escuela secundaria,
middle school la escuela intermedia
school (related to) escolar
school bus el bus escolar, 3.2
school supplies los materiales escolares, 4.1
science la ciencia, 1.2
natural sciences las ciencias naturales
scissors las tijeras, 4.1
score el tanto, 6.1; **1.1**
to **score** marcar
to score a goal meter un gol, 6.1; **1.1**
to score a point marcar un tanto, 6.1; **1.1**
scoreboard el tablero indicador, 6.1; **1.1**
scrambled revuelto(a)
scrambled eggs los huevos revueltos
screen la pantalla, **5.1**
arrival and departure screen (board) la pantalla de salidas y llegadas, **3.1**

scribble el garabato
sculptor el/la escultor(a)
sculpture la escultura
sea el mar, **4.1**
Caribbean Sea el mar Caribe
Mediterranean Sea el mar Mediterráneo
seafood los mariscos, 5.1
search: in search of en busca de
to **search** buscar
season la estación
seat el asiento, **3.1;** la butaca, **5.1**
seat number el número del asiento, **3.1**
second segundo(a)
second half (soccer) el segundo tiempo, 6.1; **1.1**
secondary secundario(a)
section la sección
security la seguridad
security checkpoint el control de seguridad, **3.1**
to **see** ver, 5.1
let's see a ver
to see a film ver una película, **5.1**
See you later! ¡Hasta luego!, BV
See you soon! ¡Hasta pronto!, BV
See you tomorrow! ¡Hasta mañana!, BV
to **seem** parecer
to **select** seleccionar
self-portrait el autorretrato
to **sell** vender, 5.2; **2.2**
to **send** enviar
sentence la oración
September septiembre, BV
serape el sarape
series la serie
World Series la Serie mundial
serious serio(a), 1.1
served servido(a)
seven siete, 1.1
seven hundred setecientos(as), 3.1
seventeen diecisiete, 1.1
seventy setenta, 2.1
to **sew** coser
shampoo el champú, **6.2**
she ella
sheet la hoja
sheet of paper la hoja de papel, 4.1
shellfish los mariscos, 5.2
ship el buque, la nave
shirt la camisa, 4.2
short-sleeved shirt la camisa de mangas cortas, 4.2
shoe el zapato, 4.2
pair of tennis shoes (sneakers) el par de tenis, 4.2
tennis shoes (sneakers) los tenis, 4.2
to **shop** ir de compras, 5.2
shopping de compras

to go shopping ir de compras, 5.2
short bajo(a), 1.1; corto(a); breve
   short pants el pantalón corto, 4.2
   short sleeve la manga corta, 4.2
   short story la historieta
   short-story writer el/la cuentista
shorts el pantalón corto, 4.2
short-story writer el/la cuentista
should deber
show el espectáculo; **(movies)** la sesión, **5.1**
to **show** mostrar (ue)
shower la ducha, **6.1**
   to take a shower tomar una ducha, **6.1**
shut cerrado(a)
shy tímido(a), 1.1
sick enfermo(a), **2.1**; mal
   to be sick (ill) estar mal
   sick person, patient el/la enfermo(a), **2.2**
side el lado
to **sigh** suspirar
to **sign** firmar
similar parecido(a), similar
simple sencillo(a); simple
since desde
sincere sincero(a), 1.1
to **sing** cantar, 3.1; **5.2**
   singer el/la cantante, **5.2**
   singles (tennis) los singles, **4.1**
   sir el señor, BV
   sister la hermana, 2.1
to **sit down** sentarse (ie), **6.1**
situated situado(a)
six seis, 1.1
six hundred seiscientos(as), 3.1
sixteen dieciséis, 1.1
sixty sesenta, 2.1
size la talla, 4.2 el tamaño; **(shoes)** el número
skeletal esquelético(a)
skeleton el esqueleto
ski el esquí, **4.2**
   ski lift el telesquí, **4.2**
   ski pole el bastón, **4.2**
   ski resort la estación de esquí, **4.2**
   water skis los esquís acuáticos, **4.1**
to **ski** esquiar, **4.1**
   to water-ski esquiar en el agua, **4.1**
skier el/la esquiador(a), **4.2**
skiing el esquí, **4.1**
   waterskiing el esquí acuático, **4.1**
skirt la falda, 4.2
sky el cielo, **4.1**
slant la inclinación
to **sleep** dormir (ue), 6.1; **1.1**
   sleeping bag el saco de dormir, **6.2**
   sleeve la manga

   long sleeve la manga larga, 4.2
   short sleeve la manga corta, 4.2
   short sleeved de mangas cortas, 4.2
slope la pista, **4.2**
   beginners' slope la pista para principiantes, **4.2**
   expert slope la pista para expertos, **4.2**
slow pausado(a)
small pequeño(a), 1.2
smoke el humo
to **sneeze** estornudar, **2.1**
snow la nieve, **4.2**
to **snow** nevar (ie)
   It's snowing. Nieva., **4.2**
so así; tan
   so much tanto(a)
soap jabón, **6.2**
   bar of soap la barra (pastilla) de jabón, **6.2**
soccer el fútbol, 6.1; **1.1**
   to play soccer jugar (ue) (al) fútbol
   soccer field el campo de fútbol, 6.1; **1.1**
   soccer stadium el estadio de fútbol
   soccer team el equipo de fútbol
social social, 1.2
   social studies los estudios sociales, 1.2
sock el calcetín
socks los calcetines, 4.2
soda la gaseosa, 5.1; la soda
soft blando(a)
software el software
some algunos(as); unos(as)
someone alguien, **5.2**
something algo
   something else algo más
sometimes a veces, 3.1; **4.1**
son el hijo, 2.1
song la canción, el canto
soon pronto
   See you soon! ¡Hasta pronto!, BV
sore: sore throat el dolor de garganta, **2.1**
soup la sopa, 5.1
source la fuente
south el sur
   southern hemisphere el hemisferio sur
South America la América del Sur
South American sudamericano(a)
space el espacio
space (related to) espacial
spaceship la nave espacial
Spain España
Spanish español(a)
Spanish (language) el español
   Spanish Club el Club de español
Spanish-speaking de habla española
to **speak** hablar, 3.1
   to speak on the phone hablar por teléfono, 3.1

English-Spanish Dictionary

special especial
spectacular espectacular
spectator el/la espectador(a), 6.1; **1.1**
speech el habla
to **spend** gastar
to **spend (time)** pasar
    to spend one's vacation pasar las vacaciones
    to spend the weekend pasar el fin de
      semana, **4.1**
  sport el deporte, 6.1; **1.1**
    individual sport el deporte individual
    team sport el deporte de equipo
  sports (related to) deportivo(a)
    sports program la emisión deportiva
  spring la primavera, BV
  squire el escudero
  stadium el estadio, 6.1; **1.1**
    soccer stadium el estadio de fútbol
  star la estrella
  state el estado
  station la estación
    subway station la estación del metro, **5.1**
  stationery: stationery store la papelería, 4.1
  statue la estatua, **5.2**
to **stay: to stay in bed** guardar cama, **2.1**
  steak el biftec
  step el paso
  stepbrother el hermanastro, 2.1
  stepfather el padrastro, 2.1
  stepmother la madrastra, 2.1
  stepsister la hermanastra, 2.1
  stomach el estómago, **2.1**
  stomachache el dolor de estómago, **2.1**
  stone la piedra
to **stop** parar, 6.1; **1.1**
  store la tienda, 4.2
    clothing store la tienda de ropa, 4.2
    department store la tienda de departamentos
    grocery store la tienda de abarrotes, la bodega
    stationery store la papelería, 4.1
    video store la tienda de videos, **5.1**
  story el cuento, la historia
    short story la historieta
    short-story writer el/la cuentista
  straw la paja
  street la calle
  string bean el ejote, 5.2
  strip la tira
    comic strip la tira cómica
  strong fuerte
  student el/la alumno(a), 1.2
  study el estudio
    social studies los estudios sociales, 1.2
to **study** estudiar, 3.1
  stuffed relleno(a)
    stuffed with relleno de

stupendous estupendo(a)
stupid estúpido(a)
stupidity la tontería
style la moda, el estilo
  in style de moda
subconscious la subconciencia
subject (school) la asignatura, la materia
subtitle el subtítulo
  to have subtitles llevar subtítulos
suburb el suburbio
subway el metro, **5.1**
  subway station la estación del metro, **5.1**
success el éxito
successful: to be successful tener éxito
such tal
suffering el sufrimiento
suit el traje, 4.2
  bathing suit el bañador, el traje de baño, **4.1**
suitcase la maleta, 3.1
  to open the suitcases abrir las maletas, **3.2**
  to pack one's suitcase hacer la maleta, **3.1**
  to pick up one's suitcases reclamar (recoger)
    las maletas, **3.2**
sum el monto
summer el verano, BV; **4.1**
sun el sol
to **sunbathe** tomar el sol, **4.1**
  sunblock la crema protectora, **4.1**
  Sunday el domingo, BV
  sunglasses los anteojos de (para el) sol, **4.1**
  sunny: It's sunny. Hace (Hay) sol., **4.1**
  suntan lotion (cream) la loción (crema)
    bronceadora, **4.1**
  superior superior
  supermarket el supermercado, 5.2
    (wholesale) supermarket el hipermercado
  supplies: school supplies los materiales
    escolares, 4.1
  sure seguro(a)
to **surf the Net** navegar la red
  surfboard la tabla hawaiana, **4.1**
  surprise la sorpresa
  surrealist surrealista
  sweet dulce
    sweet roll el pan dulce
to **swim** nadar, **4.1**
  to swim underwater bucear
  underwater swimming el buceo, **4.1**
  symptom el síntoma, **2.2**
  system el aparato; el sistema
    respiratory system el aparato respiratorio

T-shirt el T-shirt, la camiseta, 4.2
table la mesa, 5.1

English-Spanish Dictionary

folding table la mesa plegable, **6.2**
tablecloth el mantel
tablet la pastilla, la tableta, **2.2**
taco el taco
to **take** tomar, 3.1
    to take a bath bañarse, **6.1**
    to take a flight tomar un vuelo, **3.1**
    to take a hike (long walk) dar una caminata, **6.2**
    to take a shower tomar una ducha, **6.1**
    to take a trip hacer una viaje, **3.1**
    to take (clothing size) usar, 3.2
    to take notes tomar apuntes, 3.2
    to take off quitarse
    to take off (airplane) despegar, **3.2**
    to take out (secretly) escamotear
    to take part tomar parte
    to take the bus tomar el bus
    to take (shoe size) calzar
takeoff el despegue
to **talk** hablar, 3.1
tall alto(a), 1.1
tanning bronceador(a)
    tanning (suntan) lotion (cream) la loción (crema) bronceadora, **4.2**
taste el gusto
taxi el taxi, **3.1**
tea el té
    iced tea el té helado, 5.1
to **teach** enseñar
teacher el/la profesor(a), 1.2; el/la maestro(a),
team el equipo, 6.1; **1.1**
    soccer team el equipo de fútbol
    team sport el deporte de equipo
to **tear: to tear (break) to pieces** hacer pedazos
technology la tecnología
teeth los dientes, **6.1**
    to brush one's teeth cepillarse los dientes, **6.1;** lavarse los dientes
telephone el teléfono, 3.1
    to call on the phone llamar por teléfono, telefonear
    to speak on the phone hablar por teléfono, 3.1
    telephone company la compañía de teléfonos
    telephone number el número de teléfono
to **telephone** llamar por teléfono, telefonear
television la televisión, 3.1; la tele
temperate templado(a)
temperature la temperatura, **4.2**
ten diez, BV
    by tens de diez en diez
tender tierno(a)
tendon el tendón
tennis el tenis, **4.1**
    pair of tennis shoes (sneakers) el par de tenis, 4.2

to play tennis jugar (ue) (al) tenis, **4.1**
    tennis court la cancha de tenis, **4.1**
    tennis game el juego (partido) de tenis
    tennis player el/la tenista
    tennis shoes (sneakers) los tenis, 4.2
tent la carpa, la tienda de campaña, **6.2**
    to pitch a tent armar una tienda de campaña, **6.2**
term el término
terminal la terminal
terrace la terraza, 2.2
terrible terrible
territory el territorio
terror el terror
test el examen
Thank you. Gracias., BV
that que
    that is (to say) es decir
    that which, what lo que
    That's right (true). Es verdad.
the el, la
theater el teatro
    movie theater el cine, **5.1**
theatrical work la obra de teatro
their su(s)
them las, los
    to them les
then entonces; luego
there allí
    there is, there are hay
    There is nothing more we can do. No hay más remedio.
therefore por consiguente
these estos(as)
they ellos(as)
thin delgado(a)
thing la cosa
to **think** creer; opinar
    I think so. Creo que sí.
thirsty: to be thirsty tener sed, 5.1
thirteen trece, 1.1
thirty treinta, 1.1
thirty-eight treinta y ocho, 2.1
thirty-five treinta y cinco, 2.1
thirty-four treinta y cuatro, 2.1
thirty-nine treinta y nueve, 2.1
thirty-one treinta y uno, 1.1
thirty-seven treinta y siete, 2.1
thirty-six treinta y seis, 2.1
thirty-three treinta y tres, 2.1
thirty-two treinta y dos, 2.1
this este(a)
    this afternoon esta tarde
three tres, 1.1
three hundred trescientos(as), 3.1
throat la garganta, 2.1
    sore throat el dolor de garganta, **2.1**

English-Spanish Dictionary

to **throw** lanzar, 6.1; **1.1**; tirar, 6.2; **1.2**; echar
Thursday el jueves, BV
ticket el billete, el boleto, **3.1**, el ticket, **4.2**
   admission ticket la entrada, **5.1**
   to check a ticket revisar el boleto, **3.1**
   plane ticket el boleto de avión
   ticket window la boletería, la ventanilla, **4.2**
tidbits la chuchería
tie la corbata, 4.2
tied (score) empatado(a), 6.1; **1.1**
time la vez; el tiempo; la hora
   at times (sometimes) a veces, 3.1; **4.1**
   At what time? ¿A qué hora?, BV
   boarding time la hora de embarque
   every time cada vez
   to have a good time divertirse (ie), **6.2**; pasarlo
     bien
   on time a tiempo, **3.1**
   one more time una vez más
   What time is it? ¿Qué hora es?, BV
timetable el horario
timid tímido(a), 1.1
tired cansado(a), **2.1**
tissue el kleenex, **2.1**
title el título
toast el pan tostado, 5.1; **6.1**; la tostada
toasted tostado(a)
today hoy, **4.1**
   What day is it (today)? ¿Qué día es (hoy)?
   What is today's date? ¿Cuál es la fecha
     de hoy?
together junto(a)
toilet el aseo
   toilet paper el papel higiénico, **6.2**
tomato el tomate, 5.2
tomorrow mañana
   See you tomorrow! ¡Hasta mañana!, BV
ton la tonelada
tonight esta noche, **4.1**
tongue twister el trabalenguas
too también, 1.1
tooth el diente, **6.1**
toothbrush el cepillo de dientes, **6.2**
toothpaste la pasta (crema) dentífrica, **6.2**
   tube of toothpaste el tubo de pasta (crema)
     dentífrica, **6.2**
top: on top of (por) encima de, **4.1**
tortilla la tortilla
total el total, el monto
to **touch** tocar
toward hacia
towel la toalla, **4.1**
   beach towel la toalla playera, **4.1**
town el pueblo
toxic tóxico(a)
toy el juguete

traditional tradicional
trailer la caravana, **6.2**
train el tren
trainer el/la entrenador(a)
transportation el transporte
   means of transportation el medio de
     transporte
to **travel** viajar
traveling ambulante
to **treat** tratar
treasure el tesoro
tree el árbol
   family tree el árbol genealógico
triangle el triángulo
trip el viaje, **3.1**; la excursión
   camping trip la excursión de camping
   to take a trip hacer una viaje, **3.1**
trombone el trombón
trophy el trofeo, 6.2; **1.2**
tropical tropical
truck el camión
trumpet la trompeta
trust la confianza
to **trust** tener confianza en
truth la verdad
   That's true (the truth). Es verdad.
to **try** tratar de
tube el tubo
   bronchial tube el bronquio
   tube of cream el tubo de crema
   tube of toothpaste el tubo de pasta (crema)
     dentífrica, **6.2**
Tuesday el martes, BV
tuna el atún, 5.2
to **turn around** revolver (ue)
TV la televisión, 3.1; la tele
twelve doce, 1.1
twenty veinte, 1.1
twenty-eight veintiocho, 1.1
twenty-five veinticinco, 1.1
twenty-four veinticuatro, 1.1
twenty-nine veintinueve, 1.1
twenty-one veintiuno, 1.1
twenty-seven veintisiete, 1.1
twenty-six veintiséis, 1.1
twenty-three veintitrés, 1.1
twenty-two veintidós, 1.1
two dos, 1.1
two hundred doscientos(as), 3.1
type el tipo
typical típico(a)

U

ugly feo(a), 1.1
uncle el tío, 2.1

under bajo, **4.2;** debajo (de)
undershirt la camiseta, 4.2
to **understand** comprender, 5.1
underwater: to swim underwater bucear
    underwater swimming el buceo, **4.1**
uniform el uniforme, 3.2
United States Estados Unidos
university la universidad
unloading el desembarque
unoccupied libre, 5.1
until hasta
to **use** usar, 4.2
utensil el utensilio
    plastic utensil el utensilio de plástico

vacation la vacación
    to spend one's vacation pasar las vacaciones
valedictorian valedictoriano(a)
vanilla vainilla
    vanilla ice cream el helado de vainilla, 5.1
variety la variedad
various vario(a)
to **vary** variar
vegetable la legumbre, el vegetal, 5.2
vein la vena
Venezuelan venezolano(a), 1.1
version la versión
    in the original version en versión original
very muy, 1.2
    very well muy bien, BV
vest el chaleco
victim la víctima
video el video, 3.2
    to rent a video alquilar (rentar) un video, **5.1**
    video store la tienda de videos, **5.1**
view la vista
viola la viola
violin el violín
violet violeta, 4.2
to **visit** visitar, **5.2**
vital vital
vitamin la vitamina
voice la voz
volleyball el voleibol
volume el volumen
vowel la vocal

to **wait (for)** esperar, 5.1
    waiter el mesero, el camarero, 5.1
    waitress la camarera, la mesera, 5.1
to **wake up** despertarse (ie), **6.1**
to **walk** ir a pie, 3.2; andar, caminar

walk (long) la caminata, 6.2
    to take a long walk dar una caminata, **6.2**
to **want** desear, querer (ie)
    to be longing to (to want) tener ganas de
to **wash** lavar
to **wash oneself** lavarse, **6.1**
   waste el desecho
to **watch** mirar, 3.1; ver
    to watch a film ver una película, **5.1**
   water el agua, 5.2
    mineral water el agua mineral, 5.2, **6.2**
    to swim underwater bucear
    underwater swimming el buceo, **4.1**
   water (related to) acuático(a)
    waterskiing el esquí acuático, **4.1**
    water skis los esquís acuáticos, **4.1**
to **waterski** esquiar en el agua, **4.1**
   waterskiing el esquí acuático, **4.1**
   wave la ola, **4.1**
   way el camino
   we nosotros(as)
   weak débil
to **wear** llevar, 3.2; **(shoe size)** calzar
   weather el tiempo
    It's cold (weather). Hace frío., **4.2**
    It's cool (weather). Hace fresco.
    It's hot (weather). Hace calor., **4.1**
    The weather is bad. Hace mal tiempo., **4.1**
    The weather is nice. Hace buen tiempo., **4.1**
    What is the weather (like)? ¿Qué tiempo hace?, **4.1**
Web page la página Web
Wednesday el miércoles, BV
week la semana
    last week la semana pasada, **4.1**
weekend el fin de semana
    last weekend el fin de semana pasado, **4.1**
    to spend the weekend pasar el fin de semana, **4.1**
to **weigh** pesar
   weight el peso
   welcome bienvenido(a)
    You're welcome. De nada., Por nada., No hay de qué., BV
   well bien; pues, 1.1
    to do well (on an exam) salir bien (en un examen)
    very well muy bien, BV
   what? ¿qué?, ¿cuál?, ¿cómo?
    At what time? ¿A qué hora?, BV
    What a . . . ! ¡Qué... más... !
    what color? ¿de qué color?, 4.2
    What day is it (today)? ¿Qué día es (hoy)?, BV
    What is he (she, it) like? ¿Cómo es?
    What is the weather (like)? ¿Qué tiempo hace?, **4.1**

English-Spanish Dictionary

What is today's date? ¿Cuál es la fecha de hoy?, BV
What luck! ¡Qué suerte!
what nationality? ¿de qué nacionalidad?, 1.1
What's new (up)? ¿Qué hay?
What a shame! ¡Qué pena!
What size do you wear? ¿Qué número usa Ud.?, ¿Qué talla usa Ud.?, 4.2
What's the matter (with you)? ¿Qué te pasa?, **2.1**; ¿Qué tienes?
What time is it? ¿Qué hora es?, BV
when cuando, 3.2
when? ¿cuándo?, 3.1
where? ¿dónde?, 1.1; ¿adónde?, 3.2
    from where? ¿de dónde?, 1.1
which? ¿cuál?
while el rato; mientras
white blanco(a), 4.2
who? ¿quién?, ¿quiénes?, 1.1
whose? ¿de quién?
why? ¿por qué?
widow la viuda
widowed viudo(a)
widower el viudo
wife la esposa; la mujer
to **win** ganar, 6.1; **1.1**
wind el viento
windmill el molino de viento
window: ticket window la boletería, la ventanilla, **4.2**
to **windsurf** hacer la plancha de vela
    windy: It's windy. Hace (Hay) viento.
winter el invierno, BV; **4.2**
wise sabio(a)
wish el deso; la gana
to **wish** desear, querer (ie)
with con
    with a delay con una demora, **3.1**
    with himself (herself, themselves) consigo
within dentro de
without sin
    without equal sin par
woman la mujer

wool la lana
word la palabra
work la obra, el trabajo
    Let's get to work! ¡Manos a la obra!
    theatrical work (play) la obra de teatro
to **work** trabajar, 4.2
world el mundo
world (related to) mundial
    World Cup la Copa mundial
    World Series la Serie mundial
worth: to be worth valer
wounded herido(a)
to **write** escribir, 5.1
writing pad el bloc, 4.1

year el año
    to be . . . years old tener... años, 2.1
    last year el año pasado
yellow amarillo(a), 4.2
yes sí
yesterday ayer, **4.1**
    yesterday afternoon ayer por la tarde, **4.1**
    yesterday morning ayer por la mañana
you te; ti; tú; usted; ustedes; vosotros(as)
    to you le; les; ti
    You're welcome. De nada., Por nada., No hay de qué.
young joven, **2.1**
    young page (of a royal family) el/la menino(a)
    young person el/la joven, **5.1**
younger menor, 2.1
youngest el/la menor, 2.1
your tu(s); su(s); vuestro(a); vuestros(as)
    It's your turn! ¡Te toca a ti!

zero cero
    below zero bajo cero, **4.2**
zone la zona

Credits

Glencoe would like to acknowledge the artists and agencies who participated in illustrating this program: Geo Parkin represented by American Artists Inc.; Carlos Lacamara; Karen Maizel; Lyle Miller; Ortelius Design, Inc.; Andrew Shiff; David Broad and Jane McCreary represented by Ann Remen-Willis; Joe Veno represented by Gwen Walters.